R20086P2310

745 £14.95

2 DAY LOAN

CW01649123

TRADITION TODAY

INDIGENOUS ART IN AUSTRALIA

ART GALLERY OF NEW SOUTH WALES

NEW COLLEGE PONTEFRACT
R20086P2310

DEDICATED TO **TONY TUCKSON** (1921–1973), WHOSE VISION INSPIRED THIS COLLECTION.

MEMBERS OF ABORIGINAL AND TORRES STRAIT ISLANDER COMMUNITIES ARE RESPECTFULLY ADVISED THAT A NUMBER OF PEOPLE MENTIONED IN WRITING OR DEPICTED IN PHOTOGRAPHS IN THE FOLLOWING PAGES HAVE PASSED AWAY.

TRADITION TODAY
INDIGENOUS ART IN AUSTRALIA
ART GALLERY OF NEW SOUTH WALES

ART GALLERY NSW

YIRIBANA

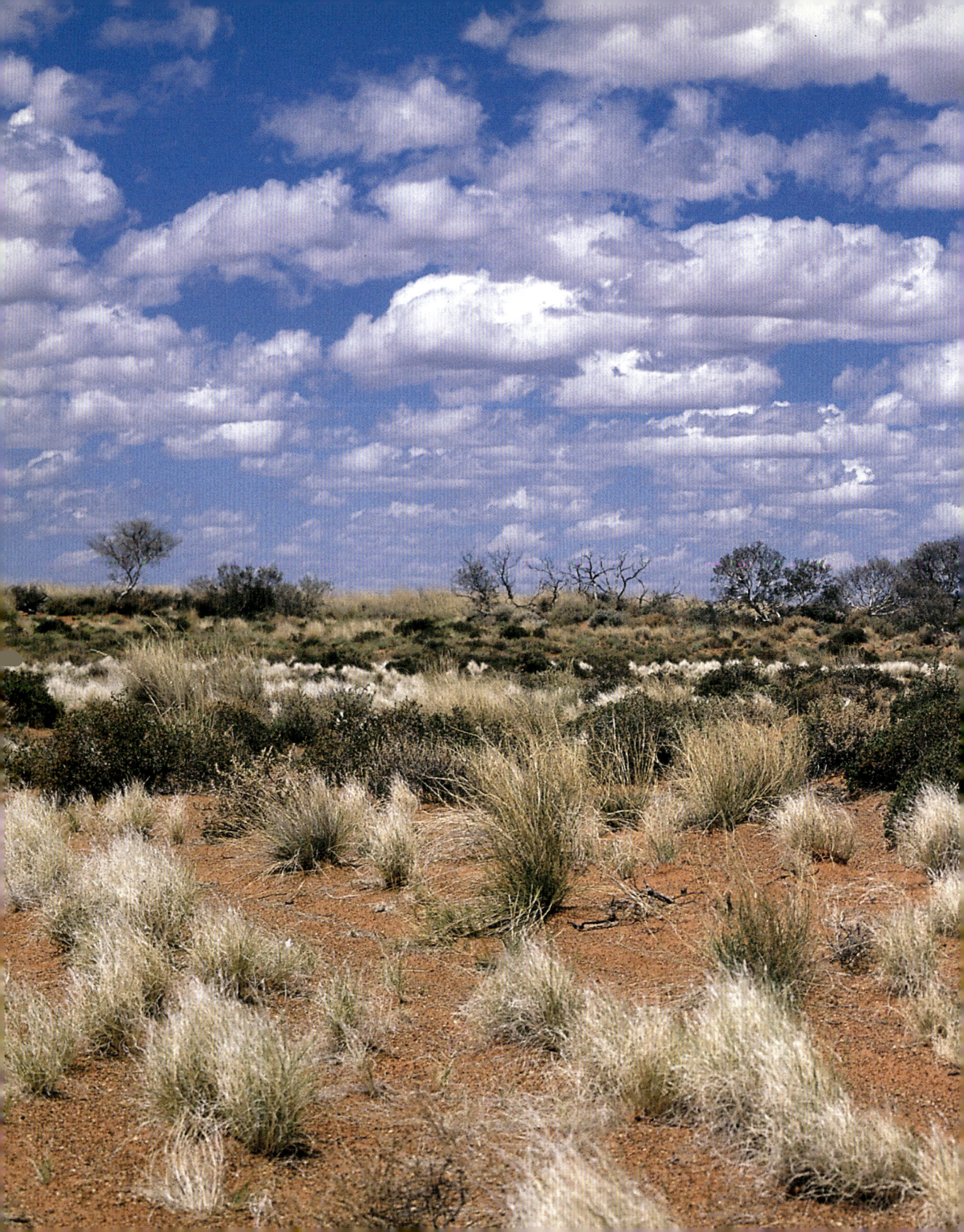

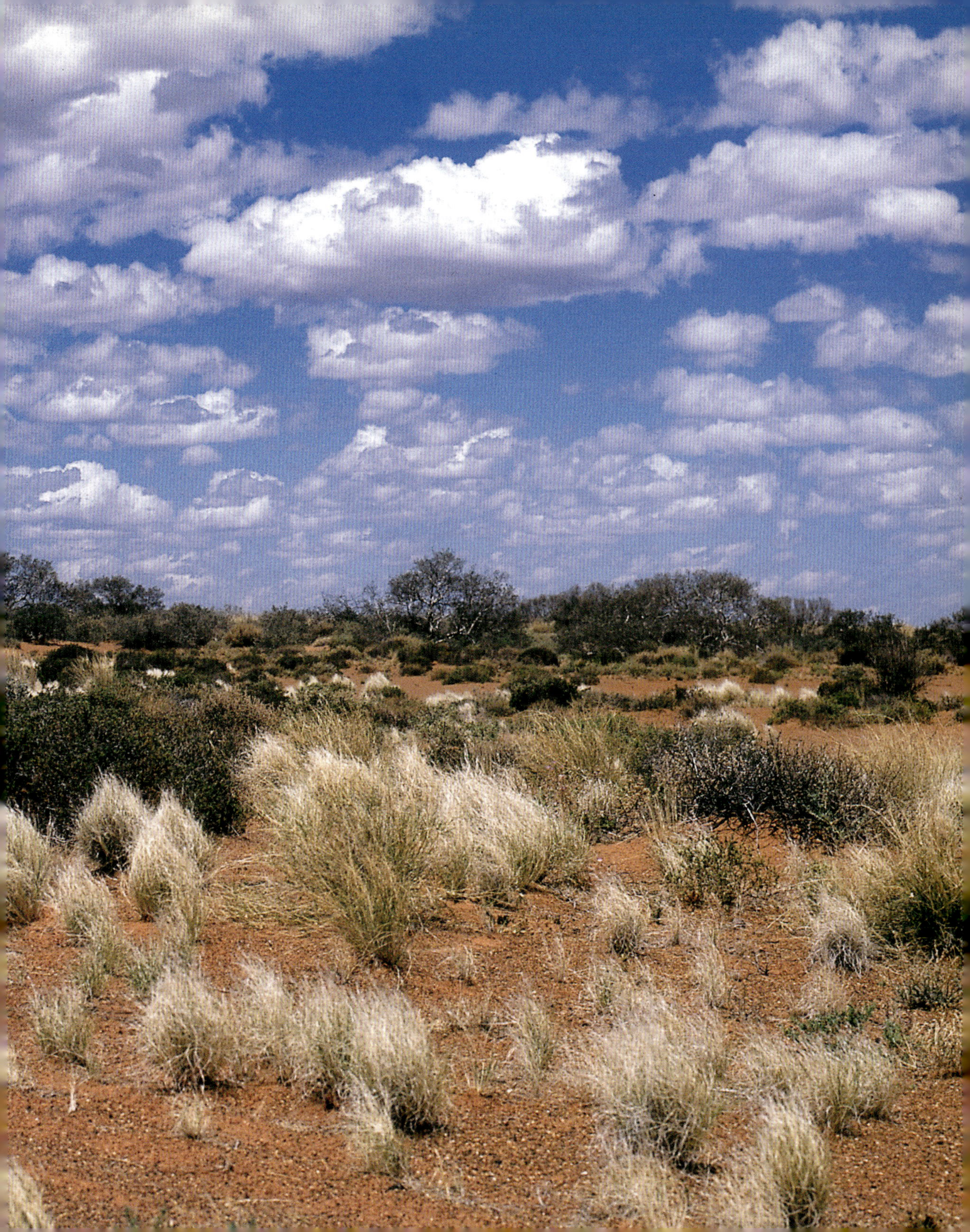

ART IS THE LIFEBLOOD OF OUR COMMUNITIES, CONNECTING US TO THE PAST, THE PRESENT AND EACH OTHER.

FOR CENTURIES, EACH GENERATION OF ABORIGINAL AND TORRES STRAIT ISLANDER PEOPLE HAS HANDED ON CULTURAL KNOWLEDGE AND TECHNICAL EXPERTISE, AND WITHIN THIS RICH TRADITION SUCCESSIVE GENERATIONS OF ARTISTS HAVE FORGED INDIVIDUAL AESTHETIC EXPRESSIONS TO MARK THEIR EXPERIENCE.

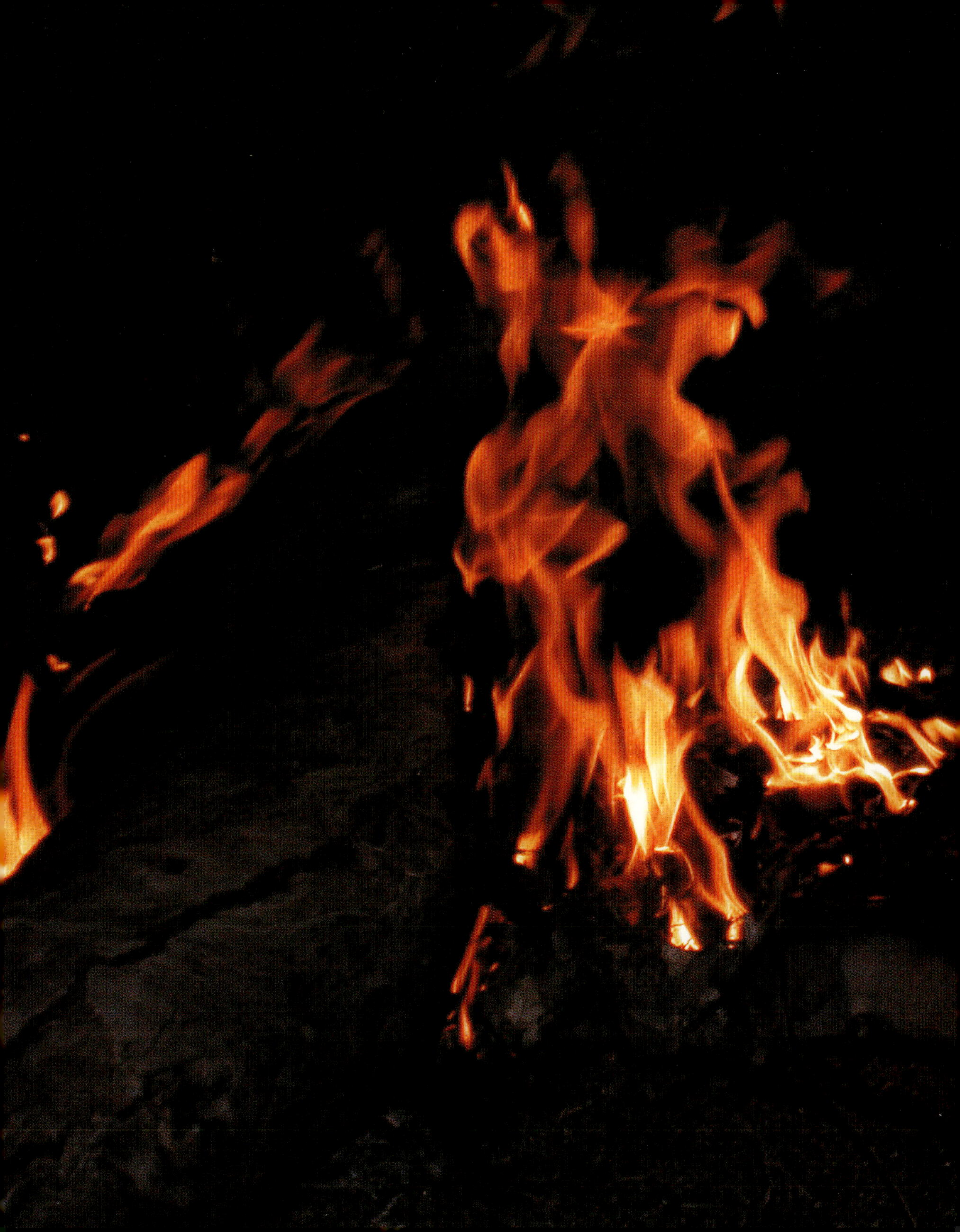

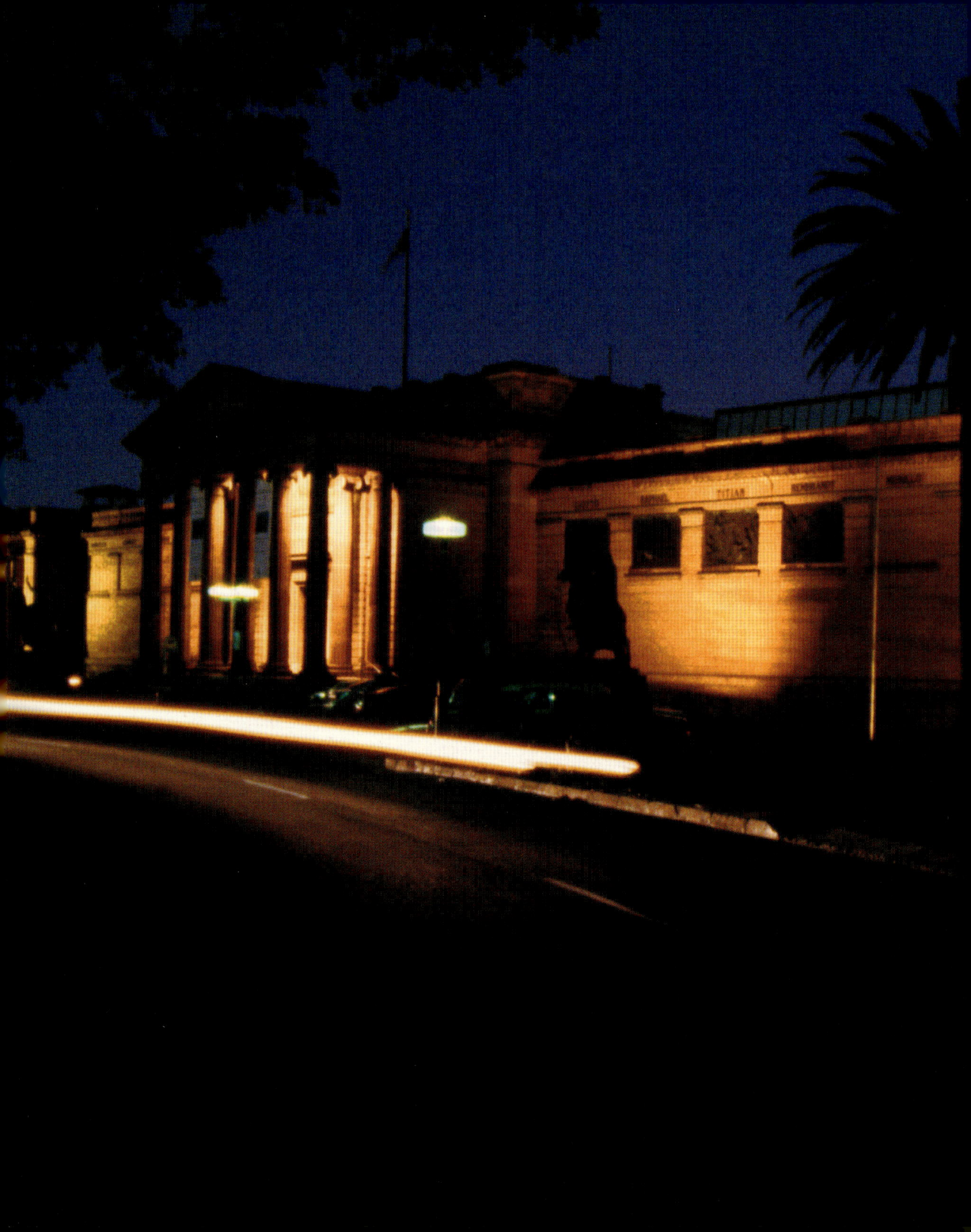
TITIAN

FOREWORD

The opening of our Yiribana Gallery in 1994 was a signal event in the history of the Art Gallery of New South Wales. As home to our Aboriginal and Torres Strait Islander art collections and of the accompanying programmes of exhibitions and events, the Yiribana Gallery is more than just a display, it is a place where the Indigenous art of Australia lives and breathes as powerfully today as it has done in the past. *Tradition Today* echoes those sentiments. This book introduces and documents the work of 77 artists represented in our extensive and growing collections of Aboriginal and Torres Strait Islander art. It will reaffirm the indelible and unique image of Indigenous art to the people of Australia and around the world.

The origins of the Art Gallery of New South Wales's collections lie in the pioneering work of a previous Deputy Director, Tony Tuckson, to whom this book is dedicated. In the 1950s and 1960s, he and Dr Stuart Scougall travelled frequently to Arnhem Land and the Tiwi Islands, meeting the communities, acquiring work, and thereby laying the foundations of the fully representative collections of today. It was their inspiration that brought to this Gallery such hallmark works as the Pukamani grave posts that at the time of their acquisition, in 1959, excited such public curiosity and debate. Over the years the collection of classic bark paintings has developed into one of the finest in the world, and these have now been joined by the wealth and diversity of contemporary Indigenous art practice. It is a diversity that on the one hand reflects the opportunities of the day, but at the same time remains staunchly devoted to its own deeply held sources and heritage.

Many people have contributed to the development of the Yiribana Gallery's collection since its inception. I thank the curators, past and present, whose expertise and care has nurtured the collection's growth, the staff who have managed the artworks, the collectors and benefactors who have made an incalculable contribution to the Yiribana Gallery, Mollie Gowing for her generous support of the Art Gallery of New South Wales's Aboriginal and Torres Strait Islander art collection, and Qantas for its continuing sponsorship of the Yiribana Gallery.

Tradition Today would not have been possible without the commitment of many people, including, first and foremost, the artists, their families and their community art centres. No less than fourteen writers from within the Art Gallery of New South Wales, other leading cultural institutions and freelance writers have written for this book. In particular, the staff of the Department of Aboriginal and Torres Strait Islander Art – Hetti Perkins, Ken Watson, Jonathan Jones and Cara Pinchbeck – have worked tirelessly to realise this project. Editor, Theresa Willsteed must be thanked for her support for the project, and also Dinah Dysart, who freely offered her expert editorial experience. We are also grateful for the support of ATSIC, the Aboriginal and Torres Strait Islander Commission.

EDMUND CAPON
DIRECTOR

This publication acknowledges the substantial and continuing support of Qantas for the Gallery's Yiribana and Torres Strait Islander programs.

QANTAS

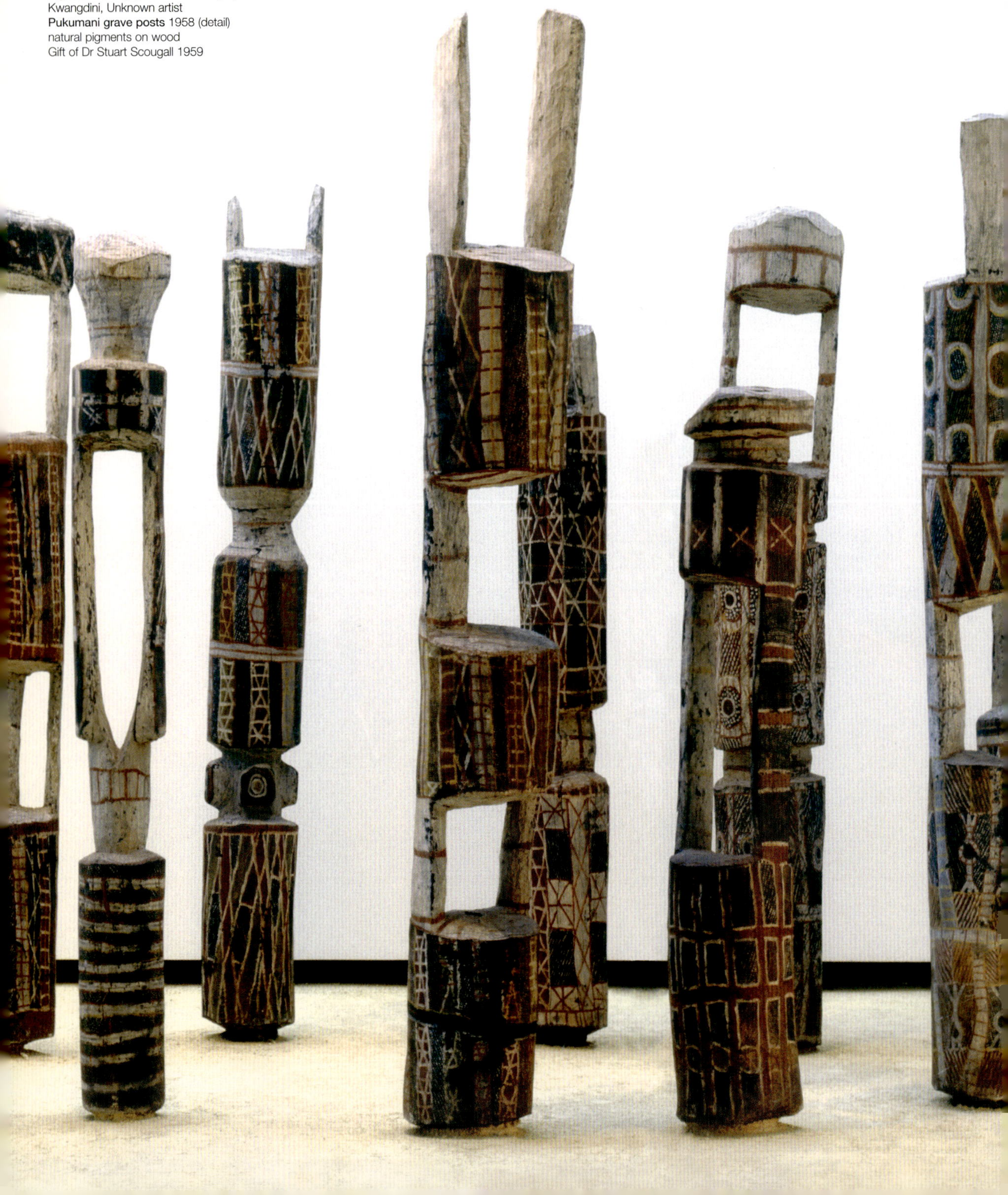

Laurie Nelson Tukialila, Bob One Galadingwama, Big Jack Yarunga, Don Burakmadjua, Charlie Quiet Kwangdini, Unknown artist
Pukumani grave posts 1958 (detail)
natural pigments on wood
Gift of Dr Stuart Scougall 1959

INTRODUCTION

The Yiribana Gallery of Aboriginal and Torres Strait Islander Art at the Art Gallery of New South Wales pays tribute to the Indigenous people who encountered the First Fleet at Port Jackson, Sydney Harbour, in 1788. 'Yiribana' means 'this way' in the language of the Gadigal clan of the Eora people, on whose country the city of Sydney now stands.

The Yiribana Gallery celebrates Indigenous Australia's age-old, yet enduring, cultural heritage and its myriad contemporary expressions. In *Tradition Today*, the works of 77 artists represented in the Art Gallery of New South Wales's extensive collection highlight the flourishing of Aboriginal and Torres Strait Islander art from the mid-twentieth century onwards, and anticipate the legacy of this extraordinary art movement in the new millennium.

Tradition Today offers a fresh insight into the history and contemporary life of Aboriginal and Torres Strait Islander communities. Each essay draws on biographical accounts of an artist's life, revealing the diversity of Indigenous experience in colonised Australia. Assembled alphabetically, the essays collectively locate the artists' diverse visual practices within an Indigenous, and international, cultural frame of reference.

From desert paintings created by small family groups living on remote Western Desert outstations and the bark paintings of the saltwater people of coastal communities, to the new media practice of 'blak city culture',[1] contemporary artists have generated a renaissance of Indigenous visual art by translating traditional symbolism in strikingly modern images. The Art Gallery of New South Wales has played an important role in the journey of Indigenous art from ethnographic obscurity to taking its place in major exhibitions, biennales and collections around the world.

Tony Tuckson, Deputy Director of the Art Gallery of New South Wales from 1950–1973 and a renowned abstract expressionist painter in his own right, was a key figure in this changing perception. Enthralled by the 'freedom of composition' that set Aboriginal art apart from the mannerism of mid-twentieth-century Western visual culture, Tuckson amassed an exceptional collection of paintings and sculpture from Aboriginal Australia's northern-most communities. Tuckson was accompanied on several expeditions to Arnhem Land and Bathurst and Melville Islands by the orthopaedic surgeon, Dr Stuart Scougall, whose professional medical interest in Aboriginal people was matched by his enthusiasm for their culture.

It took the eye of an artist to fully appreciate the aesthetic virtues of Indigenous cultural practice, and to elevate it beyond museology-based hierarchies of value then being imposed on it. The extensively documented proceeds of the Tuckson–Scougall enterprise form the foundation of the Art Gallery of New South Wales's collection of Aboriginal art. The *Pukamani grave posts*, 1959 – the centrepiece of the Tuckson collection – are a group of 17 monumental ceremonial tutini, the funerary poles unique to Tiwi culture. Their arrival at the Art Gallery of New South Wales in 1959 created a flurry of controversy around the appropriateness of their inclusion in a public art gallery collection. However, the tutini remained on permanent display, and are now installed in the atrium of the Yiribana Gallery.

It was here that young Tiwi artist, Pedro Wonaeamirri, first saw the art made by his uncles during a visit to southern city galleries with senior fellow Tiwi artist, Kutuwulumi Purawarrumpatu, in the late 1990s. Wonaeamirri was so impressed by the pristine and powerful presence of the tutini

ENTHRALLED BY THE 'FREEDOM OF COMPOSITION' THAT SET ABORIGINAL ART APART FROM THE MANNERISM OF MID-TWENTIETH-CENTURY WESTERN VISUAL CULTURE, TONY TUCKSON AMASSED AN EXCEPTIONAL COLLECTION OF PAINTINGS AND SCULPTURE FROM ABORIGINAL AUSTRALIA'S NORTHERN-MOST COMMUNITIES.

in a gallery setting that he was inspired to create his own series of tutini under commission for the biennial contemporary art survey, 'Australian Perspecta 1999'. Wonaeamirri's installation of six tutini was acquired by the Art Gallery of New South Wales, and now stand as a counterpoint to their predecessors of a half-century and as testimony to the endurance of Tiwi culture. Senior artists such as Purawarrumpatu, who was renowned for her distinctive and protean interpretations of the ceremonial body designs of her ancestors, are a source of inspiration for the younger generation.

The historically significant body of work collected by Tuckson primarily comprises a seminal group of bark paintings and associated objects by distinguished Yolngu leaders of north-east Arnhem Land. Members of the esteemed Marika family, including the late patriarch Mawalan and his son Wandjuk, participated in the Tuckson project. Along with Mawalan's daughter Banduk, a renowned printmaker, they have played a leading role as custodians of a dynamic living culture, confirming the inalienable political and moral rights of their people in the mesmerising brilliance of Rirratjingu art. Galarrwuy Yunupingu's father, Mungguruwuy, was also one of the core group of artists who created works for Tuckson. Now chairman of the Northern Land Council, Yunupingu has stated, ' ... Our painting is a political act',[2] recalling the revanchism of Indigenous artists in asserting their customary sovereignty in activities such as the presentation to the Federal Government of the historic 1963 Bark Petition and the Barunga Statement of 1988. This artistic means to a political end is a process that Yunupingu has described as 'our form of writing, writing for land ... in the form of a painting'.[3]

The legacy of pioneering Kukatja/Wangkajunga artist, Rover Thomas, may be seen in the paintings of his Gija peers, the late Queenie McKenzie, and the recent works of Paddy Bedford. A miraculous visitation through a series of dream sequences led Thomas to conceive of the Gurirr Gurirr ceremony, in collaboration with senior members of the Warmun Aboriginal community at Turkey Creek. This public performance, where the participants held aloft boards painted to depict episodes of the narrative, was the catalyst for the contemporary East Kimberley painting movement. The various strata of Indigenous experience are embedded in Gija paintings, which are created with locally mined ochres. An abstract topography of the artist's country may contain coded references to the events of the Ngarrangkarni and recent history. The unequivocal boldness of Timmy Timms's *Bedford Downs massacre*, 2000 (page 141), is symbiotic with the horror of its subject.

The systematic brutalisation of Aboriginal people on the colonial frontier is, as Gija artist Rusty Peters states, a history shared by Aboriginal communities throughout the country. Yet contemporary Indigenous art offers a generous and incredible affirmation of enduring cultural values, as portrayed in Peters' monumental autobiographical painting *Waterbrain*, 2002 (pages 118–19), which maps the life of man, from conception to adulthood. In this tour de force painting, as in much Aboriginal art, the morphing from abstraction to figuration mirrors the convergence of the seen and unseen in the Australian landscape.

The transplanted European artistic tradition of the pastoral idyll – cleared of all but the most accommodating 'natives' – has been radically refigured in the work of Indigenous artists. Ginger Riley Munduwalawala's panoramic vistas are painterly

... IN THE 1970s AND INTO THE 1980s, DURING THE OUTSTATION MOVEMENT THAT FOLLOWED THE IMPLEMENTATION OF THE NORTHERN TERRITORY *ABORIGINAL LAND RIGHTS (NT) ACT* 1976, MANY ABORIGINAL PEOPLE RETURNED TO LIVE IN THEIR TRADITIONAL COUNTRY IN SMALL COMMUNITIES SCATTERED THROUGHOUT THE VAST DESERT REGION. EACH OF THESE SETTLEMENTS IS NOW HOME TO A DISTINCTIVE ART MOVEMENT, TRIGGERED BY THE GENESIS OF THE INFLUENTIAL PAPUNYA TULA ARTISTS COMPANY.

assemblages of the natural and supernatural features of the country he knew as a jungkayi (custodian), and reveal the spiritual and physical landscape of his mother's country around the Limmen Bight River in south-east Arnhem Land. As a young stockman droving through Central Australia, Riley met the Western Aranda watercolourist, Albert Namatjira. Namatjira's paintings were among the first by an Aboriginal artist to find their way into commercial exhibitions and gallery collections. Riley's encounter with the great artist marked a turning point in his life, although it was not until decades later that he realised his dream of becoming a painter was not predicated by his ability to emulate the subtle fluidity of Namatjira's landscapes.

Namatjira was also a profound influence on the first generation of Papunya painters, who saw in his example a way out of the poverty cycle of fringe dweller existence. When equal pay legislation became operative in 1968, most Aboriginal stockmen and women were unceremoniously evicted from pastoral stations and, accordingly, their traditional lands. Amid the ensuing deprivations of life in one desolate government outpost – Papunya, 230 kilometres west of Mparntwe (Alice Springs) – the Papunya Tula art movement had its origins in the early 1970s.

Senior Papunya artists, Shorty Lungkata Tjungurrayi and Uta Uta Tjangala, were among the first of the 'painting mob' to unleash the iconic power of Pintupi symbolism. Another founding member of Papunya Tula Artists, Mick Namarari Tjapaltjarri, was arguably one of its most illustrious artists, maintaining his single-minded approach to painting for over 25 years. Always an innovator, from the late 1980s Namarari began to develop strikingly minimal abstractions of his Tjukurrpa. His work transformed desert painting, and the ascendancy of Pintupi art was confirmed through the works of Timmy Payungka Tjapangati, Turkey Tolson Tjupurrula, Ronnie Tjampitjinpa and others.

A critical turning point in Papunya Tula's history was the creation of the magnificent *Warlugulong*, 1976 (page 147), by the celebrated Anmatyerr brothers, Clifford Possum Tjapaltjarri and Tim Leura Tjapaltjarri. The scale and complexity of this prescient painting heralded the arrival of Western Desert painting as an art movement of international significance. Later in the 1970s and into the 1980s, during the outstation movement that followed the implementation of the Northern Territory *Aboriginal Land Rights (NT) Act* 1976, many Aboriginal people returned to live in their traditional country in small communities scattered throughout the vast desert region. Each of these settlements is now home to a distinctive art movement, triggered by the genesis of the influential Papunya Tula Artists company.

Since the early 1970s, government-funded art centres have been established throughout Australia. Mostly located in remote area communities, these art centres are responsible for marketing the works of their constituent artists. Much of an art centre's work revolves around supporting the cultural life of the community, organising bush trips and workshops, assisting with ceremony and documenting paintings. The Indigenous arts infrastructure has evolved in response to community priorities. Culture, country and community remain the three fundamental, inextricable tenets of Indigenous life. Community initiatives, such as the establishment of 'keeping places' or museums, support cultural maintenance priorities;

and now, through the increasing use of new technologies, these communities can also reach the global market.

When Anmatyerr elder, Emily Kame Kngwarreye, represented Australia at the 1997 Venice Biennale (with Yvonne Koolmatrie and Judy Watson), international audiences were intrigued by the contemporaneity of her gridded, webbed and striped paintings. In her earlier, vigorously expressive paintings – announcing the arrival of Kngwarreye as an artist of note – these organic trajectories were immersed in undulating fields of dots. Yet Kngwarreye's innovative style was firmly rooted in the traditions of her ancestors, and resonates with the paintings of her fellow desert artists to the west of her home community of Utopia, in Central Australia.

Not even the revolutionary nature of Papunya painting presaged the dramatic emergence of Pintupi women's art in the mid-1990s. The distinct aesthetic of this irrepressible group of artists owed more to the tactile application of body paint than the meticulous pointillism of men's ceremonial ground paintings. In works pulsating with the subterranean energy of 'women's business', Inyuwa Nampitjinpa and Makinti Napanangka insinuate their intimate relationship with country through a strategy of concealment and revelation. Women artists have played a significant role in championing the emergence of regionally distinct genres of art making, such as the fragrant fibre forms of Ngarrindjeri artist, Yvonne Koolmatrie, or the eddying pigmentation surrounding the stylised imagery of Ikuntji artist, Mitjili Napurrula. Eubena Nampitjin's richly evocative paintings have stimulated an efflorescence of paintings that capture the spirit of the vast deserts surrounding her homeland community of Wirrimanu (Balgo), in remote Western Australia.

Some of the largest Aboriginal and Torres Strait Islander communities are located within Australia's metropolitan centres, and are home to distinct cultural expressions. Born out of the extremes of dispossession suffered by Indigenous people living on the coastal fringes of the continent, this urban art movement may be seen as synchronous to the growing political empowerment of its members. Central to 'blak' visual arts – a term coined by Melbourne-based new media artist, Destiny Deacon – is the reclamation and affirmation of identity.

Portraiture has been a key conduit for the re-imaging of colonial visions of Indigeneity. Cosmopolitan artists, such as Richard Bell and Rea, place themselves in front of the camera, challenging the viewer to see past the stereotypes imposed upon Aboriginal people as either noble savages, members of a dying race, or, more recently, 'cultureless outcasts'. In Michael Riley's classic image *Maria*, 1985 (page 127), a young Aboriginal woman from western New South Wales is cast in a setting reminiscent of the historical studio portraiture that intended to document a last glimpse of a doomed race. Yet Maria's eloquent, steady gaze defies the relegation of Indigenous people to the annals of a forgotten past.

The Boomalli Aboriginal Artists Cooperative was established in Sydney in 1987 by a group of ten artists in response to the disenfranchisement of Aboriginal artists from the mainstream gallery circuit. The Cooperative has played a critical role in gaining recognition and respect for the diversity of contemporary Indigenous history, visual culture and artists. 'Boomalli' means 'to strike, to make a mark', and it is this fighting spirit that has sustained Aboriginal people since the colonial incursion of 1788. In demonstrations of the early 1970s, people proudly marched with the Aboriginal flag, which was designed by Luritja artist, Harold Thomas, in 1971. The red, black and yellow colours of the flag symbolise the land, the people and the sun. The green and blue Torres Strait flag features a dhari (headdress) and star, representing the unity of Torres Strait Islander people. In the 1990s, the Mabo and Wik findings of the High Court of Australia overturned the legal myth that Australia was 'terra nullius', confirming what had always been known and never conceded: that Aboriginal and Torres Strait Islander people belong to this land, our country.

Ricky Maynard's 'Wik' series, 2000, Mervyn Bishop's photojournalism and Brenda L. Croft's scaled-up 'family album' photographs all create a form of self-portrait, imaging the people and places that have contributed to the history and contemporary experience that unites Indigenous people. The narrative episodes in paintings by Robert Campbell Jnr and Elaine Russell animate the recent history of the mission experience in New South Wales, offering a bittersweet account of life in what were, fundamentally, refugee camps. Ian Abdulla's whimsical painted memoirs of a childhood in rural South Australia, which juxtapose images and script, are brought into sharp focus when viewed alongside Richard Bell's acerbic appropriation of the English alphabet. The radical edge of Indigenous activism, whether political or cultural, is tempered by a sense of community and 'black' humour.

Art is the lifeblood of our communities, connecting us to the past, the present and each other. For centuries, each generation of Aboriginal and Torres Strait Islander people has handed on cultural knowledge and technical expertise, and within this rich tradition successive generations of artists have forged individual aesthetic expressions to mark their experience. Indigenous art has flourished everywhere – in the missions of rural Australia, the suburbs of cities, the estuaries of Arnhem Land, the islands, deserts, ranges and waterholes – and honours the ongoing presence of the artists's ancestors.

The confident exploitation by Indigenous artists of new media practice through photography and digital imaging is matched by their experimentation in traditional forms of art making, realised in contemporary works on bark, fibre sculpture and desert painting. The visual arts offer Indigenous communities a culturally appropriate and economically viable way of living in twenty-first century Australia. Whereas painting for an outside audience was once seen primarily as a means of achieving recognition and respect for the unique and diverse traditions of Indigenous people, today Indigenous artists are transforming the cultural landscape of Australia. The Yiribana Gallery of the Art Gallery of New South Wales is proud to make a contribution to this process in *Tradition Today*.

HETTI KEMERRE PERKINS
CURATOR, ABORIGINAL AND TORRES STRAIT ISLANDER ART

SOME OF THE LARGEST ABORIGINAL AND TORRES STRAIT ISLANDER COMMUNITIES ARE LOCATED WITHIN AUSTRALIA'S METROPOLITAN CENTRES ... BORN OUT OF THE EXTREMES OF DISPOSSESSION SUFFERED BY INDIGENOUS PEOPLE LIVING ON THE COASTAL FRINGES OF THE CONTINENT, THIS URBAN ART MOVEMENT MAY BE SEEN AS SYNCHRONOUS TO THE GROWING POLITICAL EMPOWERMENT OF ITS MEMBERS. CENTRAL TO 'BLAK' VISUAL ARTS ... IS THE RECLAMATION AND AFFIRMATION OF IDENTITY.

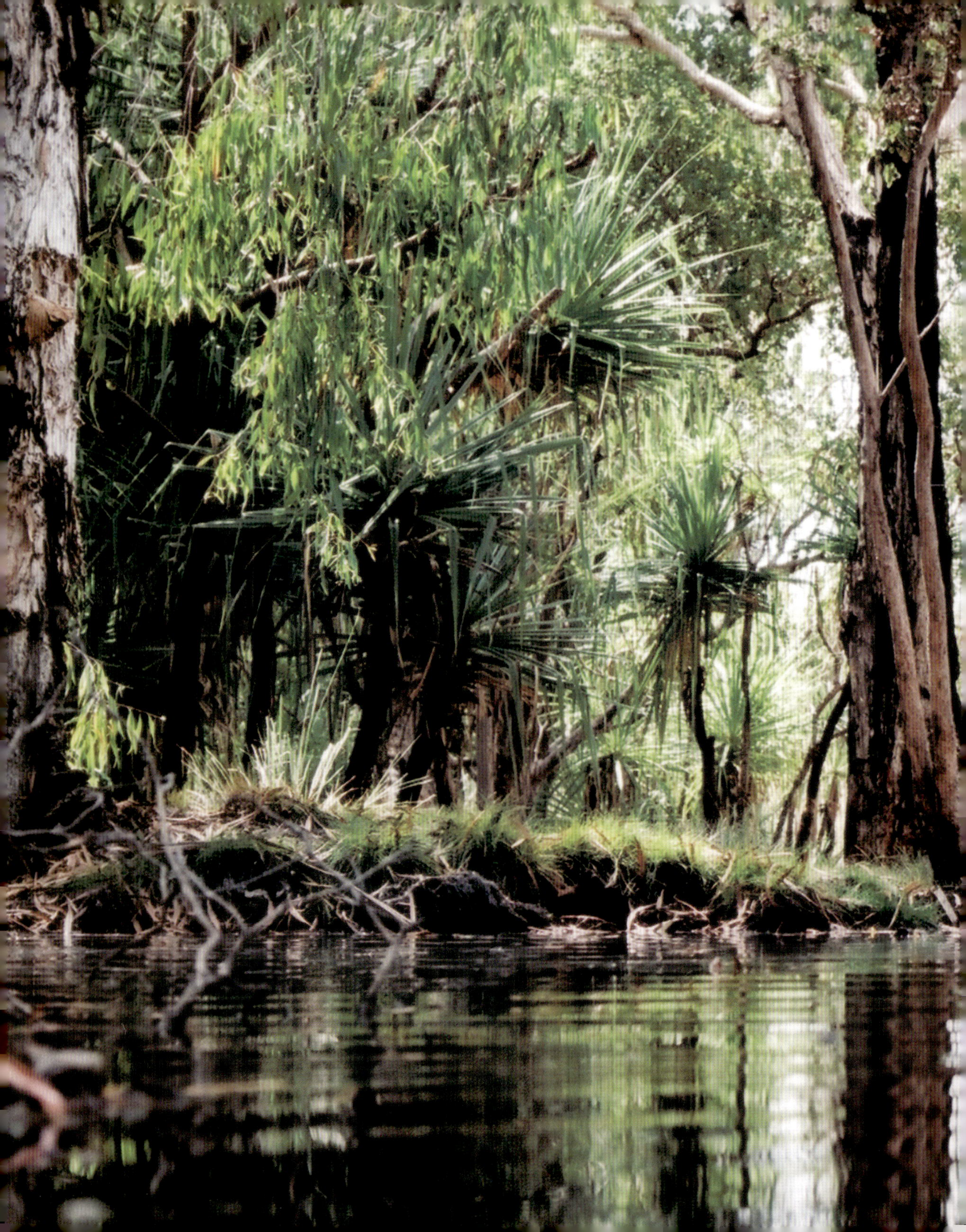

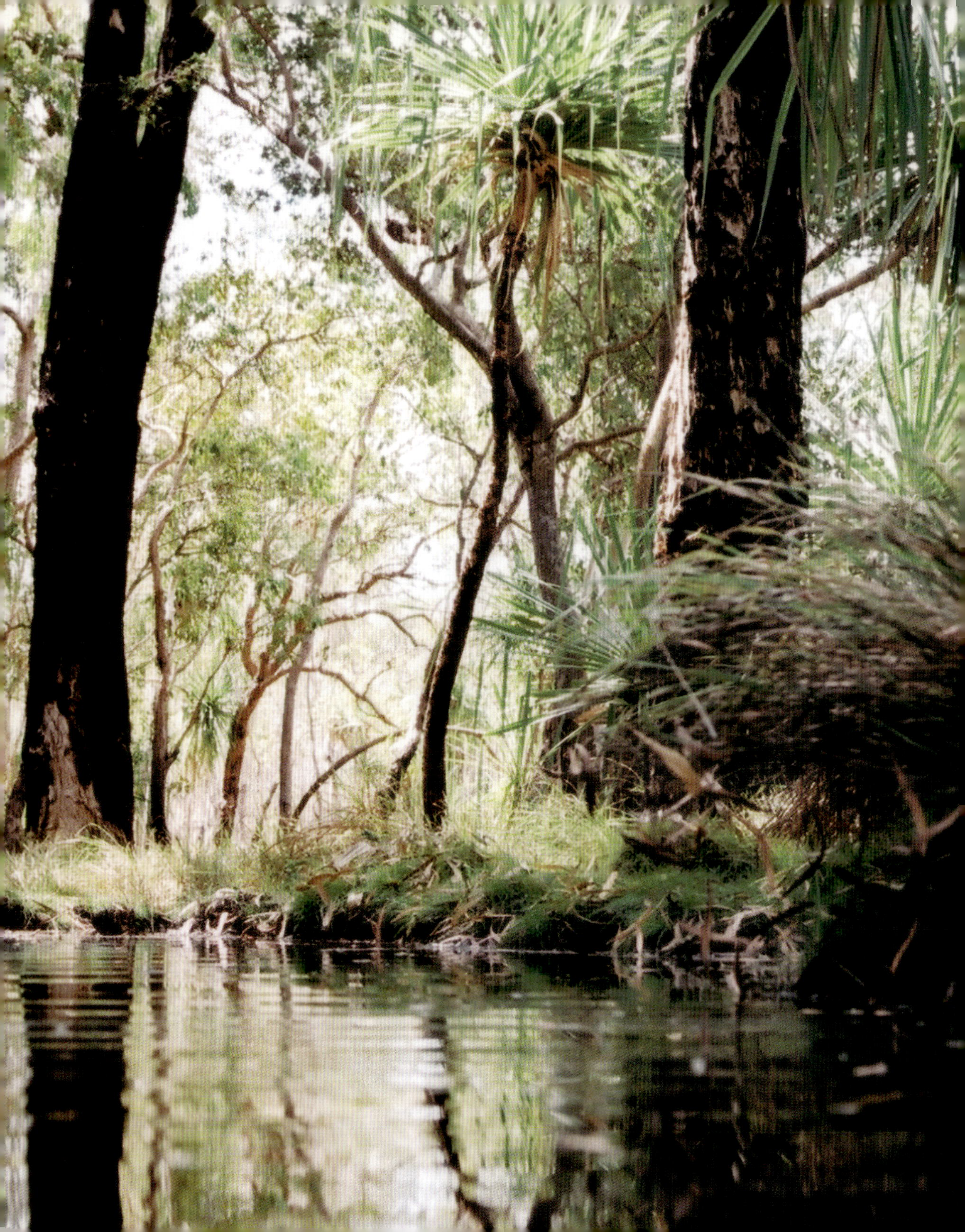

NOTES TO THE READER

The entries in this book are arranged alphabetically by the artist's last name. This may be a skin name or a surname, whichever is more commonly used as the artist's last name. Skin names identify the individual in relation to other family members and prescribe particular social obligations or roles. Artists who are known by their skin name are listed accordingly (eg Mick Namarari Tjapaltjarri is listed under Tjapaltjarri) as are artists who are more commonly known by their surname (eg Billy Benn is listed under Benn, rather than his skin name of Perrurle).

Where an artist is known by both names, the use of either surname or skin name within the artist's essay has been at the individual author's discretion eg Mick Namarari Tjapaltjarri is referred to as Namarari, whereas Timmy Payungka Tjapanangka is referred to as Tjapanangka.

The headline for each artist includes birth and, where relevant, death dates, language group(s) and the state or territory from which this language group originates.

The names used throughout are the most common and accepted names by which the artists are professionally known.

Birth and death dates for Indigenous people have not always been recorded. Where these dates are not definitive the publisher has consulted with the community and used the most widely accepted or published dates.

Notation of language groups follows the most common attribution. Where artists belong to more than one language group, this is indicated eg Pintupi/Ngaatjatjarra.

Due to changes in orthography, spellings can vary. The spelling used in this book follows the most common usage. Exceptions occur where there are regional variations eg Wagilag/Wawilak or Arrernte/Aranda. In this instance the preference of the artists or their representative has been respected.

Aboriginal names relevant to specific regions have been used throughout the book, accompanied by an English translation eg Mparntwe (Alice Springs). Exception is made for words that have more complex associations – these appear in the glossary eg Tjukurrpa.

AUTHORSHIP

Authorship of each essay is acknowledged with an individual writer's initials in the following way: George Alexander (GA), Natasha Brook (NB), Deborah Edwards (DE), Hannah Fink (HF), Vivien Johnson (VJ), Jonathan Jones (JJ), John Kean (JK), Eric Kjellgren (EK), Howard Morphy (HM), Steven Miller (SM), Hetti Perkins (HP), Luke Taylor (LT), Wayne Tunnicliffe (WT) and Ken Watson (KW).

IAN ABDULLA
PADDY BEDFORD
RICHARD BELL
BILLY BENN
BINYINYUWUY
MERVYN BISHOP
JOHN BULUNBULUN
NYM BUNDUCK & KEVIN BUNDUCK
ROBERT CAMPBELL JNR
ROBERT AMBROSE COLE
BRENDA L. CROFT
DESTINY DEACON
DAWIDI DJULWARAK
KEVIN GILBERT
WILLIE GUDABI
PHILIP GUDTHAYKUDTHAY
MITHINARI GURRUWIWI
ROY KENNEDY
EMILY KAME KNGWARREYE
YVONNE KOOLMATRIE
ANCHOR KULUNBA
CRUSOE KURDDAL
QUEENIE McKENZIE
DR PANTJITI MARY McLEAN
DR DAVID MALANGI
SAMUEL MANGGUDJA
BANDUK MARIKA
MAWALAN MARIKA
WANDJUK MARIKA
JOHN MAWURNDJUL
GALUMA MAYMURU
NARRITJIN MAYMURU
RICKY MAYNARD
TRACEY MOFFATT
SALLY MORGAN
GINGER RILEY MUNDUWALAWALA
MÄW' MUNUNGGURR
ALBERT NAMATJIRA
EUBENA NAMPITJIN
INYUWA NAMPITJINPA
MAKINTI NAPANANGKA
MITJILI NAPURRULA
NINGURA NAPURRULA
DULA NGURRUWUTTHUN
JIMMY NJIMINJUMA
LIN ONUS
OTTO PAREROULTJA
RUSTY PETERS
GLORIA TAMERRE PETYARRE
KUTUWULUMI PURAWARRUMPATU
REA
MICHAEL RILEY
ELAINE RUSSELL
NYIRLPIRR SPIDER SNELL
KEN THAIDAY
THANCOUPIE
ROVER THOMAS
TIMMY TIMMS
RONNIE TJAMPITJINPA
UTA UTA TJANGALA
CLIFFORD POSSUM TJAPALTJARRI
MICK NAMARARI TJAPALTJARRI
TIM LEURA TJAPALTJARRI
LONG TOM TJAPANANGKA
TJUMPO TJAPANANGKA
TIMMY PAYUNGKA TJAPANGATI
SHORTY LUNGKATA TJUNGURRAYI
JOHNNY WARANGKULA TJUPURRULA
TURKEY TOLSON TJUPURRULA
PRINCE OF WALES
JUDY WATSON
H. J. WEDGE
PEDRO WONAEAMIRRI
JABARRGWA WURRABADALUMBA
OWEN YALANDJA
LENA YARINKURA
MUNGGURRAWUY YUNUPINGU

IAN ABDULLA

BORN 1947
NGARRINDJERI
SOUTH AUSTRALIA

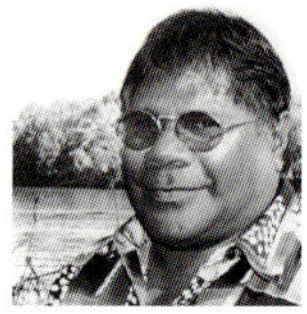

Ian Abdulla's paintings vividly recall his childhood memories of the peripatetic life of the Ngarrindjeri people of the Riverland region in rural South Australia. A hallmark of his work is the juxtaposition of text and image against a flattened foreground, in the manner of an animated narrative. Abdulla's handpainted annotations are placed dead centre at the top of his paintings, bringing a personal inflection to his stories. His experiences are shared by many Aboriginal people dispossessed of their land and marginalised into a life of seasonal work and scavenging. Yet, as *Swimming before school*, 1995, reveals, Abdulla's richly detailed paintings offer a sense of community despite the hardships of working for a subsistence livelihood on the fringes of a wealthy white farming community. The rapid degradation of the natural resources of the region, and encroaching westernisation of Nunga communities are also as subtly constant as the ubiquitous Murray River.

From his participation in a community screen-printing workshop in Glossop in 1988, Abdulla's transition to painting and increasing prominence is similar to that of many Aboriginal artists from rural or urban communities who have found a voice in the visual arts. Abdulla's work came to national attention during his first solo exhibition in 1991 at the newly established Tandanya National Aboriginal Cultural Institute in Adelaide. By actively supporting the artists of its Indigenous constituency, Tandanya was critical in the fostering of the impressive talents of Nunga artists. In 1993, Abdulla exhibited jointly with Wiradjuri artist, H. J. Wedge, at Boomalli Aboriginal Artists Cooperative, Sydney. An artist-run centre, Boomalli was set up in 1987 by a group of ten Sydney-based Aboriginal artists.

Abdulla has also produced three autobiographical picture books,[1] and undertaken commissions for 'Beyond the Pale: Adelaide Biennial of Australian art', curated by Brenda L. Croft in 2000, and the Melbourne Museum. For these projects, he created three-dimensional installations that appear as natural evolutions of his paintings. In 1991 Abdulla was named South Australian Aboriginal Artist of the Year, and was awarded an Australia Council Fellowship in 1992. As these awards and his work testify, Ian Abdulla is now counted as one of the leading figures in the flourishing of Indigenous art from Australia's rural communities. HP

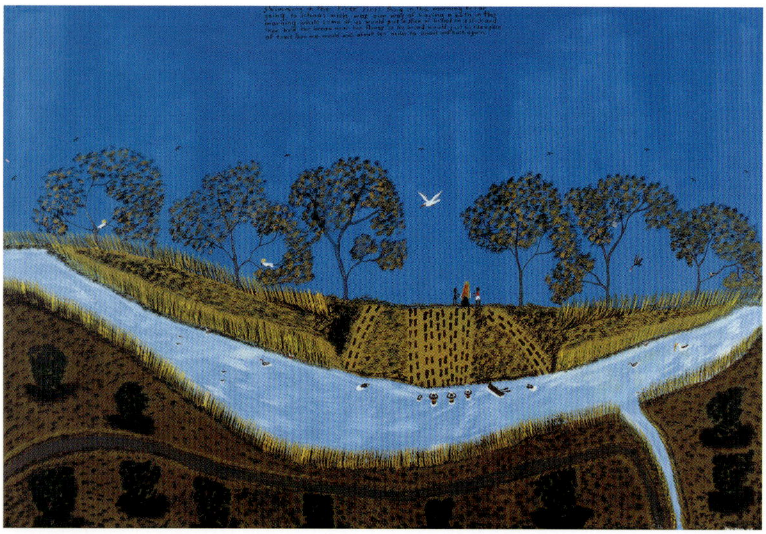

Swimming before school 1995
synthetic polymer paint on canvas
160 x 240 cm
> detail

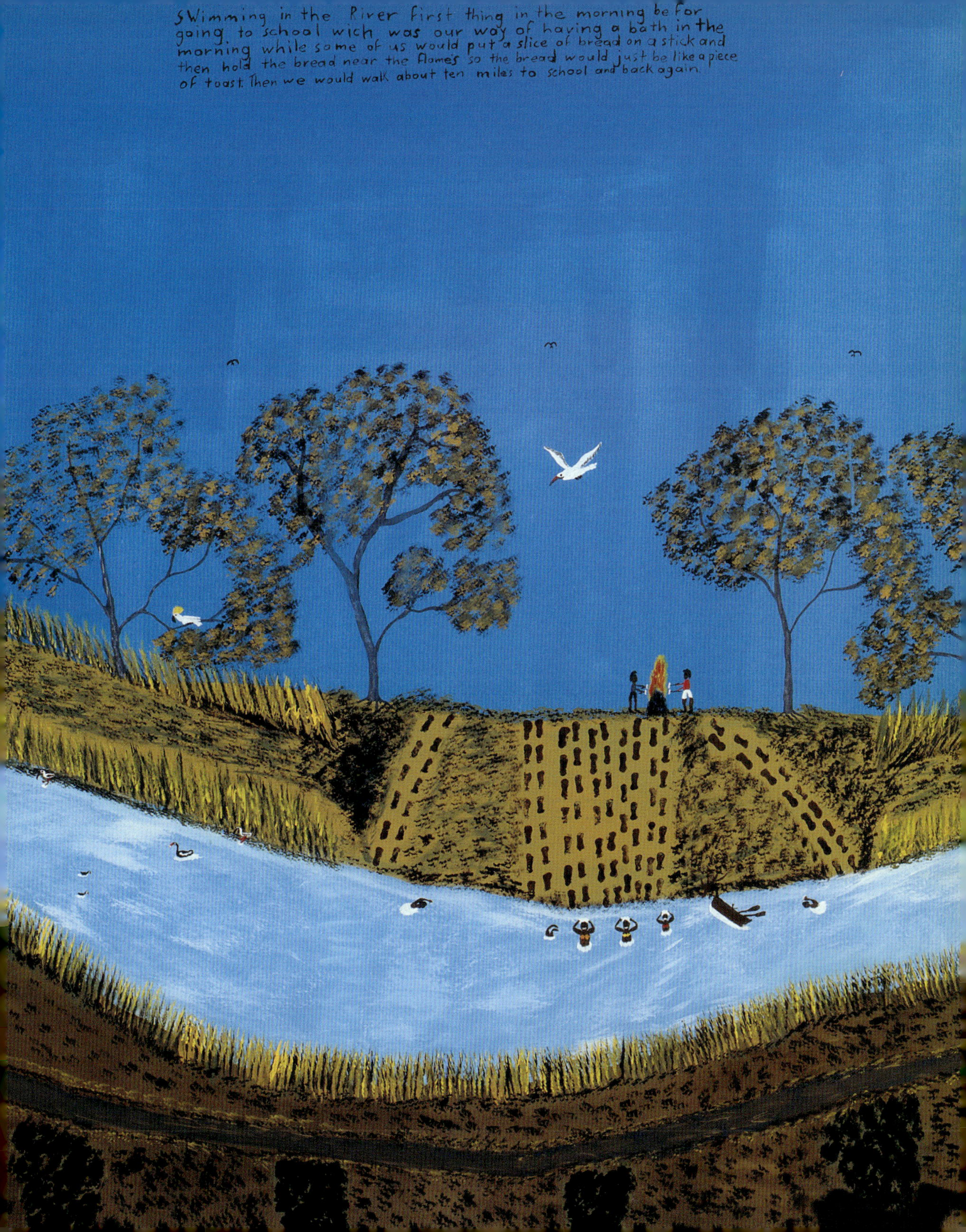
SWimming in the River first thing in the morning be for going to school wich was our way of having a bath in the morning while some of us would put a slice of bread on a stick and then hold the bread near the flame's so the bread would just be like a piece of toast. Then we would walk about ten miles to school and back again.

PADDY BEDFORD

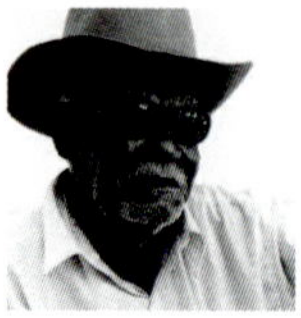

BORN c.1922
GIJA
WESTERN AUSTRALIA

A senior Gija lawman and a highly important figure within contemporary East Kimberley painting, Paddy Bedford was born on Bedford Downs Station south-west of Warmun (Turkey Creek), Western Australia. Bedford spent his youth working in the dry season as a stockman on cattle stations in or near his traditional country, including Greenvale, Bow River and Bedford Downs. Like other Aboriginal stockworkers, in the wet season he lived off the land, learning Gija culture and law and developing a reputation as an accomplished spear and boomerang fighter. In his later years Bedford moved to the main Gija community of Warmun.

For most of his life, his painting centered on the adornment of the human body, painting both himself and others for secret ceremonies and public performances. Ironically, Bedford's talents as a painter were only revealed in 1998, when an art dealer noticed a series of paintings Bedford had made on odd scraps of plywood and other salvaged materials. Originally bound for the town dump, the paintings were saved and Bedford was encouraged to try his hand at painting on canvas. Later that year he joined Jirrawun Aboriginal Arts, which was then forming at the community of Rugan (Crocodile Hole). Since then, Bedford has gone on to become one of the most renowned painters in the East Kimberley, and his work has featured in numerous solo and group exhibitions.

Bedford's spare compositions, with their large areas of monochrome ochre separated by subtly dotted lines, often resemble those of Warmun's most celebrated artist Rover Thomas. But, as is also true of Thomas's work, the apparent abstraction or minimalism of Bedford's canvases is superficial, covering a richly layered portrait of country, Ngarrangkarni and history, the significance of which is revealed through the accompanying narrative. *Untitled (Emu)*, 1999, illustrates both the seemingly abstract qualities of Bedford's painting style and the deep knowledge of Ngarrangkarni and country underlying it. At the lower left, the artist reveals the emu ancestor, who plays a prominent role in the series of sacred songs and associated country that the canvas portrays. Simultaneously 'abstract' to Western eyes and 'representational' to the painter, Bedford's work, like all East Kimberley painting, defies easy categorisation. It works in a distinctive way, simultaneously concealing and revealing the land, which sets it apart from Western landscape traditions. EK

> **Untitled (Old Bedford)** 1999
natural pigments on canvas
122.5 x 135.1 cm

v **Untitled (Emu)** 1999
natural pigments on canvas
122.2 x 135.3 cm

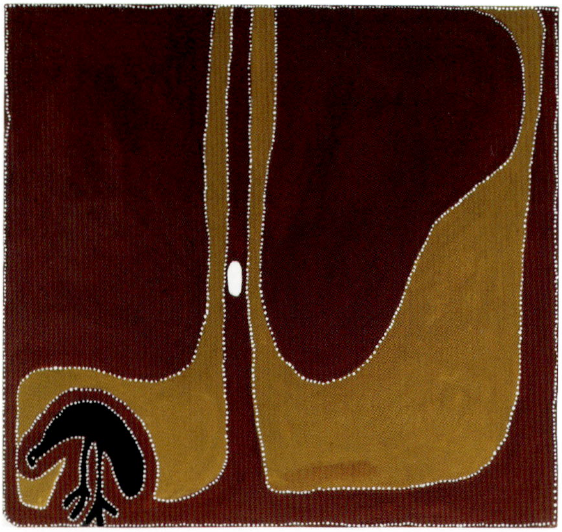

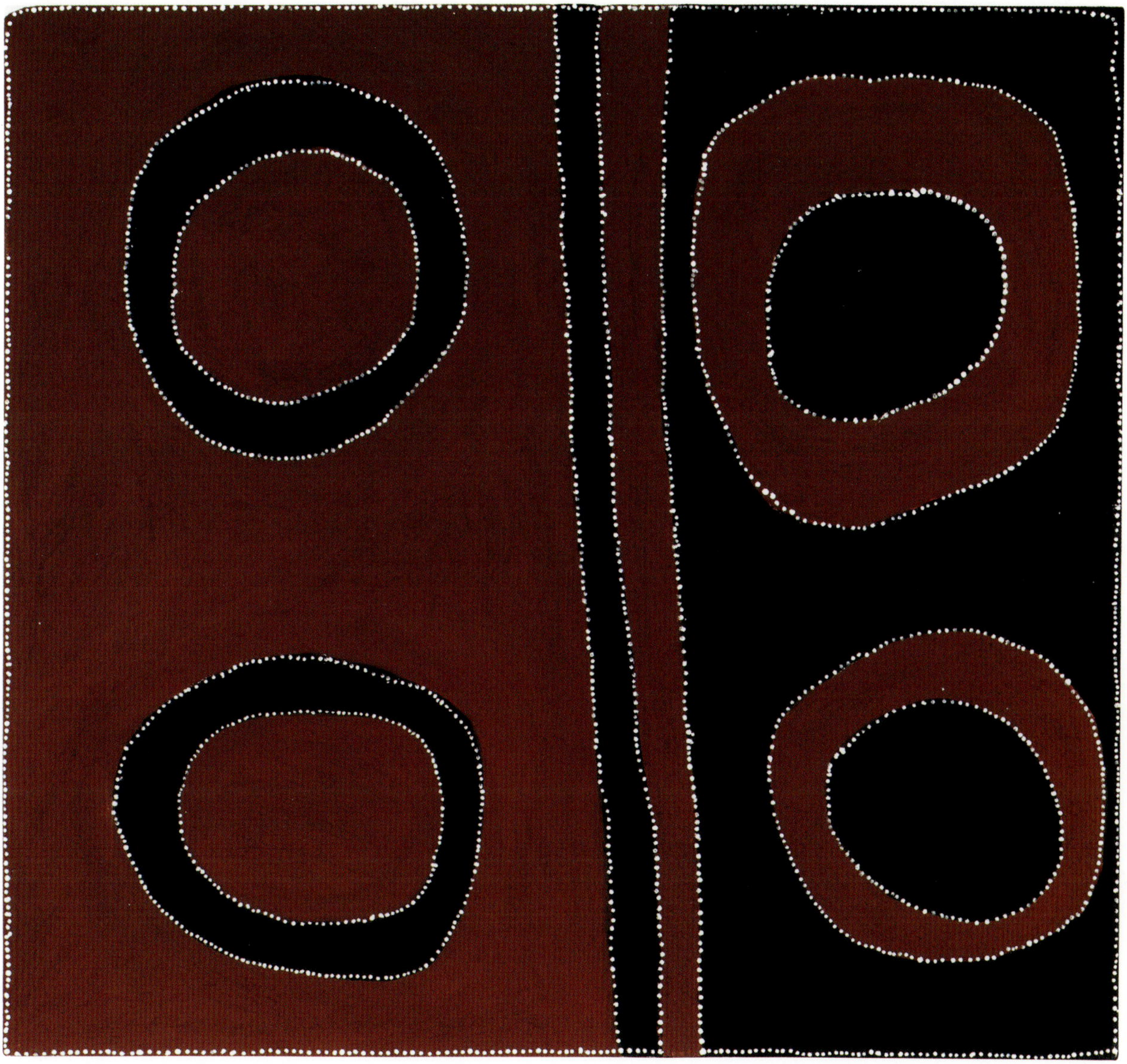

RICHARD BELL

BORN 1953
KAMILAROI
NEW SOUTH WALES

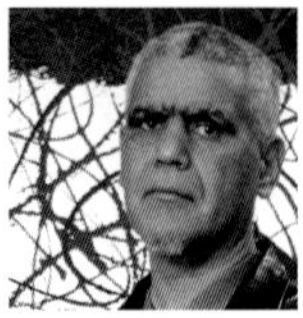

Richard Bell warns in the introduction to his unpublished 'Bell's Theorem' that his thesis will be ' ... conversational, playful, serious, tongue in cheek, moralistic, tolerant, sermonistic and informative'.[1] Aboriginal culture, Bell believes, has become a commodity, slowly being digested by Western society. Within this system, Aboriginal artists are either 'tribal' people living in the 'outback' – whose work is fair game for appropriation – or 'urban blacks' whose cultural 'authenticity' has been disenfranchised by the brutal process of colonisation. Speaking as a member of the Murri community, Bell states, ' ... Our culture was ripped from us and not much remains. Most of our languages have disappeared. We don't have black or even dark skin. We don't take shit from you.'[2] His invective is tempered by humour, however, a strategy to sugar coat the ideological pill, ensuring that his mouthful of political homily will stick in the throat.

Bell is a key figure in the collective of Indigenous and non-Indigenous artists known as the Campfire Group, established in 1993, which evolved into the Fire-Works Gallery. The programme at their Brisbane city exhibition space claims to address 'Aboriginal Art and Other Burning Issues'. The collective's mantra is one of free artistic appropriation and influence, with the political ends justifying the artistic means. Bell, the self-proclaimed 'enfant terrible' of Australian art, wilfully uses and abuses the sacred cows of painting from Jackson Pollock to Colin McCahon, describing his role as ' ... very similar to Pablo Picasso'.[3] Closer to home, Bell's paintings often make generic reference to the pictograms of rock art and desert painting. In *Devine inspiration*, 1993, a palimpsest of stencilled images and concentric circles is overwritten with an alphabet that begins with 'Abos, Blacks, Coons ... ' – an 'ABC' of racist language particular to Australia. It concludes with a withering sequence of words damning the oppressors of Indigenous people as ' ... Very Weak Xenophobic Yobbo Zookeepers'.

Bell assaults the many fronts of Australian racism, from its most covert manifestations to everyday forms, from nursery rhymes and remarks bandied around the schoolyard to the subversive use of language. Bell highjacks language, the vehicle of Western power, and drives it headlong into the class barriers that disenfranchise minority societies. As George Petelin has written, ' ... Culture for [Bell] is not something of the past but part of a daily struggle'.[4] HP

> **Devine inspiration** 1993
synthetic polymer paint and collage on canvas
239.6 x 149.6 cm

v **Pigeonholes** 1992
13 photographic panels on composition board
76 x 292 cm overall

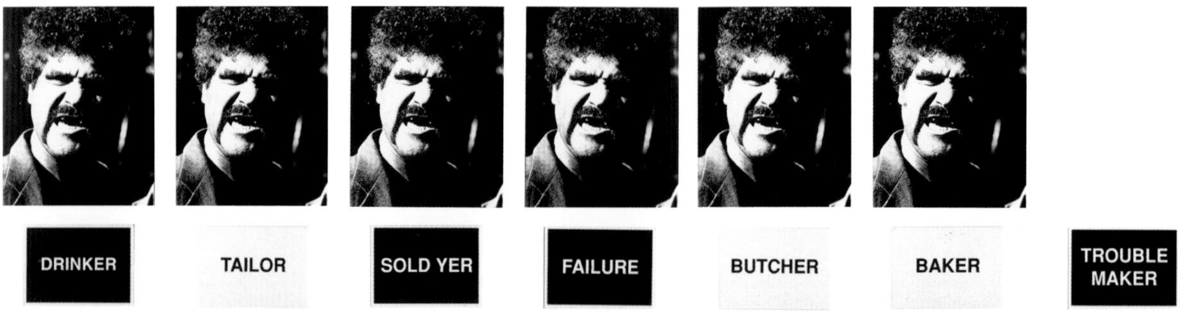

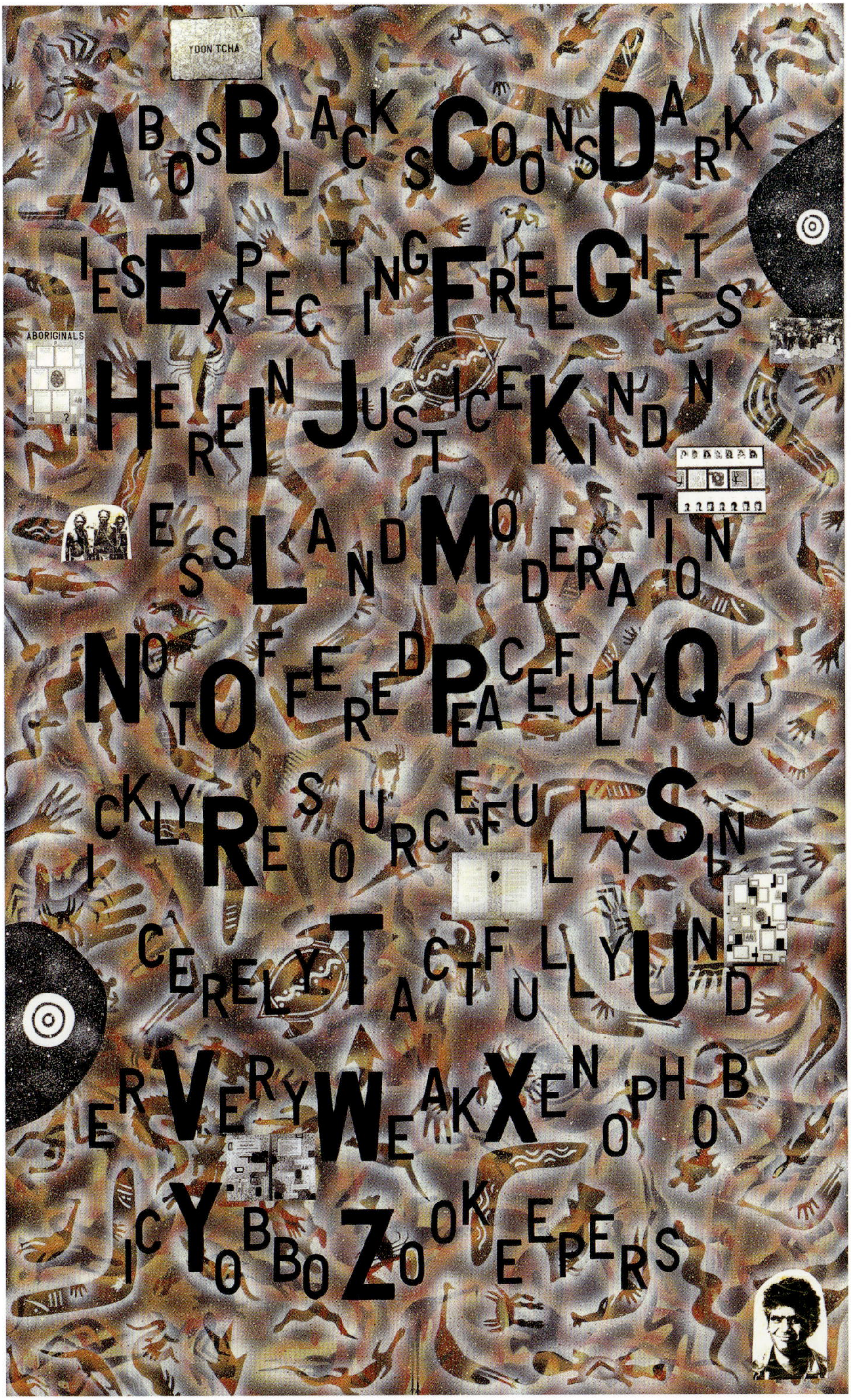

YDON'TCHA
ABOSBLACKSCOONSDARK
IESEXPECTINGFREEGIFTS
ABORIGINALS
HEREINJUSTICEKINDN
ESSLANDMODERATION
NOTOOFFEREDPEACEFULLYQU
ICKLYRESOURCEFULLYSIN
CERELYTACTFULLYUND
ERVERYWEAKXENOPHOB
ICYOBBOZOOKEEPERS

BILLY BENN

BORN 1943
EASTERN ARRERNTE
NORTHERN TERRITORY

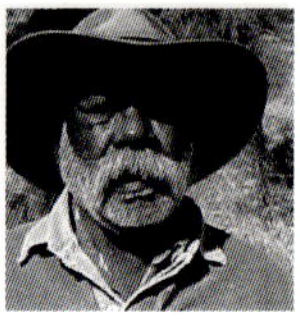

The ancient ranges that traverse the arid landscape of Central Australia, east of Mparntwe (Alice Springs), are the home of the Alyawarr and Eastern Arrernte people. This is the land Billy Benn (Perrurle) paints, his birthplace and father's country. It was here he learned the traditional art of his people from his father, and 'cousin sisters' Ally and Gladdy Kemerre. After moving to Mparntwe, he began moonlighting as an artist while employed as a gardener, metalworker and woodworker. Until recently, Benn's paintings existed in obscurity, bolted to the walls of a workshop.

Benn's paintings remain true to their origins, created on salvaged timber and, early on, were often embellished with generous coatings of estapol. Awareness of Benn's work grew when *In the bush Barrow Creek way*, c.1996, appeared in 'Desert Mob 2001', one of the annual expositions of regional Indigenous art held at the local Araluen Arts Centre in Mparntwe. Widely regarded as his most spectacular work, it is likely this painting was inspired by Benn's fond memories of droving with his cousins from his father's country Arrkngenangkerre (Mount Swann) to Barrow Creek.

Benn's tenacity inspired the establishment of Mwerre Anthurre – Bindi Centa Arts, a cooperative of artists working with a disability, and the fostering of the talents of his colleagues, including Aileen Oliver and Seth Namatjira. As a collective, the Bindi artists navigate the stylistic vernaculars of the two art movements for which Central Australian Aboriginal art is renowned: the representative watercolour landscapes of the Hermannsburg school and the interpretative symbolism of Western Desert painting. Whereas the Western Aranda artists, whose members include Albert Namatjira, create clearly defined topographical paintings saturated with the vibrant colours of the desert, Benn's expressionist landscapes are often rendered in swirling dusty hues as if emerging from a primordial dawn. Calligraphic brushstrokes suggest the bluffs and deep crevasses punctuating the ridges of this country, fringed by stands of gum trees that line wide sandy riverbeds, bleached the colour of bone. Accents of topaz and turquoise, like the intermittent flashes of brilliant birds, evoke the dramatic effects of the play of light over a vast desert panorama.

Benn's paintings are permeated by a touch of melancholy that reflects the loss of many of his family in the hard days of frontier life, yet Benn is sustained by his nostalgia for his country and driven to keep pursuing his dream of painting every hill in his country, and one day returning home.[1] HP

In the bush Barrow Creek way c.1996
synthetic polymer paint on flexi panel
30 x 244 cm
> detail

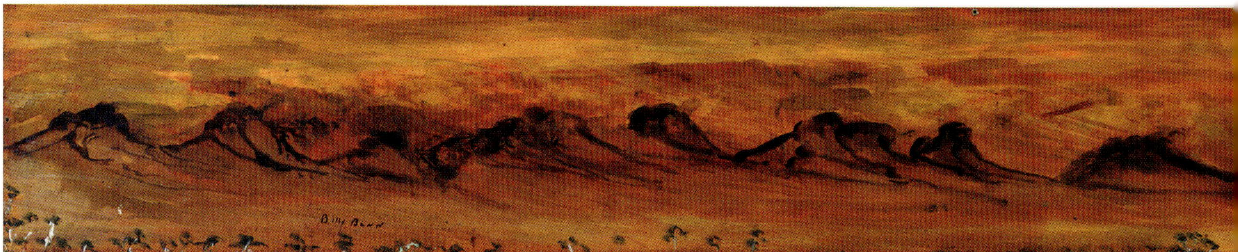

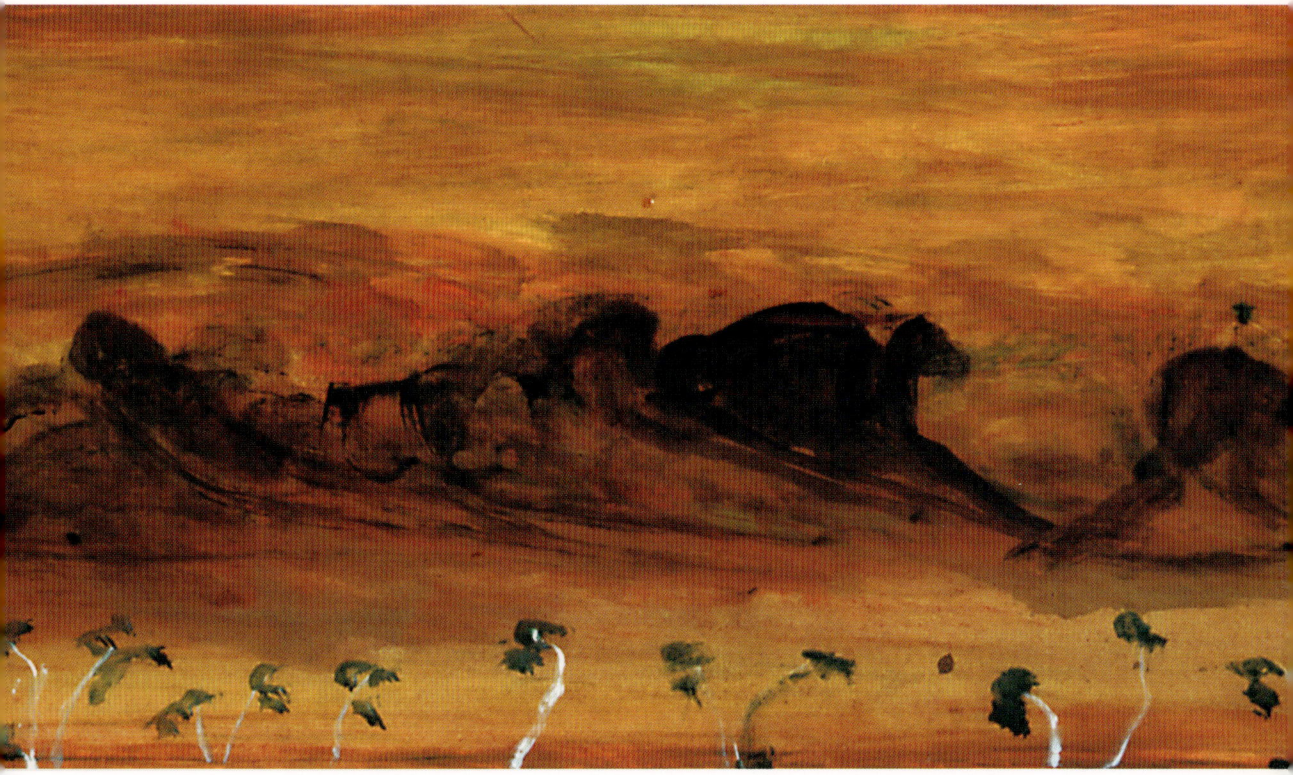

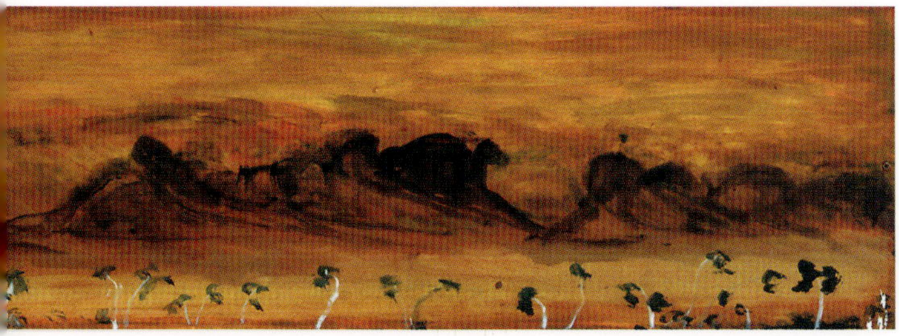

BINYINYUWUY

c.1928–1982
DJAMBARRPUYUNGU
NORTHERN TERRITORY

As a young man, Binyinyuwuy opposed the presence of the Methodist Mission at Milingimbi, established in 1923, and the adoption of balanda (whitefella) ways. Described as a 'pocket Hercules',[1] Binyinyuwuy successfully raided the mission store a number of times. However, his prodigious talents as an artist and craftsman were well known to the senior men of Milingimbi, and they encouraged Binyinyuwuy to join the group of artists then producing bark paintings for sale to collectors.

Binyinyuwuy celebrates the communal joy associated with collecting sugarbag (wild honey) in *Yirritja honey bee design (Niwuda)*, c.1960. This intricate bark painting, consisting of diamond-patterned miny'tji (sacred clan designs) painted with brilliant ochres, refers to such details as the honeycomb filled with honey, wax, pollen, dead bees and debris. The hive is ingeniously depicted, using two distinct clan designs. The black circle and pointed cone represent the built-up opening of the hive, and also refer to sacred objects made of painted and decorated wood or rolled paperbark bound with string, to signify honey in ceremony. These spectacular designs are also painted on the bodies of young Yirritja boys for their dhapi (initiation) ceremony and on men when performing in the Djambarrpuyungu and Gupapuyungu Birrkuda (honey) ceremonies.

A cloudburst of rain falls on the stylised, tropical forest in *Rain in the trees*, c.1959. Underneath this panel, sections of finely painted, multi-coloured zigzags and chevrons alternate with bands of dashes or strokes, representing the lightning and thunder clouds.

The columns of circular floral designs in *Trees and flying fox camp*, c.1950s, symbolise both the flying fox droppings and the flowers from which they extract nectar. This comparatively restrained composition successfully reduces these associated, yet divergent, realities to an identifiable visual code or abbreviation. Both paintings were collected by the Rev. Edgar Wells while he was superintendent of the mission at Milingimbi between 1949 and 1959, and were purchased by the Art Gallery of New South Wales, Sydney, in 1962.

Binyinyuwuy was a renowned fighter and great ceremonial performer. His paintings reveal his robust, meticulous character and confirm his reputation as one of the finest bark painters of his generation – a generation famous for its virtuosity in the medium. KW

> **Trees and flying fox camp** c.1950s
natural pigments on bark
48 x 29.5 cm

v left **Rain in the trees** c.1959
natural pigments on bark
74 x 39.4 cm

v right **Yirritja honey bee design (Niwuda)** c.1960
natural pigments on bark
74.5 x 35 cm

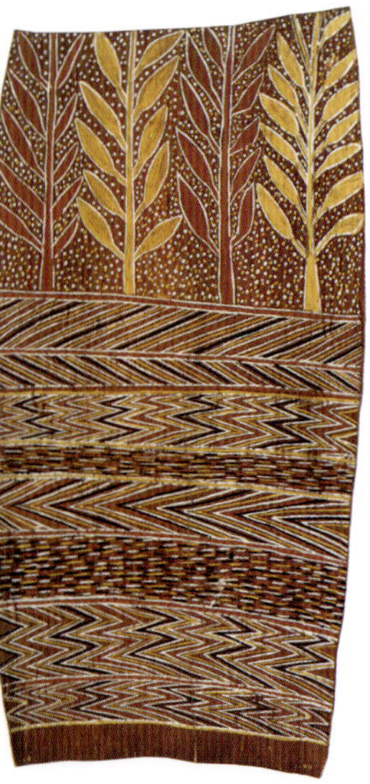

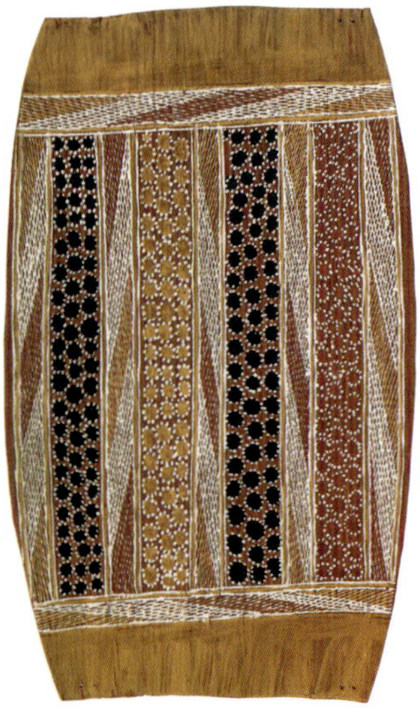

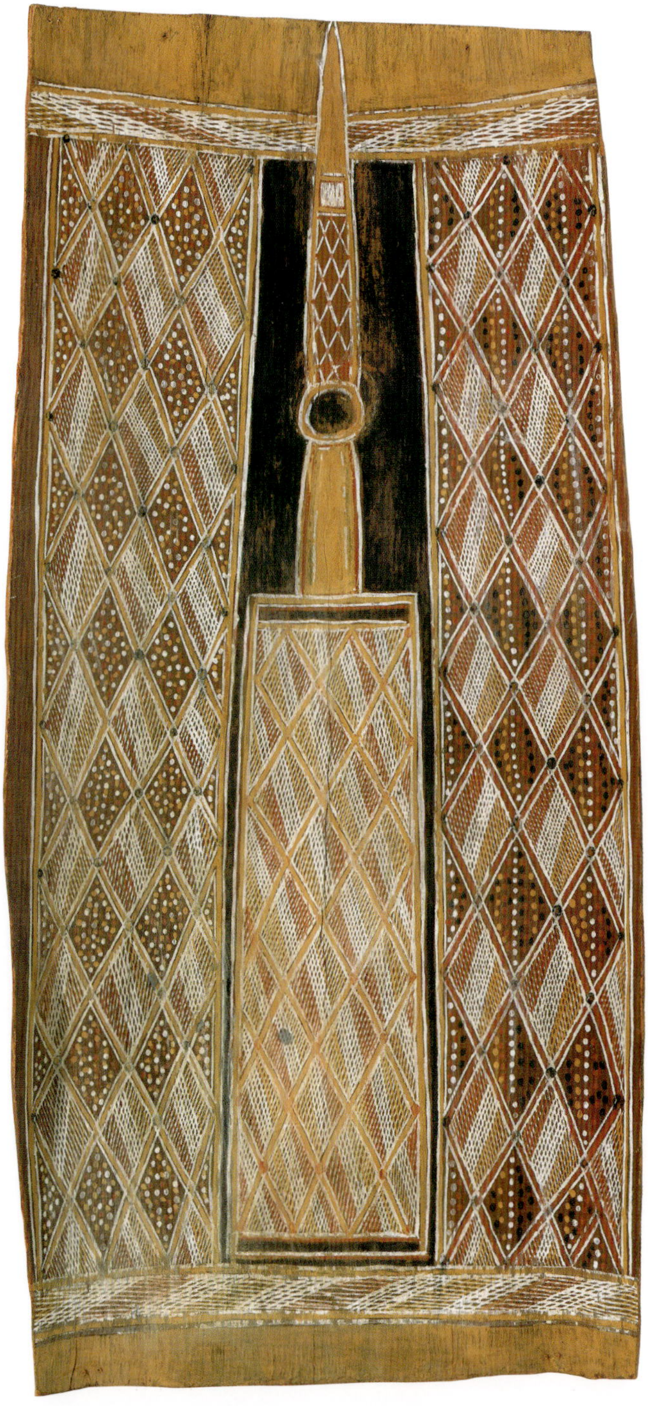

MERVYN BISHOP

BORN 1945
NEW SOUTH WALES

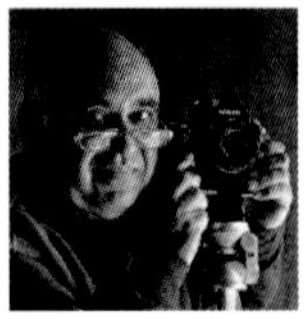

Born and raised in Brewarrina, New South Wales, Mervyn Bishop was encouraged by his mother to take his first photograph. After witnessing the 'magic' of the developing process, he became passionate about photography. In 1963 he successfully applied for a four-year cadetship at the *Sydney Morning Herald*, and completed a Photography Certificate Course at Sydney Technical College during these years. Bishop continued to work for the *Sydney Morning Herald*, and was Australia's first Aboriginal press photographer. In 1971 he won the News Photographer of the Year Award with his front-page photograph, *Life and Death Dash*, 1971. In this startling image, composition, contrast and Aboriginal social commentary combine. It is a classic example of photojournalism that has since transgressed its original context and come to insinuate the impact of religious missions within Aboriginal Australia and, in particular, on the Stolen Generations.

Bishop started work at the Department of Aboriginal Affairs in Canberra in 1974, in the early years of an important era in Indigenous self-determination. Here he covered the major developments in Aboriginal communities throughout Australia, including the historical moment in 1975 when the (then) Prime Minister, Gough Whitlam, poured a handful of earth back into the hand of Vincent Lingiari, Gurindji elder and traditional land owner. This image – representing the Australian government's recognition of Aboriginal land rights – became an icon of the land rights movement and Australian photography. In 1989 Bishop received his Associate Diploma in Adult Education at Sydney College of Advanced Education, and went on to teach photography at Tranby Aboriginal College in Glebe, Sydney and the Eora Centre TAFE (Technical and Further Education) in Redfern, Sydney.

Bishop's diverse career, combining journalistic and art photography, was celebrated in 1991 in his solo exhibition and accompanying monograph, 'In Dreams: Mervyn Bishop Thirty Years of Photography 1960–1990'. This important exhibition was curated by Tracey Moffatt and opened at the Australian Centre for Photography, Sydney, before touring nationally and internationally. The timely and intimate photographs celebrate Bishop's contribution to Australian art and photojournalism. In 2000, Bishop was presented with the Red Ochre Award from the Aboriginal and Torres Strait Islander Board of the Australia Council, in recognition of his pioneering work and ongoing influence. JJ

> **Prime Minister Gough Whitlam pours soil into the hands of traditional landowner Vincent Lingiari, Northern Territory** 1975
printed 1999
type R3 photograph
30.5 x 30.5 cm

v left **Life and death dash** 1971
gelatin silver photograph
40.4 x 30.1 cm

v right **Girl pours tea, Burnt Bridge** 1988
gelatin silver photograph
30.1 x 40.4 cm

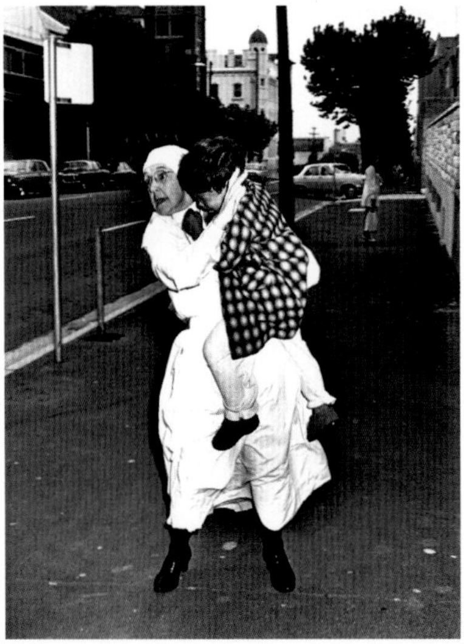

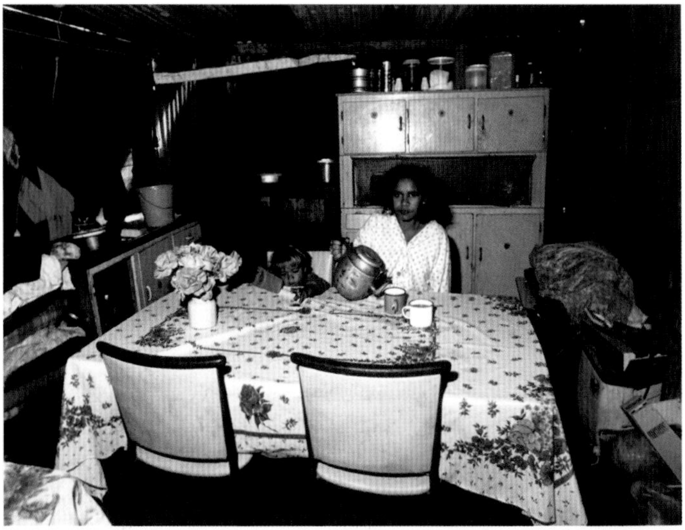

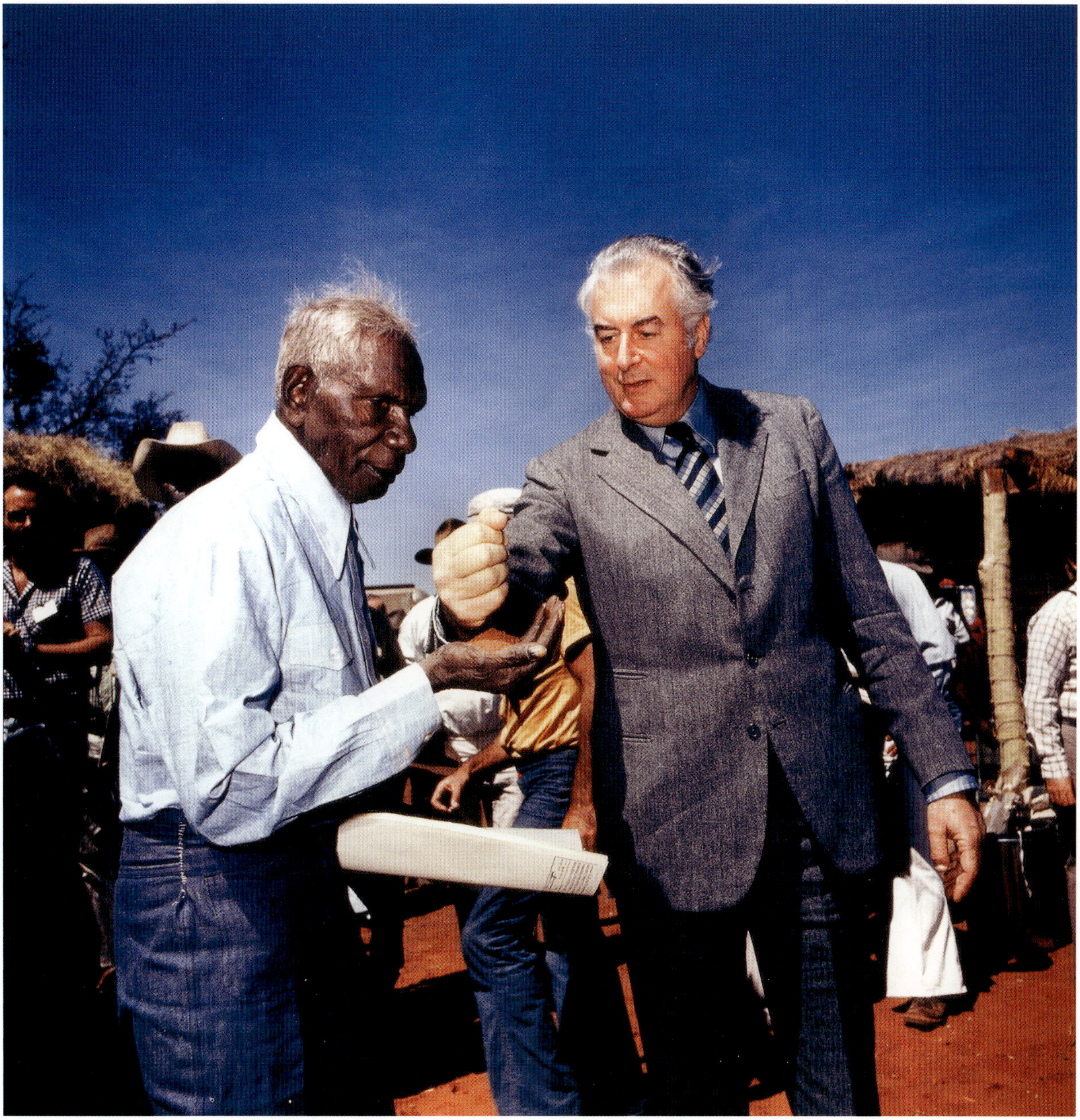

JOHN BULUNBULUN

BORN 1946
GANALBINGU
NORTHERN TERRITORY

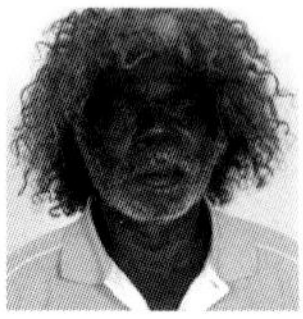

'These paintings are my Dreaming, and all the animals here are part of my Dreaming. There is the long-neck turtle ... He is the most important one because it was him who made my country and my people.' [1]

John Bulunbulun lives with his wife's family at Wurdeja, not far from the Blyth River in the Northern Territory. He is a member of the Ganalbingu clan, and one of the most important singers and ceremonial men in the northern part of central Arnhem Land. His traditional homeland lies in the Arafura Swamp area. Taught painting by his father, Bulunbulun has painted continuously since 1970, having his first solo exhibition at the Hogarth Galleries, Sydney in 1981. He received considerable publicity in 1989 when he took successful action against a Queensland T-shirt maker for illegally reproducing one of his works, a landmark case in Aboriginal intellectual property rights.

Guwaynang, the long-necked freshwater turtle, is an especially important animal in the cosmology of Bulunbulun's homeland and is the artist's own spiritual emblem. *Journey of the Guwaynang*, 2000, depicts three guwaynang travelling across their country. These animals have a number of simultaneous identities: in different stories, they are male, female or sisters. The Guwaynang story is also analogous to the more widely known ancestral history of the two Djan'kawu Sisters, who created much of the landscape in eastern Arnhem Land.

In *Journey of the Guwaynang*, Bulunbulun refers to the ancestral sisters travelling through country that contains two waterholes, shown as black circles. The bottom half of the painting refers to Bulunbulun's own Ganalbingu country, where the sisters began their journey. The thin yellow bar across the lower section represents a log at a place called Junggibarparnyamurru, which the Ganalbingu people consider to be extremely sacred. One of the sisters, shown as the yellow turtle, went on to create the country belonging to other Ganalbingu-speaking clans; the other sister created the Wurlaki-speaking clans and their country. The differences in colour and pattern of the three turtles reflect the changes in language that the Sisters instigated, and the black lines framing each turtle refer to their tracks. The turtles are depicted against a background of crosshatching and fine stripes, both wavy and straight, representing water grass. This painting displays Bulunbulun's distinctive use of white pigment and his individual style of crosshatching, which creates an overall shimmering effect. SM

Journey of the Guwaynang 2000
natural pigments on eucalyptus bark
217 x 97 cm

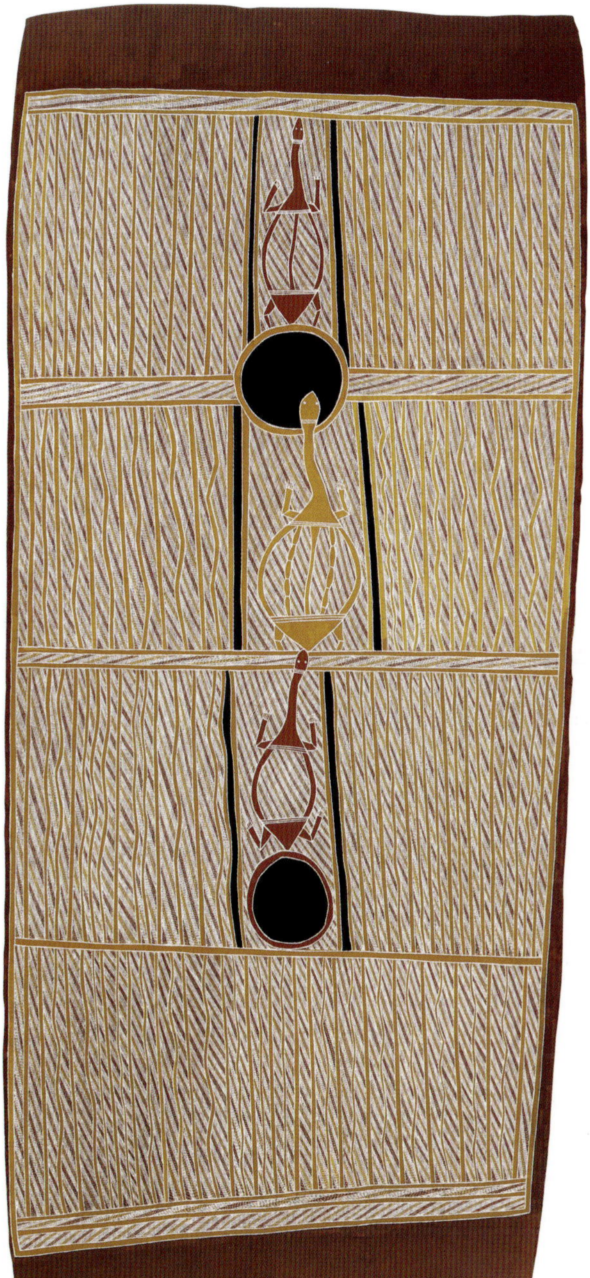

NYM BUNDUCK
KEVIN BUNDUCK

c.1907–1981
1942–1994
MURRINH-PATHA
NORTHERN TERRITORY

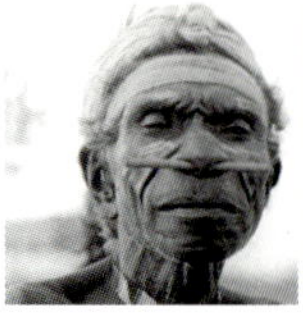

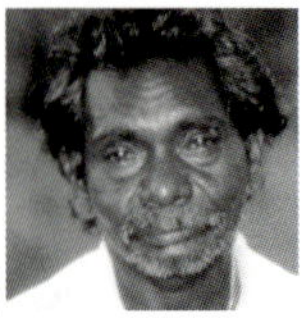

Nym Bunduck, a leader in the Wadeye (Port Keats) community, and his son Kevin collaborated on the impressive bark painting, *Emus feeding*, 1961. It depicts ancestral country during the dry season. The painting celebrates the fecundity of the natural environment and the regenerative power of the land in a region of climatic extremes. Human intervention in this process is acknowledged by the inclusion of black and green patches around the edge of the painting – these represent the scorched earth that remains after fires clear the dry undergrowth and generate new shoots. The annual burn-off is a feature of the dry season in northern Australia, where countless generations of people have continued the practice of controlled burning.

The artists depict flocks of emus feeding on flowering foliage and gathering close to the waterhole, a remnant of the creek that flows during the wet season. The dry creek bed meanders, serpent-like, around the whole landscape. Boab trees grow along the banks of the waterhole and the billabong, shown to the right. Three snakes inhabit the area around the waterhole: a female, pregnant with many eggs, a male and one of their offspring. Waterlilies and flowering vegetation are scattered across the whole field of the painting. Dotted outlines and circles indicate ceremonial connections between the Wadeye region and the East Kimberley, and also resonate with references to the ceremonial imagery of desert areas to the south of the region.

Nym Bunduck's early life coincided with the unrest caused by colonial activity in northern Australia, following the founding of the port of Darwin in 1869. To the east and south of Wadeye, pastoralists were establishing cattle stations, mining activity was underway and agricultural enterprises were starting up.

The mission at Wadeye was established on Nym Bunduck's land in 1935 to halt the drift of Aboriginal people away from their traditional lands and offer sanctuary from violent frontier conflicts. Situated on the coast, midway between Darwin and the East Kimberley, the mission promoted Christianity and discouraged Murrinh-Patha ceremonial practices. However, Murrinh-Patha people were encouraged to paint on bark and produce cultural artefacts for sale. W. E. H. Stanner, an anthropologist who was associated with the establishment of the mission, befriended Nym Bunduck, and many years later, in the 1950s, showed him topographical maps of the country. Bunduck, in turn, used paintings such as *Emus feeding* to instruct Stanner in Murrinh-Patha cultural values. KW

Emus feeding 1961
natural pigments on bark
78.8 x 179 cm
> detail

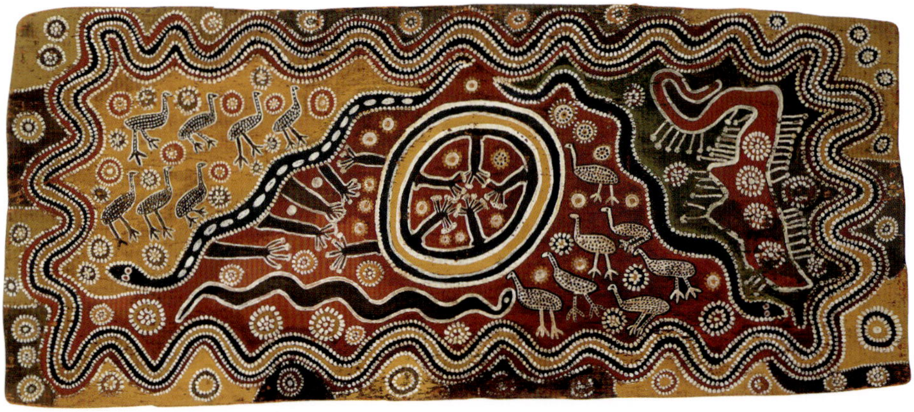

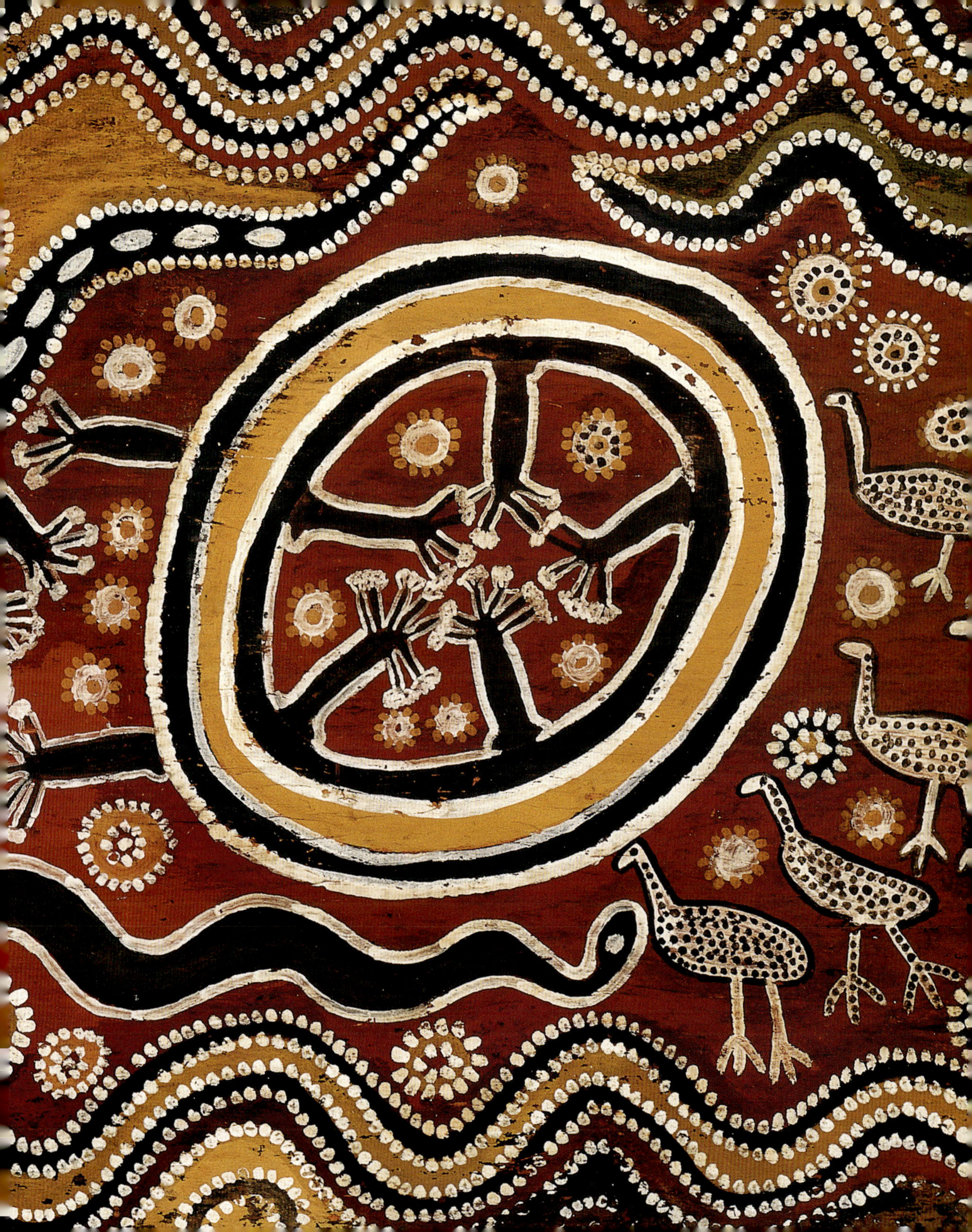

ROBERT CAMPBELL JNR

1944–1993
NGAKU
NEW SOUTH WALES

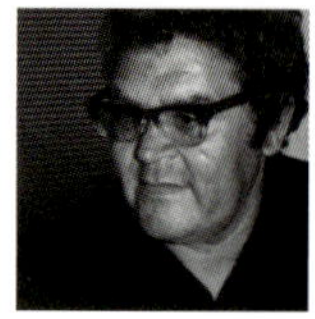

Robert Campbell Jnr's father was a boomerang-maker, and would take off with his young son into the bush around the Macleay River searching for suitable cuts of wattle or mangrove for his work. Together they would then decorate the boomerangs with birds and animals. After leaving Burnt Bridge Mission school at 14, Campbell continued to develop his artistic skills by painting local landscapes in gloss paint on cardboard, and selling them to passing tourists. After labouring at menial jobs away from home, Campbell returned to Kempsey and to painting.

Taking up canvas and artist boards for the first time, he developed his idiosyncratic approach: a bold, cartoon style in vivid colours, with all the cover-the-earth energy of a Keith Haring. Fusing sophisticated compositions with a raw, naive vision, Robert Campbell Jnr began to record the stories that he remembered from his childhood, as well as the brutal history of racism and colonialism, and the apartheid of twentieth-century Australia. *Map of the massacres of blacks on the Macleay Valley*, 1990, depicts the past rapes, murders and poisoning of waterholes. Campbell also painted Arcadian scenes of camp life, of food gathering and of Paradise lost, as in *Sunset over the Macleay overlooking Euroka*, 1990.

In all his works, the picture surface is animated by vivid decoration that recalls possum-skin cloaks and the fine engravings on Aboriginal shields, clubs and boomerangs of south-eastern Australia. The oesophagus-like red tie that appears on many of Campbell's protagonists expresses ongoing relationships with the natural and supernatural worlds, and recalls the X-ray technique of Arnhem Land rock painting. Many works form sequential narratives, such as Campbell's commemoration of the Aboriginal Tent Embassy set up in 1972 on the grounds of (then) Parliament House in Canberra.

Campbell's pictures always exude confidence and frankness, and he managed to reconcile his personal experience with public expression, despite the former typically being a realm of inarticulate pain and the latter being in danger of sloganeering. Campbell's bold imagery is a deliberate, incisive affront, but one that is also full of compassion and irrepressible humour. There is something essential in his work: a feeling of jubilation in our humanity, which might seem strange arising out of such an oppressive social order. Very few practitioners in world art encompass joy and suffering so effortlessly as Robert Campbell Jnr. GA

v left **Map of the massacres of blacks on the Macleay Valley** 1990
synthetic polymer paint on canvas
78.8 x 114.3 cm
> detail

v right **Sunset over the Macleay overlooking Euroka** 1990
synthetic polymer paint on canvas
118 x 197.5 cm

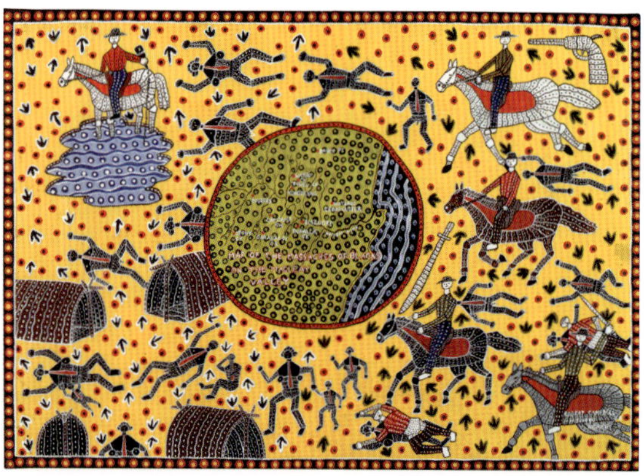

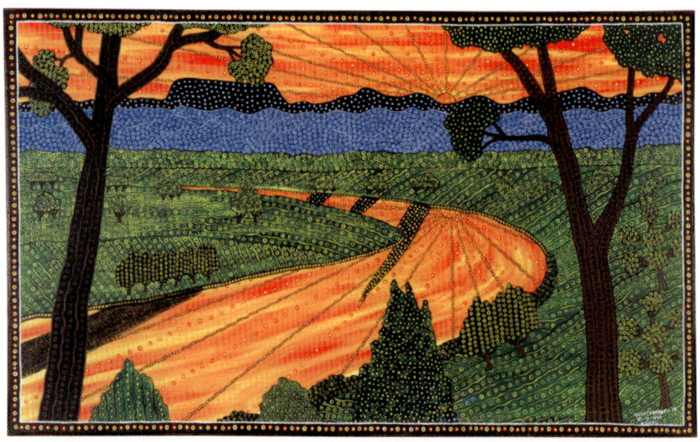

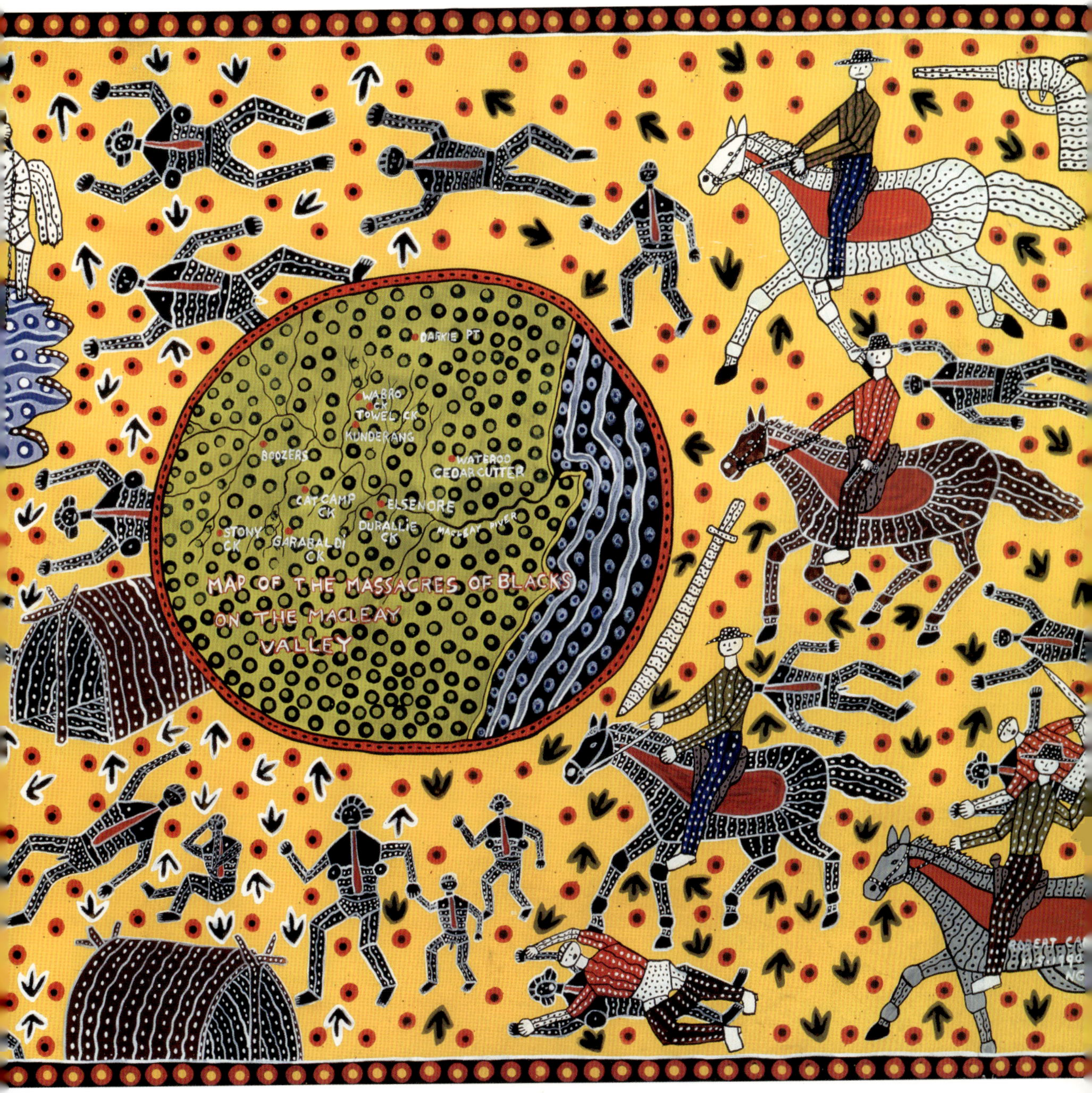
DARKIE PT
WABRO CK
TOWEL CK
KUNDERANG
BOOZERS
WATEROO
CEDAR CUTTER
CAT CAMP CK
ELSENORE
STONY CK
GARABALDI CK
DURALLIE CK
MACLEAY RIVER
MAP OF THE MASSACRES OF BLACKS
ON THE MACLEAY
VALLEY

ROBERT AMBROSE COLE

1959–1994
WARRAMUNGA
NORTHERN TERRITORY

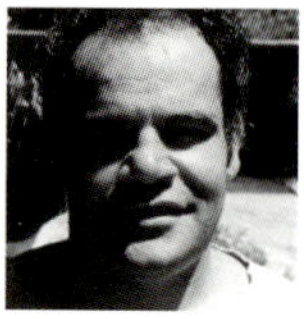

'I was born in Alice Springs. I paint my mother's and my father's country. My mother's country is Banka Banka, Warramunga people, north of Tennant Creek. Most of my paintings are from around Aputula, Finke, my father's country. His country is south of Alice Springs, the sand hills on the edge of the Simpson Desert … My images come from all over the place.'[1]

Robert Ambrose Cole was a self-taught artist who lived and worked in Mparntwe (Alice Springs). Cole's style of painting was influenced by his years growing up in an urban centre, exposed to the art movements of the Central and Western Deserts. He experimented with both acrylic dot painting and the European-influenced landscapes of the Hermannsburg water-colourists, whose proponents included Albert Namatjira and Otto Pareroultja. While Cole maintained both forms of practice, their synthesis led to his shimmering white dot paintings, in which figures and shapes emerge. These works combine a translucency and subtlety, influenced by the watercolours, with Cole's obvious stylistic affinity with dot painting.

Cole often emulated natural ochres with acrylic colours. In *Untitled*, 1993 (below left), through careful placement and very subtle variations in the size of the dots, he builds up a pattern of square forms that appear within the field. This work's intensity is similar to op art, as the viewer tries to define the grid-like shapes that emerge and retreat into the oscillating white field painted over an ochre-brown background. The tracks of lines of dots that create the grid give an almost map-like appearance to the work as the eye charts a path across its surface. At the same time, the painting remains resolutely abstract and is not connected to a particular story and place.

In *Untitled*, 1993 (right), Cole painted dots in lines that curve across the paper, defining two forms from the ochre back-ground. These two shapes have been described in many ways: as deriving from ceremonial body markings; as suggesting the dramatic gorges that cut through rock formations in the desert near Mparntwe; or as recalling the shapes of hunting boomerangs. While these may all be possible sources or references in this work, the brown shapes are also abstract, grounded in both traditional Aboriginal culture and a very contemporary painterly experimentation with colour and form. WT

Untitled 1993
Untitled 1993
both synthetic polymer paint on paper on canvas
76.5 x 58 cm
77.5 x 57 cm
> detail

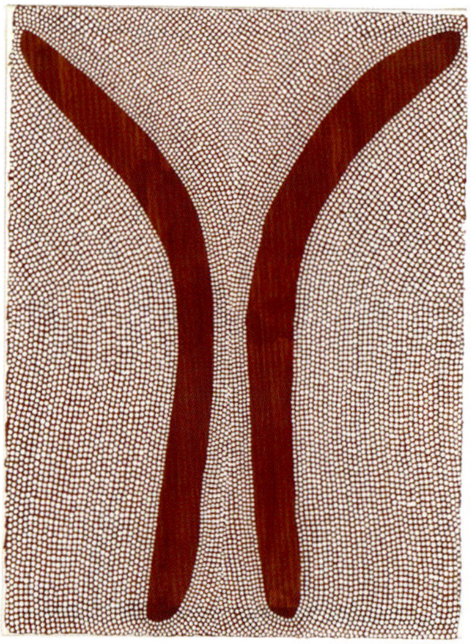

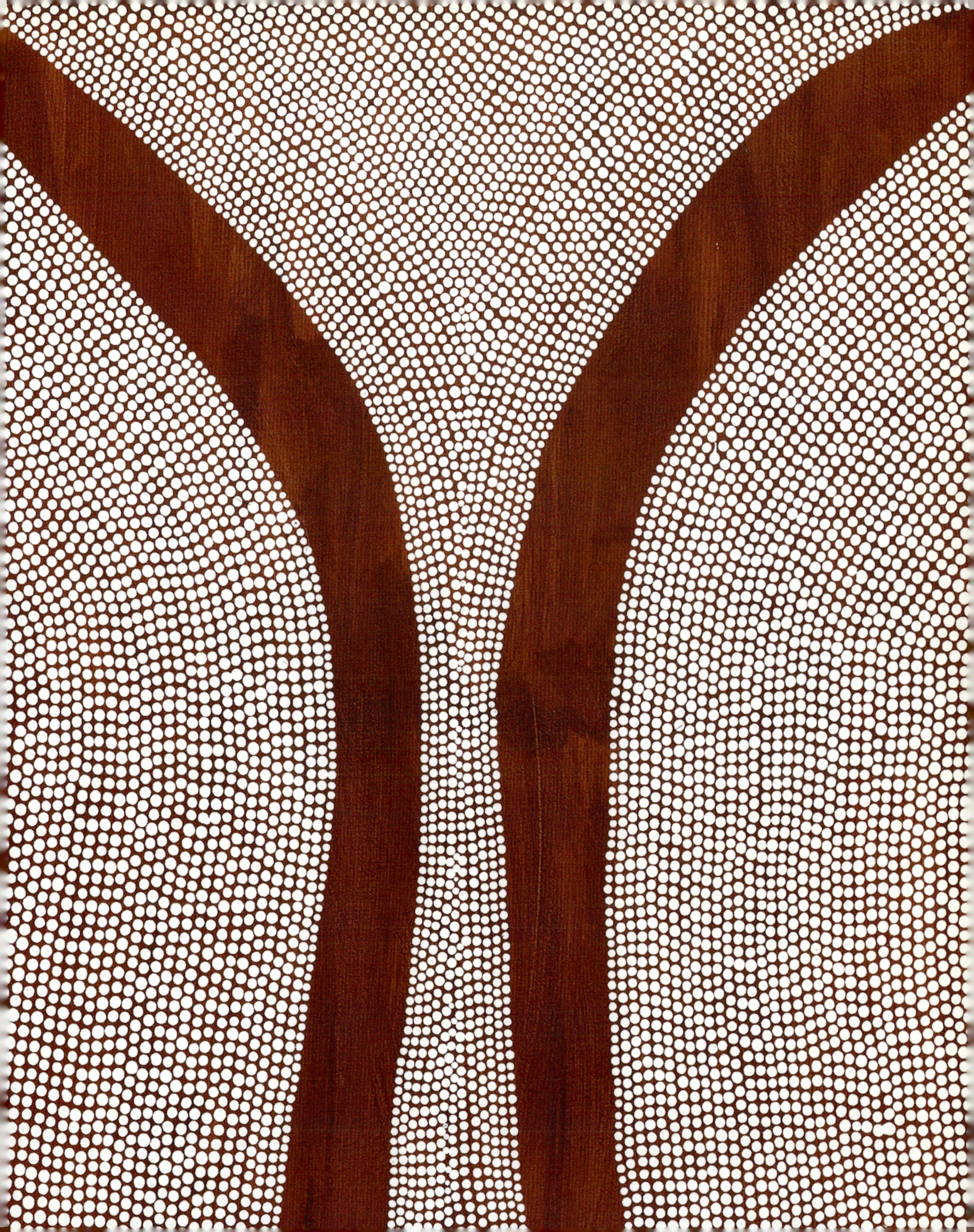

BRENDA L. CROFT

BORN 1964
GURINDJI
NORTHERN TERRITORY

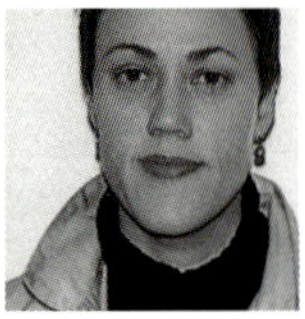

Brenda L. Croft works closely with family, friends and Indigenous community members in Sydney to create her images. In both *Shane Phillips and Noel Collett, Eveleigh Street, Redfern*, 1992, and *Mary Mumbulla and Murri Craigie*, 1993, the subjects look straight at the camera and at the viewer, directly and candidly returning our gaze.

Shane Phillips and Noel Collett, Eveleigh Street, Redfern was originally part of a collaborative work entitled *Conference Call*, 1992, made with internationally renowned African-American artist and activist Adrian Piper and exhibited at the Art Gallery of New South Wales, Sydney, in the 1992 Biennale of Sydney. Croft's photographs were taken in Redfern, Sydney, and Collett and Phillips stand at the top of Eveleigh Street wearing the jerseys of the Redfern All Blacks, the rugby league team that is a source of local pride. Contrary to the usual media depictions of this area, Croft presents a positive image of urban Indigenous communities in her strongly individual photographs of people and place, taken from an insider's viewpoint.

Mary Mumbulla and Murri Craigie is from 'The Big Deal is Black', 1993, a series of photographs of Aboriginal women and their families, taken at their homes. The personal becomes political both in the intimacy of the photographer's relationship with the families, and the strong and confident sense of self-imaging in these works. While Croft does not appear in these photographs, in depicting networks of her family and friends she has created a form of self-portrait. 'The Big Deal is Black' was first exhibited at the Australian Centre for Photography, Sydney, accompanied by audiotapes in which the subjects discussed the personal and collective memories that had shaped their lives.

Since 1998, Croft has worked with digital media to create images that layer photographs and text, exploring more directly autobiographical subject matter. History and personal memory intersect in the series 'In my mother's garden', 1998, and 'In My Father's House', 1998, which use family snapshots, religious and other imagery and language to consider Croft's experience of growing up in the suburbs with a white mother and an Aboriginal father who was stolen from his parents at the age of two under the government policy that allowed for the removal of Indigenous children from their families.

Croft wrote in the Biennale of Sydney catalogue:

'By placing myself behind the camera I am taking control of my self image and images of ourselves. I cannot, do not, take sole responsibility but challenge and attempt to reverse the expected.'[1] WT

> **Mary Mumbulla and Murri Craigie** 1993
R3 colour photograph
99.5 x 120.5 cm

v **Shane Phillips and Noel Collett, Eveleigh Street, Redfern** 1992
duratran, light box
180 x 270 x 20 cm

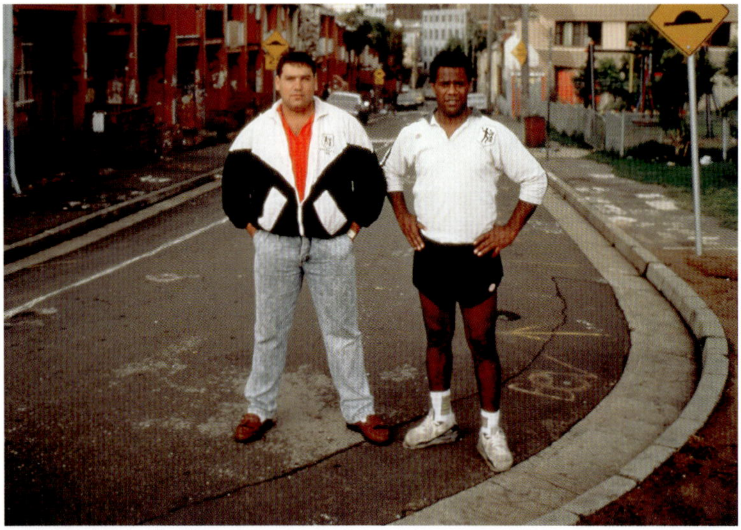

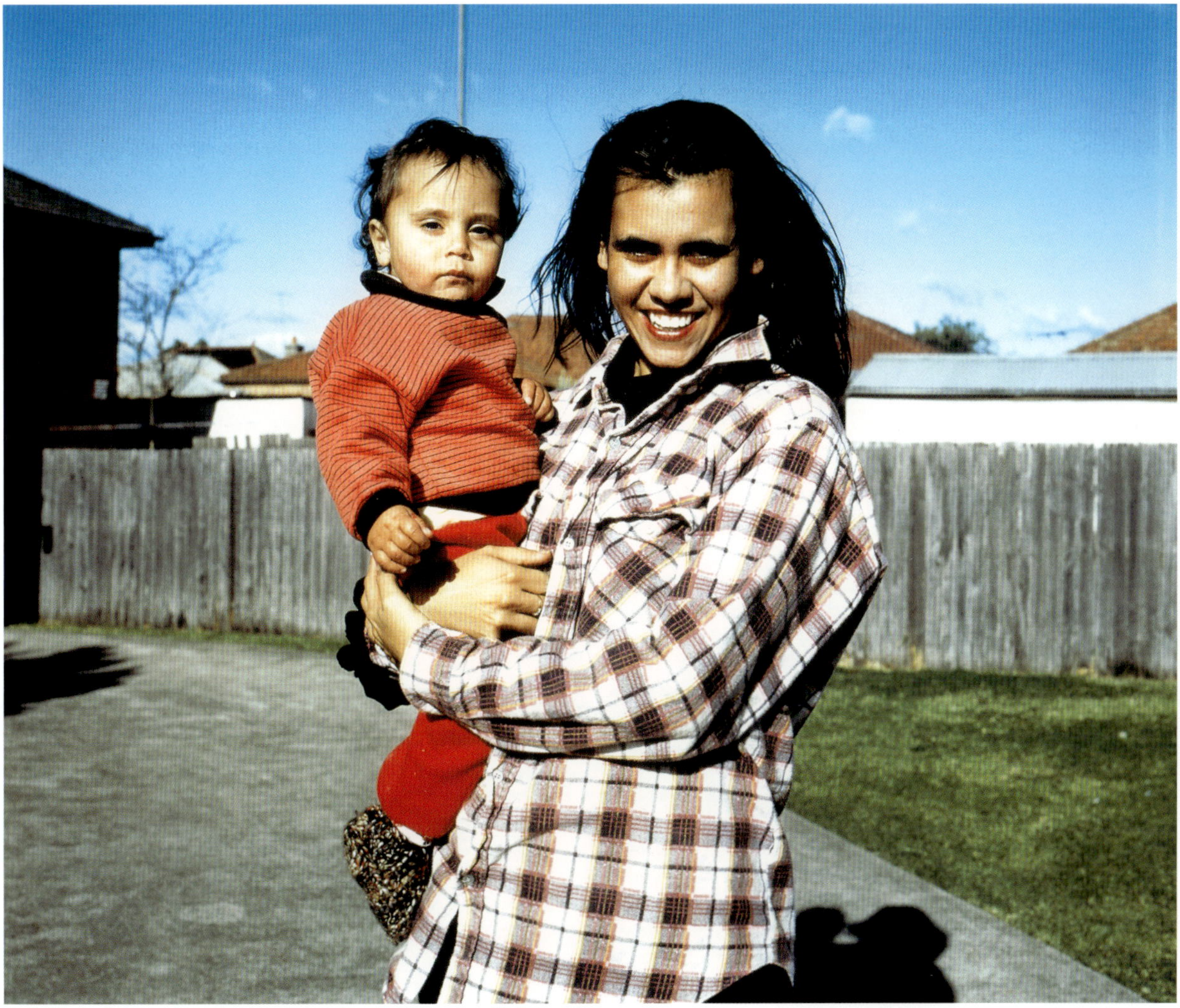

DESTINY DEACON

BORN 1957
KUKU, QUEENSLAND
ERUB, TORRES STRAIT ISLANDS

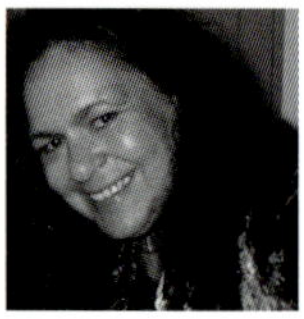

True to her name, in recent years Destiny Deacon has blazed an extraordinary trail. Since first exhibiting at the Art Gallery of New South Wales, Sydney, in 1991, Deacon has been represented in the prestigious international exhibitions Documenta, the Yokohama Triennale, the first Johannesburg Biennale and the fifth Havanna Biennale, as well as the Biennale of Sydney and Brisbane's Asia-Pacific Triennial of Contemporary Art. Like Tracey Moffatt, she is one of the few Australian artists to have established an international audience.

Deacon describes herself as 'just an old-fashioned political artist',[1] and her several careers as performer, academic and activist reflect the complexity of this role. In her installations, videos and laser-generated prints, she considers the casual cruelty of everyday racism with a humour particular to her identity. Jokes mostly rely on mocking the weak, yet in Deacon's twisted currency one cannot be quite sure who is the joker and who the joke is on. In *Dreaming in urban areas*, 1993, for example, the Goori poet Lisa Bellear appears to be annointed in tribal bodypaint, when in fact she is wearing a Blackmore's facial scrub. Deacon lampoons victimhood in works that are nevertheless full of pathos – she says she uses dolls in her work because she feels sorry for them. Her home-grown theatre of the absurd stars members from her copious collection of Aboriginal kitsch, battered thrift shop effigies that carry the burden of the grotesque incongruity between real and imagined Indigeneity. There is nothing vicarious about Indigenous suffering, however, and beneath the jest is the living hurt of a history of poverty and contempt.

Deacon's anti-art is seemingly slapdash, but is in fact thoroughly cunning. She describes herself as 'just a crappy artist', and has said that the 'worse' the art – the more unfocused or uneventful – the tougher its impact. Deacon's desultory art gives the finger to the narcissism of art making; indeed, one even gets the impression that she is only reluctantly an artist. As one series was titled, she has been 'Forced into Images'. Yet although apparently incidental, Deacon's images are far from casually acquired; in between the inaudible dialogue and unedited meanderings of the home video, the video *Taking Pictures*, 1995, shows a perfectionist at work. Deacon's beautiful portraits – of herself as Frida Kahlo, or of the Australian artists Janet Burchill and Jennifer McCamley – demonstrate the extent to which the artist works against her innate aestheticism. HF

> **Dreaming in urban areas** 1993
colour polaroid laser copies
62.5 x 56.5 cm overall

v **Waiting for Goddess** 1994
colour bubble-jet print from polaroid photograph
69.8 x 56.7 cm

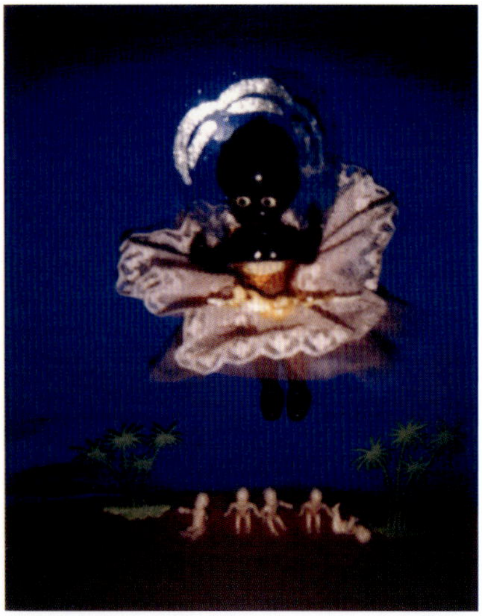

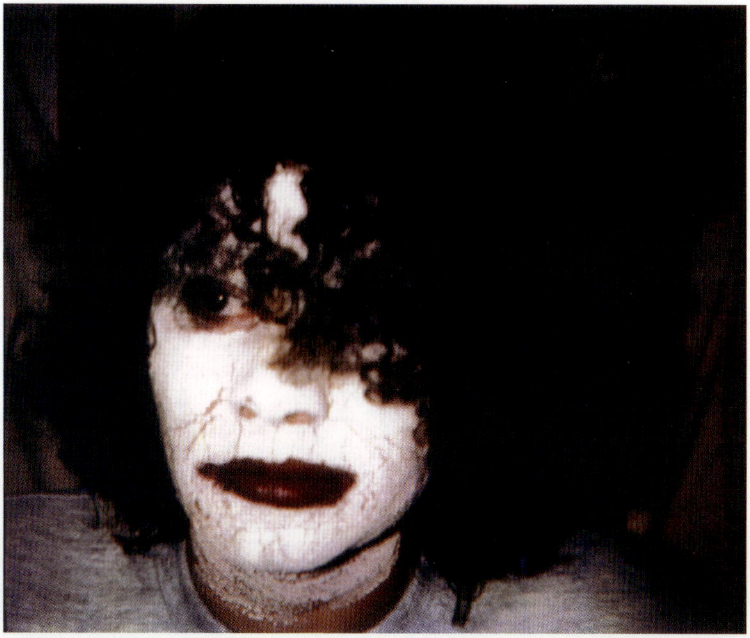

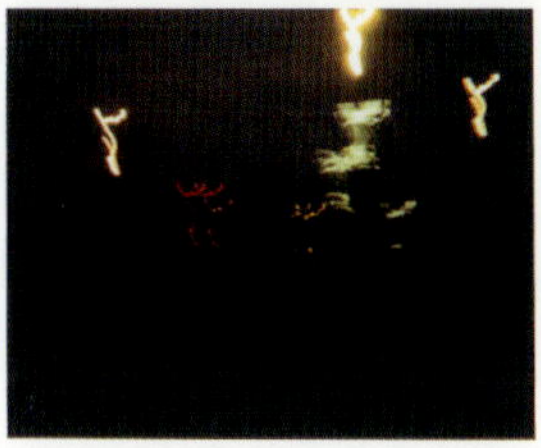

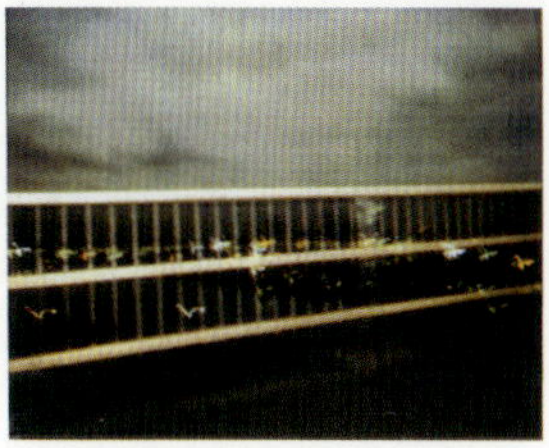

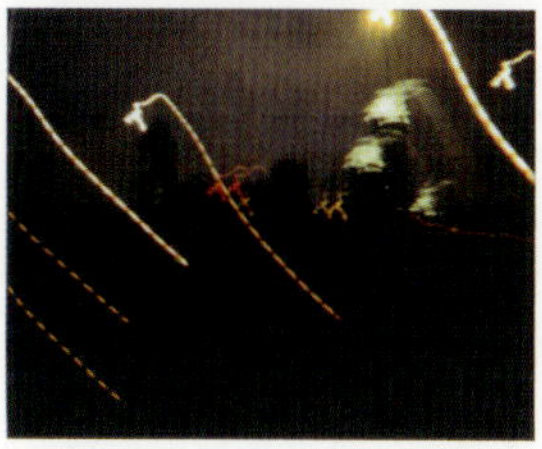

DAWIDI DJULWARAK

1921–1970
LIYAGALAWUMIRR
NORTHERN TERRITORY

Dawidi Djulwarak was born into a Liyagalawumirr family on the Arnhem Land coast in 1921.[1] Though based on Milingimbi, an island just off the mainland, Dawidi moved extensively throughout Arnhem Land, particularly after the death of his uncle, Yilkari Kitani in 1956, when he was made the senior leader of the Wagilag Sisters ceremonies – the major ceremonial cycle and painting tradition in this region. At first Dawidi was considered too young to conduct his traditional responsibilities in full, and was guided by mentors. However, from the early 1960s he became the principal authority in recording this story.

The small bark painting, *Snakes and fish anticipating rain*, was probably created in the mid-1950s, before Dawidi assumed his full ceremonial and artistic position in the community. The significance rests in the display of many qualities that distinguish his later, larger works, including his free handling of figurative elements and a very controlled, subtle use of colour.

Snakes and fish anticipating rain is divided into two fields. In one section two fish, placed between compartments of the 'fresh water grid pattern' common in central Arnhem Land iconography, swim in one direction. In the other section, seven snakes travel the opposite course, and an errant fish boldly pushes its way into this field. The dotted background, which almost fills the bark, suggests the breaking of the monsoonal rains. The Art Gallery of New South Wales, Sydney, purchased this work in 1962 from the Rev. Edgar Wells, who acquired it from the artist when Wells was superintendent of the Methodist Mission at Milingimbi from 1949 to 1959.

Most of the paintings made by central Arnhem Land artists represent the universal themes of the creation stories, sometimes obliquely denoted through more commonplace creatures and plants. *Snakes and fish anticipating rain* relates to the cycle of the seasons, which demarcates life in the monsoonal north. The work also has resonances with the story of the Wagilag Sisters, which tells of the day the two Wagilag Sisters ventured into the sacred place of Yulungul, the great python. Angered, he rose from his slumber in the lagoon, sucked in the waters, spewed forth a fierce thunderstorm and then devoured the Sisters and their children. The story records the arrival of the first monsoon season and the flooding of the earth. More importantly, it documents the foundation of the laws of social and ceremonial behaviour, and provides a means for the continued transmission of cultural knowledge. SM

Snakes and fish anticipating rain c.1950s
natural pigments on bark
44 x 17 cm

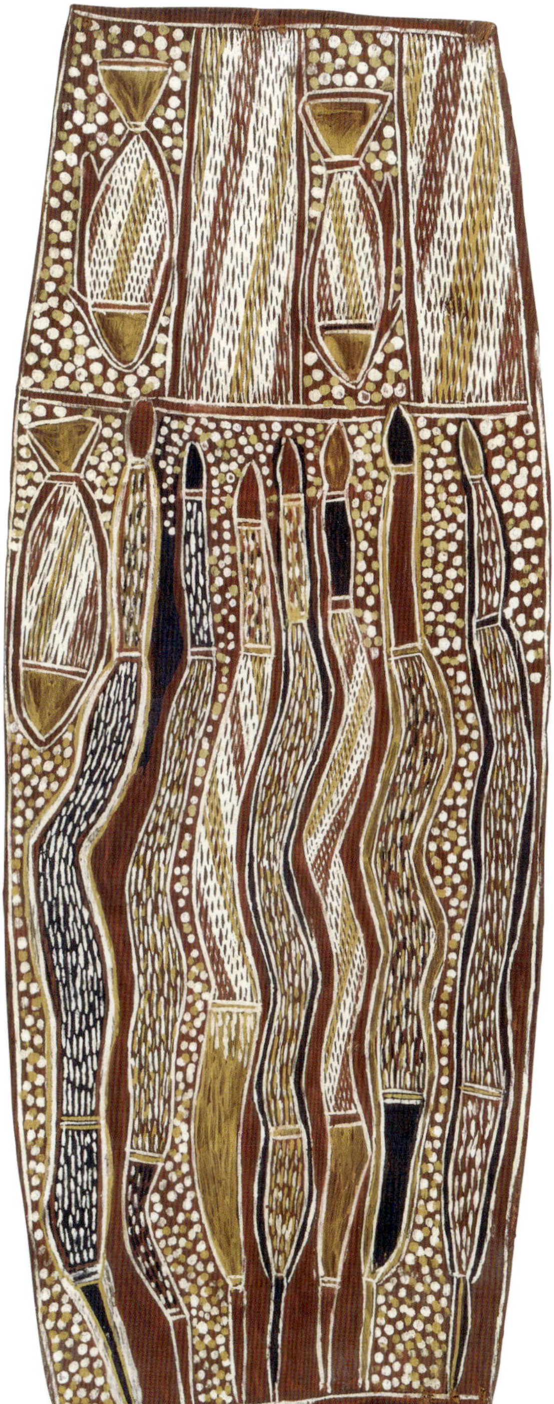

KEVIN GILBERT

1933–1993
WIRADJURI
NEW SOUTH WALES

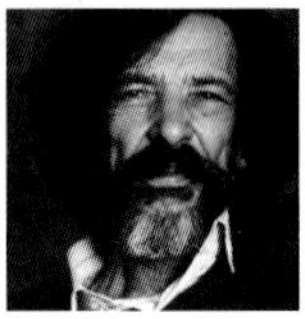

The power of art to record the highs and lows of the human condition is evident in Kevin Gilbert's work as a writer, visual artist, poet and playwright. A political activist and key creative thinker in the Aboriginal land rights and sovereignty movement, Gilbert participated in the 1972 establishment of the Aboriginal Tent Embassy in Canberra and the 'Treaty 88' campaign, which worked for a sovereign treaty between Aboriginal and non-Aboriginal Australians. Gilbert nonetheless believed that art was the tool that could most acutely expose the continual injustices suffered by Aboriginal people, and help build bridges and suggest ways forward.

Born on the banks of the Lachlan River in New South Wales, Gilbert lost his parents at an early age. He later escaped from an orphanage and lived in fringe camps with his extended family and Wiradjuri elders, where he developed his knowledge of Wiradjuri language and culture. Life on the edge in rural Australia also introduced him to those harsh factors that later became recurrent themes in his art and writing: racism, violence and alienation. On the surface, *Christmas Eve in the land of the dispossessed*, 1968, appears to be a serene work, harking back to the nineteenth-century European depiction of the Australian 'native' in his natural setting. The carefully chosen title of the work, however, evokes ideas of estrangement, want in a time of plenty, and traditional spirituality displaced by alien religion. Gilbert wrote of the work, ' ... It was the Aboriginal family sitting out under a tree, the river underneath and the hills, and in the night time, of course, the Southern Cross in the sky. But, within that, there is stillness and isolation so, to me, I can feel the isolation within that.'[1]

This was Gilbert's favourite print. It was created in 1968 in Long Bay Gaol, Sydney, while he was serving a fourteen-year prison sentence. It was one of the first prints made by an Aboriginal artist, using materials scrounged from his surroundings: ' ... old brittle lino off the prison floor' and tools made ' ... from a spoon, Gem razor blades and nails'.[2]

Gilbert believed that life for Australian Aboriginal people was too real, too close to the knuckle of oppression for abstract interpretation. Beneath the surface tranquillity of *Christmas Eve in the land of the dispossessed* is a bold statement, vibrantly drawn, of the dislocation and disparity between Indigenous and non-Indigenous peoples in Australia. SM

Christmas Eve in the land of the dispossessed
1968
printed 1990
linocut
45 x 63 cm

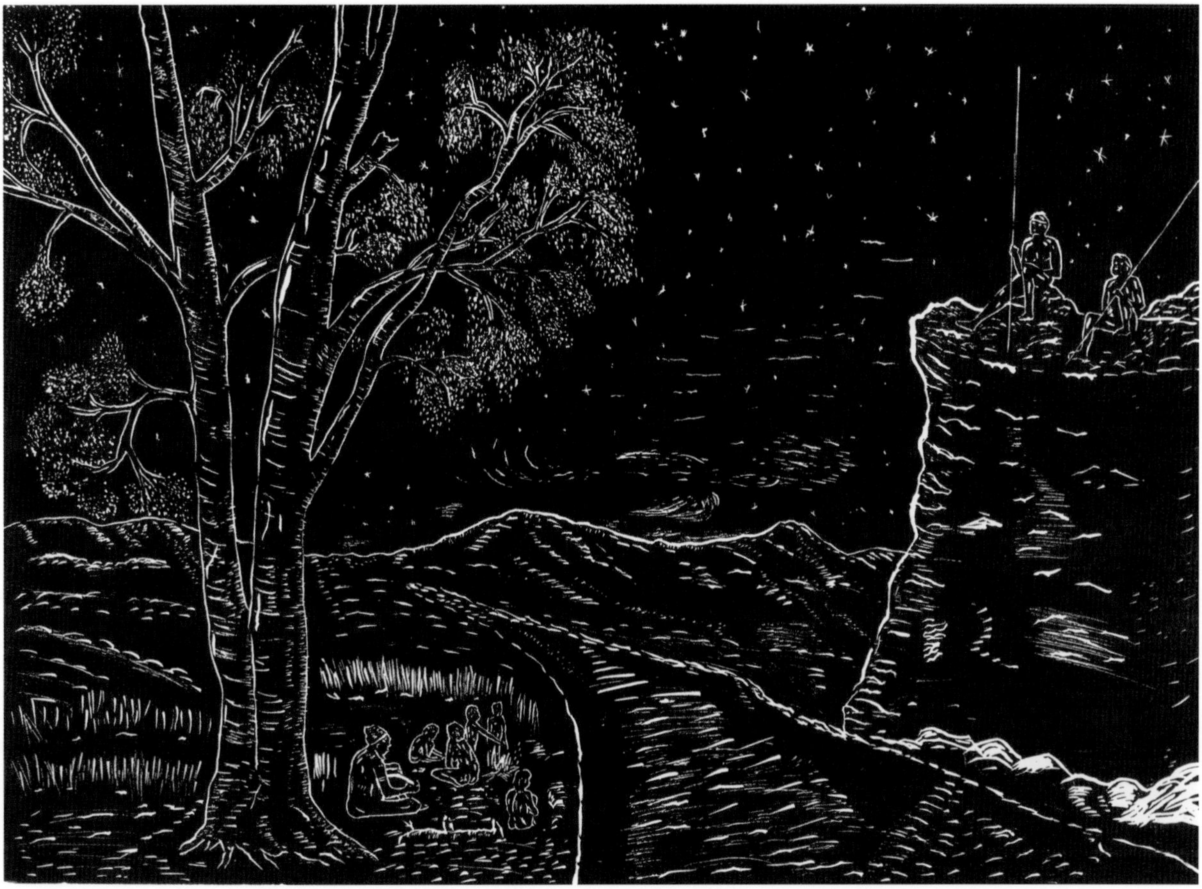

WILLIE GUDABI

c.1917–1996
ALAWA
NORTHERN TERRITORY

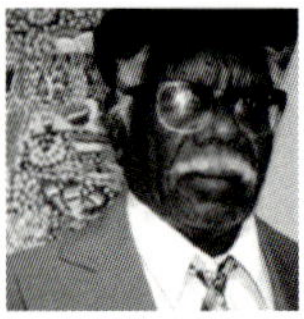

Willie Gudabi had a relatively brief career as a painter, working in collaboration with his wife Moima Willie (born c.1935) for a decade before his death. Nonetheless, he established a significant reputation with highly distinctive narrative paintings centred on initiation and mortuary ceremonies and the stories surrounding them. Gudabi was also a master carver of traditional boomerangs.

Born at Nutwood Downs Station in the Northern Territory, Gudabi grew up in Alawa country in a traditional lifestyle, on the margins of small cattle stations. He worked as a stockman on stations such as Tanumbirini, where he was initiated into the sacred life of his people. By the time Gudabi settled at Ngukurr ('place of many stones' and formerly the Roper River Mission), the settlement had a long history as a gathering point for people of different language groups during years of extreme white aggression. This diverse population was reflected in the radically distinct work of the senior artists that emerged from Ngukurr during the late 1980s. Ginger Riley Munduwalawala and Djambu Barra Barra are fellow artists who were living at Ngukurr at the time and, like Willie Gudabi, took advantage of adult education programmes to begin their painting and exhibiting careers.

Gudabi's preoccupation with death and initiation narratives and rituals of his ancestors takes a consistent form in his work – he paints extraordinarily vibrant images in segmented 'vignettes' across his canvases. The roughly illustrative forms of birds, plants, insects, animals, trees, men, masks, ceremonial events and sites of country are packed together and jostle each other over the surface. Some writers have also suggested that a number of Gudabi's paintings can also be read as maps, and sometimes illustrate inter-group boundary disputes over custodianship of country.

Notwithstanding that *Dead man ceremony*, 1993, is a mortuary painting, to a general viewer the work appears to be utterly celebratory and highlights the artist's gift as an idiosyncratic and sophisticated colourist. The 'vignettes' or patched sections in this and Gudabi's other paintings are layered, rather than sequential. They interweave, and perhaps are even cyclical in their narratives. The paintings appear to have been viewed by the artist as adjuncts and visual cues in his verbal handing down of stories and the law. They are also 'love stories' in law and the reality shared between Willie Gudabi and Moima Willie, who were married for over 50 years. Like the layered meanings in his spoken narratives, the paintings function at various levels of revelation, according to the knowledge of the viewer involved. DE

> Willie Gudabi & Moima Willie
Dead man ceremony 1993
synthetic polymer paint on canvas
237 x 136 cm

v Willie Gudabi
Gabal ritual 1990
synthetic polymer paint on canvas
126.1 x 92.1 cm

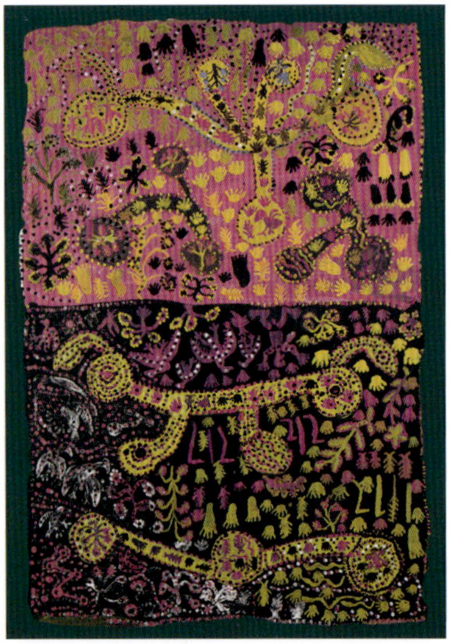

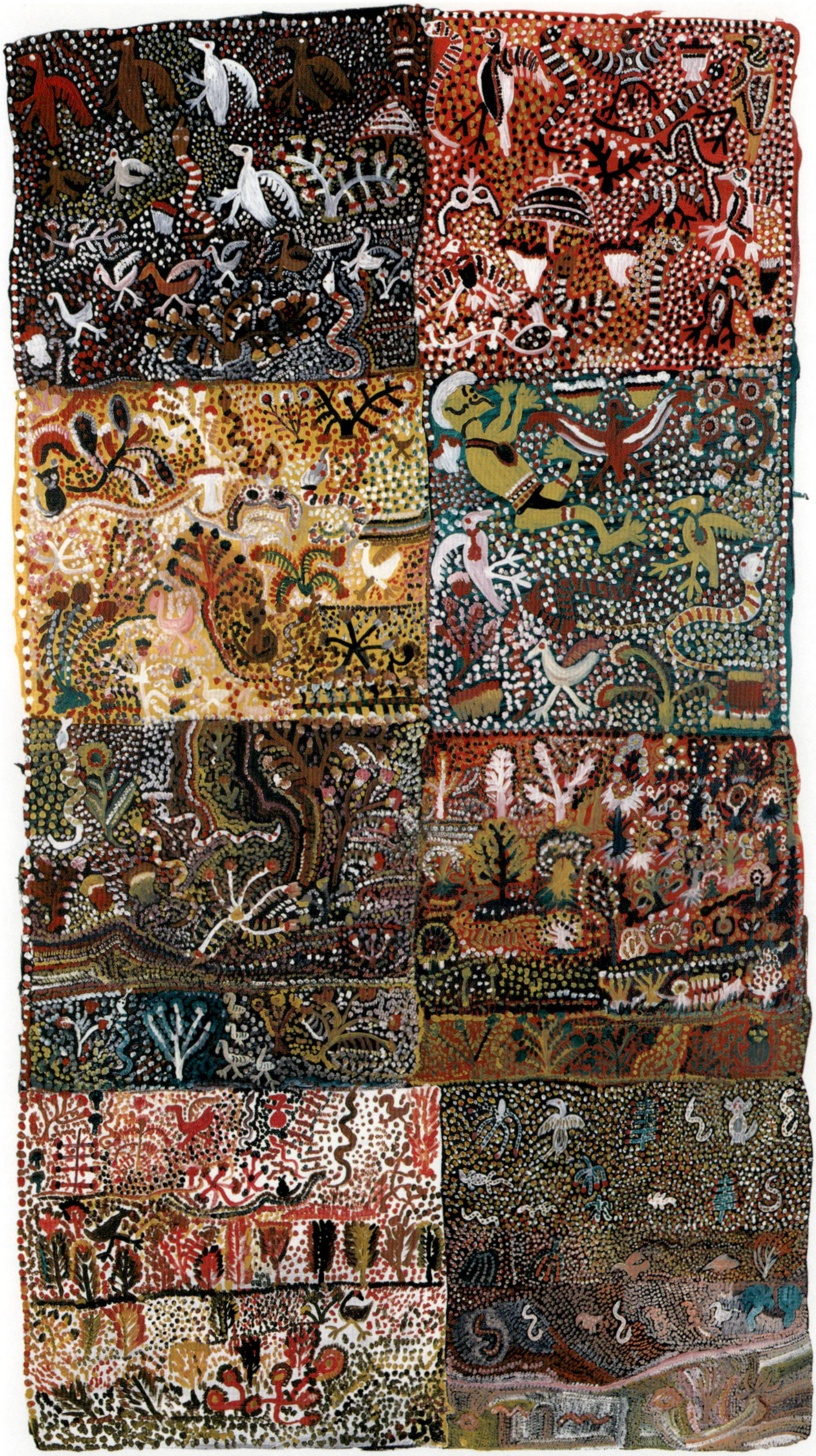

PHILIP GUDTHAYKUDTHAY

BORN 1935
GALWANUK /
LIYAGALAWUMIRR
NORTHERN TERRITORY

'There is a little creek near there, called Gunyunmirringa, and in that creek is where the practice of the first hollow log ceremony took place for the Dhuwa people. They say that this is where a crow made one of these logs ... The soul is indestructible. It stays behind ... The log is thought of as the flesh, as the skin, and putting the bones inside is like putting the soul back into the body ... This is painted with a design like a body design ...'[1]

Used as a repository for the bones of deceased people, badurru (hollow log coffins) have been created for exhibition since the 1950s. They refer potently to the spiritual universe beyond earthly existence. The shapes of the cylindrical logs lend themselves to the calm, insistent rhythm of Philip Gudthaykudthay's geometric designs, which the artist has also successfully translated onto bark paintings.

In the work *Badurru and Dindin*, 1985, equidistant black bands encircle the badurru. They define the two sections painted with distinct patterns, signifying Gudthaykudthay's clan lands at Gunyunmirringa, forested country to the east of Ramingining, Arnhem Land. The design on *Badurru (Hollow log)*, 1986 (centre), is another variation, with the rectangular grid containing unhatched diagonal stripes. Bands of yellow ochre at either end magnify its intense golden hue. *Badurru (Hollow log)*, 1986 (right), is entirely covered in Gudthaykudthay's clan design and has a band of thick black beeswax anchoring the lower edge.

Philip Gudthaykudthay was born to the east of Ramingining in central Arnhem Land. Following the death of his parents he was adopted by a Murrungun clan family and initiated around 1949 at Gatji lagoon. Gudthaykudthay has worked as a crocodile hunter, stockman and station-hand. He now lives and paints at Ramingining, his mother's country, where he is known as 'Pussycat' (a reference to the native cat, one of his ancestral totems).

Gudthaykudthay had his first solo exhibition in 1983 at the Gary Anderson Gallery, Sydney. He has had several exhibitions in the years since then, and has also exhibited in many group shows. In 1997, Gudthaykudthay participated in printmaking workshops held in Ramingining, and his paintings were included in the exhibition, 'The Painters of the Wagilag Sisters Story 1937–1997', held at the National Gallery of Australia, Canberra. KW

> left **Badurru and Dindin (Hollow log and dilly bag)** 1985
natural pigments on wood
169 x 14 cm/29.8 x 15.2 cm
v detail

> centre **Badurru (Hollow log)** 1986
natural pigments on wood
153 x 14 x 14 cm

> right **Badurru (Hollow log)** 1986
natural pigments on wood
148.5 x 13.7 x 13.7 cm

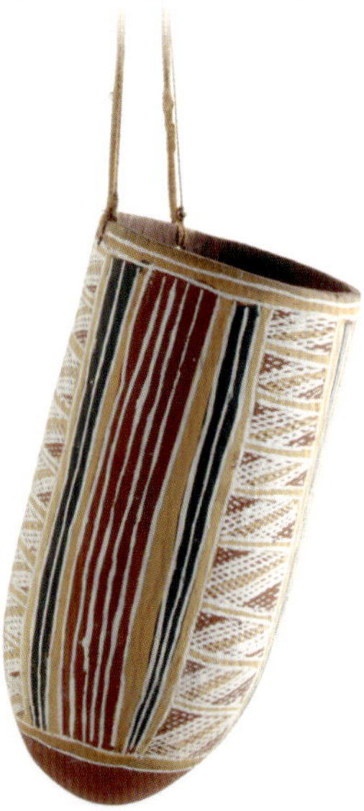

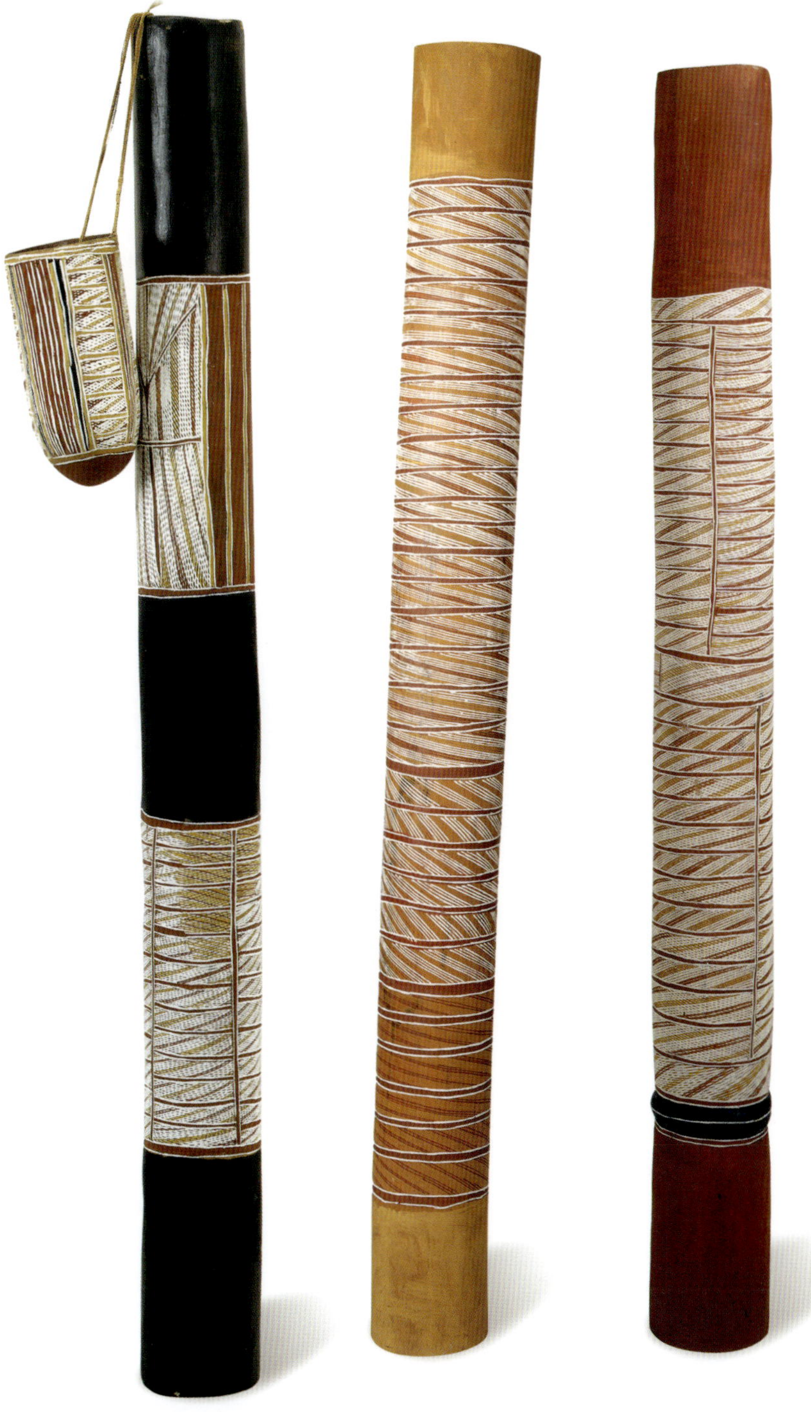

MITHINARI GURRUWIWI

1929–1976
GALPU
NORTHERN TERRITORY

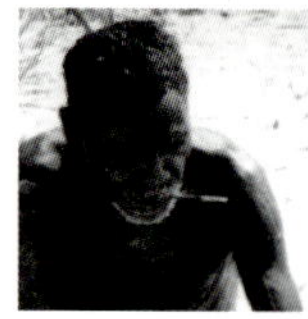

Mithinari Gurruwiwi learned to paint as a young man, with a group of Dhuwa moiety artists that also included Larrtjannga Ganambarr and Wandjuk Marika. They were taught by Wandjuk's father, Mawalan Marika, at Beach Camp in Yirrkala. Mithinari belonged to a group of the Galpu clan, and his paintings mainly represent two areas of clan land: a coastal area on Caledon Bay and the inland country of Garrimala.

Mithinari was a prolific and passionate artist, with a reputation for eccentricity. He usually camped slightly apart from other members of his community, although often surrounded by his children, and painted on the beach under a shade of palm fronds stuck into the sand. Long after other artists began using European paintbrushes, Mithinari often continued working with brushes made of frayed stringy bark when applying the background colour and drawing the main figurative components of his paintings. He infilled the design with brushes made of human hair or from the midrib of a palm frond. Mithinari painted with great speed and surety of hand. Scale was never a problem for him, and he adapted his compositions brilliantly to the size of the bark available, as in *Djaykung (File snakes)*, c.1960, and *Wuyal the Honey Man*, c.1960.

Mithinari's paintings are characterised by a diversity of forms but also have an overall coherence of stylistic elements. Yolngu art characteristically plays upon the relationship between figuration and abstraction. In Mithinari's paintings, there is often an almost complete integration of the figurative representations with the geometric clan designs, creating a flowing composition. Many of his paintings of Garrimala appear to be bursting with the vibrant life of the rich inland lake as snakes, birds and fish compete with each other among the waterlilies. In other paintings, he reduces the figurative element almost to the point of abstraction, and the energy of the works abounds in the flash of the design.

Mithinari was one of the artists who worked on the 1962 Yirrkala church panels; around the same time he painted a series of superb large barks for the collector Dr Stuart Scougall. Mithinari's works have appeared in many significant overseas exhibitions including 'Australian Aboriginal Art' in Chicago, 1972, and 'Aratjara – Art of the First Australians' in Düsseldorf, London and Humlebaek, 1993–94. Mithinari Gurruwiwi is represented in all Australian state galleries and in the Kluge-Ruhe Aboriginal Art Collection in the United States. HM

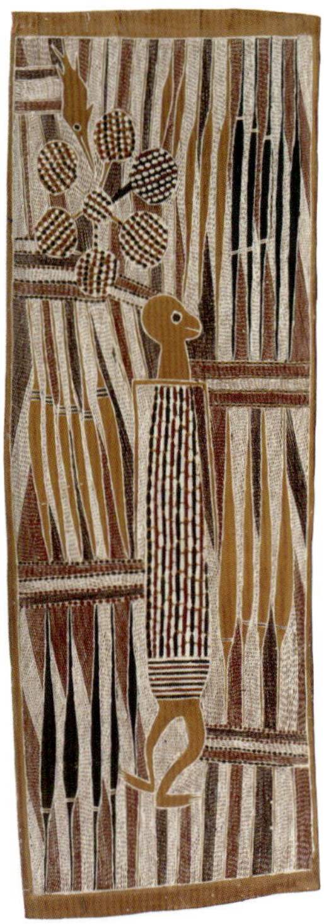

> **Djaykung (File snakes)** c.1960
natural pigments on bark
280 x 70 cm

v **Wuyal the Honey Man** c.1960
natural pigments on bark
116 x 40 cm

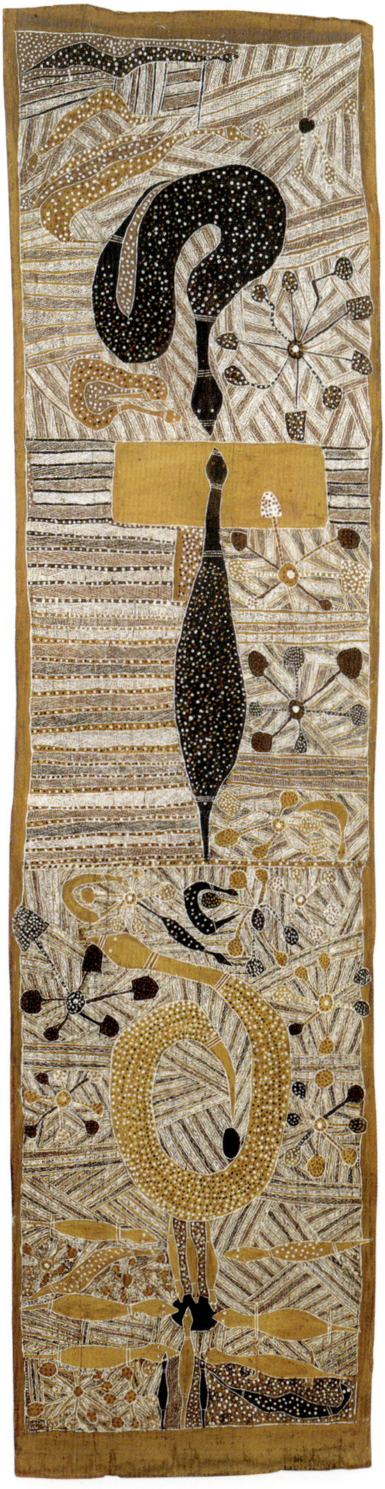

ROY KENNEDY

BORN c.1934
WIRADJURI
NEW SOUTH WALES

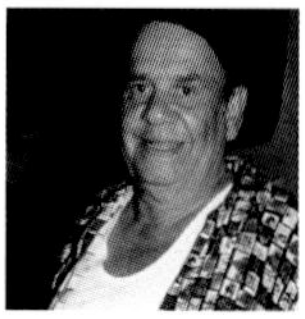

Roy Kennedy, like many contemporary Aboriginal artists, came to art late in life. As he says, ' ... I'm living proof that you're never too old to learn'.[1] Kennedy began studying painting and etching at the Eora Centre TAFE (Technical and Further Education) in Redfern, Sydney in 1995. Adult education centres such as Eora offer Aboriginal students the chance to catch up on the education denied them as children, and also to train in art making techniques. Many artists living and working in the city today, including Kennedy and fellow Eora Centre graduates H. J. Wedge and Elaine Russell, are using their newly acquired skills to reflect on their young lives on Aboriginal missions in rural Australia.

Kennedy was born on the Police Paddock Mission at Darlington Point, near Griffith in New South Wales. In his intimately detailed views of the people and places of his childhood, Kennedy's strength of vision as an artist is revealed. Pepper Tree Avenue was the arterial road leading to the mission from the highway. In *Pepper Tree Avenue*, 2001, Kennedy depicts the familiar landmarks of his childhood: the mulberry trees, the mission church – home of 'the brainwashers' – and the Murrumbidgee River. Kennedy has said, ' ... Pepper Tree Avenue was on Warangesda Mission where my mother was born in 1910. This mission was closed down in 1925, so all my people were scattered everywhere. Eventually they were moved to the mission on the police paddock, [and] from there on all the old people were classed as fringe dwellers.'[2]

Drawing on his mother's stories and his own experience, Kennedy's work documents a life of dislocation and deprivation, from the Depression years up until the abolition, in 1940, of the notorious Aborigines Protection Board that managed the missions in New South Wales. With the greater freedom that ensued, families often dispersed from the missions to find work in the surrounding agricultural communities. Kennedy recalls, ' ... wandering around doing seasonal work wherever and not finding any satisfaction with the rough life, not caring much about tomorrow'.[3] He worked as a ganger on the national railway and, like many young men, drifted towards the big city, seeking refuge in the growing metropolitan Aboriginal communities.

Kennedy's memories of mission life are bittersweet, underscored by the sense of community that saw his family through hard times. His 'Mission Series' prints chronicle his first-hand observations of a chapter of Australia's history that is finding increasing expression in the work of Indigenous artists. HP

v left **Mossgiel Weigh Station** 2001
etching
12.3 x 20.2 cm
> detail

v right **Pepper Tree Avenue** 2001
etching
23 x 28.7 cm

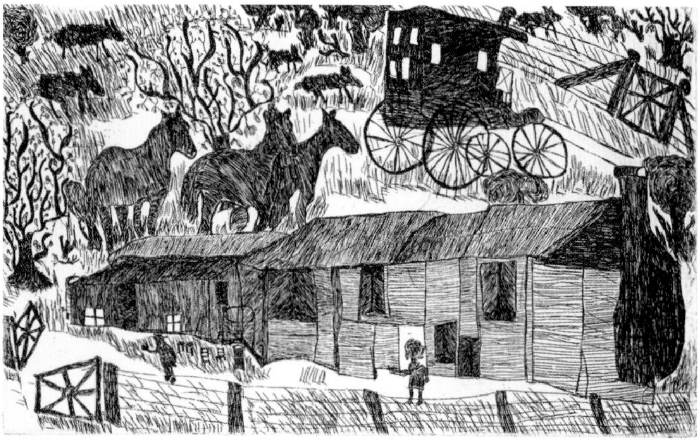

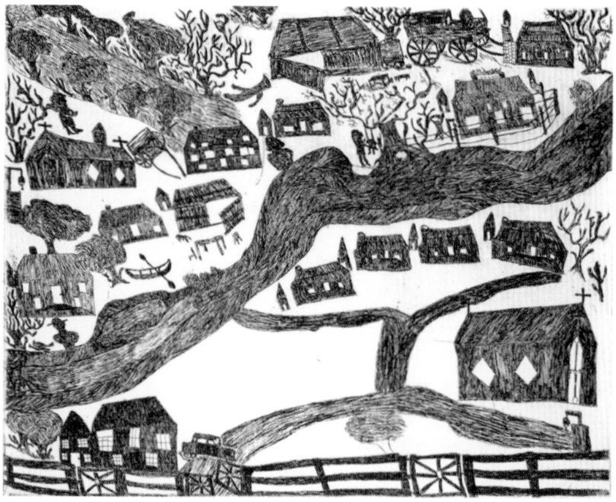

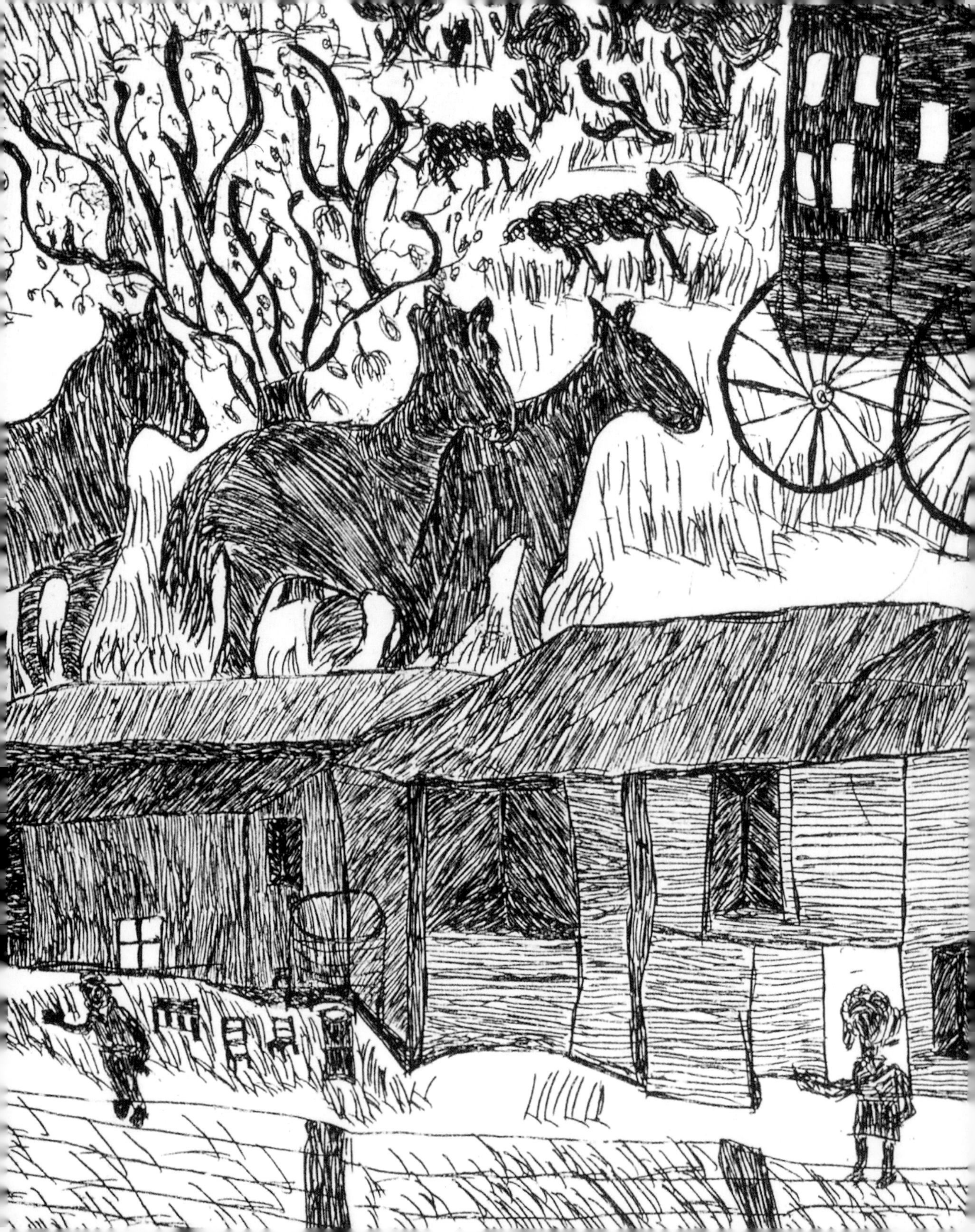

EMILY KAME KNGWARREYE

1916–1996
ANMATYERR
NORTHERN TERRITORY

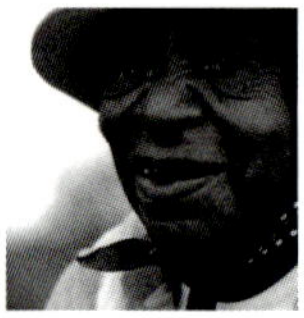

Working in a remote, north-west corner of the Simpson Desert, on land annexed by pastoral leases during the 1920s, Emily Kame Kngwarreye became, in the final decade of her life, perhaps the most celebrated and sought after Australian artist of her time.

A leading figure in eastern Anmatyerr ceremony, Kngwarreye was also the artist in whose work many white Australians first felt the force of an Indigenous art that could be seen to negotiate a space both within the aesthetics of Western abstraction and the timeless precepts of Aboriginal cultural traditions.

Kngwarreye's *Untitled (Alhalker)*, 1992 (overleaf), has been perceived as a lyrical mapping of country, a poeticising of the desert in bloom, or simply as a spectacular abstract painting. Alhalker, the desert country of Kngwarreye's birth, is anchored by a sacred rock in the form of a spectacular arched monolith, and shaped by the vagaries of the harsh desert environment. From the beginning, Alhalker remained the means and end of Kngwarreye's art.

Kngwarreye attained artistic maturity as a woman in her seventies, not long converted to the techniques of painting on canvas, but with decades of painting in a ceremonial context and activity with the Utopia Women's Batik Group behind her – as well as life as a camel handler and stockhand. In an extraordinarily prolific eight years of professional painting, she produced magnificent canvases in which she appears to have aimed for essentialist visions of the multiplicities and connectedness of her country, as imaged in terms of its organic energies. Kngwarreye's vital traceries both conform to, and seem to expand beyond, her clan codes, in abstractions of ceremonial markings and imagery of her country's flora and fauna.

During the early 1990s, Kngwarreye developed a painting technique that literally embodied her sense of the explosive, yet ordered, rhythms of the natural world: she energetically worked her canvas with fluid dots or blobs of colour that formed a pulsing layer over the 'mapped-out' underpinnings of her paintings. Later, she embraced the austerities of stripe compositions in works such as *Untitled (Awely)*, 1994, and in seething, linear 'yam Dreaming' paintings, before she created the remarkable blocky gestural abstractions of 1996, the final year of her life. DE

Untitled (Awely) 1994
triptych: synthetic polymer paint on paper laminated to canvas
100.7 x 213 cm overall
> detail

> overleaf
Untitled (Alhalker) 1992
synthetic polymer paint on canvas
165 x 480 cm

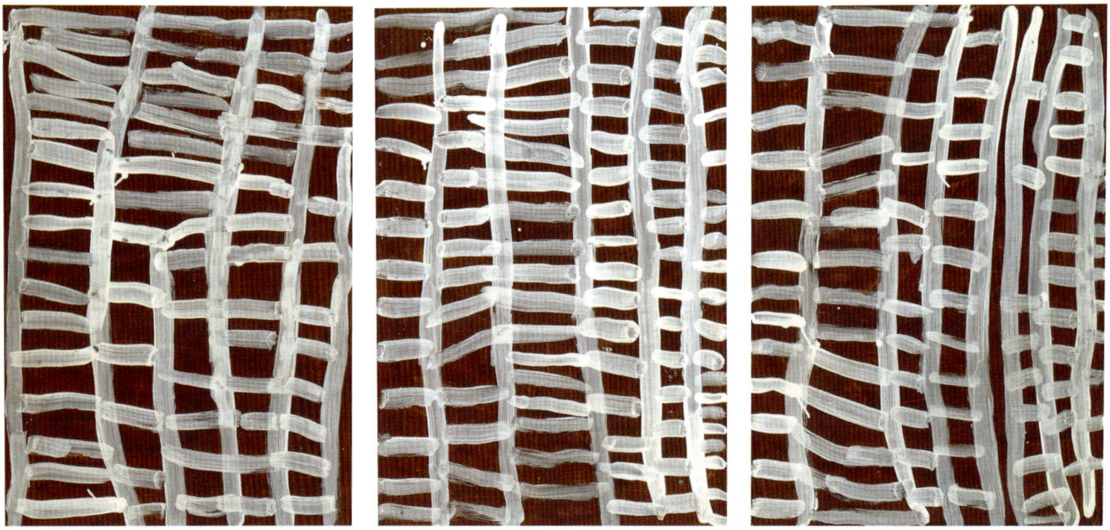

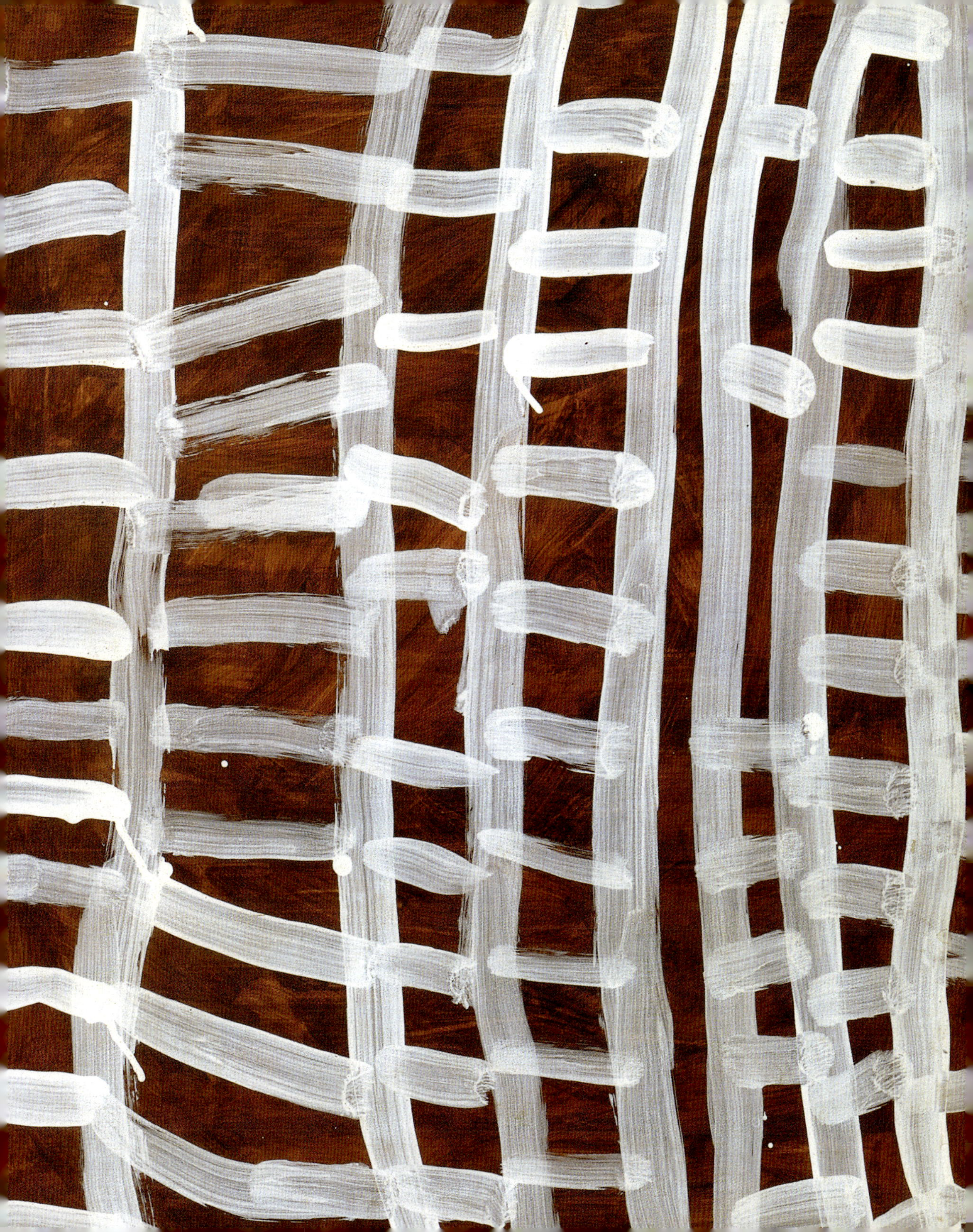

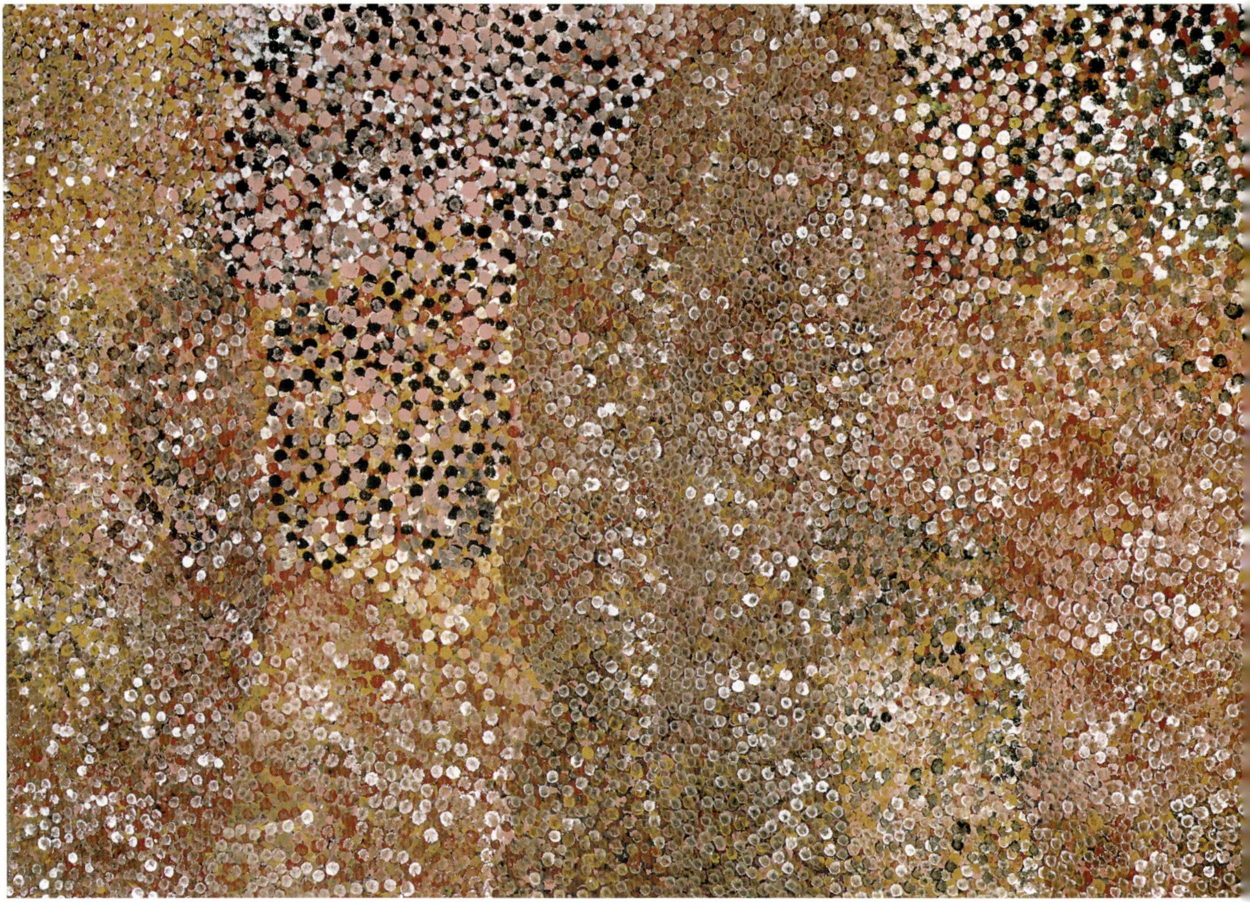

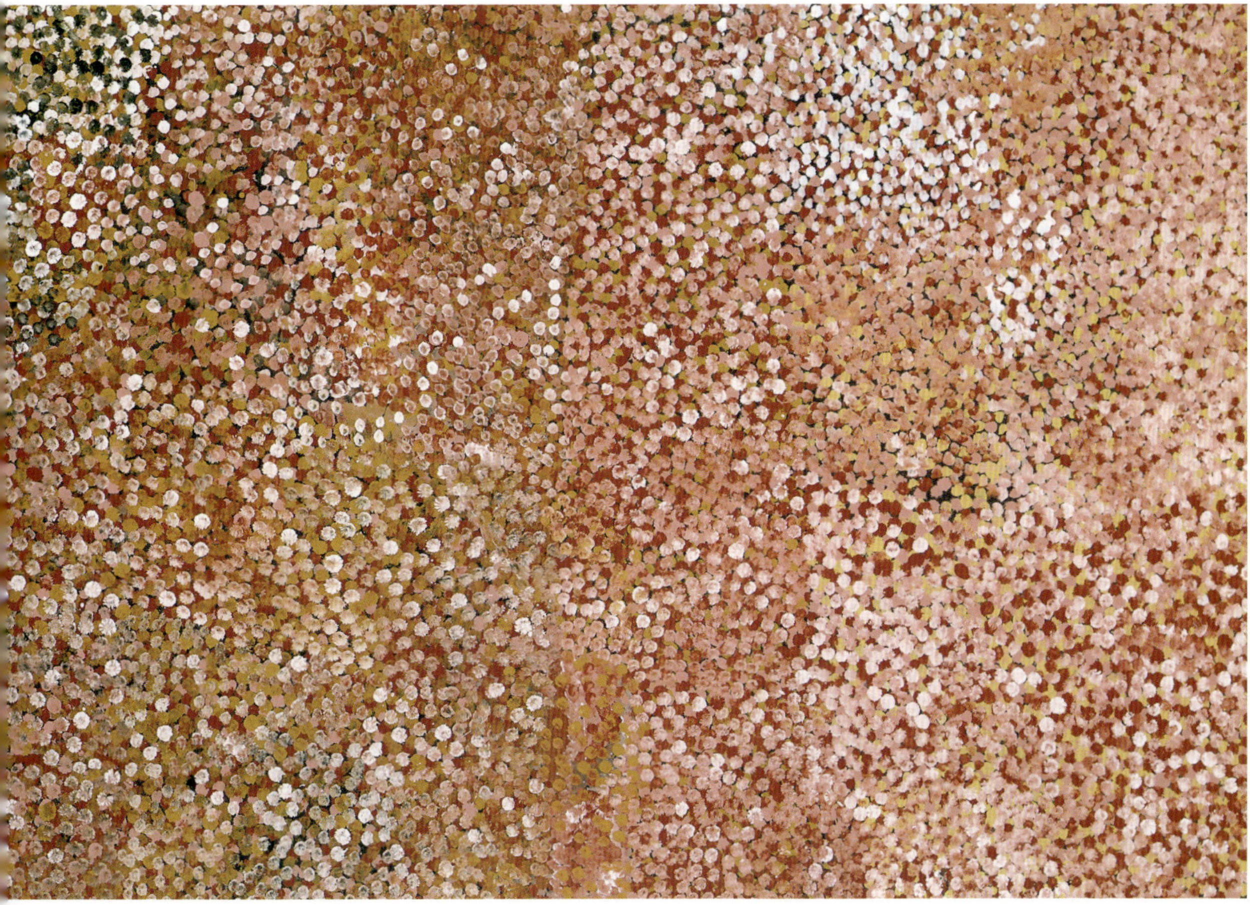

YVONNE KOOLMATRIE

BORN 1945
NGARRINDJERI
SOUTH AUSTRALIA

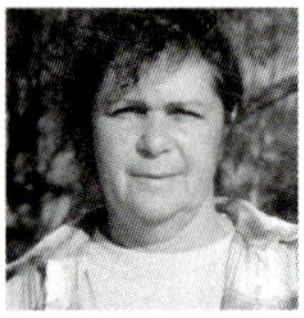

Yvonne Koolmatrie has lived all her life in Ngarrindjeri country, which ranges from the Coorong, a wetland wilderness at the mouth of the Murray River, upstream to the present day farming communities of the lower Murray Riverland. Koolmatrie grew up in the Riverland and experienced the hardship of seasonal work that became the only means of survival when Aboriginal people were denied access to their traditional lands.[1] Throughout her youth, Koolmatrie saw little evidence of the cultural practices of her ancestors that have become her life's work.

At a one-day weaving workshop in 1982, conducted by the elder, Dorothy Kartinyeri – one of the last people practicing the coiled bundle technique – Koolmatrie learned the critical first stage of Ngarrindjeri weaving. She was also instructed in the correct harvesting and preparation of sedge grass. In the once fertile environment of the Riverland, now degraded by intensive agricultural practice, suitable supplies of rushes are rare. Koolmatrie is careful not only to guard the location of her source, but also in harvesting, so as not to disturb the roots and young sedge grass plants. The subtle scent, form and hue of the finished works palpably evoke the environment of the Murray River.

Koolmatrie began to practise the weaving technique and gradually to experiment with form, extending the range of objects she had studied in the South Australian Museum ' ... to put my story in my weaving'.[2] For Koolmatrie, the near loss of the Ngarrindjeri weaving tradition crystallised a twofold responsibility: to pass on her skills and to create work of the highest possible standards so that her fibre forms will endure for future generations.

Eel trap, 1997, was first exhibited in 'fluent', Australia's representative exhibition at the 47th Venice Biennale in 1997, which also featured the work of Emily Kame Kngwarreye and Judy Watson. Created to the scale of nineteenth-century works in the collection of the South Australian Museum, Koolmatrie's eel trap does not intend to break with tradition but rather explores the possibilities of innovation. She has said, ' ... I look at different things. I might be along the river and I see different shapes and I think, that's a good way to weave. I don't sketch it, I just get my rushes and start to weave.'[3] Koolmatrie's intuitive process allows the sculptural potential of functional objects to be realised in spirited interpretations of traditional forms. HP

Eel trap 1997
sedge rushes (Lepidosperma canesens)
168 x 59 x 59 cm

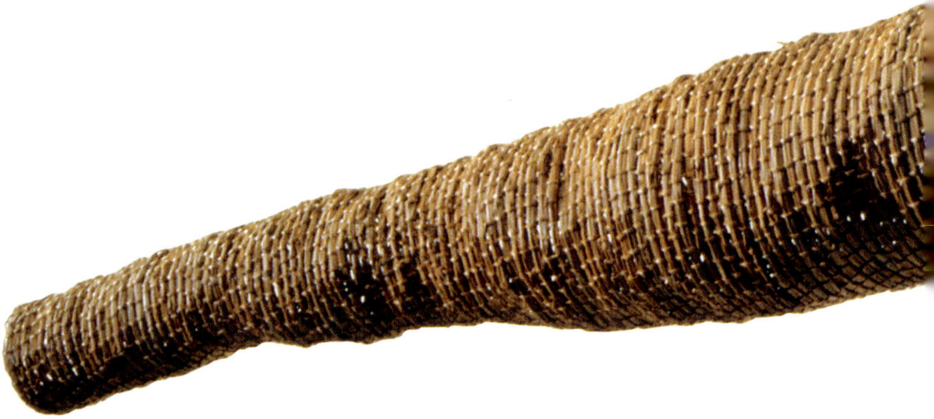

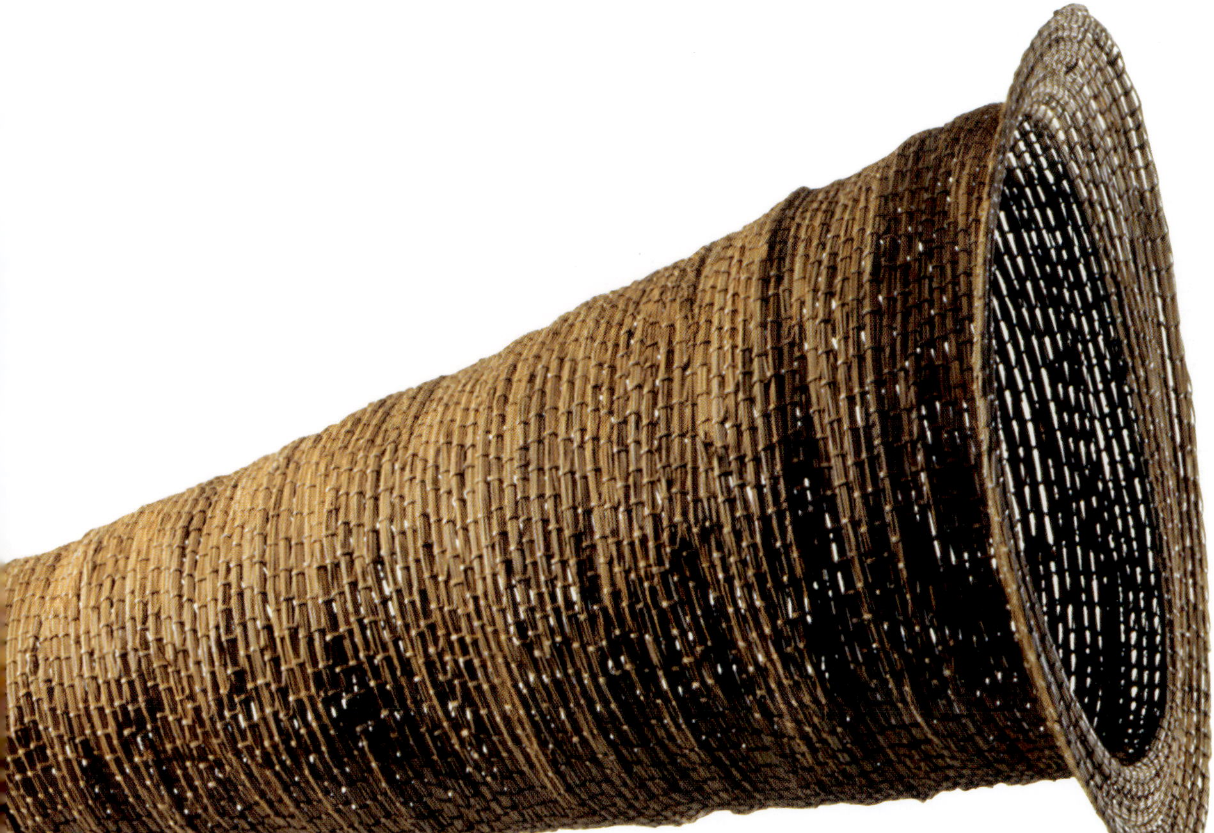

ANCHOR KULUNBA

c.1917–1996
KUNINJKU
NORTHERN TERRITORY

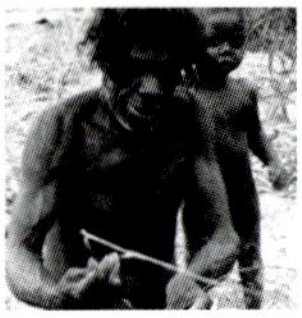

Anchor Kulunba was for many years the senior custodian of Mumeka outstation, which is adjacent to the Mann River some 40 kilometres south of Maningrida. He is the father of other senior artists John Mawurndjul and Jimmy Njiminjuma.

Anchor Kulunba spent his youth living in the bush in the Mumeka region. It was a highly mobile lifestyle that included visits to the rock country of the upper Mann River, tending to important sacred sites in his own Kurulk clan lands and movement to set up seasonal camps at Bulkay on the Tomkinson River floodplain. As a young man, Kulunba became adept at performing the regional ceremonies such as Kunabibi, Wubarr and Mardayin. During World War II, he moved to the mission at Gunbalanya (Oenpelli) – he and other Kuninjku were keen to gain access to goods such as tobacco and the new foods they could purchase there. With the development of the settlement at Maningrida in 1957, the Kuninjku were drawn back east and were actively encouraged to live at Maningrida in the 1960s. However, the Kuninjku never really enjoyed living at Maningrida, and Kulunba returned to his clan lands to establish Mumeka in 1972.

One of the attractions of Mumeka as a camp is that it is close to a number of important major food resources. From the mid-1970s until his death in 1996, Kulunba was the senior custodian of fish trapping activities on Bulkay Creek, a tributary of the Tomkinson River. This small tidal creek runs rich with barramundi fish in the early dry season. Kulunba was the sole producer of the woven conical fish trap called mandjabu that was used to trap barramundi at this place. The trap is woven from a flexible jungle vine called milil. Kulunba controlled this important activity and passed the skills of making and setting the trap to his sons. Jon Altman has documented Kulunba's skills in this activity in a number of publications.[1] As the Maningrida Arts cooperative developed through the 1980s, a number of art advisers recognised the skills involved in this unique weaving process and encouraged Kulunba to also make the traps for the art market. Kulunba's traps were often included in group exhibitions of woven and twined artefacts, the rough texture of the milil contrasting with the fine work involved in women's fibre art. LT

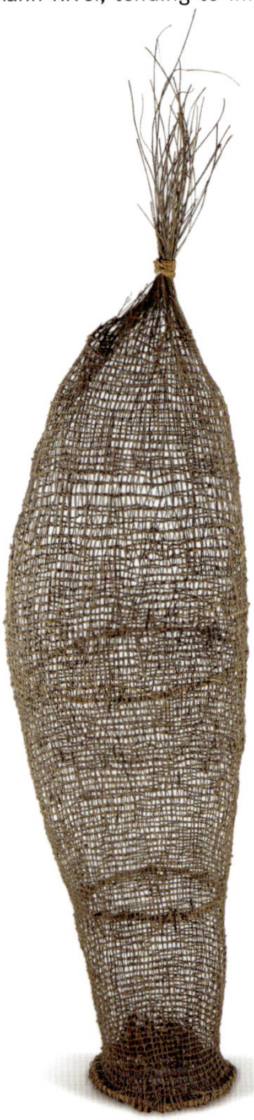

Mandjabu (Conical fish trap) 1985
wood, milil vine
290 x 48 x 70 cm
> detail

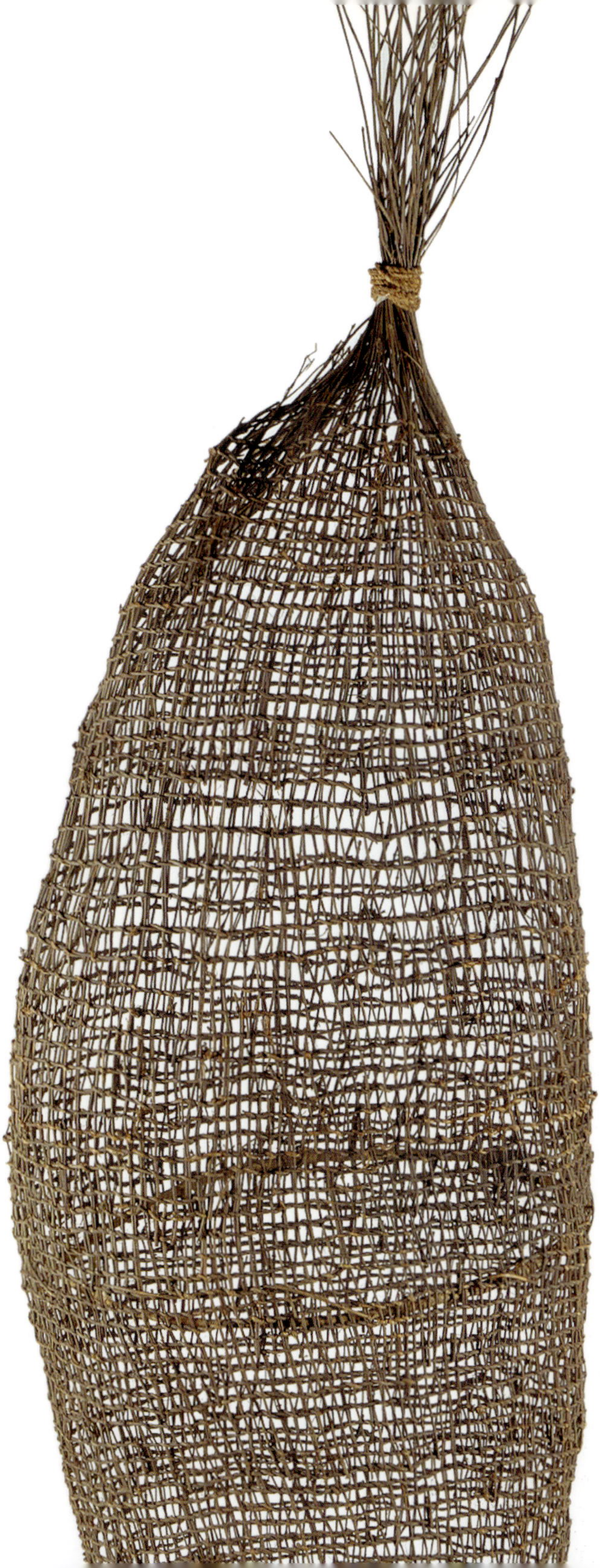

CRUSOE KURDDAL

BORN 1964
KUNINJKU
NORTHERN TERRITORY

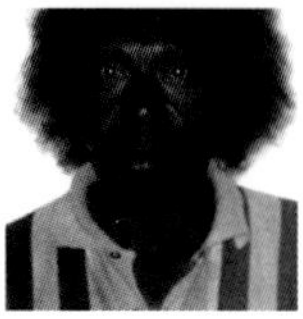

Crusoe Kurddal maintains a sculptural practice that was invented by his father, the famed Kuninjku singer and artist Crusoe Kuningbal. Crusoe Kuningbal was broadly recognised as a virtuoso at singing and dancing stories associated with the mimih spirits, and he developed a way of representing these spirits in sculptural form for use in a Kuninjku trade ceremony called Mamurrng. Mamurrng is performed to promote good relations between different language groups and the trade of different items made by the respective groups. Humour is used throughout the ceremony to foster these amicable relations. Kuninjku people still smile with pleasure as they recall Kuningbal's hilarious performances and evocative singing. The dances performed around the tall, slender mimih sculptures are one of the more humorous elements in the ceremony. Kuninjku language speakers from western Arnhem Land tell many stories about the profane activities of these spirits. Part of the humour surrounding them relates to the mimih's elongated form – they are said to be so thin that a slight wind can break their necks. They slip through the cracks in the rock country to enter their own lands, which exist inside the rock.

In the 1960s, Kuninjku people began performing Mamurrng at Maningrida on special public occasions, and the white people in the town came to recognise Kuningbal's skills as the carver of these unique sculptural mimih forms. Kuningbal was encouraged to market his sculptures, and they became increasingly popular throughout the late 1970s and early 1980s. When he died in 1984, his two sons, Crusoe Kurddal and Owen Yalandja, maintained their inherited skills of making mimih. Kurddal, in particular, continued using the red base colour and dotted patterning that his father had used. In the mid-1980s Kurddal was encouraged to make much larger sculptures than those of his father, and there are now monumental mimih in many public collections. From the late 1980s many Kuninjku people began to carve similar figures, but Kuningbal's two sons lead the way as innovators in these sculptural representations. LT

Mimih spirits c.1985
natural pigments on wood
272 x 15 x 15 cm
270 x 19.5 x 14 cm
270 x 14 x 14 cm
v detail

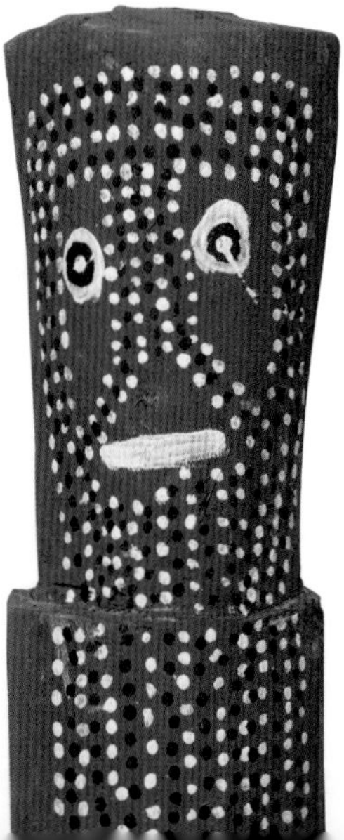

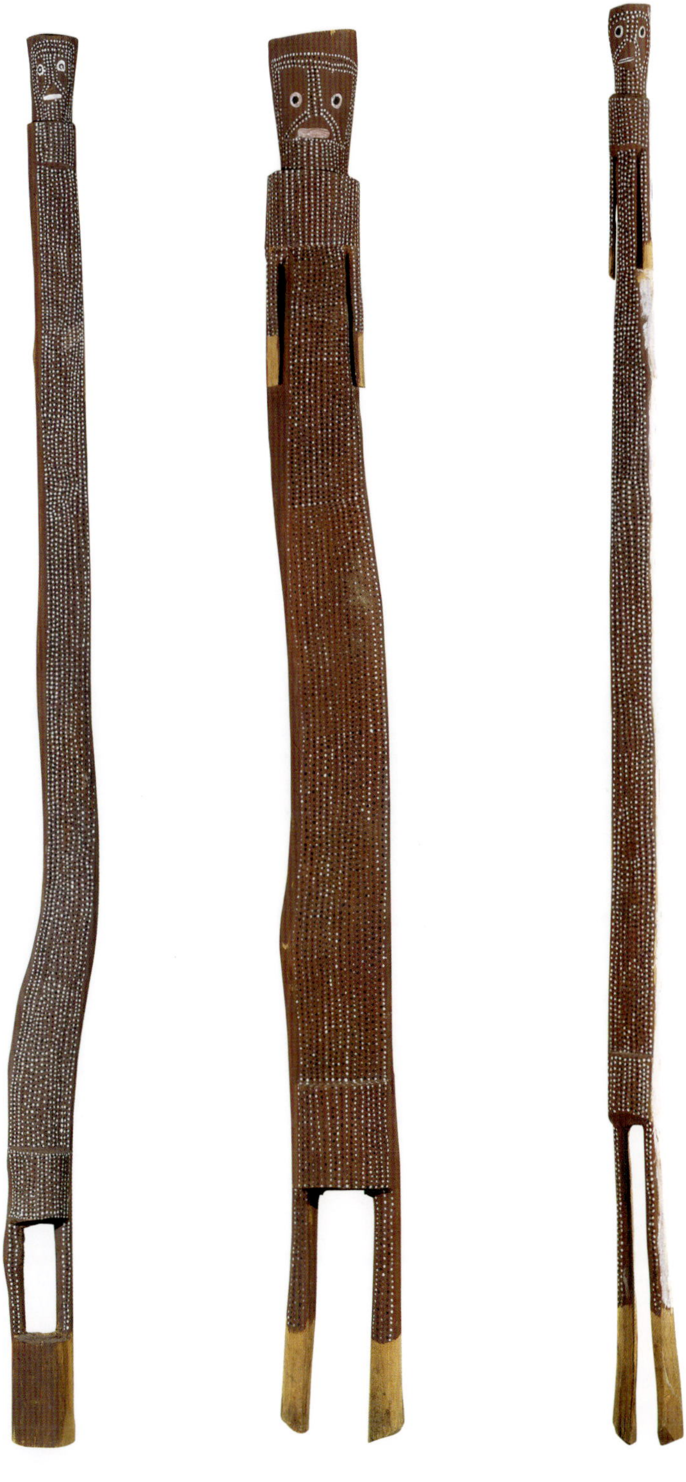

QUEENIE McKENZIE

c.1925–1998
GIJA (MALNGIN/GURINDJI)
WESTERN AUSTRALIA

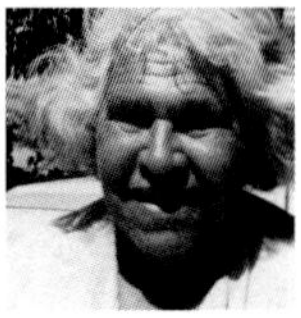

One of the most prominent painters of the Warmun (Turkey Creek) community, Queenie McKenzie was born at Texas Downs Station. The daughter of an Aboriginal woman and a gardiya (white-fella) father, in her youth McKenzie was at the centre of a series of tense encounters between her mother and local government authorities. They sought to take her from her family, following the assimilation policies of the time. On each occasion, McKenzie's mother strongly resisted, even rubbing charcoal on the young girl in an attempt to conceal her lighter skin. As a young woman, McKenzie worked as a goatherd and later as a cook in the cattle mustering camps of Texas Downs. In her later years she moved to Warmun, where she became one of the most senior figures in Gija women's law and ceremony. After witnessing the success of the male Warmun artists, and with the encouragement of Rover Thomas, in 1987 McKenzie was the first woman to begin painting in her community.

In little more than a decade of active painting, Queenie McKenzie emerged as a prominent and compelling commentator on the Aboriginal experience. Participating in numerous solo and group exhibitions, she created works that range in scope from the creation of the world, through the violent encounters of the colonial era, to the present day. Many of McKenzie's paintings are autobiographical: depicting episodes from her life with her own people and with gardiya, on the remote cattle stations of the East Kimberley. McKenzie created a remarkable visual history of a life spent in two worlds: the sacred landscape of the Ngarrangkarni, and her working life on Texas Downs Station.

Untitled, c.1994, is typical of McKenzie's bold, detailed landscapes, which depict the rugged hills of her home country in and around Texas Downs Station. The work also reflects McKenzie's distinctive use of a formal perspective in which she visually compresses the features of the landscape so that she can include multiple sites associated with the particular Ngarrangkarni or historical incident she is portraying. Hence, all the features she includes might not necessarily be visible to an observer standing at a given point on the ground; and, although she portrays actual hills and other geographic features, in this, as in many of McKenzie's works, their physical spatial relationships are rearranged and adapted to illustrate the underlying narrative that unites them. EK

Untitled c.1994
natural pigments on canvas
80 x 100 cm

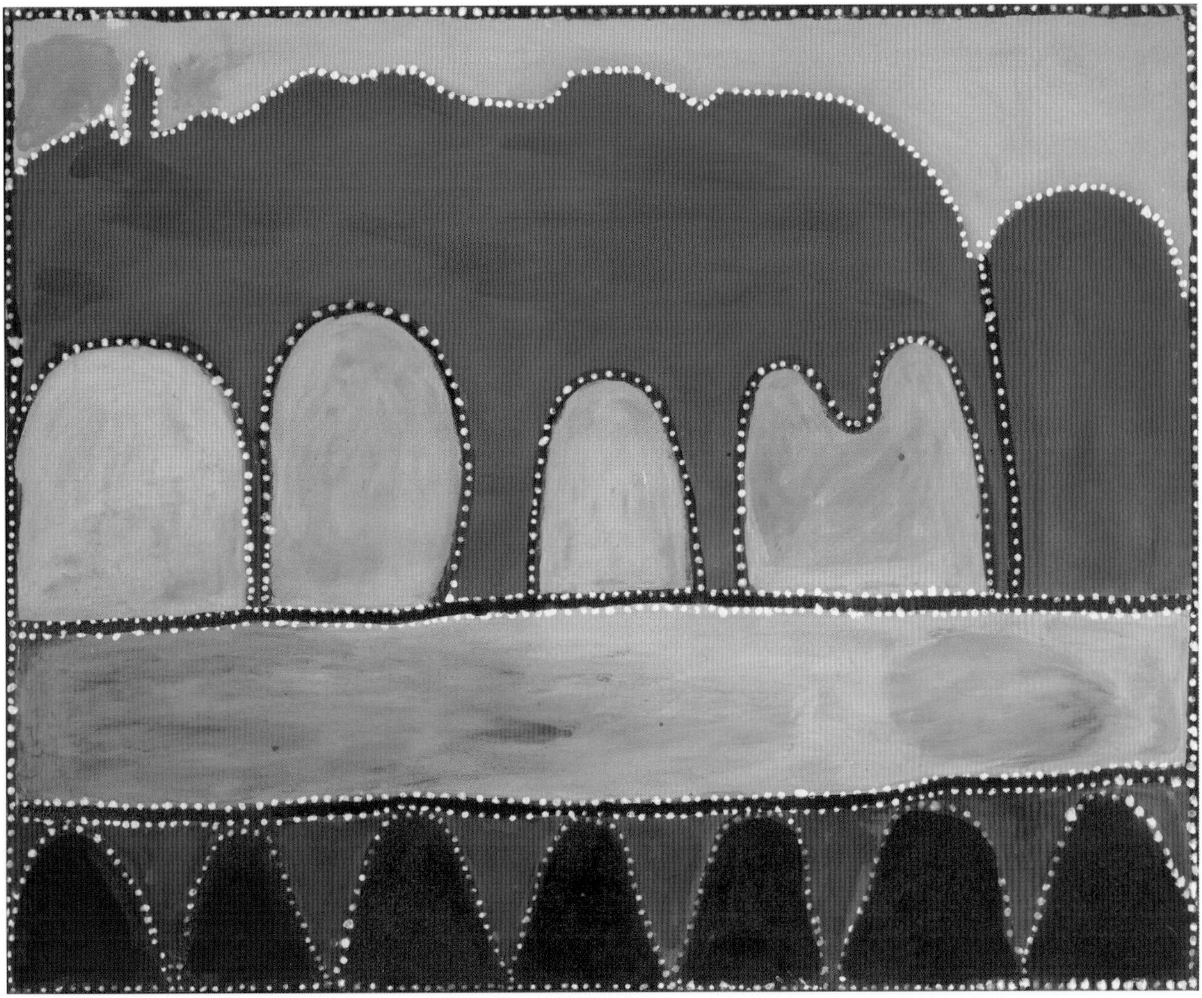

DR PANTJITI MARY McLEAN

BORN c.1930
NGAATJATJARRA
WESTERN AUSTRALIA

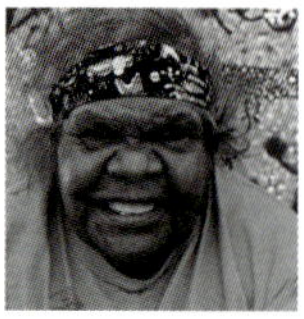

Dr Pantjiti Mary McLean's paintings are infused with the vibrancy, life and bounty of her country, Ngaatjatjarra land in the central deserts of Australia. *Hunting Grounds*, 1993, depicts walku (the ripe quandong fruit), the ripples on the surface of the waterholes, the scampering of the nyintaka (goanna) and the laughter and song of her people. Wira (carved wooden dishes) of gathered bush foods and blooming flowers cover the surface and surround the lively subjects. The aerial view of this idyllic group adds a charmed dimension to the uniquely stylised figures that are the artist's hallmark.

Pantitji now resides at the Ninga Mia community in Kalgoorlie, Western Australia. She began painting in her fifties, usually producing paintings in a methodical, Western Desert 'dot painting' style and quandong root pokerwork artefacts. In the early 1990s, Pantitji was encouraged by fellow artist, Nalda Searles, during a two-year public art project, to further develop her own style. She takes great joy in producing her anecdotal paintings of the day-to-day narratives of her childhood in her grandmother's country, Kaltukutjara (Docker River) in the Northern Territory, and her father's country, around Papalungkuta (Blackstone) in Western Australia.

To make her paintings, Pantitji lays paper or canvas on the ground and sits and paints from various points around it and on it, creating a multi-directional composition. No specific character or element is isolated, or described as having greater significance than another. Everybody and everything plays an important role in this artist's stories.

Pantitji's paintings of daily activities include the human and animal tracks that cross the same plane, seamlessly merging the past and the present. Her 'borderless' pictures are imbued with a sense of great wellbeing and of the continuation and harmony of the life cycle.

Pantitji's significance as a contemporary artist is enhanced by her roles as a mother, a respected elder and a community educator, for which she was awarded an Honorary Doctorate of Letters from the Curtin University of Technology, Perth, in 2001. Pantitji's distinctive paintings are alive with optimistic symbols of the shifting relationship between art and country, and give us a privileged insight into traditional Aboriginal beliefs in a modern context. NB

Hunting grounds 1993
synthetic polymer paint, charcoal and ochre on paper
138.5 x 261 cm
> detail

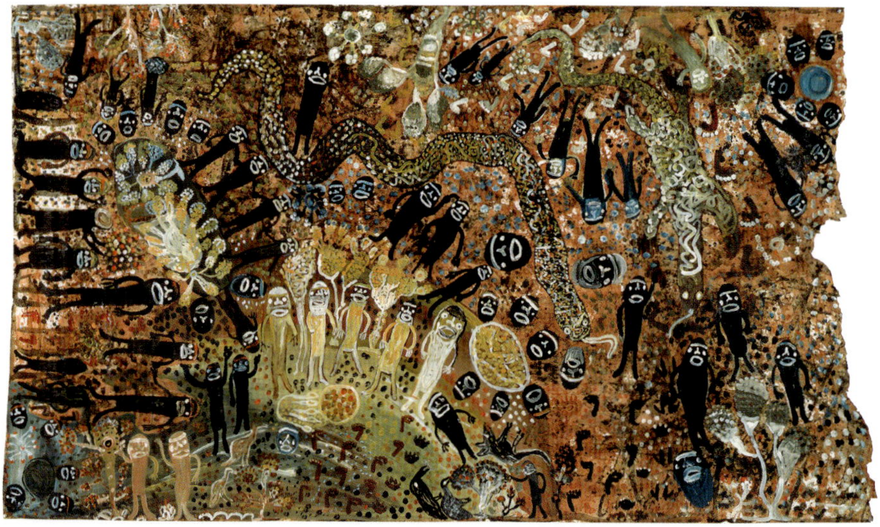

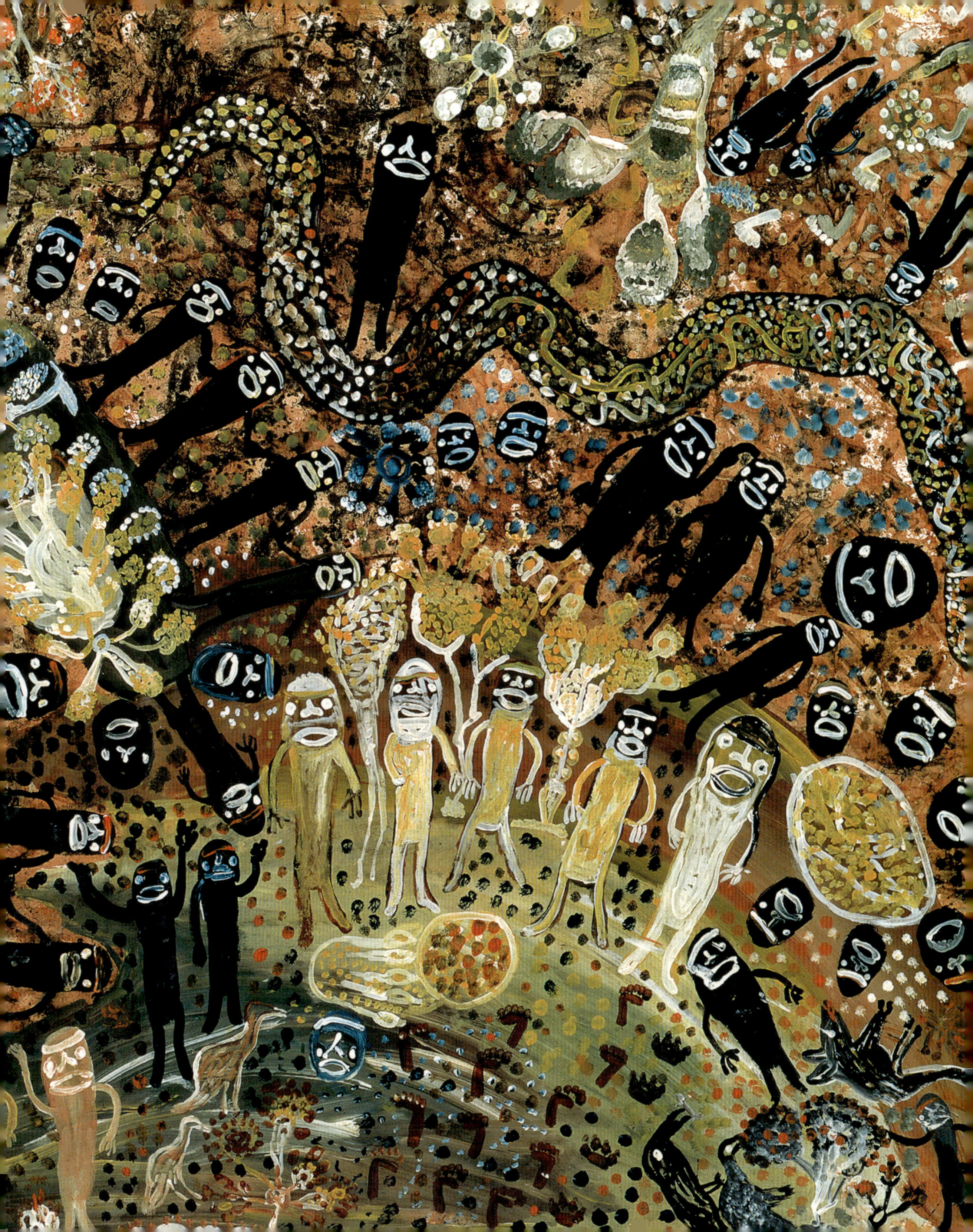

DR DAVID MALANGI

1927–1999
MANYARRNGU
NORTHERN TERRITORY

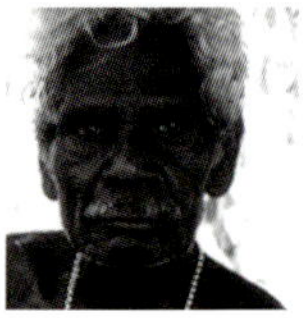

Dr David Malangi was born in central Arnhem Land the year after the Methodist Mission was established at Milingimbi. His early years were spent in this area, where he received initiation into Manyarrngu culture from his parents and extended family. He began painting in earnest after World War II. In Australia, Malangi is probably best known as the artist whose work was featured, without his knowledge or permission, on the one dollar note in 1966. He was also one of the first Aboriginal artists to have his work included in an international exhibition of contemporary art, at the Biennale of Sydney in 1979. In 1988 he collaborated on *The Aboriginal Memorial* – a group of 200 log coffins now on permanent display at the National Gallery of Australia, Canberra – to mark 200 years of European occupation of Australia. Malangi was honoured with the Australia Council Emeritus Award in 1998.

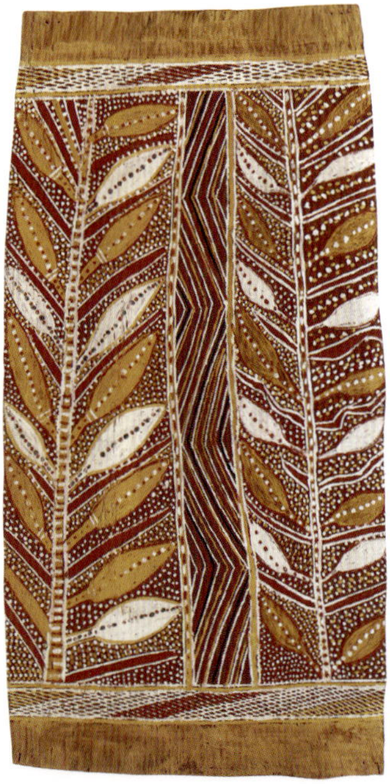

Gunmirringu funeral scene, 1983, was one of eight bark paintings that the artist exhibited in the 1983 Australian Perspecta at the Art Gallery of New South Wales, Sydney, as an incontrovertible land rights statement. The works were created and put together after discussions with the artist about his concerns for the safety of his sacred sites, under threat from mining and commercial fishing. Gunmirringu, the great ancestral hunter, is central in Malangi's art. Here, Gunmirringu is shown lying in state. His clansmen are around him, holding clapsticks, singing ceremonial songs and dancing. Darrpa, the deadly brown snake, which bit and killed Gunmirringu, is shown alongside. Around him also are the spoils of his last hunt: yams, nuts and a butchered kangaroo, which commonly refers to the death of a person. Gunmurringu's was the first funeral, and this story tells of how death came into the world. It is enacted through ceremony and art to assist the passage of the soul after a member of the clan dies. In this composition, the ceremony is framed within two flowering stringy-bark trees. These trees often refer to the raga, or white berry bush, under which Gunmirringu sat, cooking his food, when the snake struck.

The beautiful small bark, *Food pattern of trees*, is a more direct reference to the raga. It is a much earlier painting than *Gunmirringu funeral scene*. Its overall design is more intricately wrought and its colours softer than later, more characteristic, barks by Malangi. SM

> **Gunmirringu funeral scene** 1983
natural pigments on bark
156 x 73.7 cm

v **Food pattern of trees** c.1960
natural pigments on bark
57.5 x 31.1 cm

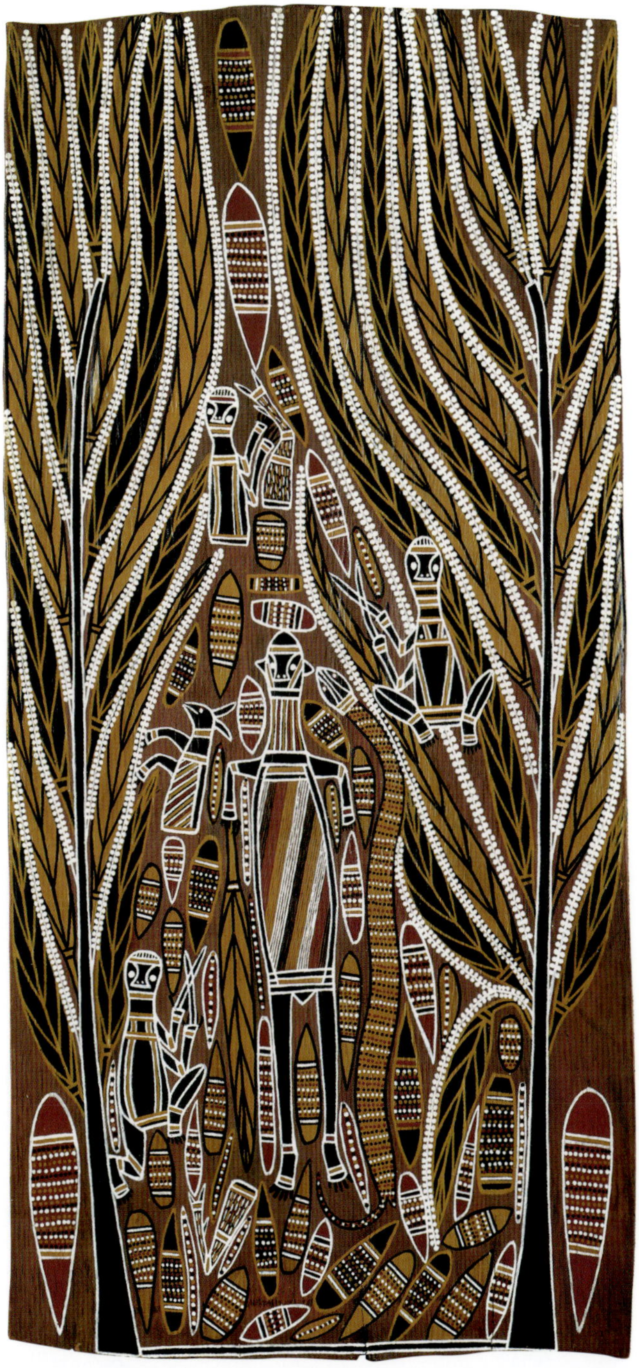

SAMUEL MANGGUDJA

1909–1983
KUNINJKU
NORTHERN TERRITORY

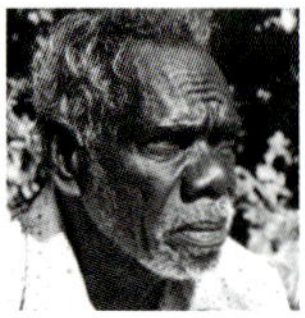

Samuel Manggudja (Garnarradj) was born in the Gumaderr River region of western Arnhem Land, and spent his early years living a traditional lifestyle. His father took him to Goulburn Island Mission as a young boy and he attended school there. Later, in 1930, he went to join his promised wife in Gunbalanya (Oenpelli), where he lived for the rest of his life. Manggudja had strong knowledge of ceremonial matters, and was a key assistant in the research work conducted by the anthropologists Ronald and Catherine Berndt in Gunbalanya in the late 1940s. Ronald Berndt collected a number of paintings by Manggudja in 1947, and these are now housed in the Berndt Museum of Anthropology at the University of Western Australia, Perth.[1] Manggudja's work in the Art Gallery of New South Wales, Sydney, is part of the extensive gift by Dr Stuart Scougall, and dates from 1960. These works characteristically feature dotted infill for the figures, a style that relates strongly to the rock art of Manggudja's clan lands. It was only later, in the 1970s, that the crosshatched infill, borrowed from ceremonial painting, became an ubiquitous style in the western Arnhem Land region.

Manggudja's painting, *Man with leprosy*, 1961, relates to many rock paintings that were the product of sorcery practices. Paintings of figures with elongated or detached limbs are said to have been used to magically transfer these afflictions to a nominated victim. Once the image was created, the name of the victim was called out over the painting. *Figure with the long fingers*, 1960, relates to paintings of the namorrorddo, or shooting star spirit, that is said to grasp the souls of the living with its clawed hands and rush away across the sky with them.

Manggudja continued to develop as an artist throughout the 1970s and his works were included in exhibitions arranged by the then Aboriginal Arts Board of the Australia Council and in its *Oenpelli Bark Painting* publication of 1979.[2] Samuel Manggudja served on the Aboriginal Arts Board from 1973 to 1975. LT

> **Man with leprosy** 1961
natural pigments on bark
75 x 39.7 cm

v **Figure with long fingers** 1960
natural pigments on bark
34.5 x 103.5 cm

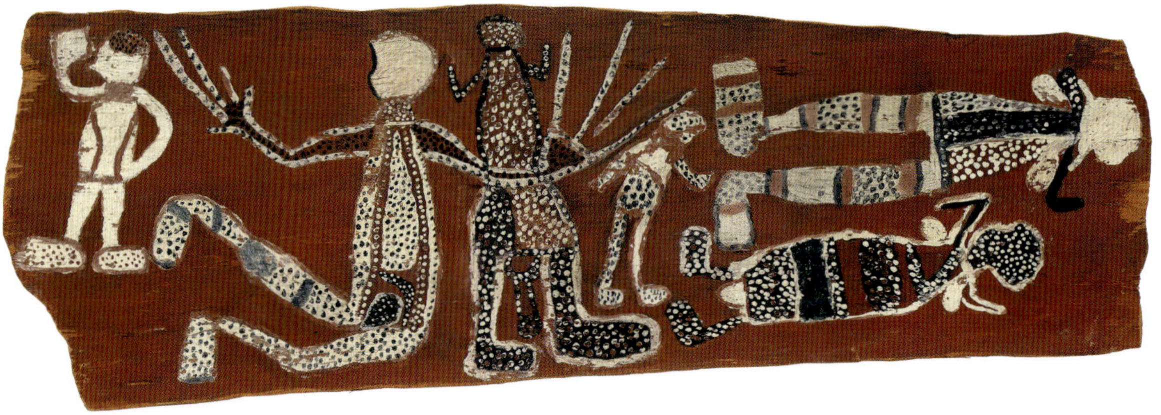

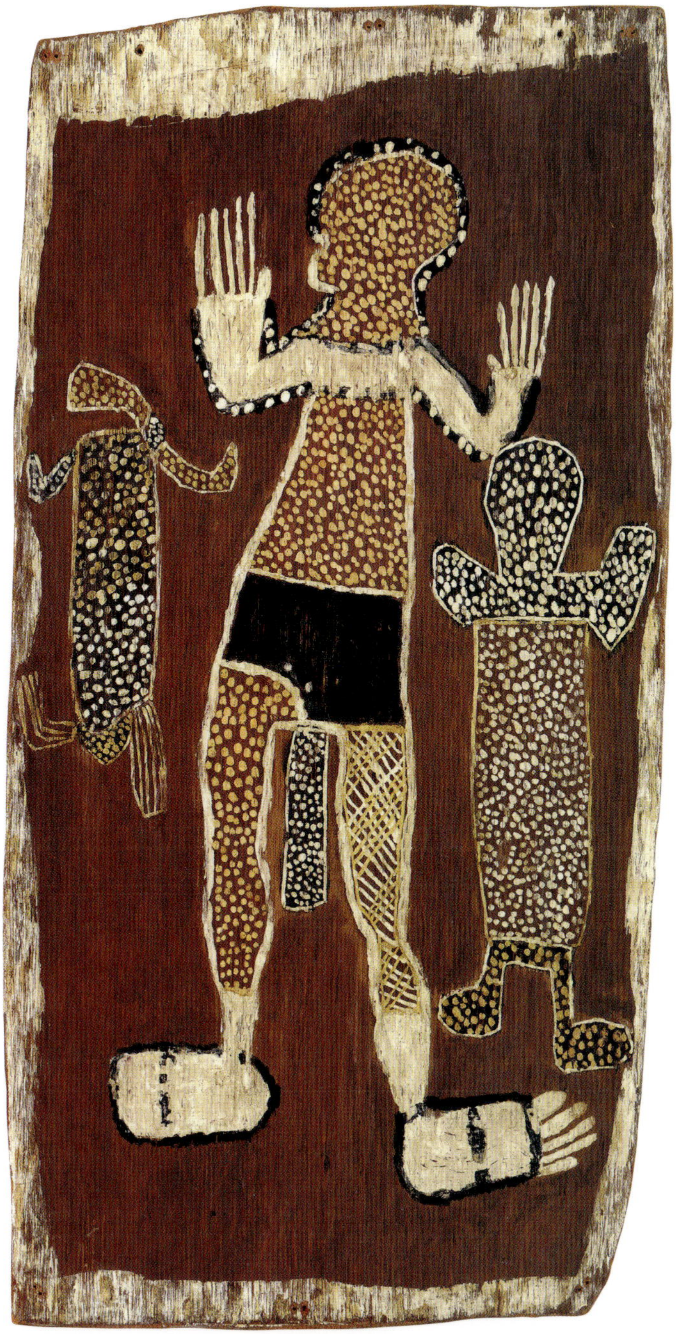

BANDUK MARIKA

BORN 1954
RIRRATJINGU
NORTHERN TERRITORY

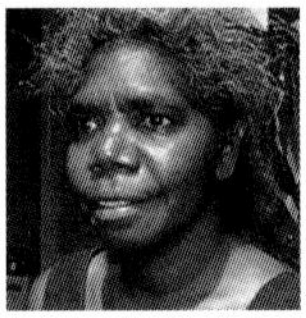

Banduk Marika is the youngest daughter of Mawalan Marika, and sister of Wandjuk. Banduk Marika and her sisters are among the first Yolngu women to be encouraged by their male relatives to paint ancestral creation stories. Marika's medium of choice, linoprint, enables her to depict the ancestral stories in a new way, while respecting the law. Carving the design into the lino blocks echoes the practice of precisely incising clan designs onto wooden objects such as ancestral figures, Macassan pipes and message sticks.

Marika's print *Miyapunuwuy Yarru Yan – Turtle hunting at Dhambaliya (Bremer Island)*, 1987, illustrates key aspects of the story of two ancestral hunters who harpooned turtle and prepared them in the traditional way on Ruwakpuy Beach. Gakarrarr, the land seagull, was spearing fish nearby and caught wind of this. Sneaking up, he grabbed some meat and was in turn caught by the hunters and thrown onto the fire. *Wawalak Wulay, Djan'kawu Creation*, 1987, shows scenes from the Wawilak Sisters and Djan'kawu song cycles. Because she is a Rirratjingu woman, Marika is intimately associated with Yalangbara and other important clan land in the region.

As a traditional landowner at Yirrkala, Marika has inherited responsibilities that have shaped her life. She was educated at Yirrkala and moved to Darwin in 1972. She later moved to Sydney in 1980 to pursue her career as an artist. In 1984 she was artist-in-residence at the Canberra School of Art, and in 1985 she was artist-in-residence at Flinders University, South Australia. In 1988, Marika returned to Yirrkala to be the manager of Buku-Larrngay Mulka Arts Centre and Museum.

Marika combines her familial responsibilities with her activities as an artist and cultural activist. She has travelled as a delegate and speaker to many national and international conferences. In 1994, a Federal Court judgement awarded Marika (and seven other Aboriginal artists) damages against a company that illegally reproduced their work on carpets produced in Vietnam. Consequently, she featured in *Copyrights*, a documentary made in 1997 that explored Indigenous principles of copyright. Among Marika's many accomplishments have been appointments to the boards of the National Gallery of Australia, Canberra, and the Museums and Art Galleries of the Northern Territory, Darwin. She was also a member of the Aboriginal and Torres Strait Islander Arts Board of the Australia Council. In 2001, Marika was the recipient of the Aboriginal and Torres Strait Islander Arts Board's prestigious Red Ochre Award for lifetime achievement. KW

above **Wawalak Wulay, Djan'kawu Creation** 1987
linocut
23.3 x 41.4 cm

below **Miyapunuwuy Yarru Yan – Turtle hunting at Dhambaliya (Bremer Island)** 1987
linocut
28.7 x 48.2 cm

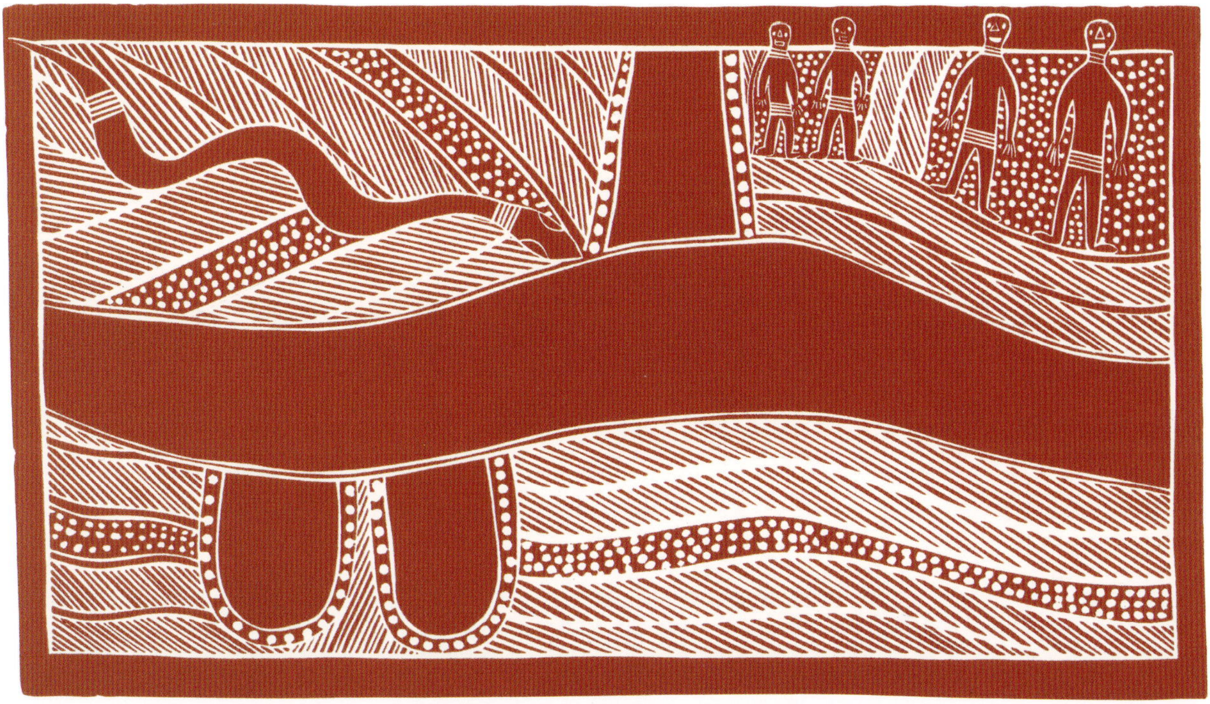

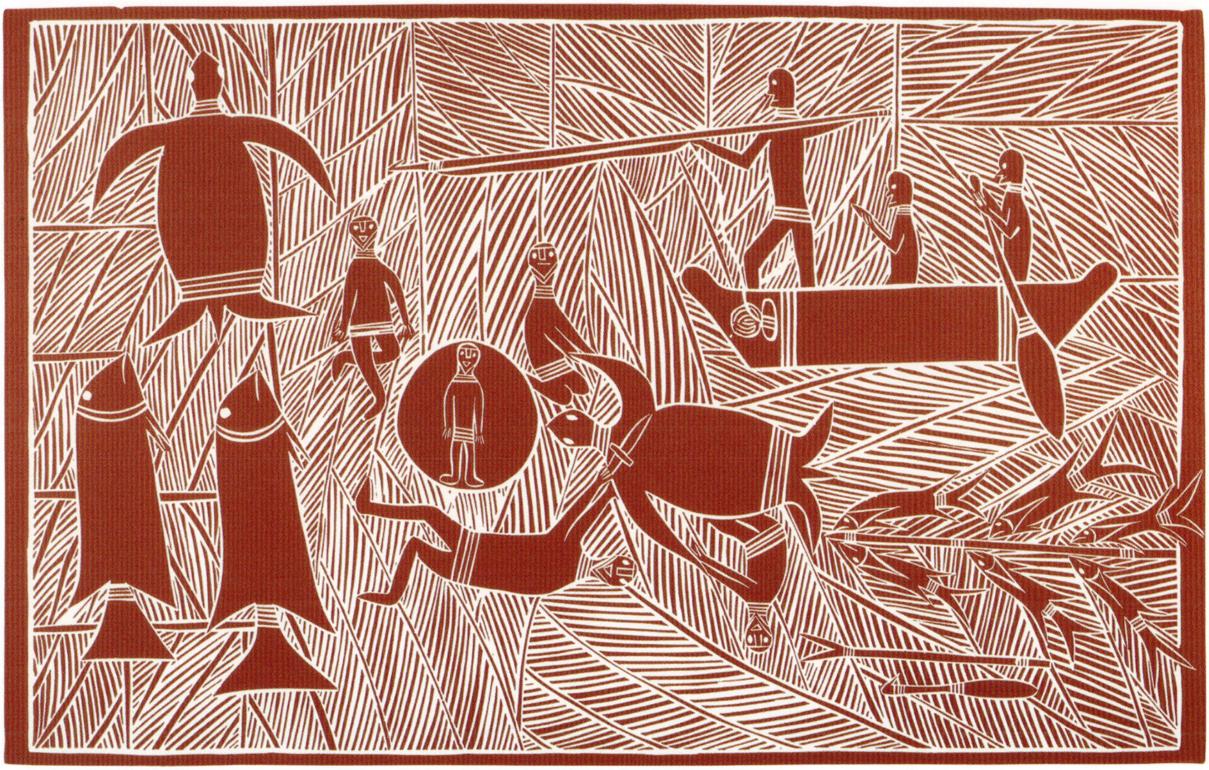

MAWALAN MARIKA

c.1908–1967
RIRRATJINGU
NORTHERN TERRITORY

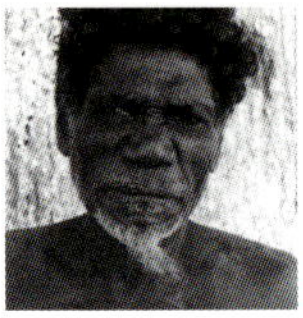

The Djan'kawu, a man and two sisters, are the primary ancestral creator beings for the Dhuwa moiety of central and north eastern Arnhem Land. Yalangbara, where the Djan'kawu landed after their canoe journey from Burralku (an island to the east), is the most important location painted by Mawalan Marika. The Marika family consider themselves to be Mayarr Mayarr – the children of the Djan'kawu. In a series of five large bark paintings, Marika depicted the Djan'kawu journey by canoe across the sea, and their activities after they landed at Yalangbara. These paintings are considered to be the most comprehensive visual narratives of the Rirratjingu ancestral song cycle in existence.

Djan'kawu creation story, 1959, portrays the verses from the song cycle that tell of the Djan'kawu Sisters travelling to different locations and giving birth to the Dhuwa clans. The lower panel refers to the Sisters giving birth at Arnhem Bay and later at Milingimbi, above. Marika also includes eight mawalan (sacred digging sticks) that the Djan'kawu plunged into the ground, creating waterholes, sacred trees and food-bearing plants. To the right of this, the Djan'kawu watch a sunrise and sunset. The top panel shows the death of the Sisters at Galiwin'ku (Elcho Island), while Djan'kawu the man is shown at Yalangbara contemplating the mawalan and singing.

The two carved, wooden *Djan'kawu, ancestral being[s] of the Dhuwa moiety*, 1960, are painted with ceremonial body designs and decorated with human hair, feathered pendants and bark aprons. Marika's figures are rare, three-dimensional representations of these miraculous ancestors.

Marika was a great law man with extensive sacred knowledge. He led key parts of the Djan'kawu and Wawilak ceremonies, which are the basis for most of his paintings. Marika also painted other subjects, including depictions of Murruruma, a Rirratjingu songman and cultural hero, and hunting scenes. He occasionally painted Macassan subjects, recalling the trepang fishing fleets that worked around the north coast of Australia until they were banned in 1907. Marika was one of the first artists at Yirrkala to begin painting barks for sale, and was also one of the first leaders and artists from Arnhem Land to visit the southern Australian cities. Marika strongly protested against the activities of mining companies in his country, through letters written by his son, Wandjuk Marika, to the Federal Government in Canberra. Mawalan Marika will be remembered as a passionate advocate for his people's cultural and land rights. KW

> **Djan'kawu creation story** 1959
natural pigments on bark
188 x 64.8 cm

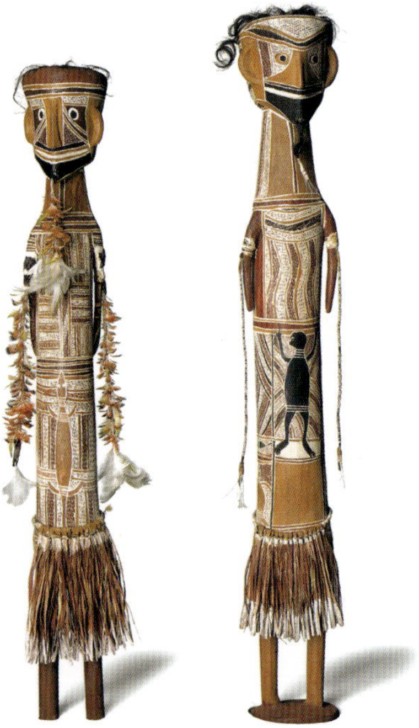

v **Djan'kawu, ancestral being of the Dhuwa moiety** 1960
Djan'kawu, ancestral being of the Dhuwa moiety 1960
both wood, human hair, bark fibre, parakeet feathers, white feathers, natural pigments
74.3 cm
81 cm

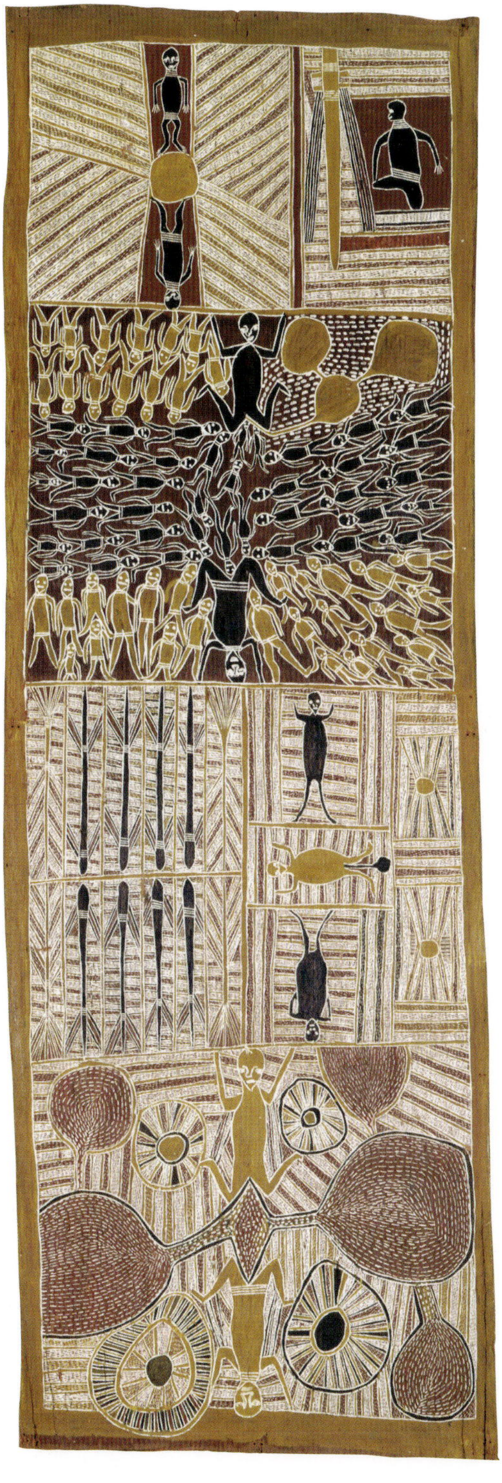

WANDJUK MARIKA

c.1927–1987
RIRRATJINGU
NORTHERN TERRITORY

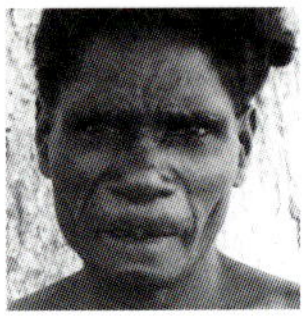

'Painting is very important. It's the design or symbol, power of the land.' [1]

Wandjuk Marika was born on Dhambaliya (Bremer Island), the eldest son of Mawalan Marika. His early life was influenced by the increasing intrusion of balanda (whitefella) influence and activity in Arnhem Land. After the establishment of Yirrkala Mission in 1935, increasing numbers of academics, mining representatives, hunters, fishermen and art enthusiasts visited the region.

Marika grew up learning the skills associated with his future responsibilities as a leader of the Rirratjingu clan and Dhuwa moiety. His father taught him to hunt and his ceremonial obligations regarding the two major Dhuwa ancestral song cycles – the Djan'kawu Story and the Wawilak Sisters. Marika was also one of the first students, and later an assistant, at the Yirrkala Mission school. His facility with English enabled him to interpret Yolngu culture for visiting anthropologists and art collectors, including Charles Mountford and Ronald and Catherine Berndt. Marika started painting on bark when he was in his mid-teens, working with his father.

The beginning of the Djan'kawu song cycle is characterised by descriptions of constant paddling, the rocking of the canoe in which the Djan'kawu travelled, and numerous marine observations. Approaching Yalangbara, the Djan'kawu feel the warmth of the rising sun upon their backs. This moment is wonderfully captured in Marika's bark painting *Djan'kawu Story (The sun rising)*, 1959, which depicts the dazzling sun as it comes over the horizon.

In the painting *Sea life (Dreaming of the artist's mother)*, 1959, Marika demonstrates his association with his mother's Warramirri clan, and depicts a variety of marine species swimming over the field of miny'tji (sacred clan designs) representing the sea. The dots on the tentacles of the Portuguese man-of-war jellyfish represent its poison buds – the poison they emit is said to heat the water and calm the sea.

Throughout his life, Marika wrote letters on behalf of the eastern Arnhem Land clan leaders, including his father, to the Federal Government, protesting unsuccessfully the mining activities that were threatening Yolngu sovereignty over their lands. He travelled extensively in Australia and overseas as a member, and later chairman, of the (then) Aboriginal Arts Board of the Australia Council (1973–79). The unauthorised reproduction of *Djan'kawu creation story*, 1959 (see previous page), on a tea towel disturbed him to the extent that he stopped painting for a number of years. Marika became a key advocate for the legislative protection of Indigenous intellectual property rights. KW

> **Sea life (Dreaming of the artist's mother)**
1959
natural pigments on bark
102.9 x 62.9 cm

v **Djan'kawu Story (The sun rising)** 1959
natural pigments on bark
44.8 x 32.4 cm

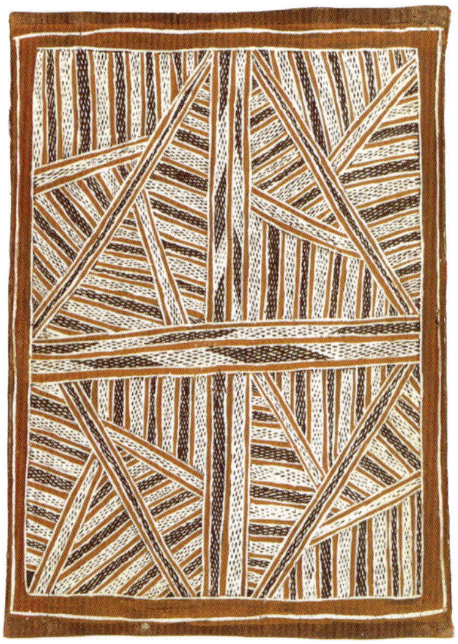

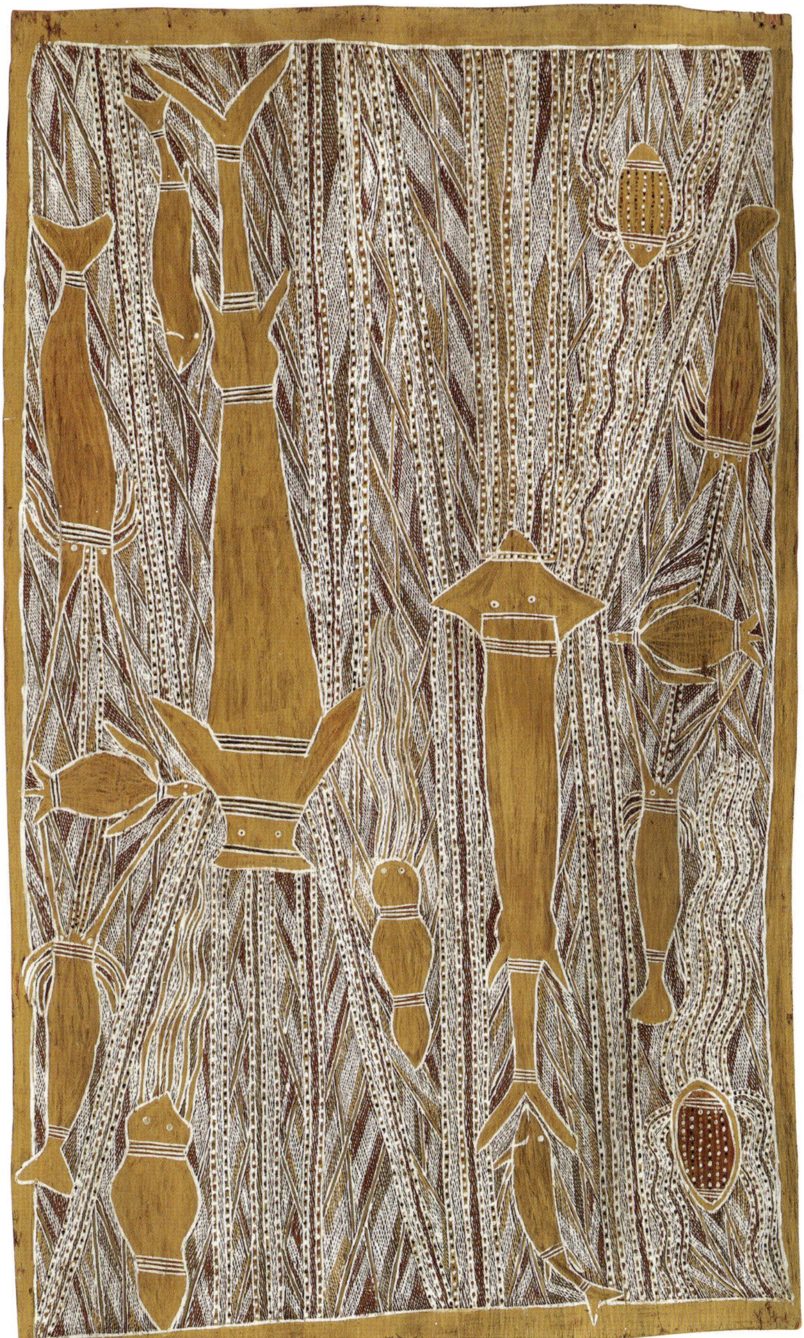

JOHN MAWURNDJUL

BORN 1952
KUNINJKU
NORTHERN TERRITORY

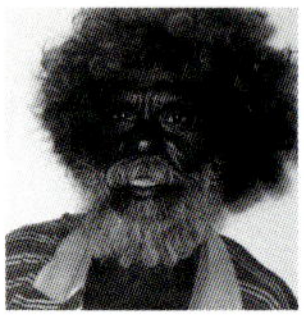

John Mawurndjul is one of the most experimental bark painters in Arnhem Land. Mawurndjul grew up in his country near Mumeka on the Mann River. He lived for a considerable time in the newly established Aboriginal town of Maningrida in the 1960s, but returned to Mumeka from 1972. Today he moves regularly between Maningrida and his outstation at Milmilngkan, south of Maningrida. He was taught to paint by his father, Anchor Kulunba, his brother Jimmy Njiminjuma and his uncle Peter Marralwanga. Mawurndjul's early work of the late 1970s reveals his meticulous attention to detail and very fine rarrk (crosshatching) technique.

Many of his early works are relatively small images of the rainbow serpent Ngalyod in snake-like form, or of the yawkyawk, mermaid-like creatures that were devoured by Ngalyod in Mawurndjul's clan lands. However, in the late 1980s Mawurndjul began to produce larger paintings of this subject, which evoked the powerful twists and turns of the body of Ngalyod. The iridescent rarrk across Ngalyod's body captures the almost electric, radiating power of this being. In other paintings, Mawurndjul experimented with complex interactions of figurative forms, particularly in depictions of Ngalyod involved in the act of biting or swallowing the yawkyawk. Sometimes Mawurndjul shows the dismembered bodies, and at other times they may be merging together. In essence, the imagery of the rainbow serpent swallowing these other beings is a reference to site creation, of the yawkyawk joining with Ngalyod inside the earth and investing it with their everlasting power.

More recently, Mawurndjul has emphasised the geometric aesthetic in Kuninjku painting. He has produced works that comprise grids of crosshatching with circles representing waterholes enmeshed in the grid. These paintings relate to Mardayin body paintings, and focus attention upon the abstract representation of features of the associated landscape. In the context of the Mardayin ceremony, these geometric body designs are said to physically connect initiates to the sacred power of the ancestral beings who made their clan lands. Mawurndjul has said that he is not simply reproducing ceremonial designs in works such as *Mardayin ceremmony,* 2000, but that he is also creating new forms of patterning and composition. Mawurndjul has travelled the world with his art, and studied collections of early bark painting in cities as far afield as Paris. Through his art, Mawurndjul draws upon and extends Kuninjku traditions to promote a wider understanding of his culture. LT

> **Mardayin ceremony** 2000
natural pigments on bark
170 x 78 cm

v **Yawkyawk (Young girl's spirit)** 1985
Yawkyawk (Young girl's spirit) 1985
both natural pigments on bark
50.5 x 27 cm
47.5 x 25.9 cm

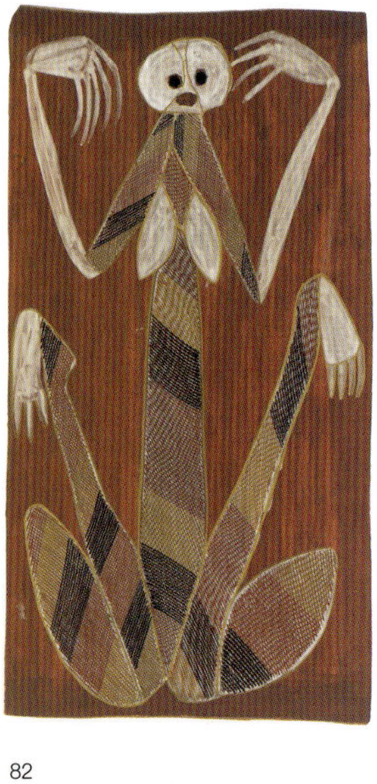

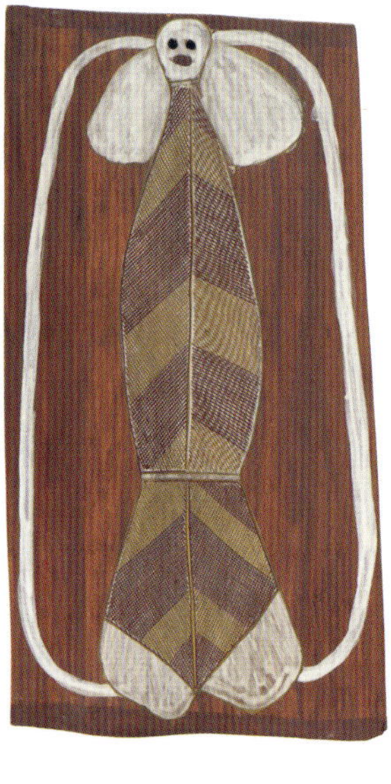

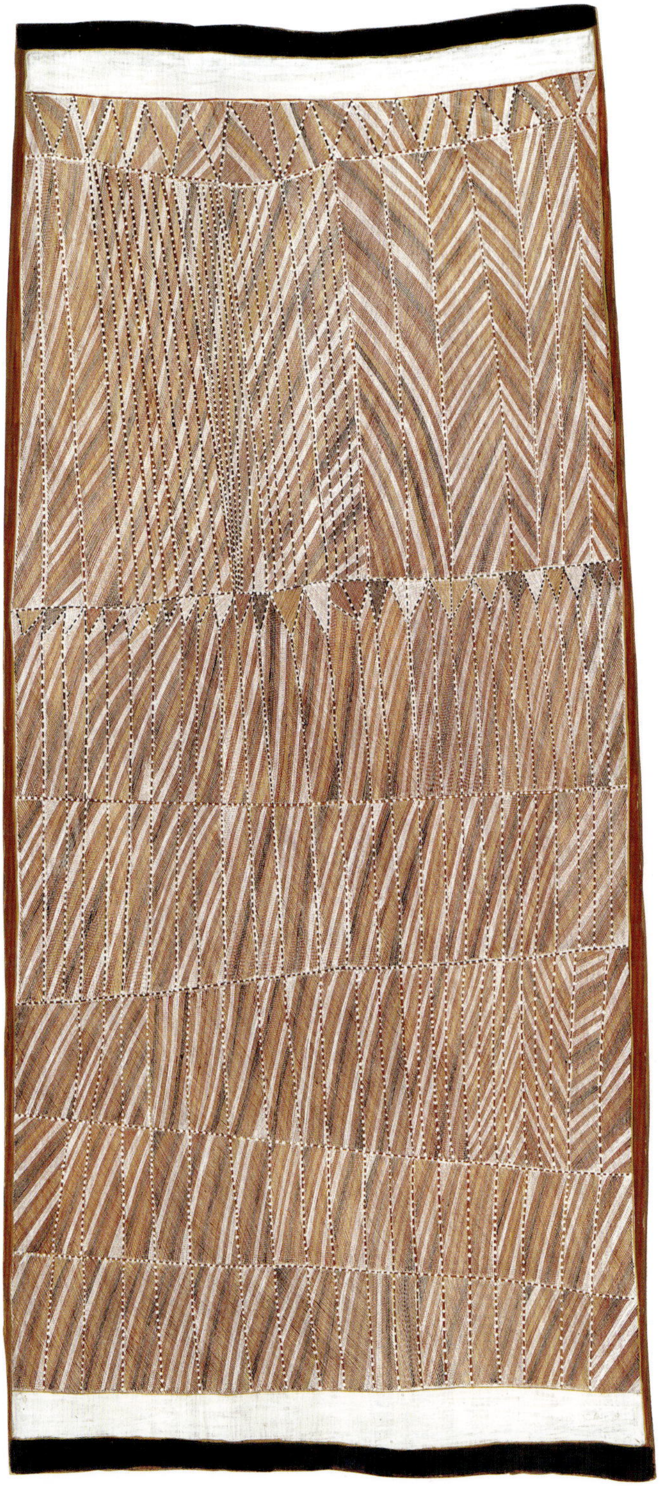

GALUMA MAYMURU

BORN 1951
MANGGALILI
NORTHERN TERRITORY

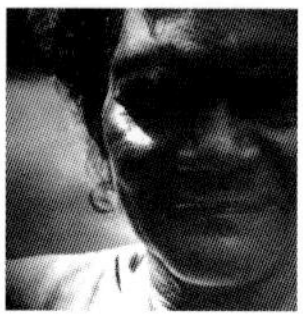

Galuma Maymuru is the daughter of Narritjin Maymuru. She grew up at Yirrkala Mission in north-east Arnhem Land. Since 1974 Galuma has lived either at the homeland centre of Yilpara or at Dhuruputjpi in her husband Dhukal Wirrpanda's Dhudi Djapu clan country, close to her own Manggalili clan lands. For ten years she was the community's schoolteacher, before becoming a full-time artist.

Her first solo exhibition in 1999 at the William Mora Galleries, Melbourne, was subtitled 'In memory of Narritjin', acknowledging the debt she owed to her father, who taught her to paint and carve. With her father's encouragement, she was one of the first generation of Yolngu women to become major artists. 'He'd say "this is our painting and I'm telling you about the paintings for in the future when I am passed away you can use them".'[1] She learned by watching Narritjin paint and then worked on small bark paintings herself, practising the techniques ' ... until my hand got better, putting it into my mind'.[2]

Galuma stresses the intellectual energy she invests in her art, from her engagement with the landscape through the ancestral designs, and then creating the final image on the bark or as a carving. Her work is multi-layered, recreating the lives of the ancestral beings in the landscape at Djarrakpi, among them the ancestral woman Nyapililngu as she wanders in the sand dunes at Djarrakpi, and the hunter Muwandi poised on a rock spearing yambirrku (parrot fish). Many of Galuma's finest paintings and carvings – such as *Nyapilingu ga Guwak*, 1999, and the *Sacred digging stick*, 1999 – emphasise the transformational nature of the spiritual world, with figures appearing from and disappearing into a back-ground pattern of Manggalili clan designs that represent the moving surface of the rivers, sand and sea. To Galuma, art is an act of memory and a process of transmission, in which she passes Manggalili law on to new generations of her clan. Equally, it is a spiritual and aesthetic exploration of her homeland. HM

left **Nyapilingu ga Guwak** 1999
natural earth pigments on wood
130.5 cm

right **Sacred digging stick** 1999
natural earth pigments on wood
113 cm

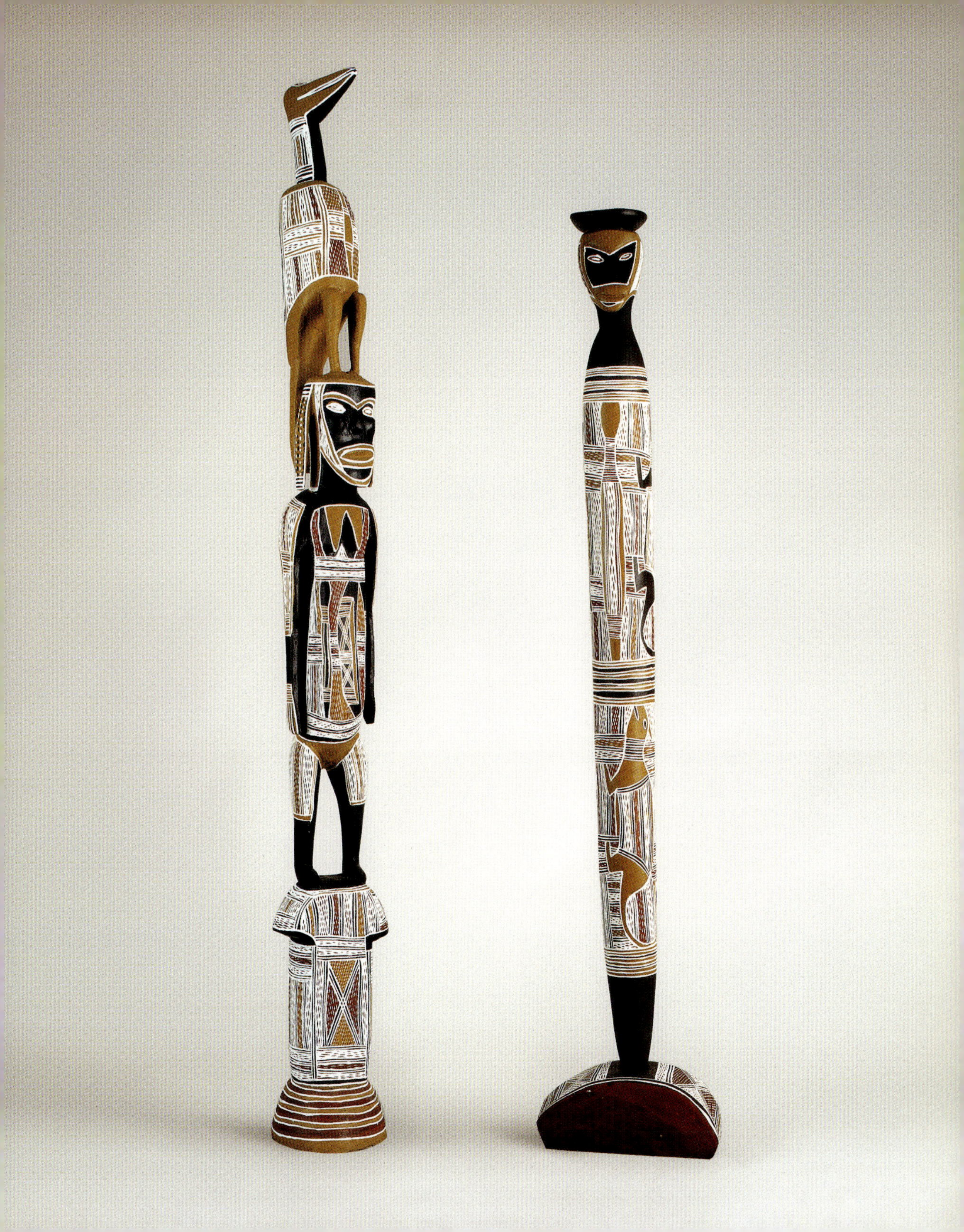

NARRITJIN MAYMURU

c.1916–1981
MANGGALILI
NORTHERN TERRITORY

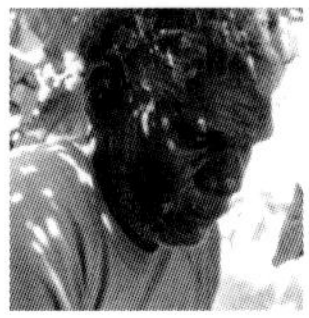

Narritjin Maymuru's life encompassed some of the major events of Australian and Northern Territory history. He was a great intellectual and ceremonial leader. Within his community he was often called on to assume the role of mediator, bringing disputants together. Above all he was an artist with a passion for making things. He would work late into the night while his family slept, bent double over a sheet of bark, painting by the light of an unshaded bulb.

Narritjin's earliest surviving paintings and carvings were completed for the anthropologists Ronald and Catherine Berndt in 1946, and in 1948 and 1952 he produced a number of works for Charles Mountford (who led the American–Australian Scientific Expedition to Arnhem Land in 1948). During the 1950s Narritjin painted very little, and mainly produced polished hardwood carvings. However, by the early 1960s he had become one of the most prolific and renowned Yolngu artists. In 1962, Narritjin suggested that two great painted panels should be placed on either side of the Yirrkala church altar, and was one of the artists who painted these extraordinary works.

In 1963, Narritjin Maymuru and a group of Yolngu dancers performed in Sydney and Melbourne, in a tour organised by the Elizabethan Theatre Trust, and a solo exhibition of Narritjin's paintings was also held in Sydney. Narritjin developed a close relationship with the Melbourne art dealer Jim Davidson, and his art became well represented in museums and galleries in Australia and overseas, in particular in the United States. In 1978, with his son Banapana, Narritjin was jointly awarded a Creative Arts Fellowship from the Australian National University, Canberra.

Narritjin Maymuru was an innovative artist, although he always worked within the canons of Yolngu art. His paintings are known for their complex symbolism. Many of them represent ancestral stories in narrative form, and symbolic connections are often conveyed by subtle visual puns. Similar elements occur across the paintings, with different but related meanings. Narritjin's art is characterised by its diversity, intricacy and great attention to detail, as seen in *Djert* (*The sea eagle*), c.1958. Yet within his corpus there are also works of profound simplicity, in which he condenses imagery into key motifs. Narritjin Maymuru saw art as a means of communicating ideas and knowledge – to an audience outside his community as a means of widening understanding of Yolngu culture, and to younger generations of Yolngu as a way of ensuring the continuity of their ancestral law. HM

Djert (The sea eagle) c.1958
natural pigments on bark
90 x 47 cm

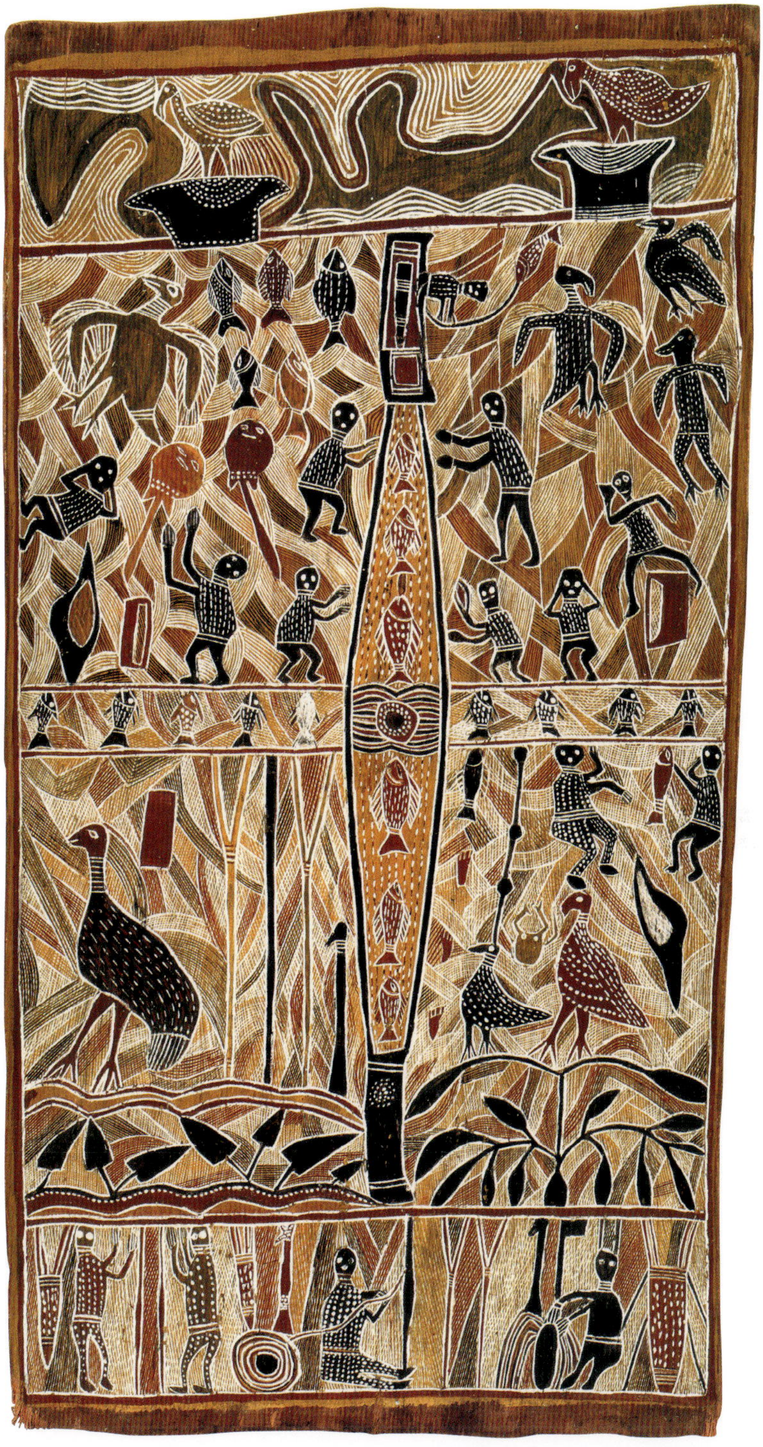

RICKY MAYNARD

BORN 1953
TASMANIA

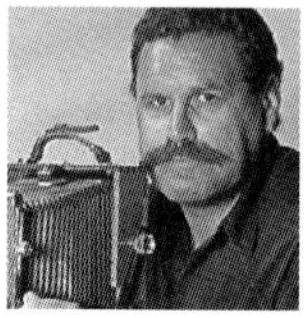

Strangely underestimated, perhaps because his work has circulated more in the realm of documentary photography than art, Ricky Maynard has produced some of the most compelling images of contemporary Aboriginal Australia over the last two decades.

Largely self-taught, Maynard began his career as a darkroom technician at the age of sixteen. He first established his reputation with the 1985 series 'Moonbird People', an intimate portrayal of the muttonbirding season on Babel, Big Dog and Trefoil Islands in his native Tasmania. The 1993 series 'No More Than What You See' documents Indigenous prisoners in South Australian gaols. He is the recipient of numerous grants and commissions, including a 1990 Commonwealth Government Award to study at the International Centre of Photography in New York. In 1997 he received the Australian Human Rights Award for Photography and is a recipient of the Mother Jones International Documentary Award.

The owner of an enviable collection of antique cameras, Maynard is a lifelong student of the history of photography, particularly of the great American social reformers Jacob Riis, Lewis Hines, Dorothea Lange and Walker Evans. He is interested in the power of the uninflected image – of sheer veracity – as an agent of record and change. Maynard's images cut through the layers of rhetoric and ideology that inevitably couch black history (particularly Tasmanian history) to present images of experience itself. 'To know the meaning of a culture you must recognise the limits and meaning of your own,' the artist explains. 'You can see its facts but not its meaning. We share meaning by living it.'[1] Maynard's photographs are, he says, about 'leaving proof' – about ' ... life in passing and in complicated times'.[2]

The word 'Wik' has come to denote a historic decision of the High Court of Australia rather than the name of the Indigenous peoples from the western Cape York Peninsula in northern Queensland. In his intimate portraits of elders from these communities, Maynard aims to unpick this abstraction. Etched on each face is the complexity of an unspoken life story, delineated, one imagines, by hardship, perseverance and the burden – and wealth – of an extraordinary living memory. As he wrote in his artist's statement for the exhibition 'Returning to Places that Name Us' in 2001, ' ... I wanted a presence and portraits that spoke, and through this process to present an idea, rather than preach messages.'[3] In this series, Maynard achieves his aim of capturing meanings that no other medium could convey. HF

> **Wik Elder, Arthur** 2000
gelatin silver photograph
96.1 x 121.4 cm

v **Wik Elder, Gladys** 2000
gelatin silver photograph
95.3 x 121.7 cm

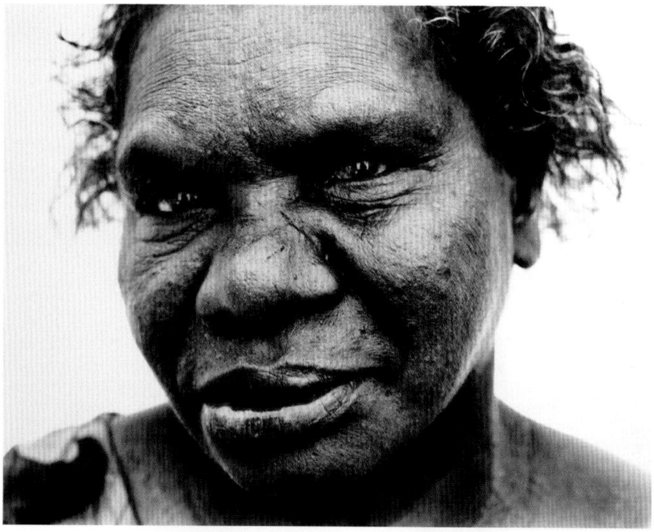

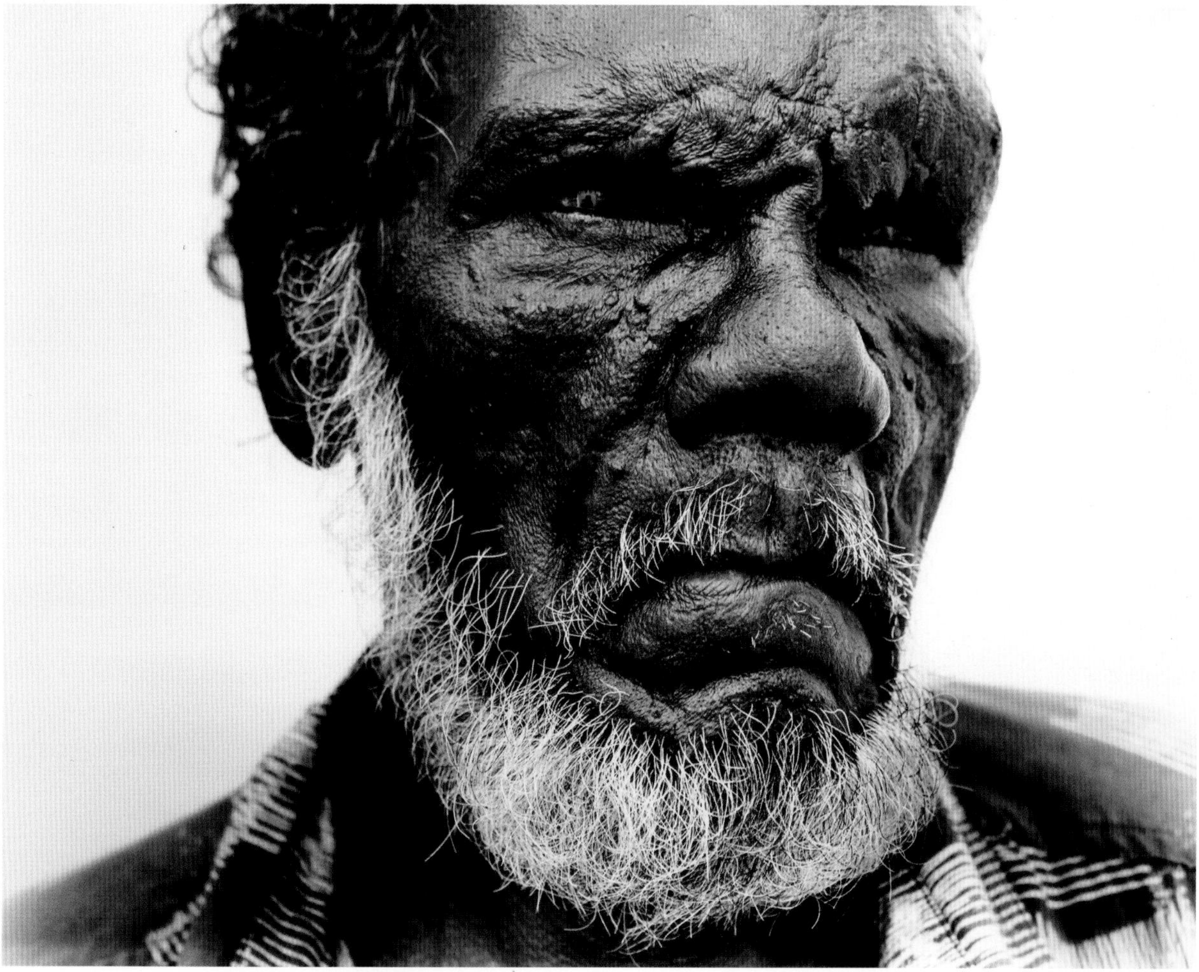

TRACEY MOFFATT

BORN 1960
QUEENSLAND

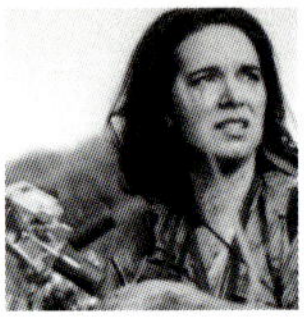

Tracey Moffatt is probably Australia's most successful artist ever, both nationally and internationally. She is certainly one of the few Australian artists to have established a global market for her work. A filmmaker as well as photographer, Moffatt has held around 100 solo exhibitions of her work in Europe, the United States and Australia. Her films, including *Nightcries – A Rural Tragedy*, 1990, and *Bedevil*, 1993, have been screened at the Cannes Film Festival, the Dia Centre for the Arts in New York and the National Centre for Photography in Paris.

Over the last 25 years Moffatt has produced a cohesive body of work, from her celebrated 1989 series 'Something More' to the more recent 'Fourth', 2001. Each series devolves upon an unwritten narrative – a story is implied, but never stated. Part of the artist's project is to dismantle the conventions of storytelling, paradoxically by using artifice alone to tell her tales. At the same time, the power of her work derives from the persuasions of myth. Moffatt's subjects touch on deep-seated, implacable issues, on the wounds that never heal – hence the title of her tragicomic series, 'Scarred for Life', 1994. Based on true stories told to the artist, this series captures both the pain and the restless energy at the heart of suburban life. Possibly Moffatt's best work to date, its potency is due to the fact that, as the artist has explained, ' ... everyone has a tragic tale to tell'.[1]

Like the work of Destiny Deacon, Moffatt's art is sharpened with pain and humour. In works such as 'Something More' and, most explicitly, 'Laudanum', 1999, she engages the rhetorical confusions of racism through the sado-masochistic dynamic of the colonised subject. Indeed, her avowed ambivalence about being categorised as an Indigenous artist is at odds with her commitment to the fostering of Aboriginal culture, and to the central place of Indigeneity in her work. This seeming contradiction – an apparent moral inconsistency – is resolved in her dedication to the accoutrements of success: as much as Moffatt's work is about pain, it is also about glamour. Moffatt's vision is essentially theatrical, and one might argue that being an art-star – with all its attendant posturing – is as much a part of her practice as the art itself. HF

> **Something More 1**
from the series 'Something More' 1989
cibachrome photograph
103 x 133 cm

v from left
Doll birth, 1972
Birth certificate, 1962
Useless, 1974
from the series 'Scarred for life' 1994
photolithographs
80 x 60 cm each

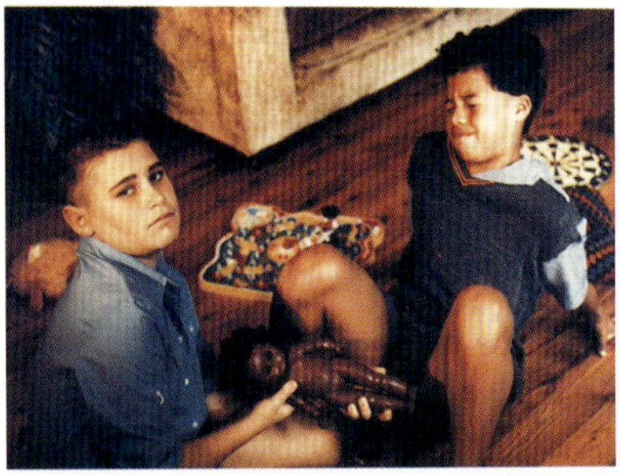

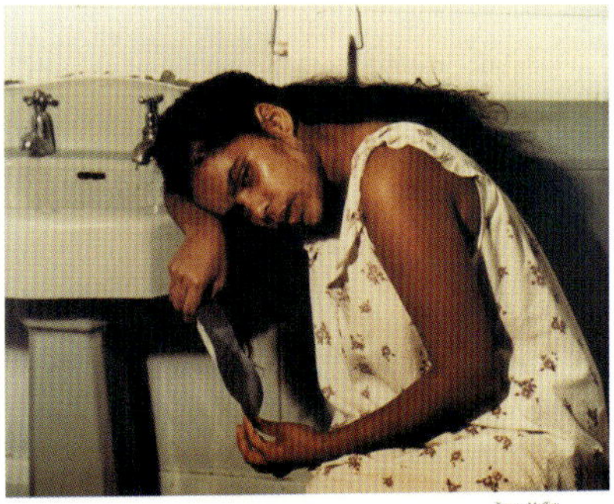

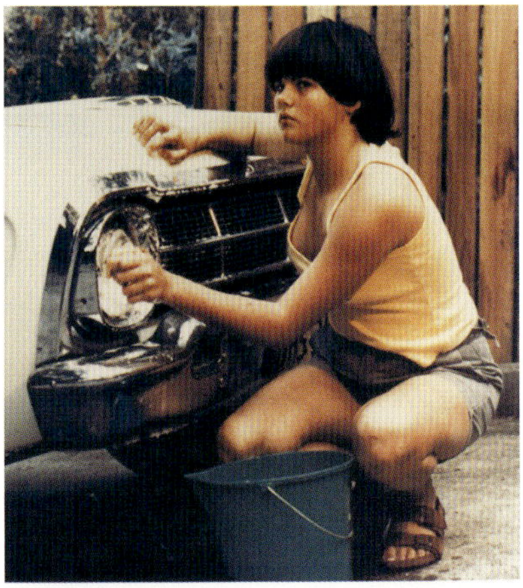

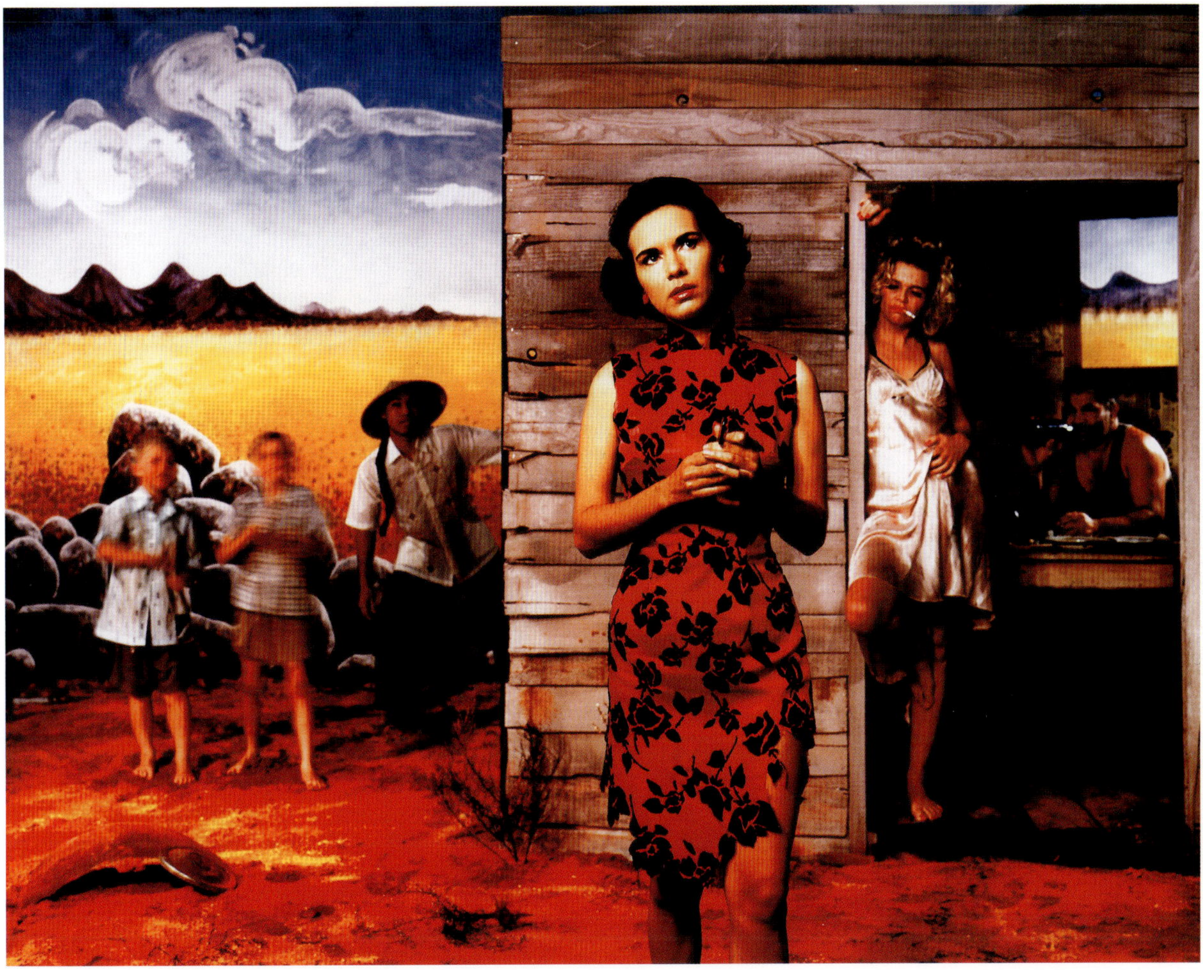

SALLY MORGAN

BORN 1951
PALKU / NYAMAL
WESTERN AUSTRALIA

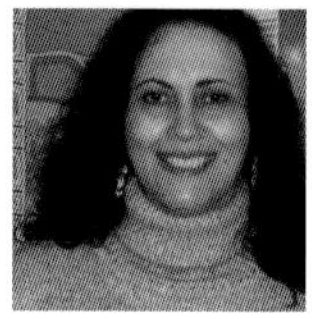

Sally Morgan belongs to the Palku and Nyamal peoples of the Pilbara. Her family was part of the Stolen Generation and she grew up in Perth, unaware of her Aboriginal heritage. Until the age of 15 she was led to believe that she was of Indian descent. This experience of hidden origins and her subsequent quest for identity were the inspiration for her 1987 autobiography, *My Place*.[1] While researching her family history for this book, Morgan's childhood interest in art was rekindled. In 1986, Sally Morgan held her first exhibition at the Birukmarri Gallery in Fremantle. She is currently Director of the Centre for Indigenous History and Arts at the University of Western Australia, Perth. She has continued to write, publishing children's stories, another book and a play.

Citizenship, 1987, is Morgan's most widely known print. It was made for the 'Right Here, Right Now Australia 1988' exhibition held at Adelaide's Experimental Art Foundation, which presented an alternative perspective on Australia's 1988 Bicentennial celebrations. The text at the bottom of the print refers to the *Natives (Citizenship Rights) Act* of 1944 (Western Australia), which required Aboriginal people to apply to become 'citizens' of their own land. This Act allowed for magistrates to provide certificates of citizenship to Aboriginal people ' ... deemed to be no longer a native or Aborigine'. Strict conditions applied: Aboriginal people had to adopt the manner and habits of 'civilised whites', they were not allowed to freely associate with other Aboriginal people and their citizenship papers could be summarily revoked for infringements of these conditions. Jack McPhee, Morgan's grandfather, recalled, ' ... We used to joke about the whole thing among ourselves ... We all called our papers a Dog Licence: we thought that was a better name for it than Citizenship.'[2]

Printmaking has a long history as a medium for social criticism and commentary. Morgan's cartoon-like work has a graphic quality that belies its serious intent. *Citizenship* is an unusual symbolic image for the abuse of Aboriginal people, and all the more memorable because of this. The dog Morgan depicts, which has been compared with Anubis, the jackal-headed Egyptian god of death, evokes ideas of servility and suggests that even this animal is better treated than Aboriginal people in their own land. SM

Citizenship 1987
screenprint
58.7 x 36.3 cm

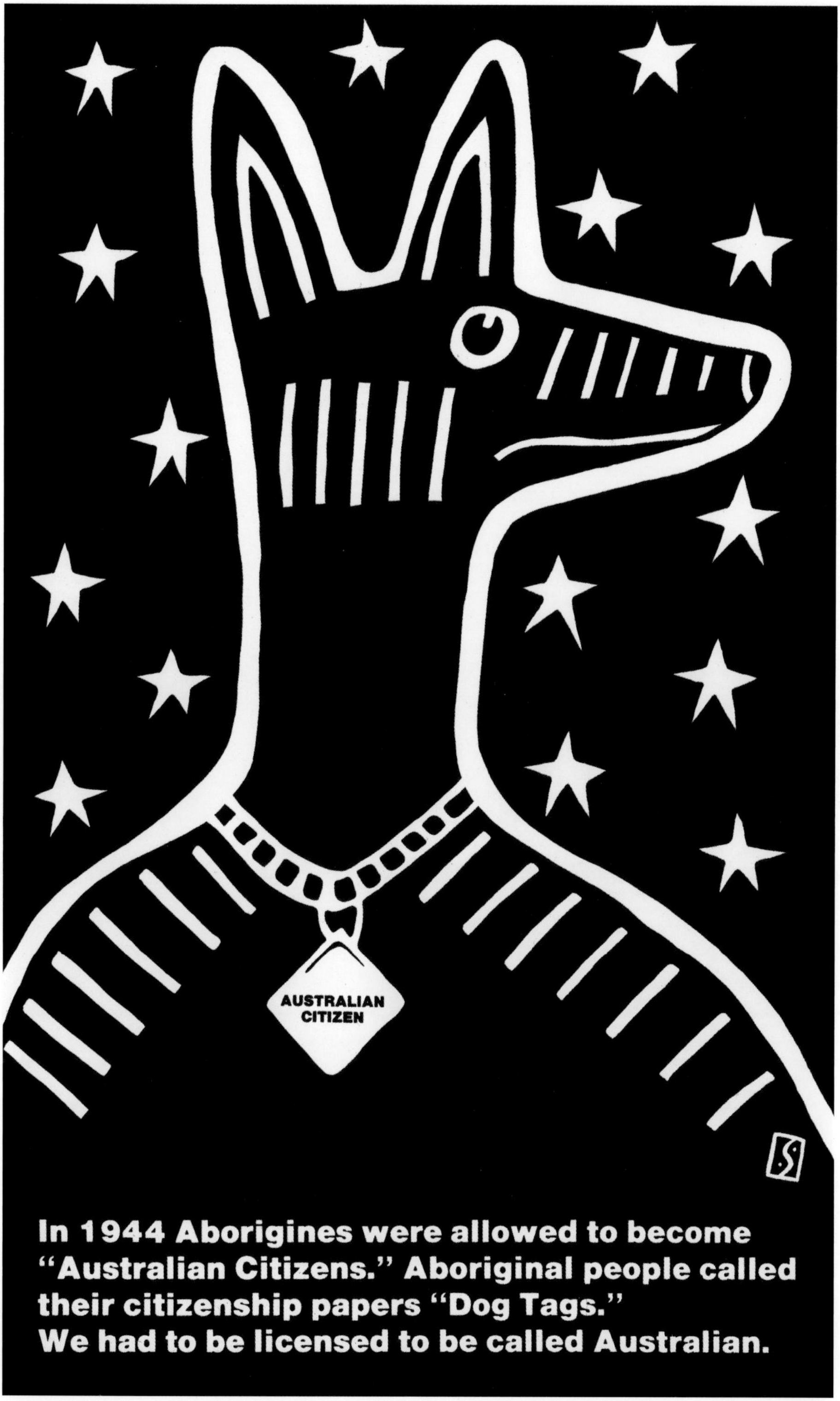

In 1944 Aborigines were allowed to become "Australian Citizens." Aboriginal people called their citizenship papers "Dog Tags."
We had to be licensed to be called Australian.

GINGER RILEY MUNDUWALAWALA

c.1937–2002
MARA
NORTHERN TERRITORY

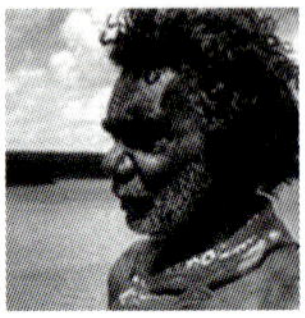

Ginger Riley Munduwalawala painted his mother's country, focusing on the weather-worn rock formations known as the Four Archers near the mouth of the Limmen Bight River in south-east Arnhem Land. Using bright, luminous and often contrasting colours and strong flattened forms, Riley depicted this landscape and its ancestral beings: Garimala the snake, who created the Four Archers; Ngak Ngak the white-breasted sea-eagle and guardian figure; the ceremonial shark's liver tree; the Four Archers themselves; and the Limmen Bight River. Riley's extraordinary creativity allowed him to reinvent this subject matter again and again, expressing in his work his vision of physical geography, creation knowledge and ancestral sites. His strong sense of place enabled this overview, and he painted, he has said, as if he was, '... on a cloud, on top of the world, looking down ... From the top I can see country right down to where I come from.'[1]

Riley saw the work of western Aranda watercolourist Albert Namatjira as a young man in the 1950s. This meeting with Namatjira made a lasting impression, and much later inspired Riley to pursue painting in acrylics when the Northern Territory Education Department offered a painting course at Ngukurr, where Riley was living, in 1987. Riley rapidly developed his own very distinctive style and iconography and, after initially exhibiting with the other Ngukurr-based painters, he established an independent career at the Alcaston Gallery, Melbourne. Riley exhibited both nationally and internationally, and was awarded an Australia Council Fellowship in 1997, the same year that the National Gallery of Victoria, Melbourne, mounted a retrospective of his work.

In *Nyamiyukanji, the river country*, 1997, Riley depicts the dramatic rock formations that rear up out of the Gulf country landscape and are known as the Ruined City.[2] This is Riley's grandfather's country, near the Nathan River. As in many of his works, Riley has painted the rocky outcrops and surrounding land in bands across the painting, while the river winds diagonally up to the sea. At the top of the painting, the bright blue sky, which is not differentiated from the sea at the mouth of the river, has large, wet season clouds raining on the landscape. In Riley's work, clouds or the sun usually represent his mother. Ngak Ngak appears in the foreground and, on the right, Garimala travels across the country. This place exists in Riley's creation knowledge as much as it does in the landscape. WT

> **Nyamiyukanji, the river country** 1997
synthetic polymer paint on canvas
185 x 201.5 cm

v **Ngak Ngak and the Ruined City** 1998
synthetic polymer paint on canvas
193 x 249.3 cm

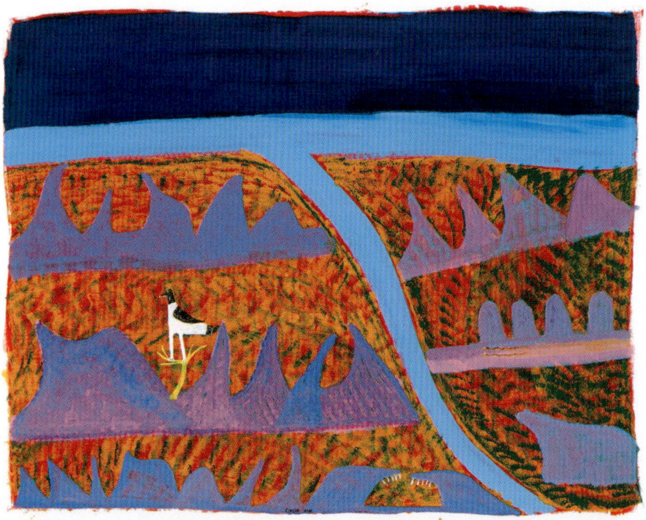

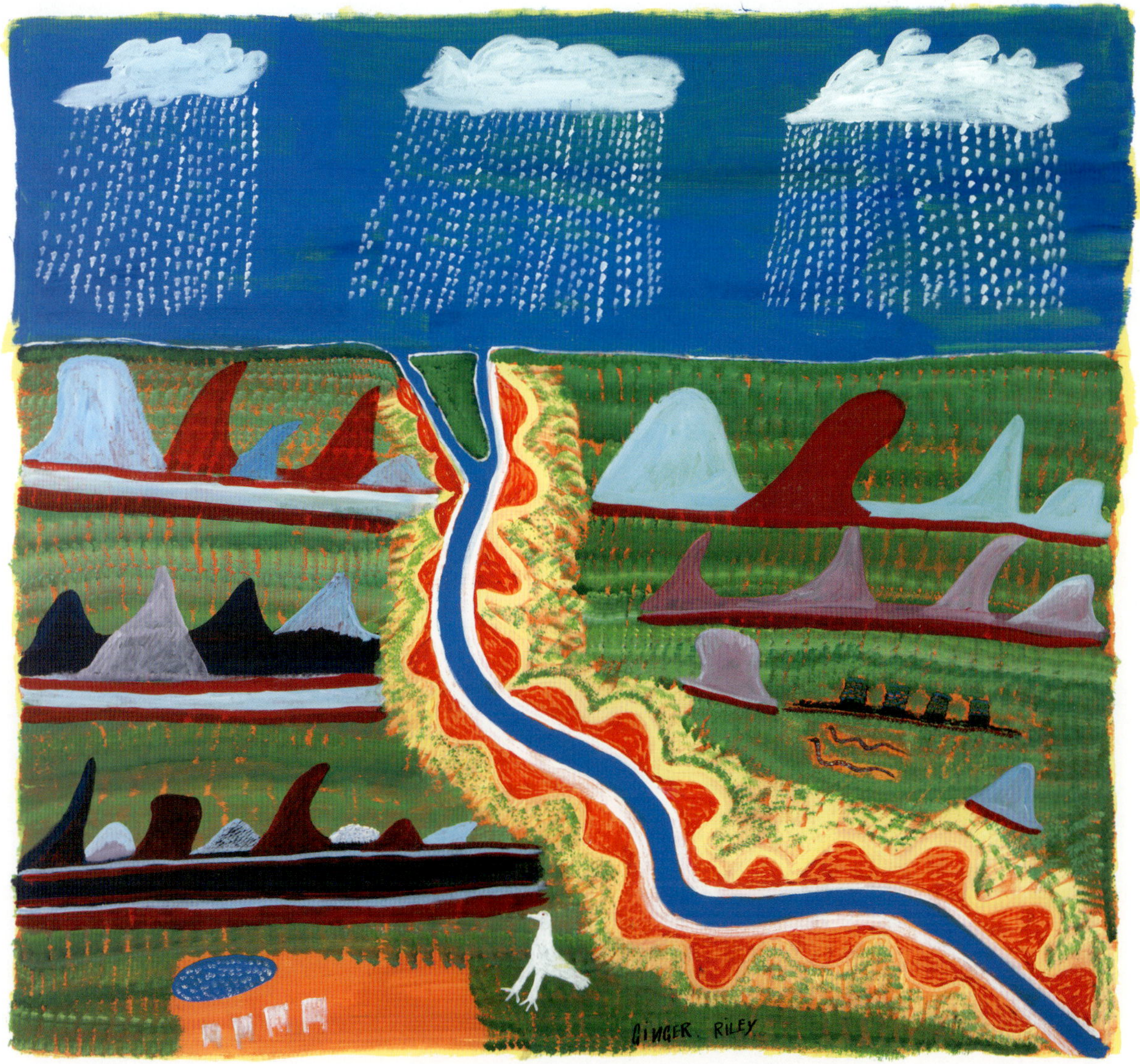
GINGER RILEY

MÄW' MUNUNGGURR

c.1910–1976
DJAPU
NORTHERN TERRITORY

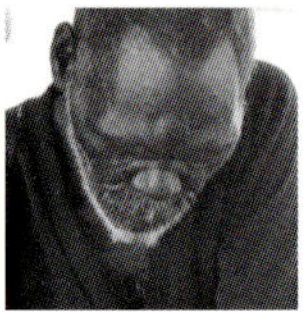

Mäw' Mununggurr's life spanned a crucial era in the history of the Yolngu people of north-east Arnhem Land. He was one of the older sons of Wonggu Mununggurr (c.1880–1959), the famous Djapu clan leader who led resistance to incursions on his land before the establishment of the Methodist Yirrkala Mission in 1935. Mäw' was imprisoned for a year in Fannie Bay Gaol in Darwin following a skirmish at Caledon Bay in 1933 in which the crew of a Japanese pearling boat were killed. During World War II he was a member of Donald Thomson's Aboriginal observer force, patrolling the shores of Arnhem Land looking for any signs of Japanese invasion. Wonggu, in collaboration with his older sons including Mäw', painted for Thomson an enormous bark painting of the main settlement site, *Wandawuy: Wet season painting*, 1942, now in the Melbourne Museum.

After the war, Mäw' settled at Yirrkala, making frequent visits to his country around Caledon Bay and Trial Bay. He was a prolific painter, producing works for anthropologists Ronald and Catherine Berndt in 1946 and 1947, and for Charles Mountford's American–Australian Scientific Expedition to Arnhem Land in 1948. Mäw' produced bark paintings throughout his life, and during his final years he worked intensely to help his clan establish Wandawuy. Painting for sale was only a minor part of his artistic output. Mäw' was a great singer, dancer and ceremonial leader, and was frequently called upon to produce paintings of his own clan and his mother's clan in ceremonies. He was a leader of the spectacular Dhanbul (Morning Star) exchange ceremony – which he depicts in *Banumbirr (Morning Star ceremony)*, 1948, and *The Morning Star ceremony*, c.1960 – and took it to Groote Eylandt and Numbulwarr.

Mäw's style of painting is often reserved. Many of his early paintings comprise multiple figurative representations of fish and animals, with broad areas of crosshatching in a single colour. These paintings were in continuity with some of the earlier Yolngu barks representing daily scenes that were among the first produced for the Rev. Wilbur Chaseling, who established Yirrkala Mission. Towards the end of his life, Mäw's paintings emphasised the story of Mäna, the Djapu shark, and the shark itself often provided the dominant image. He also continued to create the paintings of his mother's clan, the Munyuku, and related Yirritja moiety clans. HM

> **Banumbirr (Morning Star ceremony)** 1948
natural pigments on bark
120.6 x 64.2 cm

v left **The Morning Star ceremony** c.1960
natural pigments on bark
120.6 x 64.2 cm

v right Wonggu Mununggurr (attrib.)
Untitled c.1930s
natural pigments on bark
69.5 x 72 cm

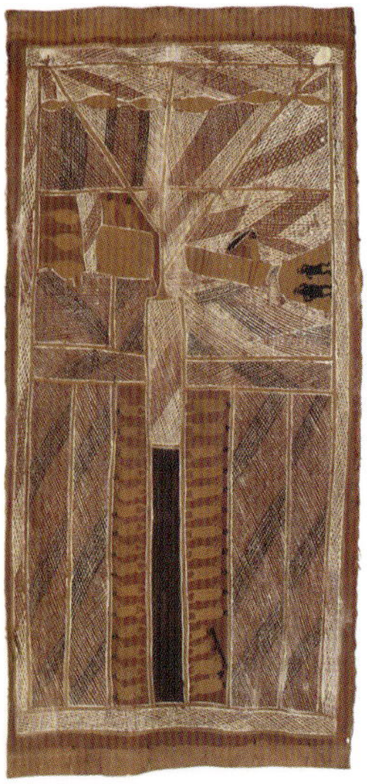

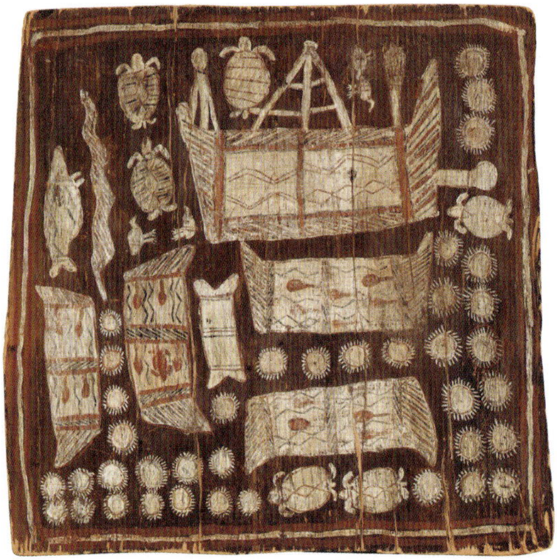

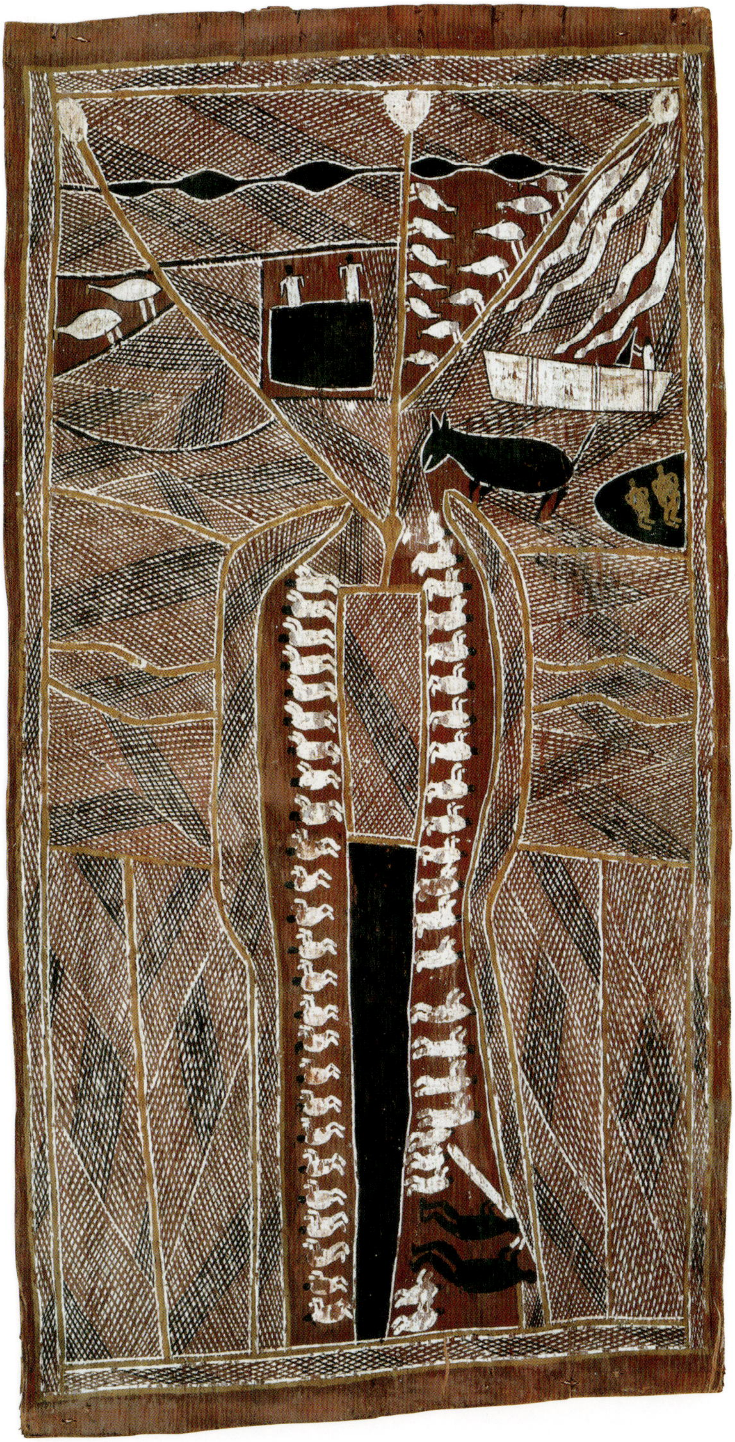

ALBERT NAMATJIRA

1902–1959
WESTERN ARANDA
NORTHERN TERRITORY

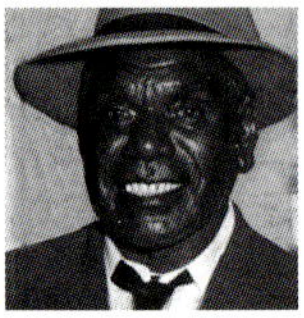

Although not the first Aboriginal artist to work in a European style, Albert Namatjira is certainly the most famous. Ghost gums with luminous white trunks, palm-filled gorges and red mountain ranges turning purple at dusk are the hallmarks of the Hermannsburg school. Hermannsburg Mission was established by Lutheran missionaries in 1877 on the banks of the Finke River, west of Mparntwe (Alice Springs). Namatjira learnt watercolour technique from the artist, Rex Battarbee.

Initially thought of as having succumbed to European pictorial idioms – and for that reason, to ideas of European privilege over the land – Namatjira's landscapes have since been re-evaluated as coded expressions on traditional sites and sacred knowledge.[1] Ownership of country is hereditary, but detailed knowledge of what it 'contains' is learnt in successive stages through ceremony, song, anecdote and contact. Namatjira's father's country lay towards Mount Sonder and Glen Helen Gorge, in the MacDonnell Ranges, and his mother's country was in the region of Palm Valley in Central Australia. In Namatjira's paintings, the totemic connections to his country are so indelible that, for example, Palm Valley the place and *Palm Valley*, c.1940s, the painting seem to intersect, detailing Namatjira's artistic, cultural and proprietorial claim on the land.

Namatjira's skills in European watercolour painting were interpreted as evidence of the potential success of assimilation policies. In 1957, Namatjira became the first Aboriginal person to be granted conditional Australian citizenship. This entitled him to limited social freedoms and to live in Mparntwe, although he was prohibited from purchasing land. His relations, including his children, were not permitted the same privileges. After an incident in 1958 that didn't directly involve the artist, Namatjira was charged with supplying alcohol to members of the Aboriginal community – at the time, it was illegal for all Aboriginal people, except Namatjira, to possess and consume alcohol. Namatjira was sentenced to six months labour at Papunya and this, exacerbated by the authorities' refusal to allow him to purchase the land of his ancestors, caused him profound despair. He served only two months, and died shortly after.

The more recent, dramatic success of the nearby Papunya Tula movement must be read against the history of its predecessor, the Hermannsburg school, which has endured for half a century. Recently, the centenary of Namatjira's birth was celebrated with a major retrospective at the National Gallery of Australia, Canberra. GA

> **Palm Valley** c.1940s
watercolour
37 x 54.2 cm

v **Catherine Creek, Northern Territory** c.1950
watercolour
37 x 37 cm

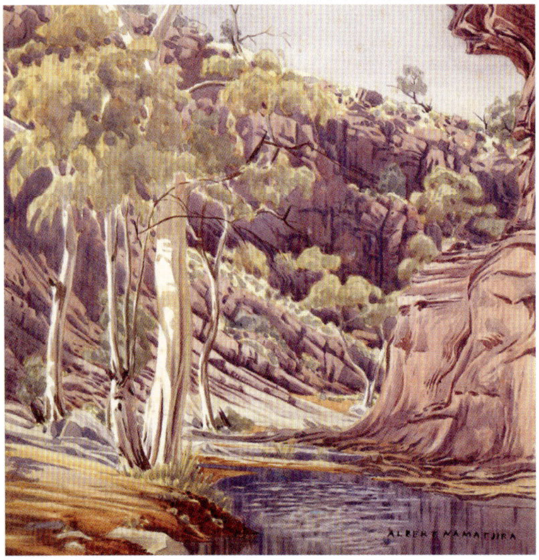

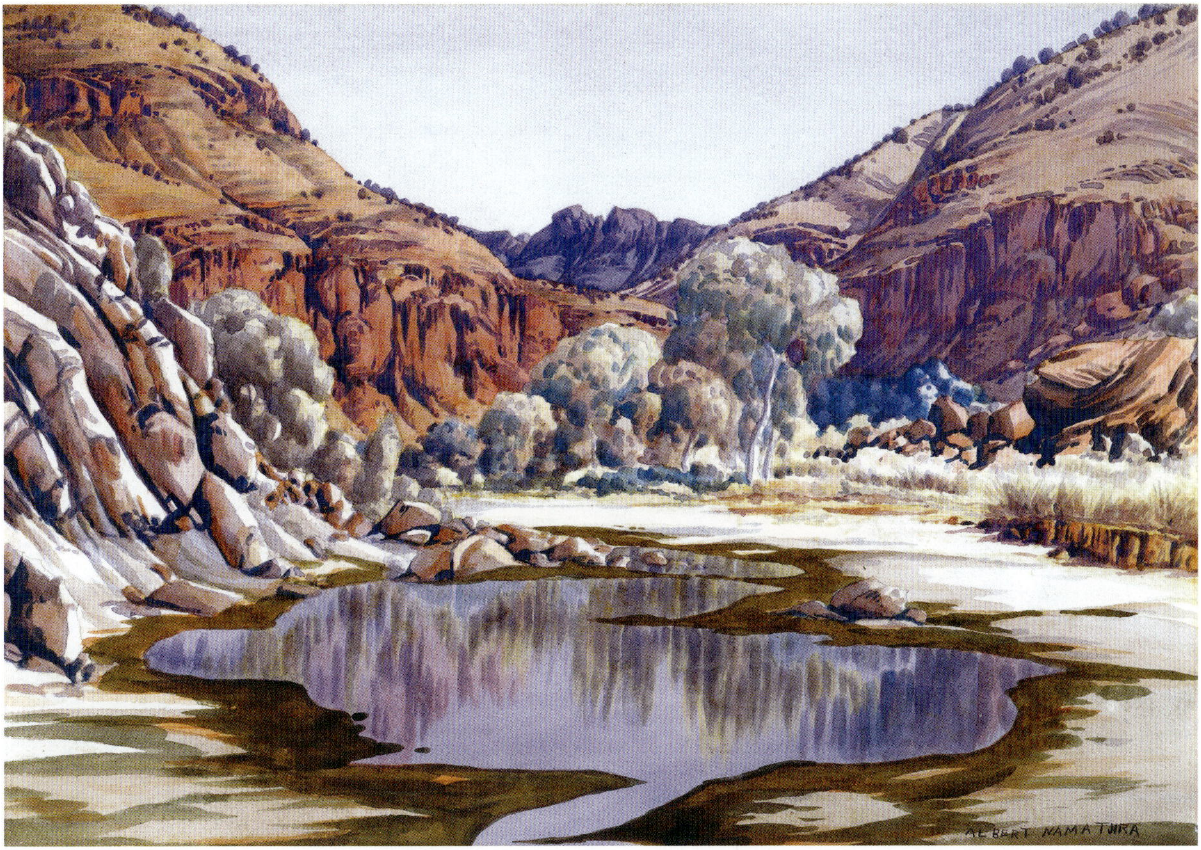
ALBERT NAMATJIRA

EUBENA NAMPITJIN

BORN c.1925
WANGKAJUNGA
WESTERN AUSTRALIA

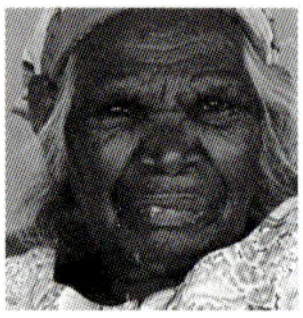

Eubena Nampitjin was born in Tjinndjaldpa, south of Jupiter Well in the Great Sandy Desert, Western Australia. This area, on the Canning Stock Route and over 350 kilometres inland from Port Hedland, is one of the most remote places in Australia. Nampitjin had little contact with non-Indigenous Australians until the late 1940s, when she travelled to Old Mission with her children and first husband. She moved with the mission in 1963 to its present site at Balgo, or Wirrimanu as it is traditionally known. Nampitjin is an elder of the Wangkajunga people, a custodian of women's law and the most senior woman artist working in the area. While at the mission, she has regularly returned to live in her country for extended periods.

Nampitjin started painting in 1986, when women were becoming more broadly included in the growing art movement centred on Wirrimanu. During that year she painted three canvases, one of which was included in the exhibition 'Art from the Great Sandy Desert' at the Art Gallery of Western Australia, Perth, at the end of 1986. Further impetus to paint came in 1989, when the new arts organisation, Warlayirti Artists, was formed. Nampitjin, her husband Wimmitji Tjapangarti and their daughters all painted, often collaboratively. Nampitjin was awarded the Open Painting prize in the Telstra National Aboriginal and Torres Strait Islander Art Award in 1998.

To outsiders, Nampitjin's homeland in the heart of the Great Sandy Desert may appear desolate on a map; but for the artist, it provides her impetus to paint and is full of life and significance. The surface of *Pinyu*, 1991, is a metaphor for the surface of her country. She represents its sacred rocks, which are associated with Kurinyin, a dingo from the Tjukurrpa. She also depicts a number of waterholes that the artist and her family used when she was younger, and the women's dancing tracks. *Pinyu* was painted during a transitional period for the artist, between her early works, from 1988–90, which were distinguished by their strongly defined forms and web of complex dotted fields and her later, more fluid style, in which she manipulates colour exuberantly. Christine Watson has observed, ' ... the 1990–92 works, though at this time using a lighter-hued palette of yellow, pink and white, and delicate dotting applied with painting sticks, are rich and subliminal, even-grained textures that continue in the higher-keyed site-path works of late 1992–94.'[1] SM

Pinyu 1991
synthetic polymer paint on canvas
100 x 50 cm
> detail

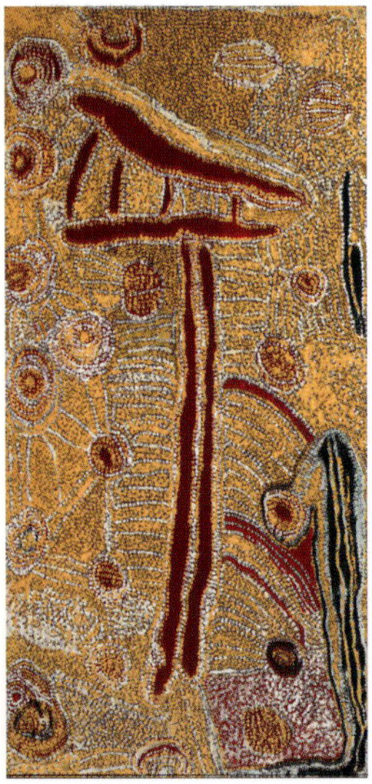

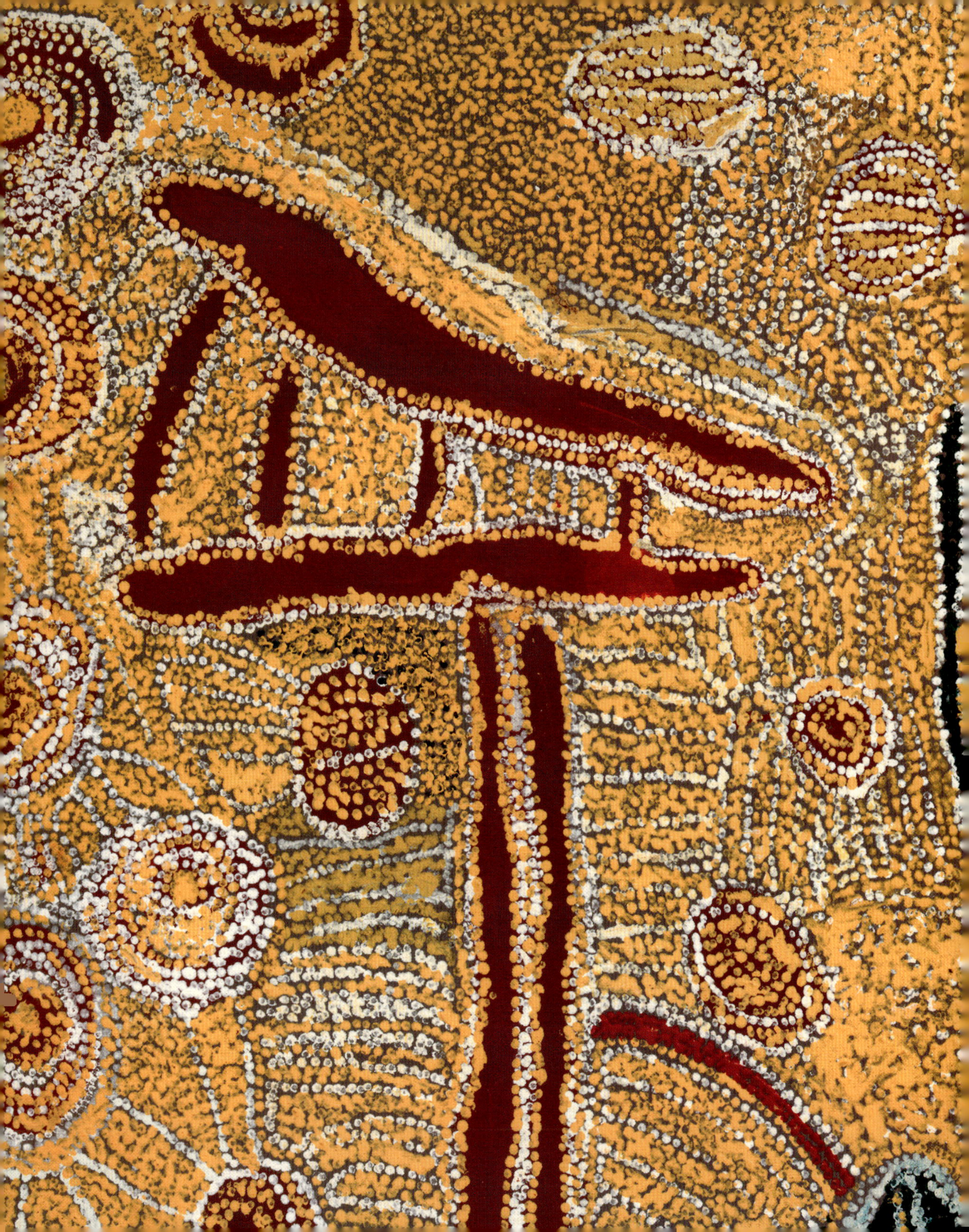

INYUWA NAMPITJINPA

c.1922–1999
PINTUPI
NORTHERN TERRITORY / WESTERN AUSTRALIA

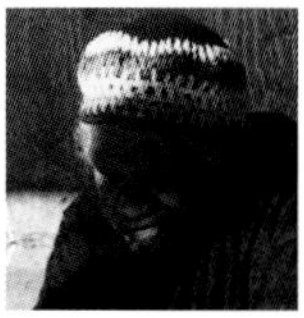

Inyuwa Nampitjinpa was among a group of Pintupi people who made their weary way into Ikuntji (Haasts Bluff) settlement just before Christmas 1956. They had walked hundreds of kilometres from west of the salt lake of Karrkurutintjinya (Lake Macdonald) to experience first-hand the supplies of food and water on offer at the settlement under the new government administration that had replaced the Lutheran missionaries. Nampitjinpa already had four children – three sons and a daughter – with her elderly husband Rartji Tjapangati. Nine years later, Rartji Tjapangati passed away in Papunya, and Nampitjinpa re-married. Her second husband was Tutuma Tjapangati, one of the most senior men in the founding group of artists painting at Papunya in 1971. Nampitjinpa and her family moved back to the Pintupi homelands community of Walungurru (Kintore) soon after its establishment in 1981.

Tutuma Tjapangati was such a prolific and ebullient painter that it is doubtful Nampitjinpa would have been called upon to assist him, but when she took up painting her style owed much to his freewheeling, energetic approach. Nampitjinpa became involved with the Haasts Bluff/Kintore women's painting project in 1994. As an elder of the community, she assumed a supervisory role regarding the portrayal of women's ceremonial subject matter, reminiscent of that taken by the senior men early on in the history of the Papunya movement.

In 1997 Nampitjinpa had an operation to remove cataracts, which dramatically improved her eyesight, and she began painting regularly. Nampitjinpa's paintings helped establish the signature style of senior women's painting at Walungurru. Their dense, tactile surfaces, applied with a roughness and sheer volume of paint, exceeded those of any previous practitioners in the Desert style. As seen in *Untitled (Pukunya)*, 1999, her work retained only the most basic elements of traditional imagery, referencing rockholes, campsites and women's utensils simplified to the point of abstraction. The large permanent water site of Punkilpirri, south west of Tjukula, was a recurrent subject.

Until her death, the artist sustained a creative energy that resulted in her first solo exhibition at Gallery Gabrielle Pizzi, Melbourne, in June 1999. The paintings were still up on the walls of the gallery when Nampitjinpa passed away. Her legacy remains in the paintings of her daughters, Walangkura Napanangka and the late Pirrmangka Napanangka. VJ

Untitled (Pukunya) 1999
synthetic polymer paint on canvas
153 x 122 cm

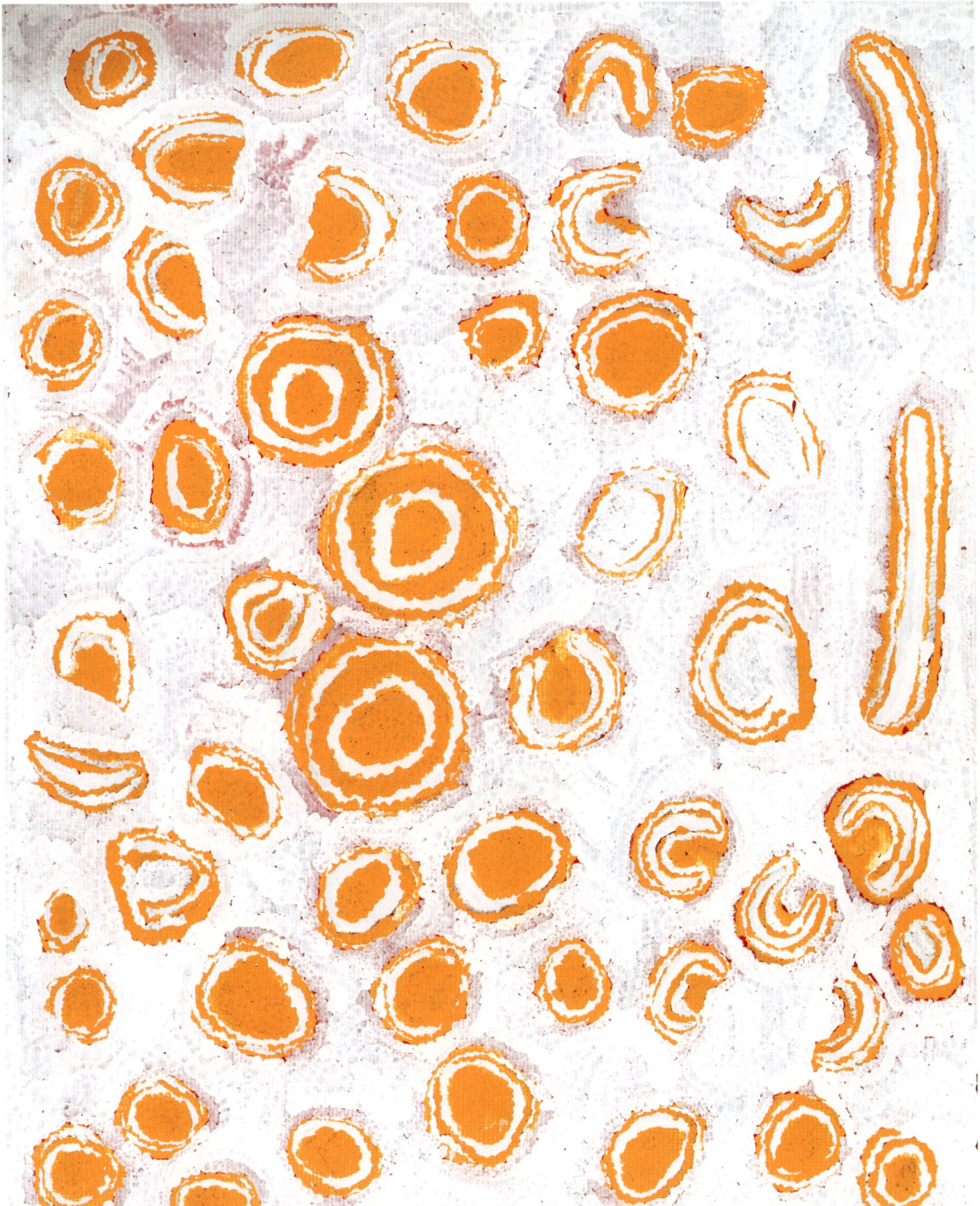

MAKINTI NAPANANGKA

BORN c.1930
PINTUPI
NORTHERN TERRITORY / WESTERN AUSTRALIA

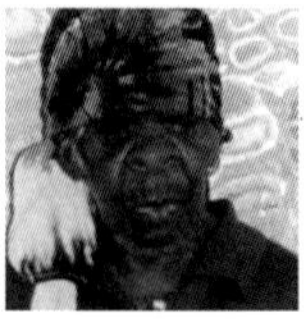

Makinti Napanangka is the most senior woman painting with the renowned Papunya Tula Artists. As with other Pintupi women now exerting their considerable influence on Australian art, Napanangka worked on the collaborative Haasts Bluff/Kintore women's painting project. This series of major paintings, completed in 1994 and exhibited at the Tandanya National Aboriginal Cultural Institute in Adelaide, marked the beginning of Pintupi women's participation in the Western Desert art movement as independent artists. Up until then, women had largely worked as collaborators on paintings by their husbands and other close male relatives. Napanangka joined Papunya Tula Artists in 1996.

Most senior practitioners of Western Desert art led a traditional bush life in their desert homelands until their first contact with white Australians as young adults. Napanangka's life has followed the same course and, as with most Pintupi people, she has returned to live close to her country at Walungurru (Kintore), a small Aboriginal community established during the outstation movement, more than 500 kilometres west of Mparntwe (Alice Springs).

Napanangka is a familiar presence at the Papunya Tula arts centre in Walungurru, often the first to arrive with her pack of camp-dogs to begin a day of intense painting. Even when her eyesight faltered, Napanangka's enthusiasm for painting on canvas remained undiminished. When she recovered, her work showed renewed vigour, and was exhibited in the major retrospective 'Papunya Tula: Genesis and Genius' at the Art Gallery of New South Wales, Sydney, in 2000. *Untitled*, 2000, contains all the hallmarks of Napanangka's style, owing more to the gesture of hand-painting ochre onto the body for women's ceremonies, than to the meticulous application of dots that characterises men's ceremonial and contemporary art making.

Napanangka's paintings often depict designs associated with the travels of the Kungka Kutjarra (Two Ancestral Women). The lines entering the upper section of *Untitled*, 2000, represent the handspun, hair-string skirts worn by women during ceremonies. The celebratory nature of these performances is expressed in the hedonistic play of colour and form across the painting's surface. Napanangka's art personifies the ongoing presence of Pintupi cultural traditions in the contemporary painting movement. HP

Untitled 2000
synthetic polymer paint on canvas
153 x 122 cm

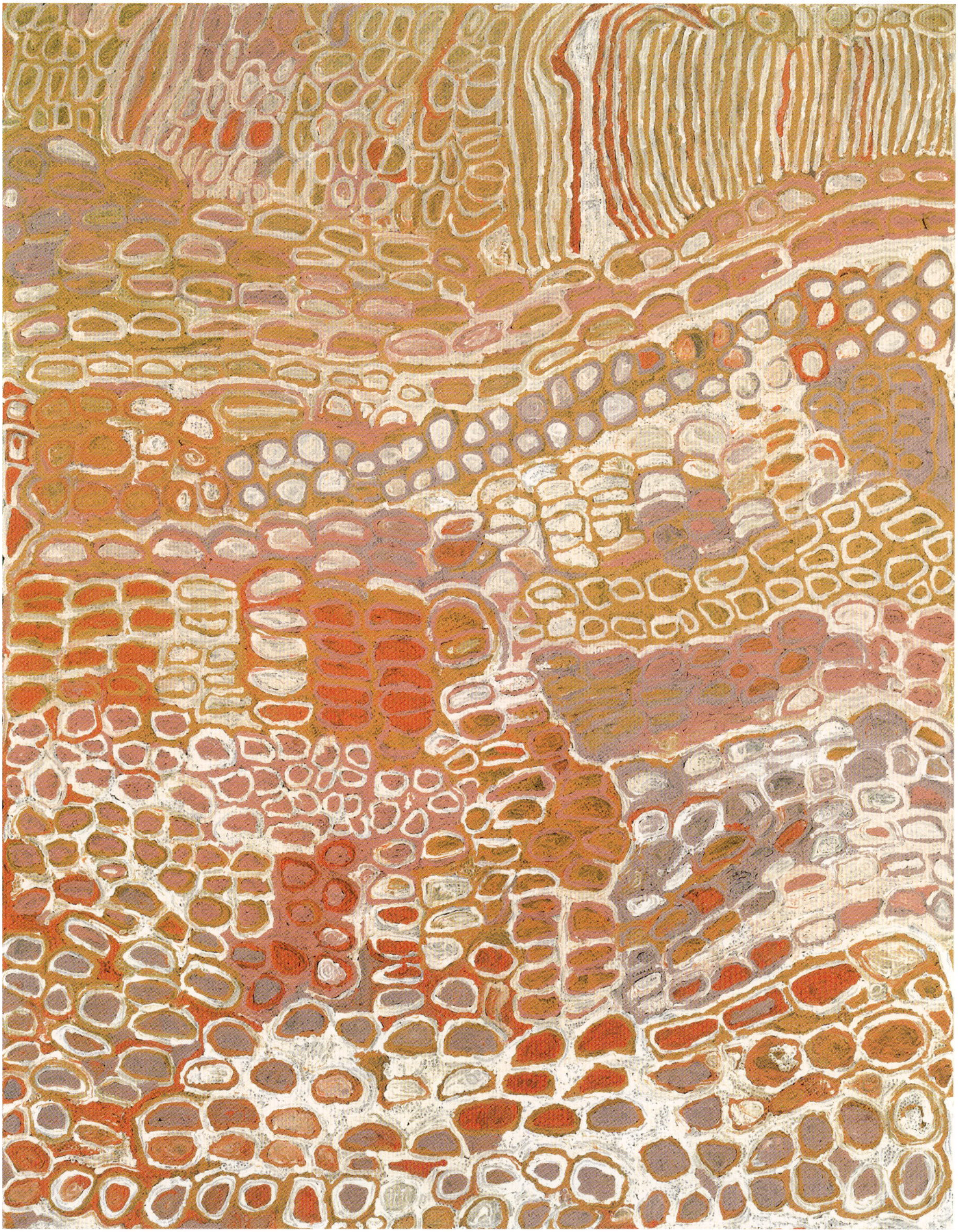

MITJILI NAPURRULA

BORN c.1945
PINTUPI
NORTHERN TERRITORY / WESTERN AUSTRALIA

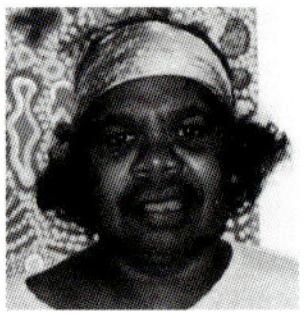

Mitjili Napurrula was born in Ikuntji (Haasts Bluff) after her mother Tjunkayi Napaltjarri, came in from the desert with her mother, a Pintupi/Luritja woman from Yumari. Dispossession and drought were only two of the factors that led to a series of migrations from the desert to mission or government settlements in the mid-twentieth century. Following the outstation movement of the late 1970s and early 1980s, Aboriginal communities sprang up throughout the region, each home to a distinctive art movement. Despite being the first ration depot in the region, Ikuntji was one of the last communities from which this widespread renaissance of cultural affirmation emerged.

Like many of her generation, Napurrula witnessed the genesis of the Papunya Tula art movement and the artistic contribution made by members of her immediate family. Tjunkayi Napaltjarri and her sister Wintjiya made small craft items for Papunya Tula Artists, until venturing into painting independently on 'Minyma Tjukurrpa' – the 1994 Haasts Bluff/Kintore women's painting project. Napurrula's brother, Turkey Tolson Tjupurrula, was one of the founding members of the Papunya Tula Artists cooperative.

Napurrula and Tjupurrula had the same father, Tupa Tjakamarra, from whom they inherited the right to paint works related to Ilyingaungau in the Gibson Desert. This site, south of Walungurru (Kintore), some 520 kilometres west of Mparntwe (Alice Springs), is where the artist's Mutikatjirri ancestors assembled their kulata (spears) for a conflict with the Tjukula men. Allusive works that refer to the straightening of kulata by Tjupurrula are among the landmark paintings of the movement's 30-year history.

The paintings of Napurrula and her husband, Long Tom Tjapanangka, have come to be understood as archetypical of Ikuntji art since they began to work with the arts centre in 1993. Napurrula remembers, ' ... After I got married, my mother taught me my father's Tjukurrpa in the sand, that's what I'm painting on the canvas'.[1] In Napurrula's major untitled painting of 1999, coagulated white pigment eddies around abstract forms that refer to the spearwood trees. The tightly structured patterning of the key motifs and bold use of colour demonstrates the artist's confidence in her individual artistic vision within a family of superlative artists – and the cultural heritage that continues to inform the myriad expressions of Western Desert artists. HP

> **Untitled** 1999
synthetic polymer paint on canvas
183 x 198 cm

v **Nullanulla and alcatjari (bush sultanas), Ualki** 1994
synthetic polymer paint on canvas
91 x 137 cm

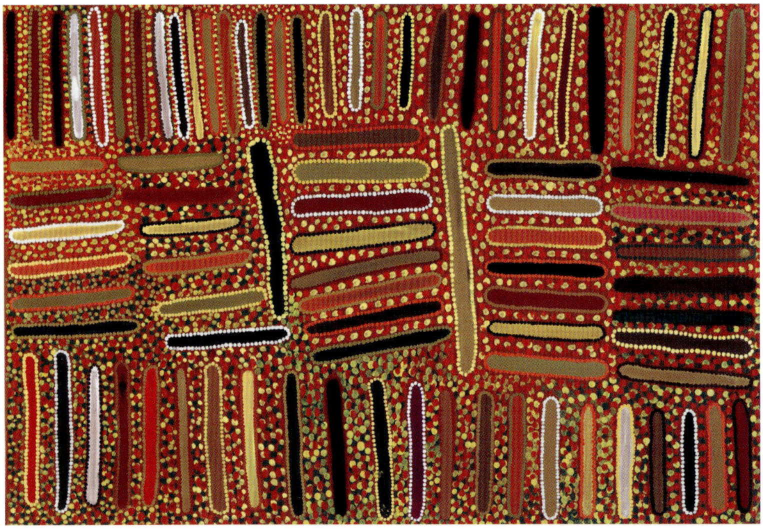

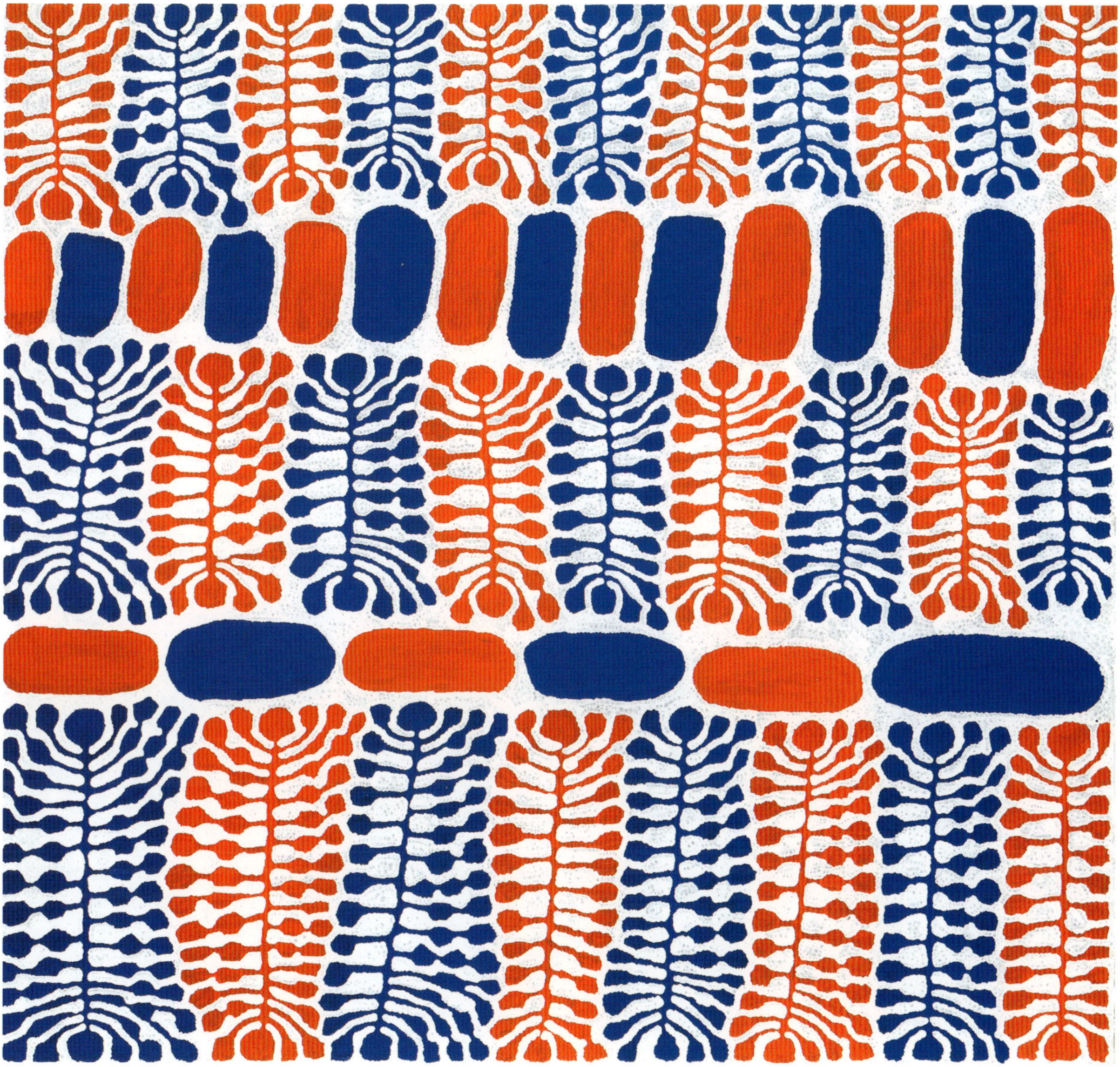

NINGURA NAPURRULA

BORN c.1938
PINTUPI
NORTHERN TERRITORY / WESTERN AUSTRALIA

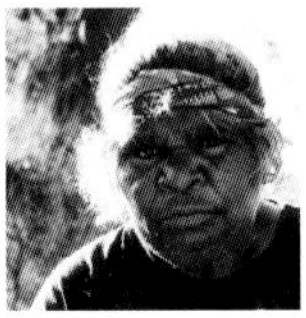

Ningura Napurrula was a young woman in her mid-twenties when she took her first journey out of the Gibson Desert in 1962 to Papunya with the Northern Territory Welfare Branch patrol. After their son received medical treatment at Papunya, Napurrula and her husband Yala Yala Gibbs Tjungurrayi were transported by another patrol back to their own country, close to the present day site of Kiwirrkura. The following year, Napurrula and Tjungurrayi walked back to Papunya with their whole family group as part of a general migration of Pintupi people from their country.

Yala Yala Gibbs Tjungurrayi became one of the founders of Papunya Tula Artists in the early 1970s, and one of the exponents of the classic Tingari painting style that dominated Pintupi men's painting until the early 1990s. In the 1980s, the family moved back to the newly established Pintupi township of Walungurru (Kintore), then to Muntarti outstation in Western Australia, before returning to Walungurru. Here, Napurrula and Tjungurrayi's other two wives began assisting Tjungurrayi in infilling the backgrounds of his canvases with the meticulous, precisely placed dots that characterised the Tingari style.

Napurrula first painted in her own right in 1995, in the second year of the Haasts Bluff/Kintore women's painting project. Following Tjungurrayi's death in 1998, her painting activity increased dramatically. Her bold, intricate linework and dense monochrome infilling – as seen in *Untitled (Wirrulnga)*, 2000 – are reminiscent of Tjungurrayi's earliest works. Wirrulnga is an important women's rockhole site east of Kiwirrkura. Napurrula's work is strongly charged with the seriousness of women's business, echoed in the distinctive paintings of fellow Papunya Tula Artists, Makinti Napanangka and Inyuwa Nampitjinpa. Napurrula and Tjungurrayi's sons, Morris Gibson Tjapaltjarri (Mawitji) and Adam Gibbs Tjapaltjarri, now carry on their mother's and father's work in their own paintings. VJ

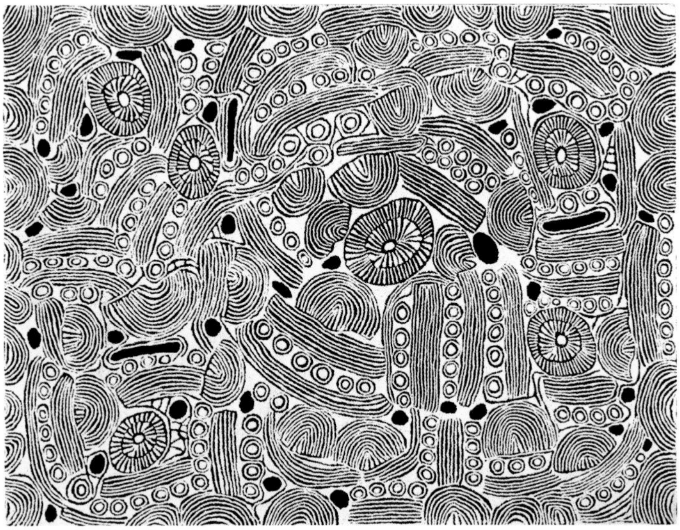

Untitled (Wirrulnga) 2000
synthetic polymer paint on canvas
183 x 244 cm
> detail

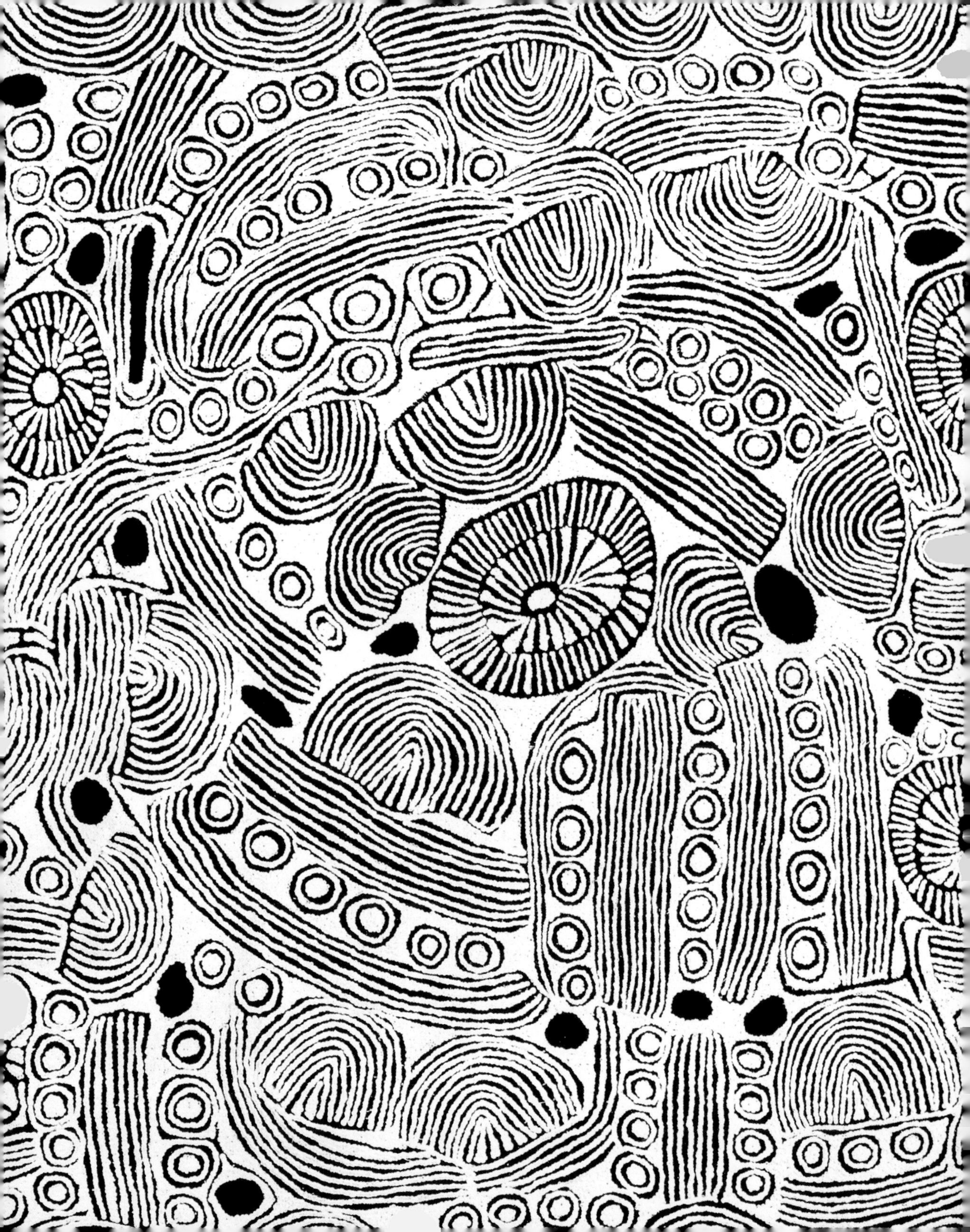

DULA NGURRUWUTTHUN

c.1936–2001
MUNYUKU
NORTHERN TERRITORY

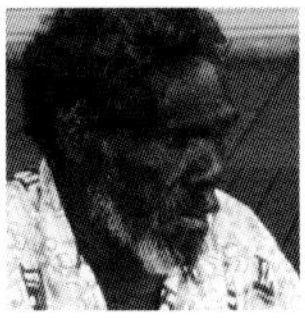

'It is for the Yolngu that we paint ... We are working on our Law. This is interpreting our wisdom, our foundation, and the sinews of Yolngu. This is a true story, not lies. And this hair on my head is true. The truth comes out of this hair brush.'[1]

In this quote, Dula Ngurruwutthun reflected on the significance of painting and the tradition of making the paintbrush out of several strands of human hair. Completed days before the artist's death, *Untitled*, 2001, is layered with meaning referring to the ancestral story and depiction of saltwater country. The painting is also imbued with a poignant reflection on mortality. Dula has painted his own essence into his depiction of the spirit bones of Mirinyungu, the ancestral whale.

In Wangarr times, Mirinyungu lived in the ocean at Yarrinya in Munyuku clan country. The whale's 'brothers', Munyuku spirit men, killed Mirinyungu with garapana (stone knives), severing the tail and cutting the body into long strips, contaminating the beach. The bones of Mirinyungu – that is, its essence or soul – are said to have become part of Garapana, a sacred rock in the ocean.

Consequently, the character of the salt-water at Yarrinya, represented here by the miny'tji (sacred clan designs), is 'rough with the odour of death hanging over it'.[2] In this bark painting, the bones occupy a sea composed of radiating waves of dotted miny'tji traversed by mysterious currents. In reality, Garapana, a dangerous, forbidden place, lies below this water. Here, it is revealed on the surface of the water, as a strange, anthropomorphic arrangement of whale bones. An additional layer of meaning is Dula's identification as a Munyuku clan member, with custodianship responsibilities at Yarrinya.

Dula painted for an outside audience from the early 1960s. He was the son of Djimbaryun and the brother of Gambali Ngurruwuthun. The three men were djirrakay, or ceremonial specialists, for both Dhuwa and Yirritja people in north-east Arnhem Land. Dula performed an essential role in education and ceremonial business for both moieties. He advised on the development of the major exhibition, 'The Painters of the Wagilag Sisters Story 1937–1997', held at the National Gallery of Australia, Canberra, in 1997, and on the collection and exhibition 'Saltwater, Yirrkala Bark Paintings of Sea Country', at the Australian National Maritime Museum, Sydney, in 2000. KW

Untitled 2001
natural pigments on bark
181 x 105 cm

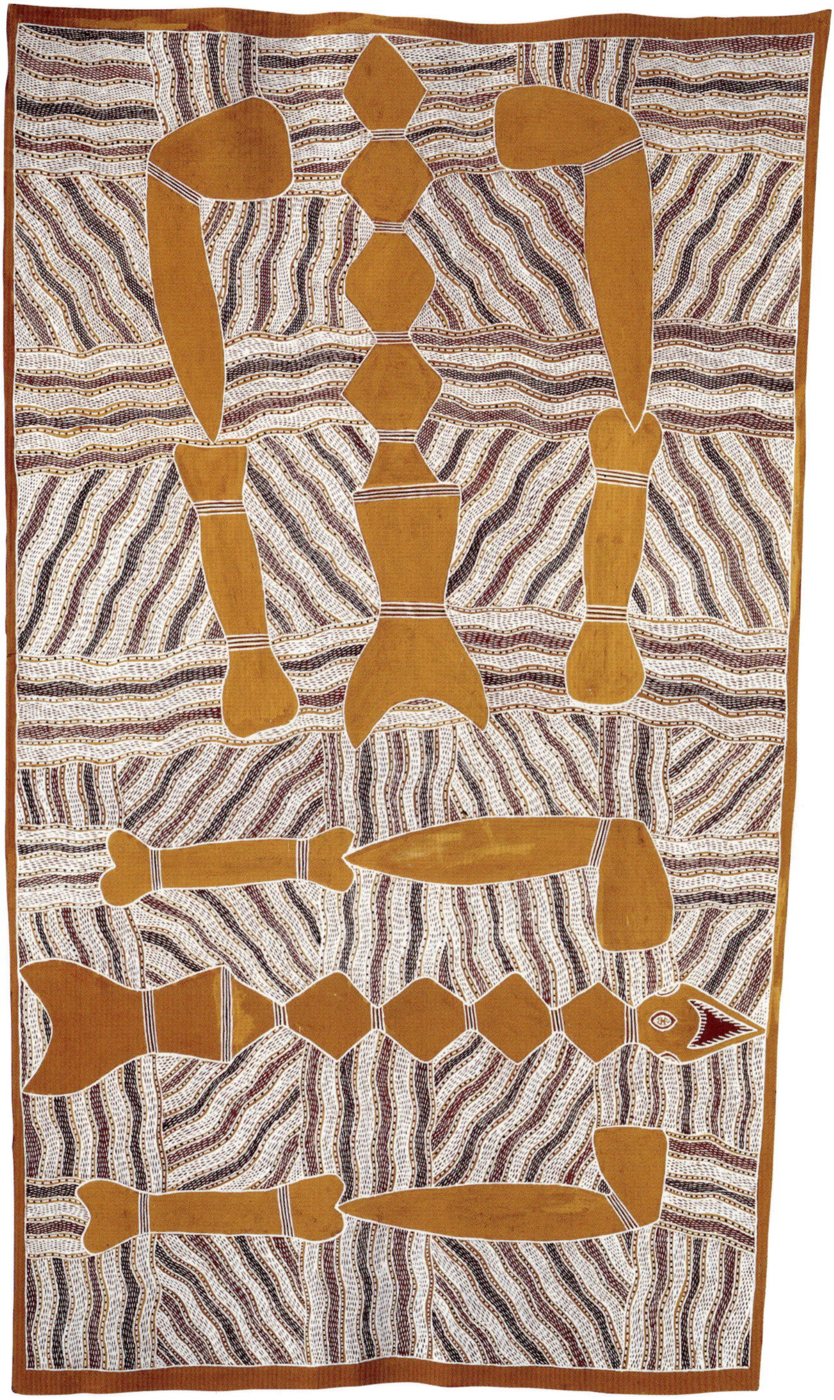

JIMMY NJIMINJUMA

BORN 1945
KUNINJKU
NORTHERN TERRITORY

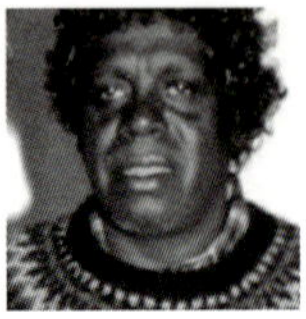

Jimmy Njiminjuma is currently one of the most senior artists in the western Arnhem Land region. For many years he lived with his father, Anchor Kulunba, at Mumeka outstation. Njiminjuma says that his father and his uncle Peter Marralwanga showed him how to paint. In the 1980s Njiminjuma took a strong role in teaching his younger brother John Mawurndjul the art of bark painting. Njiminjuma has now established an outstation at Kurrurldul on Mimarlar Creek, a tributary of the Tomkinson River, south of Maningrida.

Njiminjuma is adept at painting a number of subjects, and one of his recurring themes is the yawkyawk. These figures are understood to be a kind of female water sprite, and the Kuninjku often paint them with the forked tail of a fish and long flowing hair likened to the trailing waterweed of freshwater streams. In *Yawkyawk*, 2000, Njiminjuma depicts the form of the spirit being, embedded in the sacred landscape of Milmingkan, in his clan lands. The rarrk (crosshatched) designs at the left of the painting represent the banks of the waterhole, and the fork-tailed figure is shown outlined against a field of rarrk that represents the site.

Part of the creativity in Njiminjuma's painting is evident in his ability to construct complex figures that merge with the geometric background designs. These designs have their basis in the body paintings of the Mardayin ceremony, in which the participants are marked with images of the landscape that is their birth heritage. In bark paintings, the incorporation of geometric designs and figurative elements reveals Kuninjku beliefs in how certain landscape forms were moulded by the creative actions of ancestral beings. The ancestral beings entered the earth at these special places and exist there still as an animating life force. LT

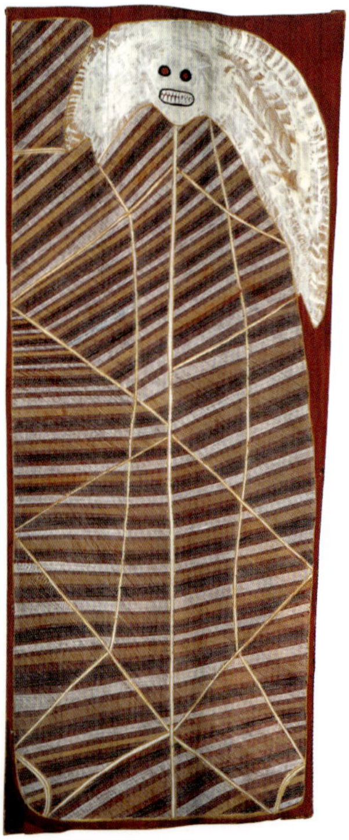

Yawkyawk 2000
natural pigments on bark
157 x 63 cm
> detail

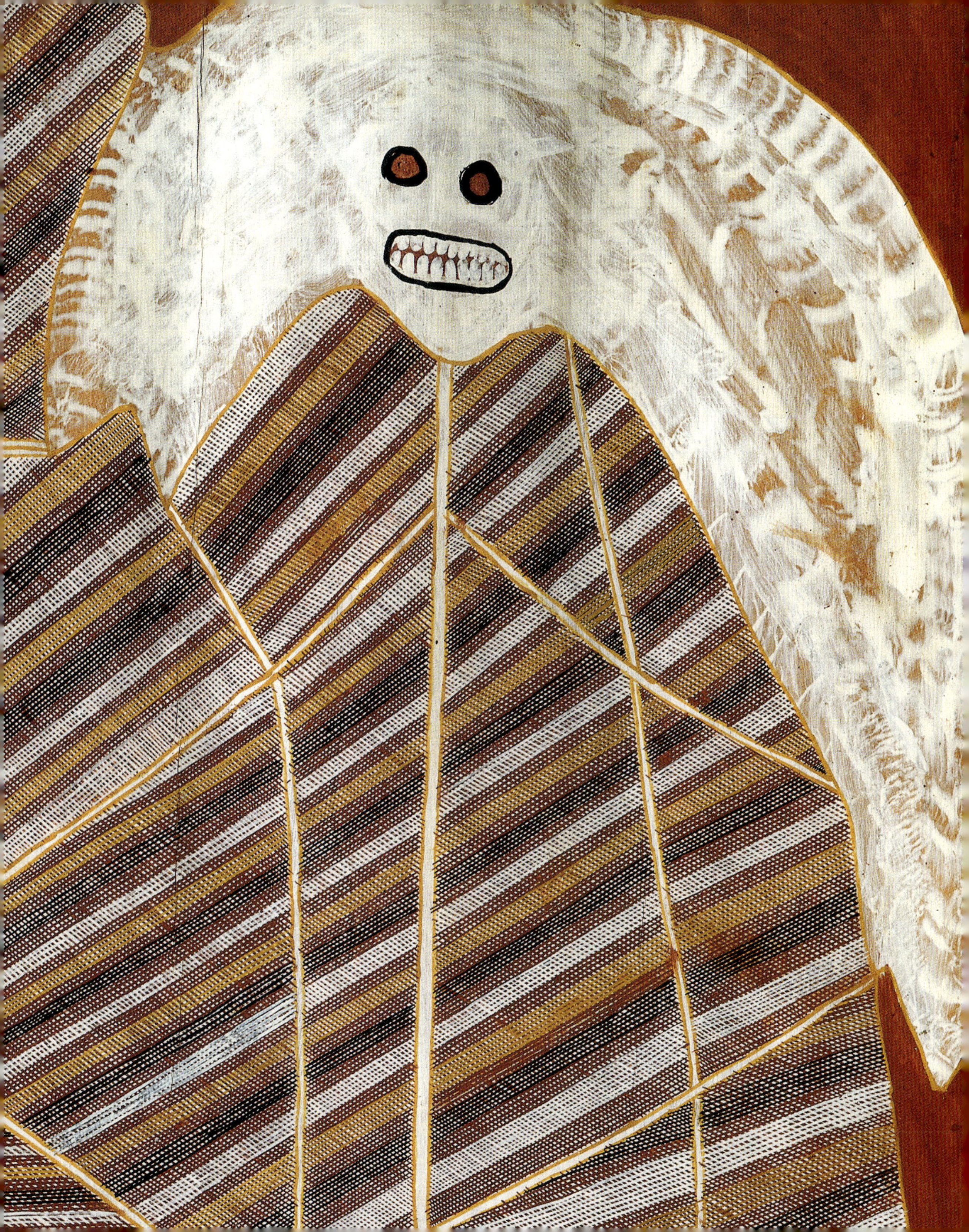

LIN ONUS

1948–1996
YORTA YORTA
VICTORIA /
NEW SOUTH WALES

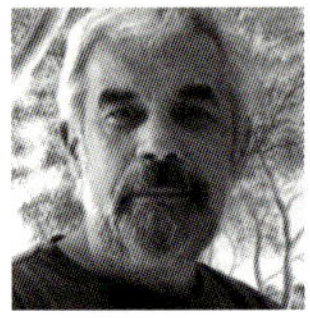

Yorta Yorta painter, sculptor and activist, Lin Onus developed a distinctive visual language from a combination of traditional and contemporary Aboriginal imagery.

Lin Onus was unjustly expelled from school on racist grounds at the age of 14, yet later attended university. He worked as a mechanic and spray painter, before managing his father's boomerang workshop in Melbourne. A self-taught artist, Onus forged a brilliant career and held exhibitions throughout the world.

Onus's political commitment was inherent in his work. His Scottish mother was a member of the Communist Party, while his Aboriginal father, Bill, and uncle Eric were leading lights in the Aboriginal rights movement of the 1950s and 1960s.

After a visit to Maningrida in 1986, Onus began his long and close association with the late Djinang artist, Djiwul 'Jack' Wunuwun and other central Arnhem Land artists, including John Bulunbulun. Onus then developed his signature style of incorporating photorealism with Indigenous imagery. It is a virtuoso effect, in which the landscape is overlaid with traditional Indigenous iconography, reflecting his strong ties with his father's community at Cummergunja Mission, on the Murray River. Onus's works from this period often have a riddling, Magritte-like quality. A memorable motif in his work is the breaking up of a seamless surface into jigsaw puzzle pieces – a metaphor for the sense of dislocation he felt, caught between black and white, urban and rural, worlds.

In Onus's sculptures, irony, wit and whimsy are the predominant features. *Fruit bats*, 1991, is made up of a flock of fibreglass sculptures of bats decorated with rarrk (crosshatching), hanging on a Hills Hoist clothes line. Beneath this icon of Australian suburbia are wooden discs with flower-like motifs, representing the bat droppings. In this powerful installation, the sacred and the mundane combine. The work was inspired by Murrungun-Djinang imagery, which Onus was given permission to use. In *Fruit bats*, the artist shows a head-on collision between two contrasting sets of values, and throws in a few inversions of his own. The backyard – suburban Australia's haven of privacy – becomes spooked by the formidable presence of these noisy animals. The pre-colonial bats seem to have taken over and reclaimed their place, in a story worthy of Alfred Hitchcock. GA

Fruit bats 1991
polychromed fibreglass sculptures, polychromed wooden disks, Hills Hoist clothes line
250 x 250 x 250 cm overall
v detail

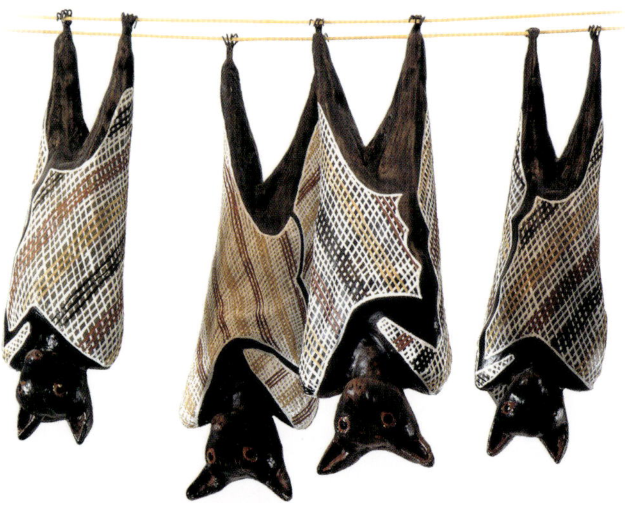

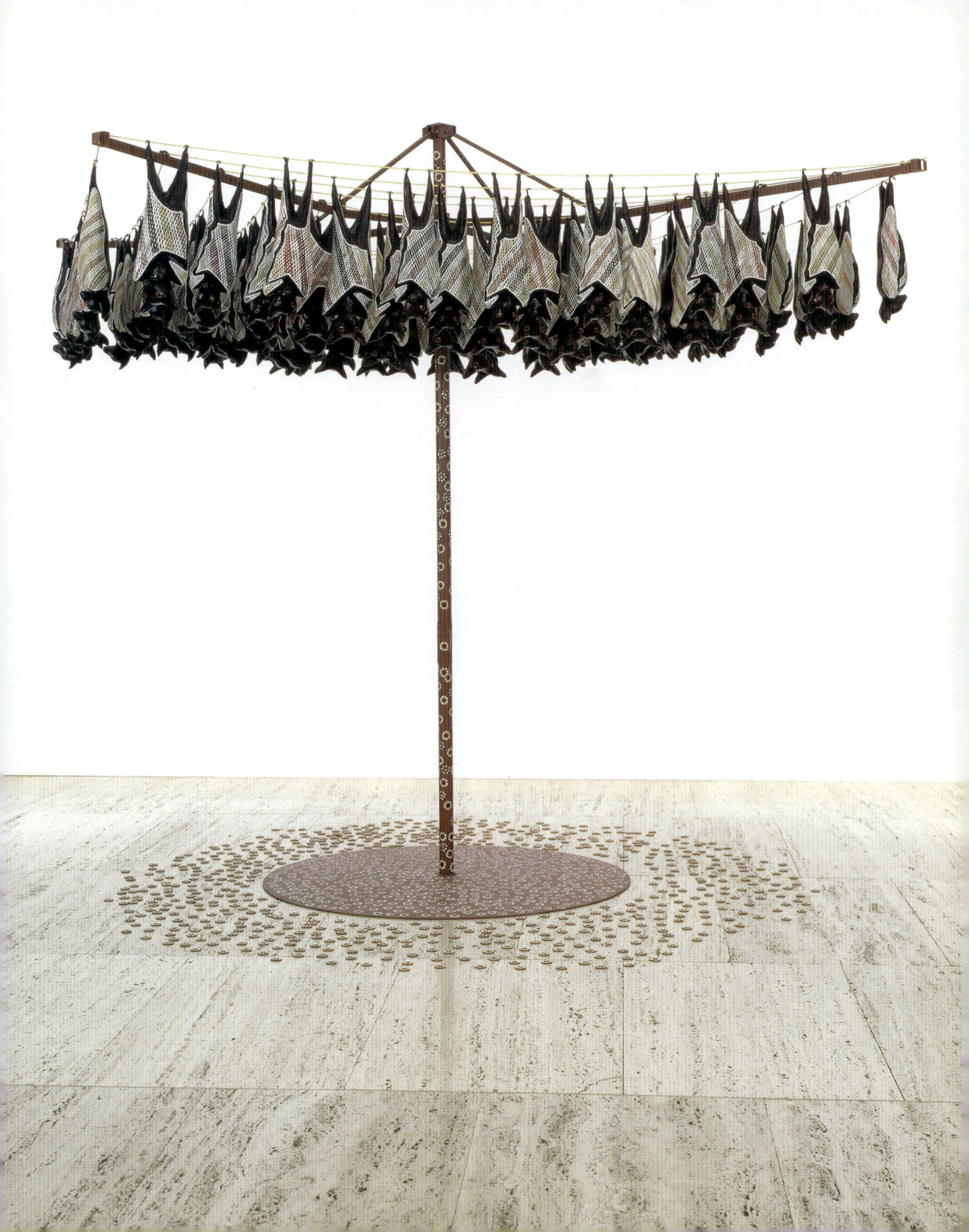

OTTO PAREROULTJA

1914–1973
WESTERN ARANDA
NORTHERN TERRITORY

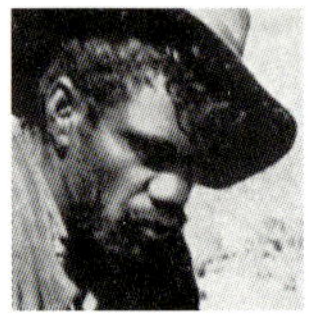

Otto Pareroultja and his brothers Reuben and Edwin worked and painted at the Lutheran Hermannsburg Mission in Central Australia. Initially influenced by their countryman, Albert Namatjira, and by Rex Battarbee, the Melbourne water-colourist who worked closely with the Hermannsburg artists, the Pareroultja brothers developed their own distinctive styles within a modern European land-scape idiom. In their paintings, the desert landscape is less representational than in Namatjira's work, and is animated by their use of vigorous, sinuous lines, dynamic areas of repeated patterning and strong colours massed together.

A white ghost gum in front of distant mountain ranges is a common motif of the Hermannsburg school. In an untitled study of two gum trees, painted at the height of the Hermannsburg movement, Pareroultja cropped the image so that the focus is drawn to the trunk of a mature tree. The trees are not isolated, however – Pareroultja merges them into the landscape and the sky by continuing the blue and purple tones in the shadowing and markings on their trunks, creating an integrated image of the land. The aged tree next to the sapling could suggest a narrative subject matter, contrasting maturity and endurance with youth, but it is more likely that Pareroultja depicts the rigours of this landscape without sentiment.

Contemporary commentators saw the parallel lines and concentric circles often used by the Pareroultja brothers in their watercolours as being distinctly Aboriginal motifs, signalling a modern Aboriginal art movement. Battarbee claimed that elements of Otto Pareroultja's work were derived from Aboriginal rock art and from the designs on tjurunga (sacred objects). The linguist, T. G. H. Strehlow, singled out Pareroultja's depiction of ghost gums as being, ' ... in close harmony with Ancient Aranda ... tales, according to which many of these old gums had arisen from poles abandoned on their travels by their original totemic ancestors.'[1] Strehlow also commented that Pareroultja's watercolours are capable of reproducing ' ... the same kind of distinctive Aranda feeling for balance, love of repetition and design, and sure sense of rhythm, that give such glorious vitality to their best verse'.[2]

Pareroultja's paintings undoubtedly draw on his intimate knowledge of his land and culture. Some recent commentators on the Hermannsburg school suggest that these artists drew on sacred ancestral knowledge in their paintings; other writers continue to see the work of artists such as Pareroultja as a remarkable regional development within a European landscape tradition. WT

> **The hills behind Hermannsburg** c.1954
watercolour
31 x 52 cm

v **Untitled landscape** c.1950s
watercolour
33.5 x 28 cm

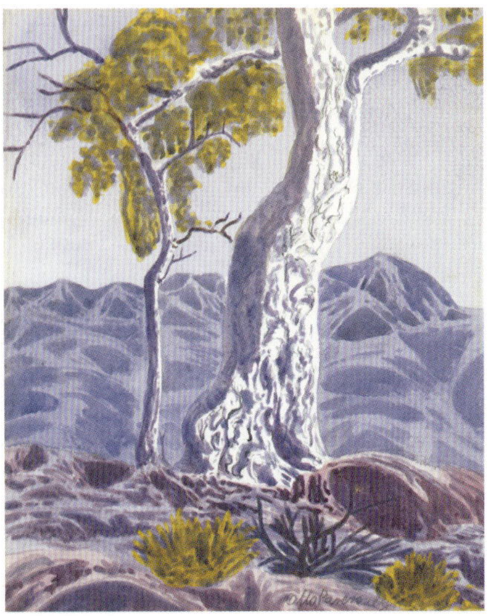

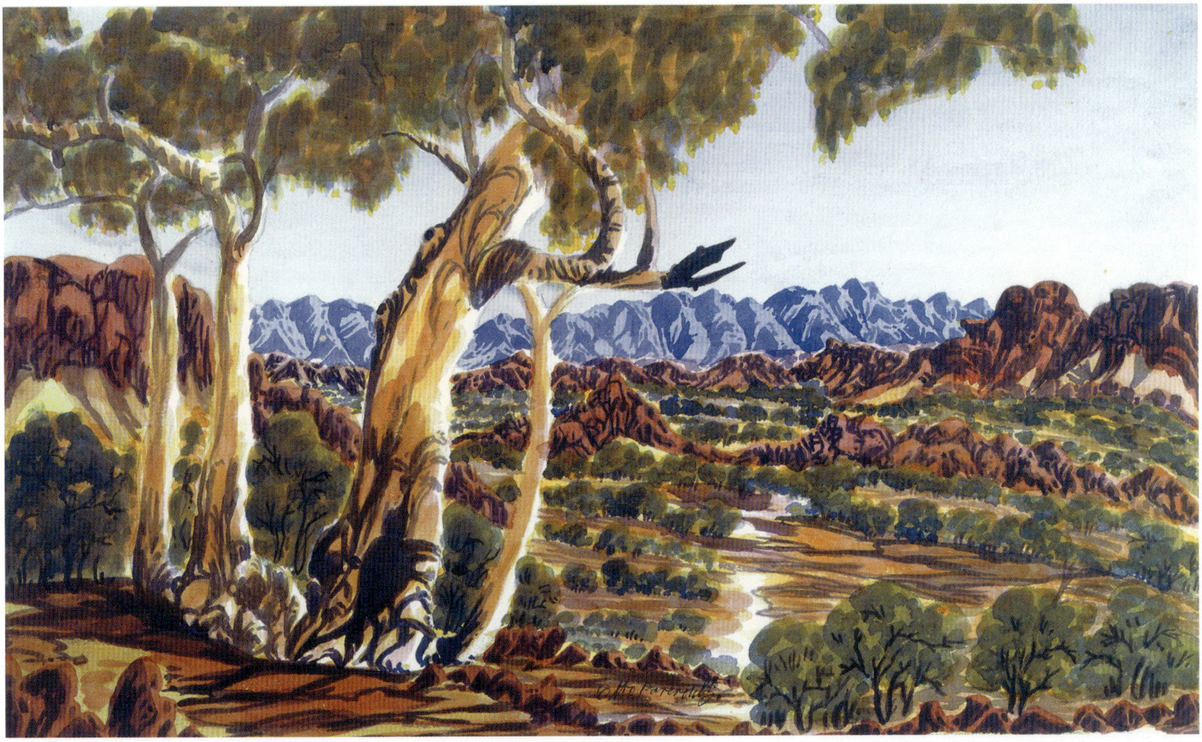

RUSTY PETERS

BORN 1935
GIJA
WESTERN AUSTRALIA

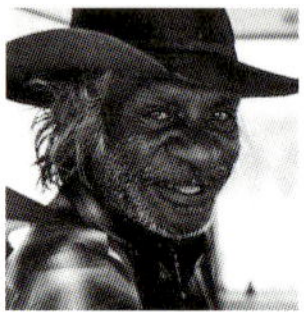

Rusty Peters, like many East Kimberley painters, spent his youth working as a stockman on cattle stations throughout the Kimberley, and earned a reputation as an accomplished horse breaker. Along with other Gija community elders, Peters was influential in establishing the Ngalangangpum bicultural school – the first school at the main Gija community Warmun (Turkey Creek) – ensuring that instruction in Gija law and culture was prominent in the curriculum.

In 1989, Peters moved to Kununurra, where he worked as an assistant at Waringarri Aboriginal Arts, a community-owned Aboriginal art cooperative. He often worked closely with Rover Thomas, the East Kimberley's most renowned painter and a co-founder of the regional contemporary painting movement. Although Peters occasionally produced small canvases during this period, he did not begin painting in earnest until 1998, after he had left Waringarri to join the newly founded Jirrawun Aboriginal Arts. Since then he has had a series of successful group and solo exhibitions, including the 2000–02 travelling exhibition 'Two Laws ... One Big Spirit', in which he collaborated with artist Peter Adsett.[1]

In his most ambitious canvas to date, the immense, twelve-metre long *Waterbrain*, 2002, Peters departs from the specific themes of country and Ngarrangkarni that normally form the focus of East Kimberley painting. Instead, he chooses to explore the cycle of life and learning that is universal to all peoples. Read from left to right, the canvas presents a chronology of the process of birth, growth and learning from conception to adulthood. At the lower left are waterweeds among which, according to Gija belief, the spirits of unborn children reside before entering the mother's womb to become the spirits of human beings. The next panels deal with birth and infancy, when a child moves from crawling, to walking, to running, although his or her brain has yet to begin to absorb the teachings of his or her culture. The large circular motif at the centre shows the adult brain – the child has grown up and is beginning to have his or her own ideas. The next panels deal with the education that transforms a child into a full member of adult society. As a symbol of the culmination of the individual's education, in the final panels Peters depicts the artefacts his elders taught him to make and which, before the coming of European settlers, all Gija men needed to know how to create in order to survive. EK

Waterbrain 2002
8 panels: natural pigments on canvas
180 x 1200 cm overall
> detail

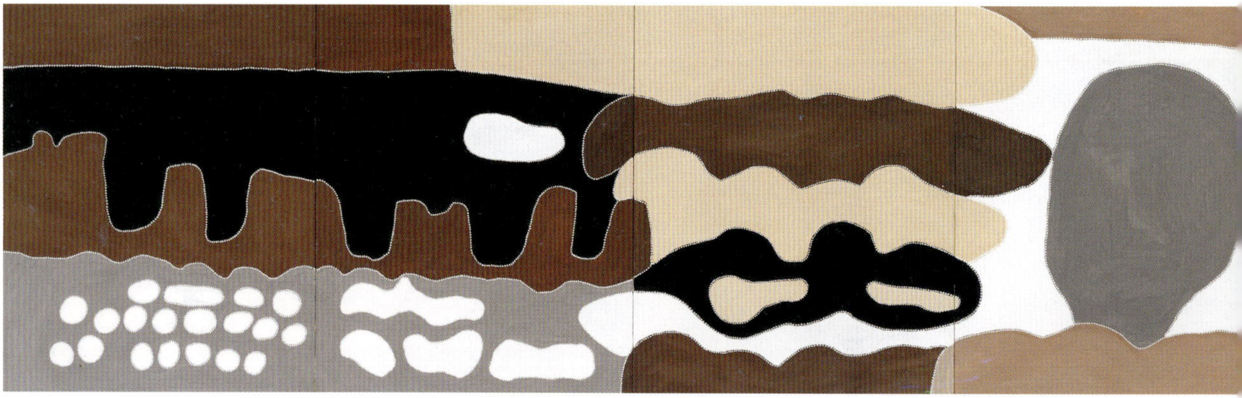

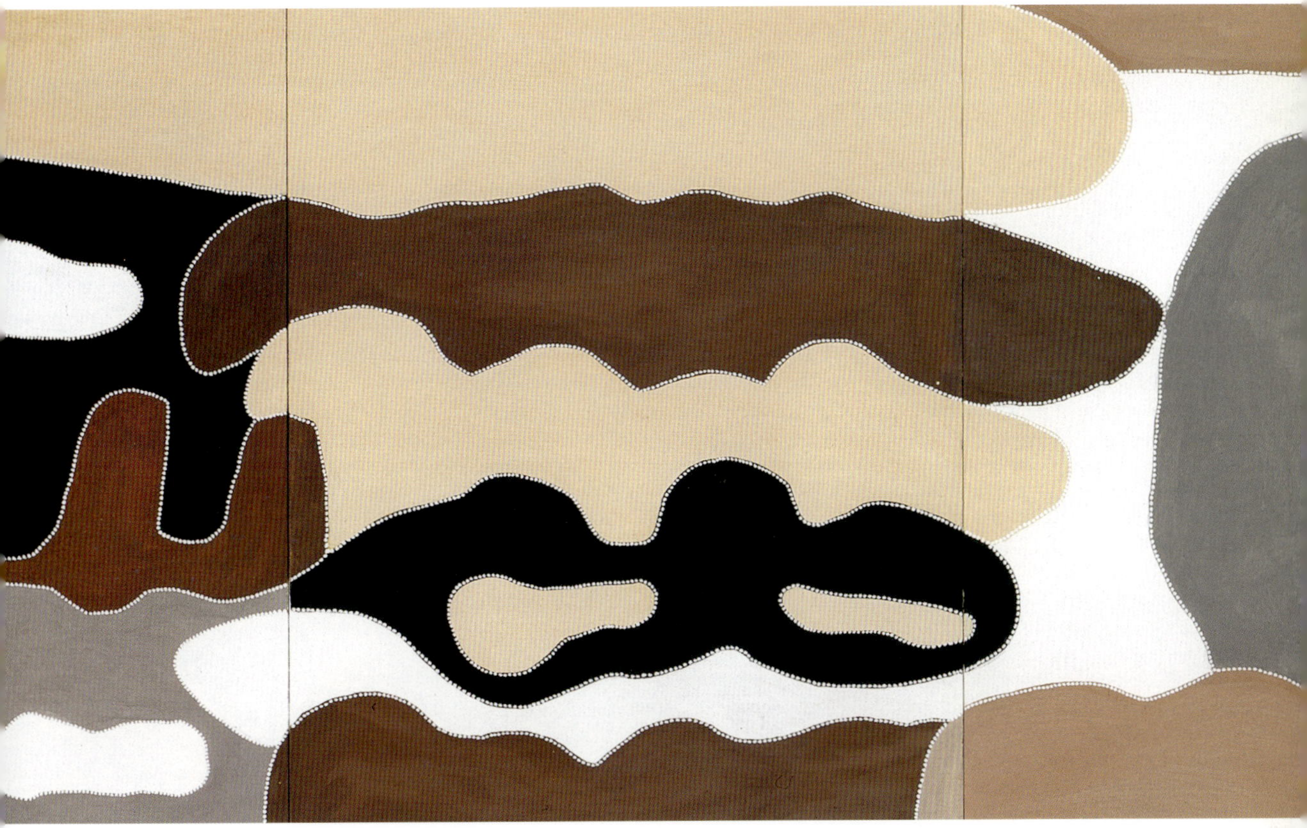

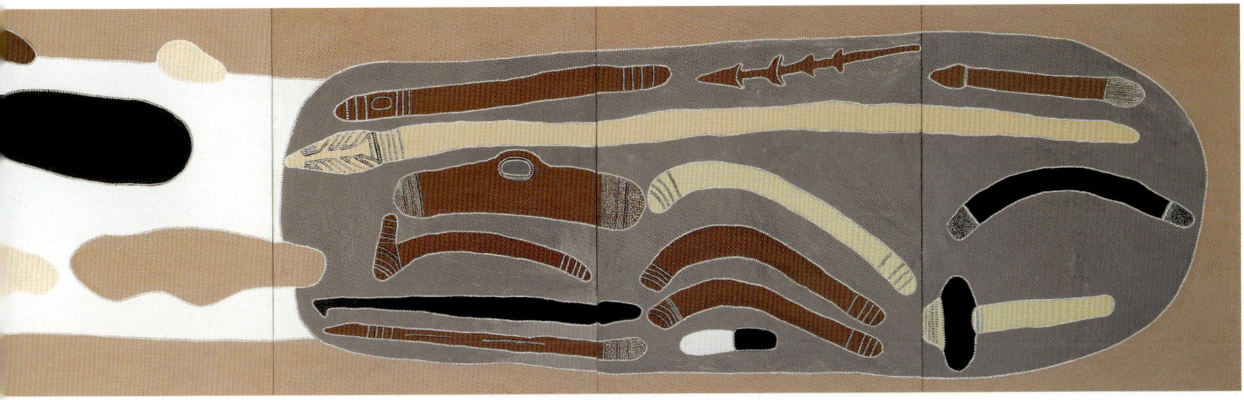

GLORIA TAMERRE PETYARRE

BORN 1938
ANMATYERR
NORTHERN TERRITORY

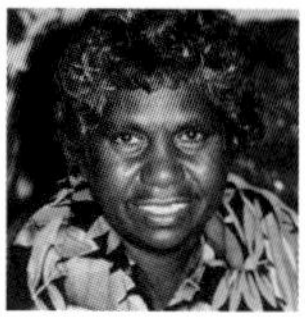

Since her first solo exhibition in 1991, Gloria Tamerre Petyarre has been regarded as a leading artist in the Utopia community, and has exhibited widely in Australia, Europe, North America and Asia. Like Emily Kame Kngwarreye, Petyarre first came to prominence as a batik painter in the late 1970s, before taking up painting on canvas in the late 1980s. As various commentators have noted, this use of sophisticated batik-making techniques, combined with the early referencing of body marking associated with women's ceremonies, shaped the unique forms of Utopia painting in the 1980s. Petyarre, one of four renowned painter sisters, is considered to have taken various forms based on ceremonial markings and her Altyerr or Akngannety stories to abstraction more consistently than many of her contemporaries.

Petyarre is an experimental artist renowned for her diversity and mastery as a colourist. Her work is anchored in 'awely' – a term that not only describes women's ceremonial body painting but also the wider concept of 'women's business'. For example, Petyarre's major, 21-panel work, *Awely for the mountain devil lizard* (*Twenty-one women*), 1996, refers simultaneously to ceremonial body painting as sourced in stories relating to Arnkerrth, the mountain devil lizard, and to a larger cosmology that is foundational in Petyarre's painting. Arnkerrth is a major subject, of particular importance to Petyarre, and her ability to constantly re-invent its visual representations has been widely recognised.

These panels, which could form an installation, reveal a great deal about the positioning of Petyarre's work both within traditional Aboriginal culture, and in dialogue with contemporary art practices. Her painterly abstractions of 21 women seem to make tangible the movement, energy and rhythms of ceremonies in which women themselves embody the creative act. They can also be viewed as forming an abstract series that conforms to the classic canons of Western modernism, with the use of serial units, repetition, a lack of focal point, an underlying grid structure and close-toned optical effects.

In her paintings throughout the 1990s, which progressively increased in size and painterly precision, Petyarre created some of the most significant recent Aboriginal artworks. They are spectacular paintings, in which she has lately been supplanting her dots and lines with elongated drop-forms in feathery layers that move over the surfaces of her work with the velocity of wind in foliage or the fluidity of water currents. DE

Awely for the mountain devil lizard (Twenty-one women) 1996
21 panels: synthetic polymer paint on canvas
294 x 490 cm overall
> detail

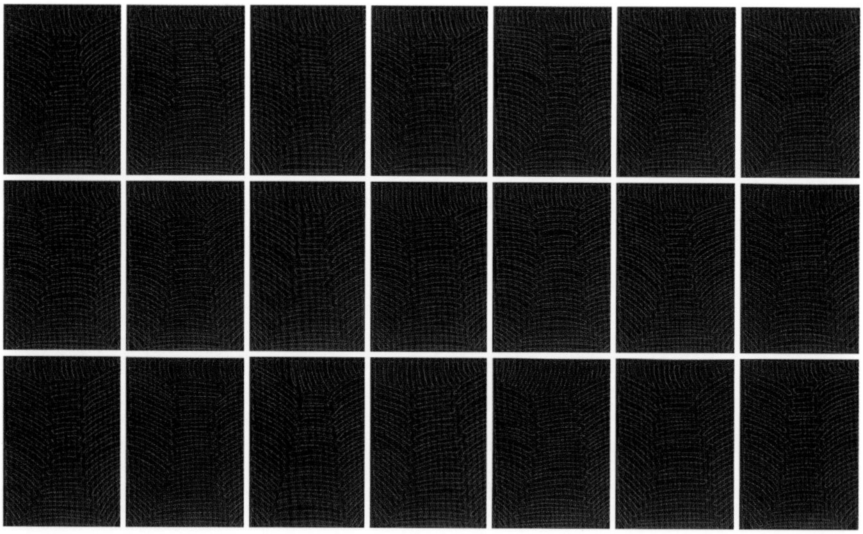

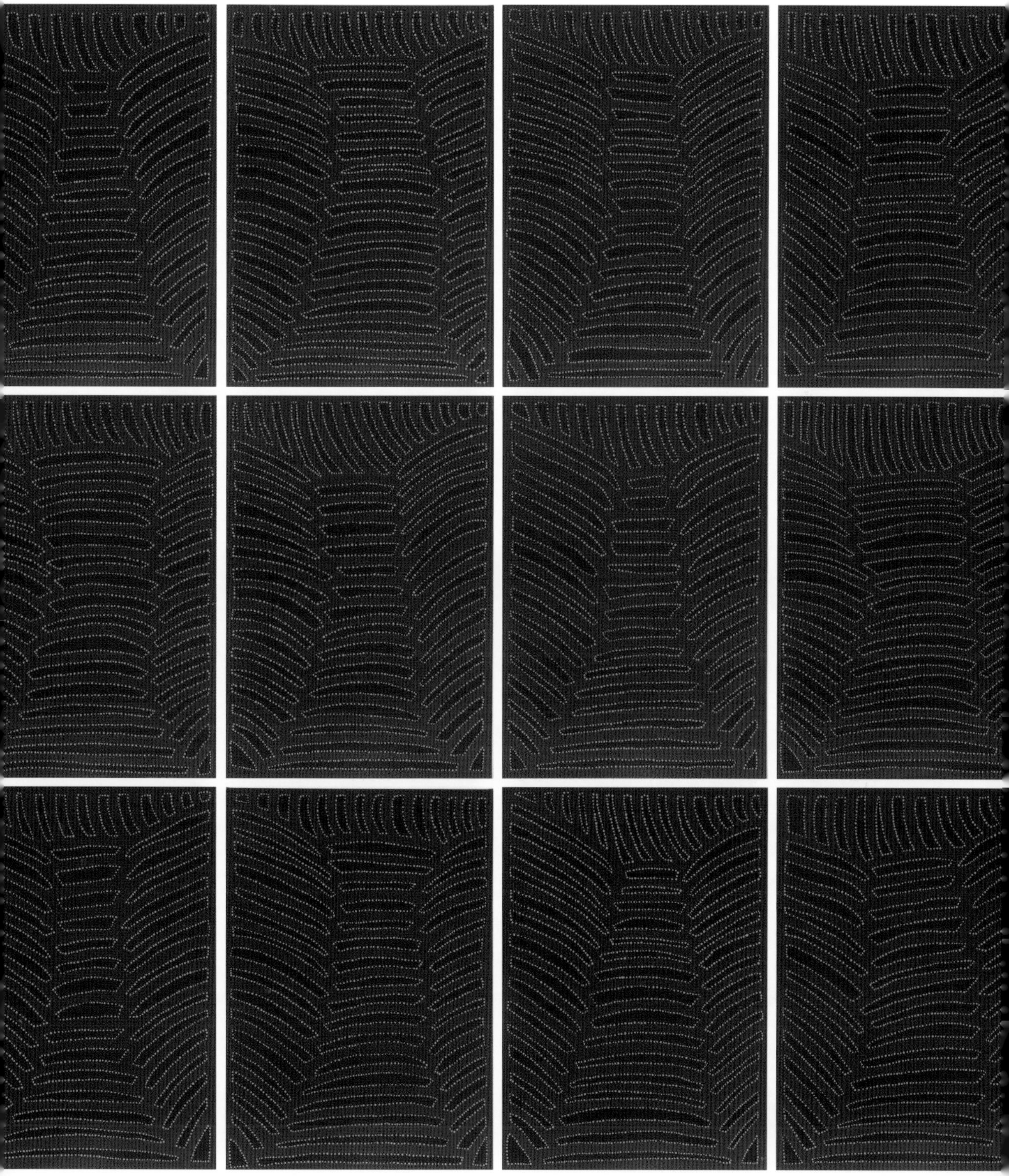

KUTUWULUMI PURAWARRUMPATU

c.1928–2003
TIWI
NORTHERN TERRITORY

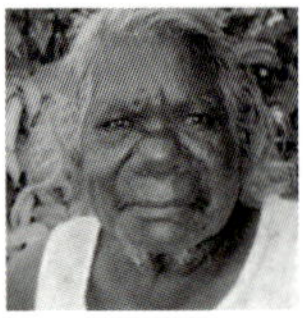

Even within the distinctive island culture of the Tiwi people of Bathurst and Melville Islands, Kutuwulumi Purawarrumpatu's work stands apart. The Tiwi people share a visual language known as jilamara (design) based on innumerable configurations of mulypinyini pwanga (lines and dots). These designs are individually conceived and used as body markings in ceremonial performance, and also transcribed onto sculptures and paintings. A central tenet of Tiwi culture is the Pukumani funerary ceremony, which commemorates the death of the ancestor Purukuparli and celebrates the lives of those who have passed away. For this elaborate memorial to the deceased, monumental tutini (grave posts) are carved and decorated with natural ochres. At the culmination of the ceremony, after many of days of song and dance, the tutini are erected at the gravesite. Left to the elements, these solemn clusters of bloodwood sculptures stand as majestic sentinels to the endurance of Tiwi beliefs. Pukumani is the wellspring of contemporary Tiwi art, and its influence may be traced to the Indigenous mainland communities of Arnhem Land.

Purawarrumpatu, commonly known as Kitty Kantilla, was a stalwart of Tiwi tradition, well-versed in the nuances of her culture. Her work is stamped with her imprimatur as a senior member of the community, yet also discloses a radical artistic spirit. Purawarrumpatu began working as an artist, outside of a ceremonial context, after moving from the mission on Bathurst Island to a widows' camp at Paru, in her mother's country on Melville Island. Here, she and other senior women formed the 'Paru Mob', carving distinctive, and usually figurative, sculptures. When working with ironwood became too strenuous, Purawarrumpatu turned to painting and etching for Jilamara Arts and Crafts.

The Tiwi people established Jilamara Arts and Crafts at Milikapiti in 1989 to ensure the maintenance of their cultural heritage. Purawarrumpatu and fellow artist members, such as the late Taracarijimo Freda Warlapinni and Pedro Wonaeamirri, adhere to Jilamara's aesthetic standard of using a restricted palette of red, black, yellow and white ochre, thereby honouring the traditions of their ancestors. In her paintings, however, Purawarrumpatu often inverted the usual practice of painting on a black ground, instead executing fields of geometric designs and massed colour on a white surface.

Purawarrumpatu's art embraces the conundrum of meaning and abstraction in enigmatic images that do not easily oblige literal translation. Refusing to be drawn into interpreting her work for an outside audience, she maintained that ' ... it's from the old times'.[1] HP

> **Untitled** 1997
natural pigments on canvas
92 x 94 cm

v left **Untitled** 1997
natural pigments on paper
57 x 75.5 cm

v right **Untitled** 1997
etching
19.5 x 88.4 cm

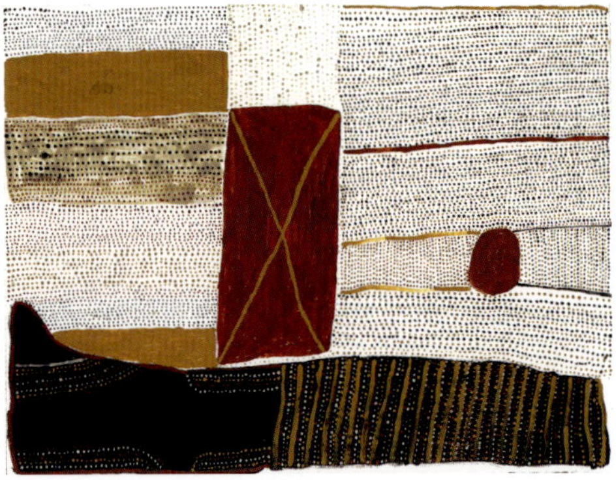

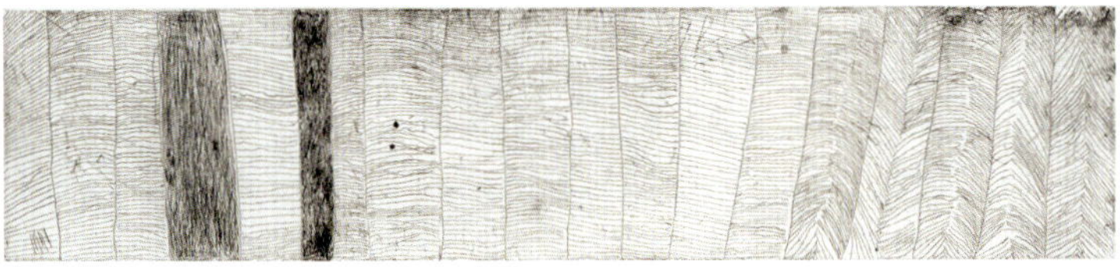

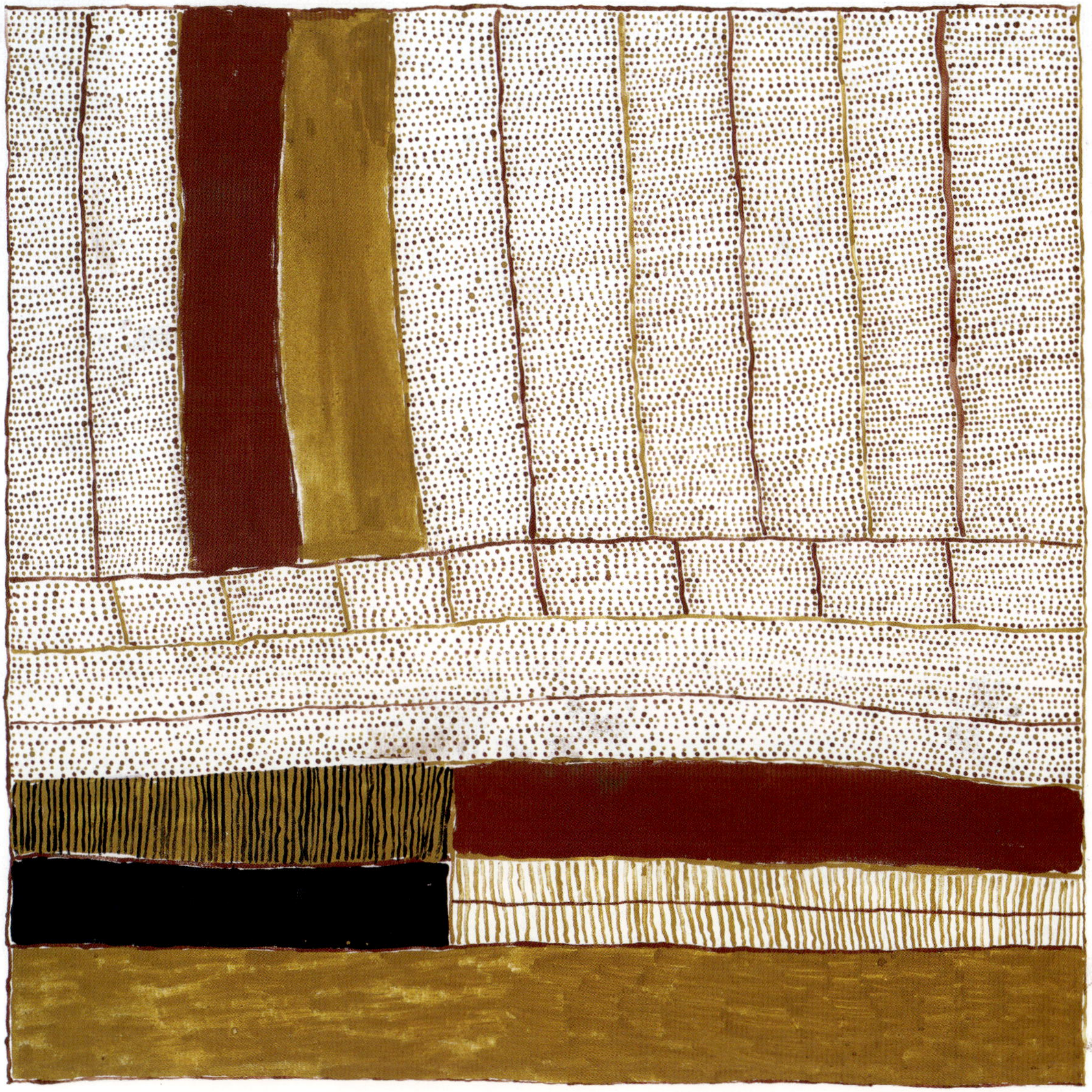

REA

BORN 1962
GAMILAROI / WAILWAN
NEW SOUTH WALES

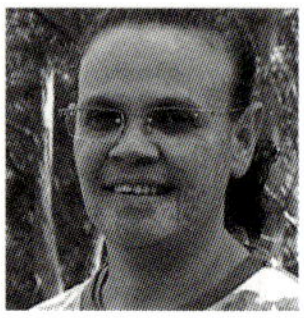

One of Rea's earliest memories is of looking through family photographs that her mother kept in a biscuit tin. The connections between memory and photography, and between personal experience and political history are central to Rea's work as a digital media and installation artist. She layers text, image and colour to explore the representation of the black body and, in particular, the black female body. Words and sentences are often an important component of her practice, through which she traces how attitudes to race are embedded in language itself. Rea's use of pop culture references and her acute awareness of how images circulate in the mass media enhance the impact of her work.

The colours and text that Rea has chosen to use in the series 'Highly coloured – my life is coloured by my colour I–VI', 1994, are coded references to the artist's childhood memories. Rea has written about these works:

'In each [image] I am revealed in different ways … The red is the gun at my head because that is how you feel when you are frustrated, angry and isolated. Purple and yellow are my mother's favourite colours … [Every] house we went into, [Mum] always painted the kitchen purple and yellow. I gave the yellow colour to my Uncle, who died in custody… I [put] yellow roses on his grave. He used to go and get [vouchers] from St Vinny's to feed and clothe us. The blue and green is about growing up … the struggles and insecurity, which is the text and not separate from the image … "Green, I wish I could be seen".'[1]

The central image is a life-size photograph of the artist herself, with her face obscured by a camera as she looks back at the audience through a lens. Rea's self-representation turns the tables on the viewer, causing us to question both the subject and object of this work. The history of ethnographic and anthropological observation of Aboriginal people as 'other', photographed as the passive subject of the Western gaze, is disrupted by denying the desire to see the face in this portrait and by including the process – the image of the camera – in the final work. The camera implicates the viewer as the subject of the work as much as the artist herself, making clear our role in constructing meaning around this image. WT

∨ from left
Mum, she said can I have an orange
Yellow reminds me of the roses which I put on my Uncle's grave
She was in the midst of a purple patch or else she could have been standing in her mother's kitchen
Green, I wish I could be seen
Red there's a gun at my head
Blue moon I saw you standing alone…
From the series 'Highly coloured – my life is coloured by my colour I–VI' 1994
computer-generated photographs on perspex
185 x 58.5 cm each
> detail

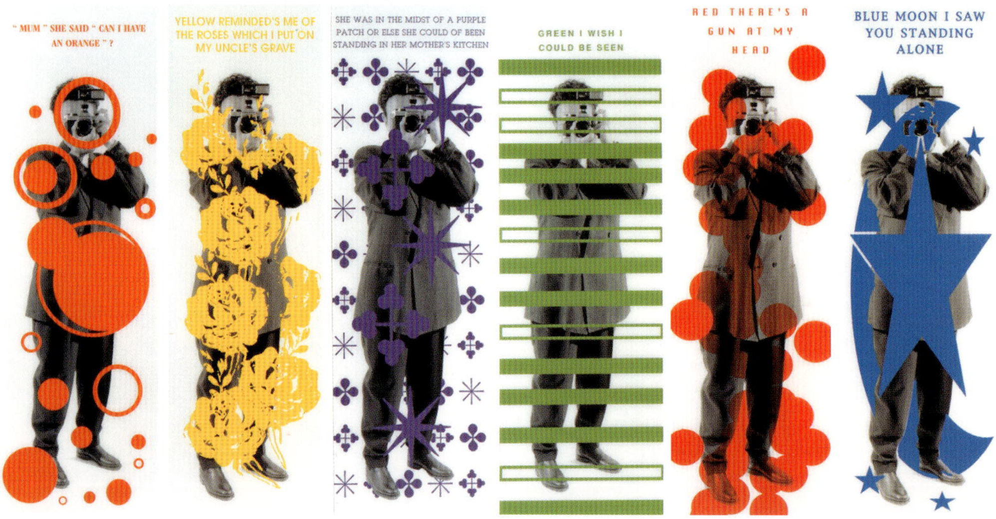

YELLOW REMINDED'S ME OF THE ROSES WHICH I PUT ON MY UNCLE'S GRAVE

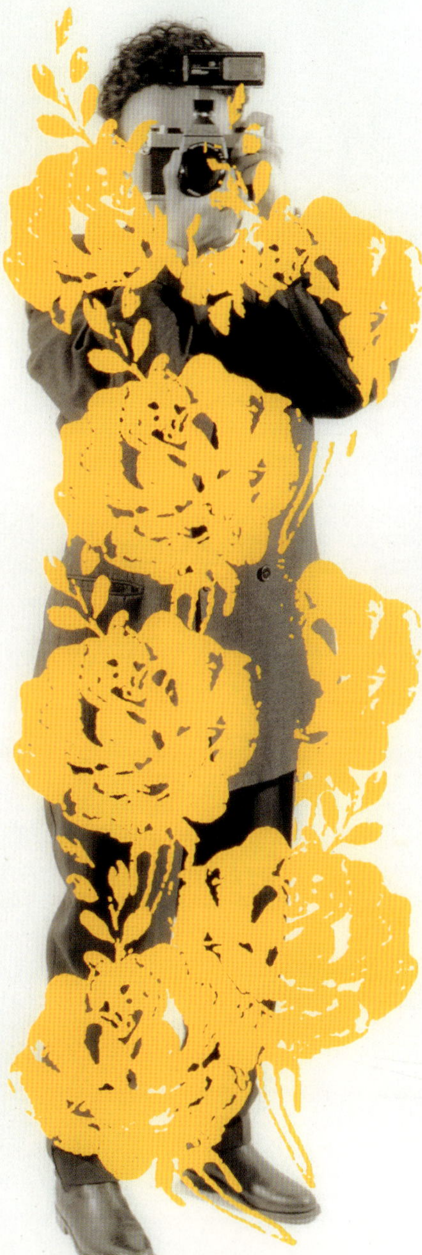

RED THERE'S A GUN AT MY HEAD

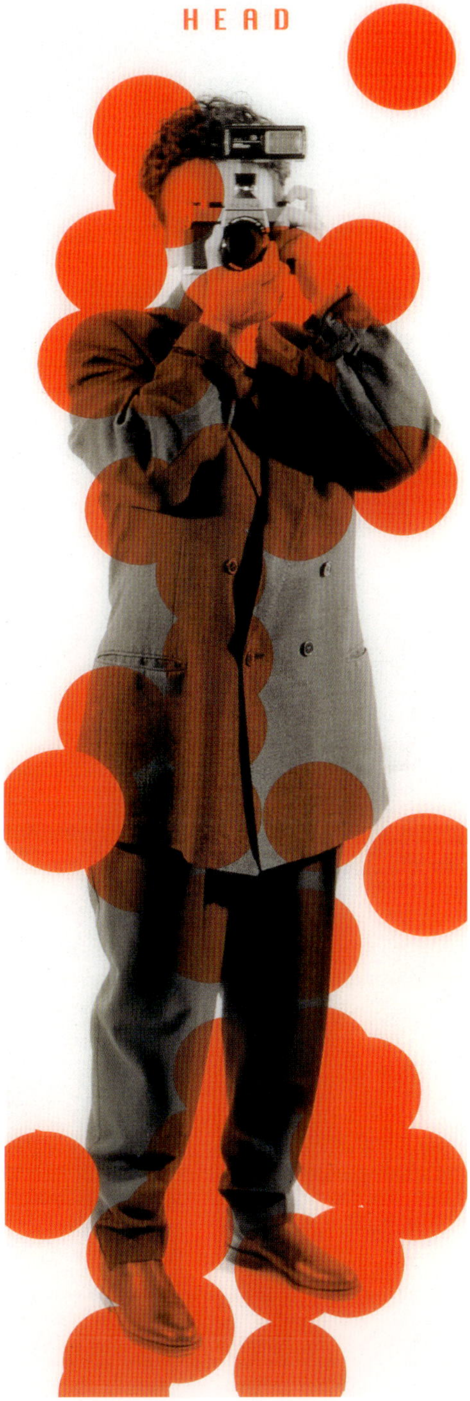

MICHAEL RILEY

BORN 1960
WIRADJURI / GAMILAROI
NEW SOUTH WALES

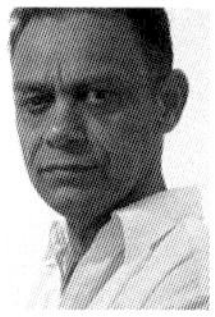

Michael Riley's career started in 1982, when he enrolled in a photography workshop at the Tin Sheds Gallery, University of Sydney, and later became the photographic technician at the Sydney College of the Arts. Riley's family and friends are his constant inspiration, and his work is characterised by a strong sense of intimacy that inherently challenges the negative portrayal of 'otherness' in historical ethnographic portraiture.

In 1986, Riley was included in the first exhibition of Indigenous photography at the Aboriginal Artists Gallery, Sydney, exhibiting five portraits of black women, one of which – *Maria*, 1985 – seemingly appropriates historical depictions of Truganninni, the woman martyred as the last of the Aboriginal people in Tasmania. In 1986, Riley and nine other Sydney-based artists established Boomalli Aboriginal Artists Cooperative. He worked concurrently at Film Australia, where he wrote and directed his first film *Boomalli: Five Artists*, 1988, followed by the highly acclaimed *Dreamings*, 1988, a documentary made for the exhibition of Aboriginal art at the Asia Society Galleries, New York.[1]

Riley continued to celebrate Aboriginal women in 'Portraits by a Window', 1990 and the 1991 series 'A Common Place – Portraits of Moree Murris'. From 1993 Riley's work focused on self-abuse as a symptom of colonisation, represented in 'Sacrifice', 1993, a series of images of icons, such as Aboriginal hands displaying stigmata. He was commissioned by the Museum of Sydney in 1996 to create *Eora*, a permanent video display dedicated to the people of Sydney. In this work, he presented a subversive juxtaposition of traditional and contemporary Aboriginal culture.

Riley surveyed the environmental destruction of his country as a metaphor for the encroachment on Aboriginal culture in his film *Empire*, 1997, and the photographic series 'Fly Blown', 1998. These works juxtaposed images of Christianity and roadkill with the parched Australian environment, and were shown as a satellite exhibition of the 1999 Venice Biennale. Riley returned to community portraits in 1999, with the series 'Yarns from Talbragar', depicting members of his father's Wiradjuri community in Dubbo and echoing his 1991 Moree series, which centred on his mother's Gamilaroi family. Riley's first digital series, 'Cloud', 2000, was included in Photograhica Australis at ARCO in Spain, the Fourth Asia-Pacific Triennial of Contemporary Art at the Queensland Art Gallery, Brisbane, and the 2003 Festival of Sydney. Isolated against an emblematic blue Australian sky, a cow, a bible and a boomerang each symbolise pastoralism, religion and Aboriginality – questioning who belongs within Australia. JJ

> **Maria** 1985
gelatin silver photograph
45.5 x 47.9 cm

v from left
Untitled (crucified hands)
Untitled (water)
Untitled (row of eight fish)
from the series 'Sacrifice' 1992
gelatin silver photographs
22 x 15.5 cm
15.5 x 22 cm
15.5 x 22 cm

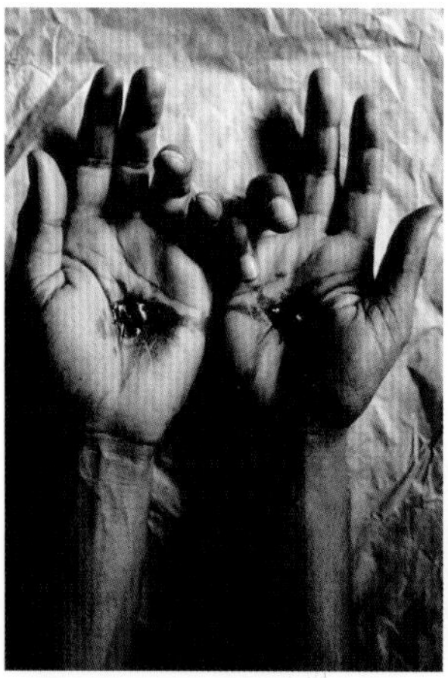

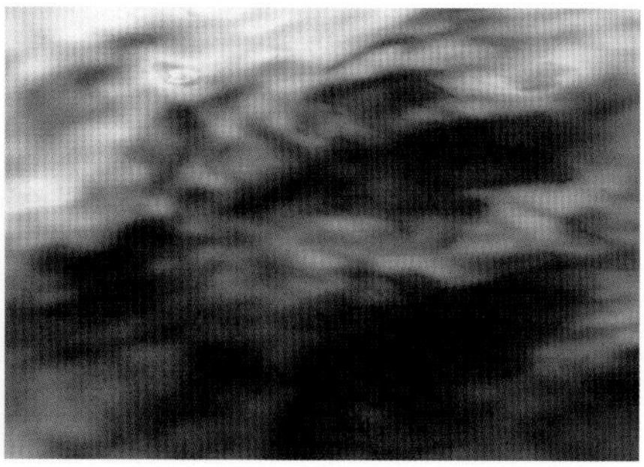

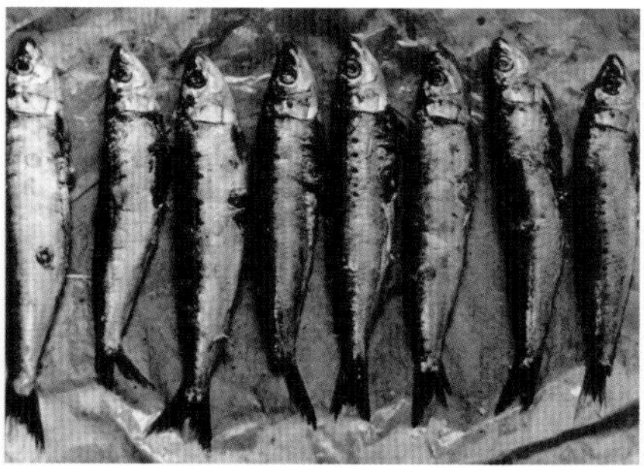

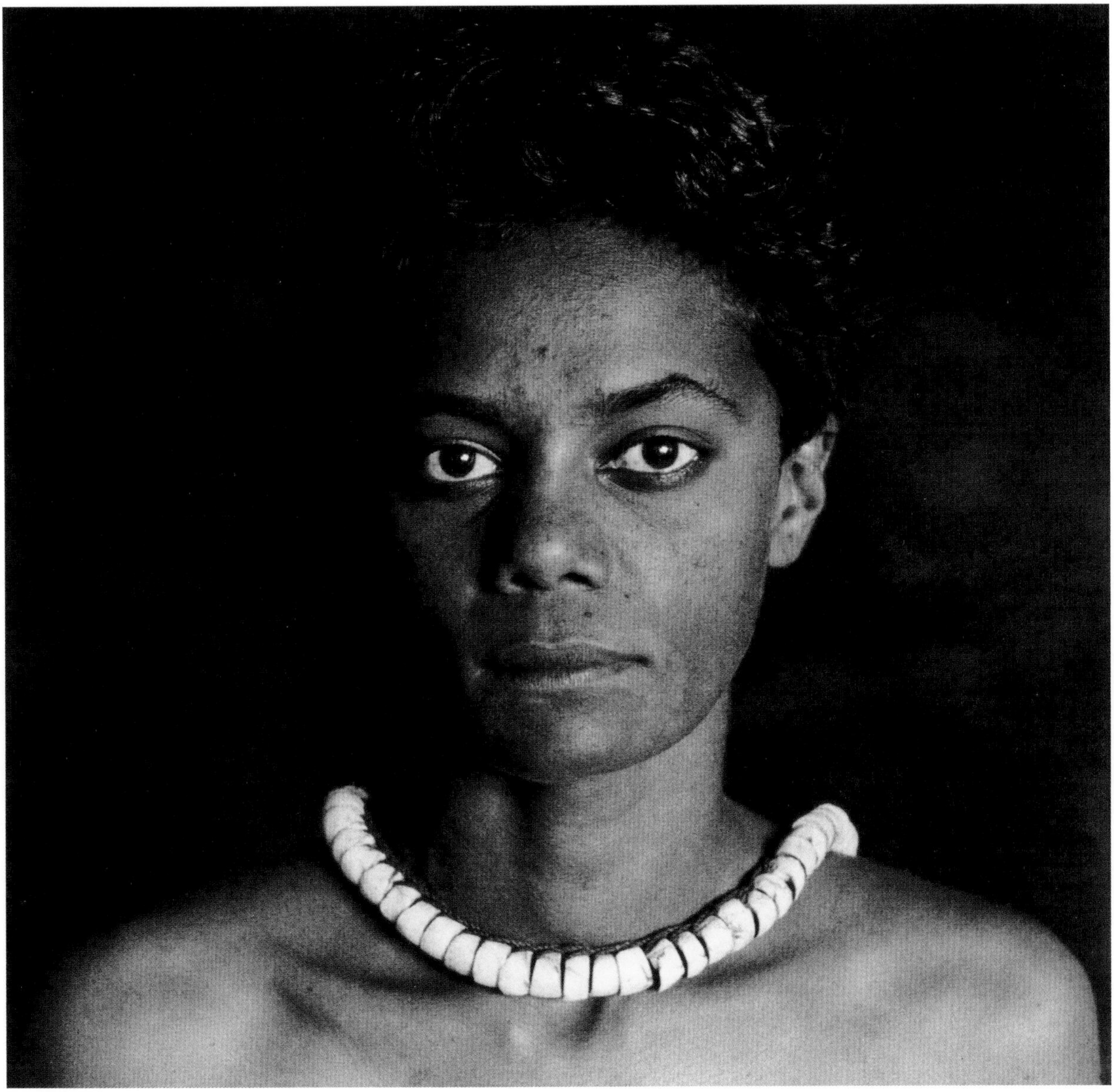

ELAINE RUSSELL

BORN 1941
KAMILAROI
NEW SOUTH WALES

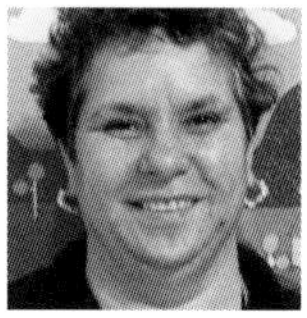

Elaine Russell was born at Tingha, New South Wales, and spent her early years at La Perouse in Sydney. Her family then moved to the Murrin Bridge Mission, on the Lachlan River, near Lake Cargellico, New South Wales.

Russell developed an early interest in art, and particularly loved drawing. When she was around 12 years old she entered the local art competition and won the first prize of a trip to the Philippines. Her mother refused to allow Russell to go, fearing that it was part of the government assimilation policy to have her daughter removed from the family. Russell can remember children 'disappearing' from the Murrin Bridge Mission, never to be seen again. Elaine Russell didn't begin her formal artistic career until 1993, at the age of 52, when she enrolled in the Certificate of Visual Arts course Eora Centre TAFE (Technical and Further Education) in Redfern, Sydney. That year, Russell also became a member of Boomalli Aboriginal Artists Cooperative, and participated in several group exhibitions. One of these was 'Narratives' in 1994, with the late Kerry Giles, Peta Lonsdale and Dr Pantitji Mary McLean, which highlighted common concerns within the diversity of practice and experience of contemporary Aboriginal women artists.

Russell's illustrative paintings of mission life, such as attending school and routine inspection days, are animated in her bold and colourful style. Working from an abundance of rich memories and experiences, in common with artists such as H. J. Wedge, Ian Abdulla and Robert Campbell Jnr, Russell depicts the human reality of the suppressive conditions on the mission. She has stated that she '... just paint[s] about her childhood, rations, bush food, how we lived.'[1]

In 2000 ABC Books published Russell's *A is for Aunty*, an alphabetical account of mission life for children. It encourages literacy and an awareness of Aboriginal history in the younger generation, Russell's target audience. She communicates the injustices of the colonial era and the segregation of Indigenous people on missions in a non-confronting way.

Elaine Russell portrays many social issues that might otherwise be avoided, or even whitewashed, acting as a catalyst for crossing cultural barriers. JJ

above **Inspection day** 1994
synthetic polymer paint on cardboard
73.5 x 99.9 cm

below **Lachlan River, our childhood dreams** 1994
synthetic polymer paint on cardboard
73.2 x 99.9 cm

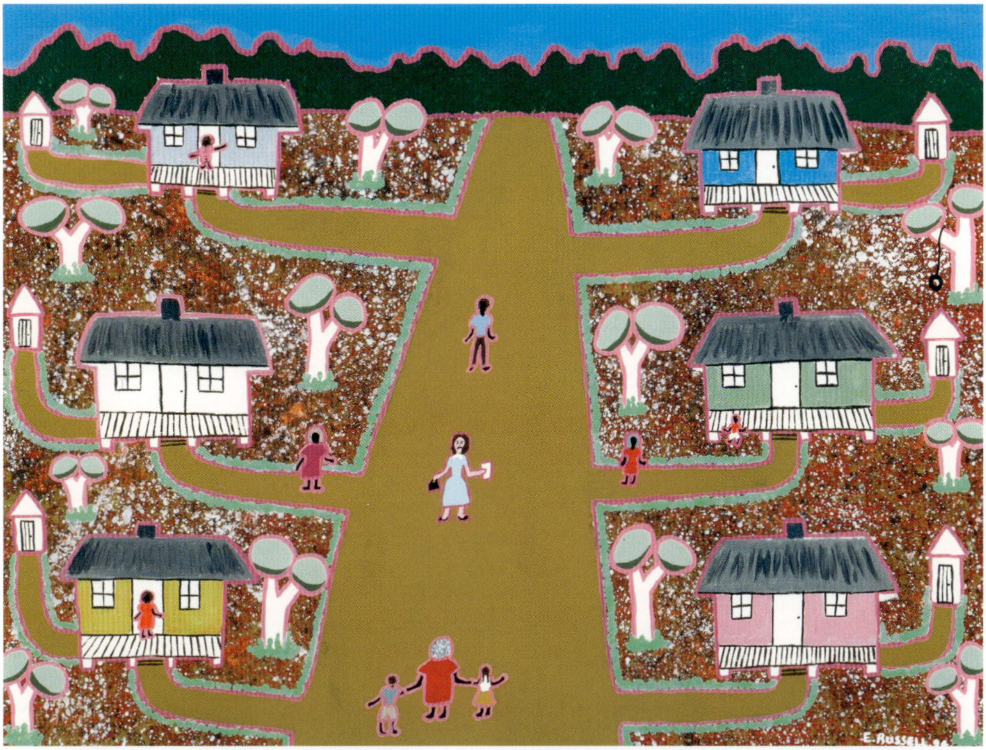
E. RUSSELL.94

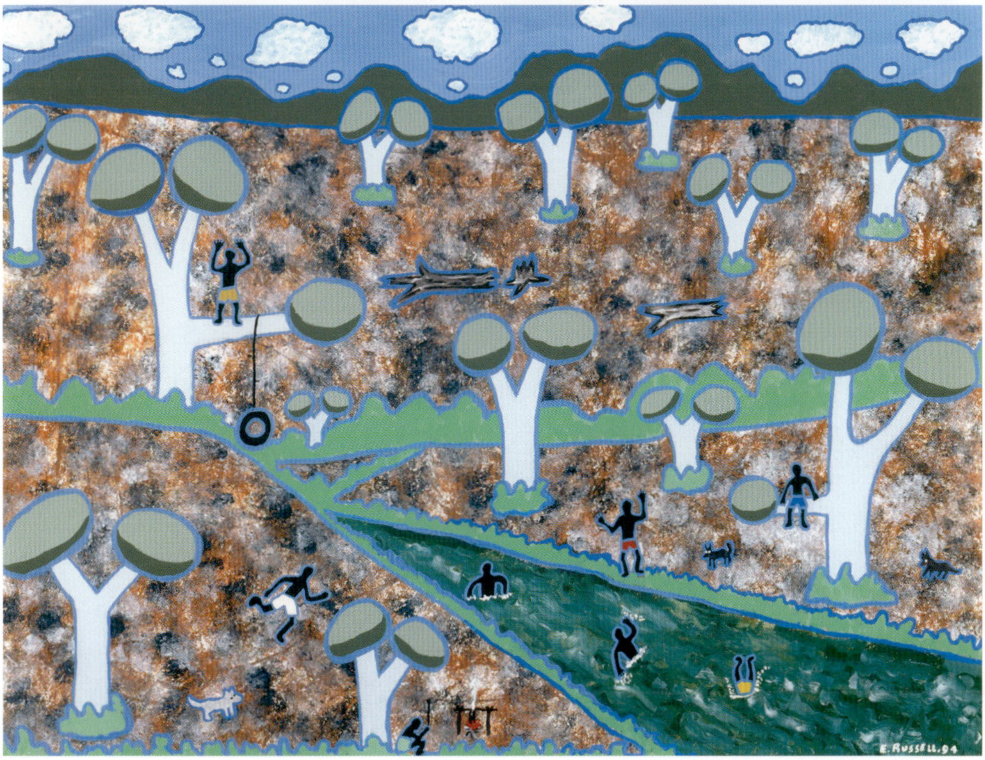
E. RUSSELL.94

NYIRLPIRR SPIDER SNELL

BORN c.1925
WANGKAJUNGA
WESTERN AUSTRALIA

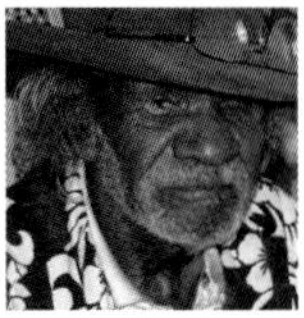

A Wangkajunga ceremonial leader, dancer and visual artist, Nyirlpirr Spider Snell is one of the few remaining elders born at Yurramaral, an important permanent waterhole on the south-eastern side of the Canning Stock Route in the Great Sandy Desert. As a young man, Spider developed skills as a stockman, handling horses and cattle on Christmas Creek Station. His true apprenticeship began before that, however, when three senior men taught him the key dance ceremonies that he still performs today. In 1998, Spider danced on the *Ngurrara canvas* in Canberra. This giant painting resulted from the collaboration of 50 artists and claimants over two weeks, and was made in support of the Ngurrara group's Native Title claim.

As a key custodian, Spider communicates with his ancestors through Kurtal, the Snake Spirit, who lives in a sacred water-hole. In the old days, this jila (spring) provided the only reliable source of water in all seasons. Water in the desert means life, and Kurtal is a 'living water' as well as the moral protector of land-use rights for the people in the area.

Kurtal is present, living in the water. Kurtal's story cycle includes his journey as a man, travelling south-west and south-east through the region. Kurtal and other ancestors moved all through the desert country, coming to rest in a number of different key sites. Through ceremony and song, the Wangkajunga elders make rain by interacting with Kurtal.

The acrylic painting, *Kurtal*, 1996, is a self-portrait of Spider dancing the Kurtal ceremony. The figure wears the long black rain cloud called kutukutu as a headdress, accompanied by other black clouds outlined in white and red. These wilarn (horse-shoe shaped clouds) can appear in a clear blue sky to signal the approach of rain. The kutukutu is the first rain that follows the wilarn, and can be a fierce rainstorm. Works by Spider's brother, the late Jarinyanu David Downs, also depict this subject matter.

Spider makes kutukutu headdresses for performances from human hair, grass string and wool. Over the last few years, he has been passing on his knowledge of these important dances to his grandchildren. GA

Kurtal 1996
synthetic polymer paint on paper
74.5 x 105 cm

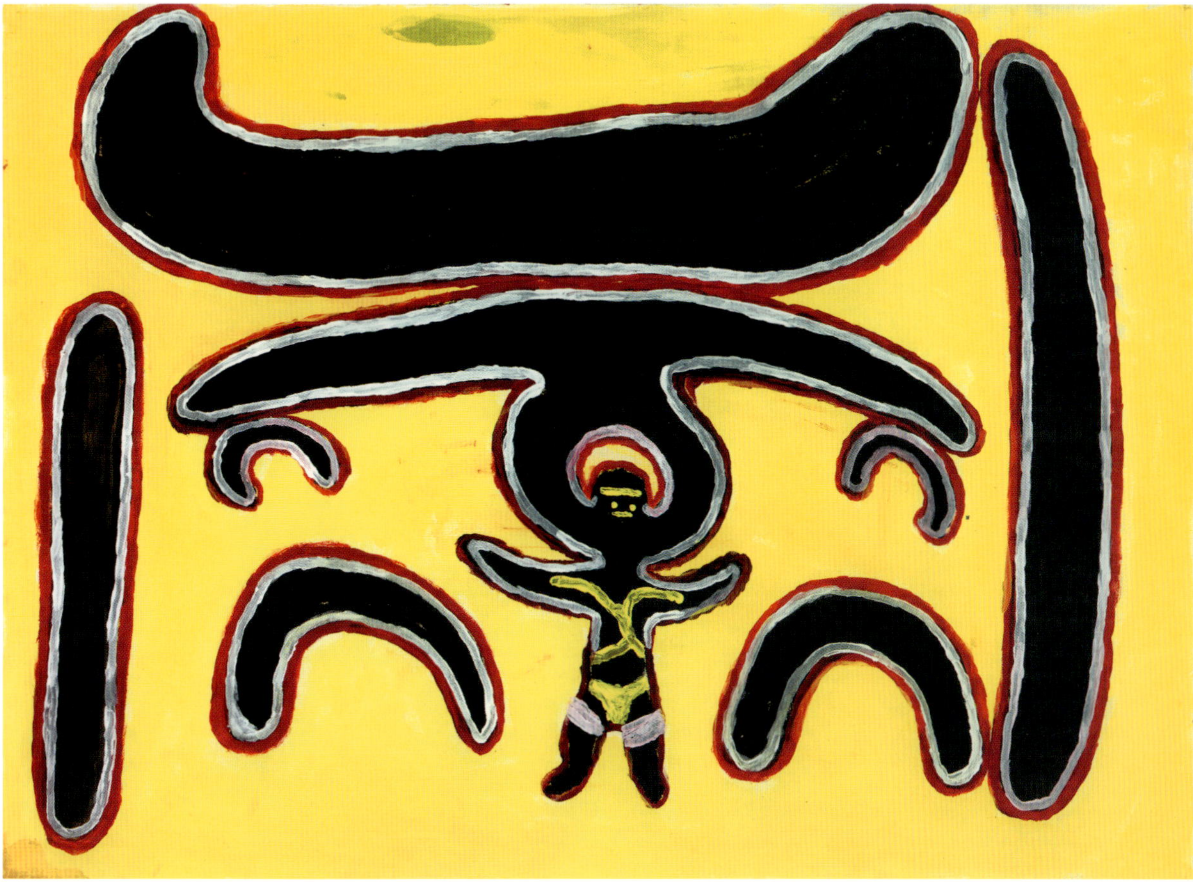

KEN THAIDAY

BORN 1950
MERIAM MIR
TORRES STRAIT ISLANDS

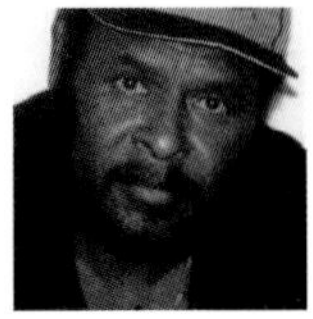

The Torres Strait Islands are situated between Cape York in Queensland and Papua New Guinea. Ken Thaiday was born on Erub (Darnley Island), in the eastern group of the Islands. Thaiday's childhood on Erub involved fishing for crayfish, coral trout and mackerel, tending gardens of sweet potatoes, cassava and sugar cane, and participating in ceremonial performances at weddings, feasts and tombstone unveilings. Like many Islanders, Thaiday's family settled in Cairns on the mainland when he was a teenager. His father, Tat, was an important dancer, and as a young man Ken Thaiday attended dance ceremonies and made drawings and paintings that were the foundation of his later masks, headdresses, and hand-held 'dance machines'.

In 1987, Thaiday began constructing dance artefacts for the Darnley Island Dance Troupe. These 'mobilised artefacts', as he calls them, are used in ceremonial performances, and connect with Islander traditions and clan identity. Each island group has its own performances, and although using modern materials (e.g. plastic piping and enamel paint) these objects are used as they were in the past. Some are percussion instruments that feature the sun and evening stars rising and falling, or hibiscus plants opening and closing, or large wooden fish with painted scenes of island life that switch from day to night at the turn of a handle.

Thaiday's best known works are his hammerhead shark dance headdresses. These objects extend high above the dancer's head and down to the upper chest. They are made of wire, plastic, plywood and strips of black bamboo, and are decorated with a ruff of white feathers that represents the foam breaking as the shark surfaces. Animated by the dancer pulling on strings, the jaws of the shark-effigy snap open and shut, as if swimming in search of food. The gyrating dancers in the shark headdresses are an impressive and menacing sight. Torres Strait Islanders have a maritime salt water culture, and the shark is an important totem. Not only is the shark a food source, but it is also a symbol of law and order.

In constructing these objects, Thaiday is contributing to the ongoing cohesiveness and strength of Islander culture. They have a pivotal role in ceremonial life, especially in sacred performances that reach back to the Malu-Bomai spirituality of pre-colonial times, and reaffirm Islander culture's benign relationship with the supernatural. GA

Beizam (shark) dance mask 1996
plywood, black bamboo, string, plastic, paint, glass, feathers
86.7 x 106 x 71 cm

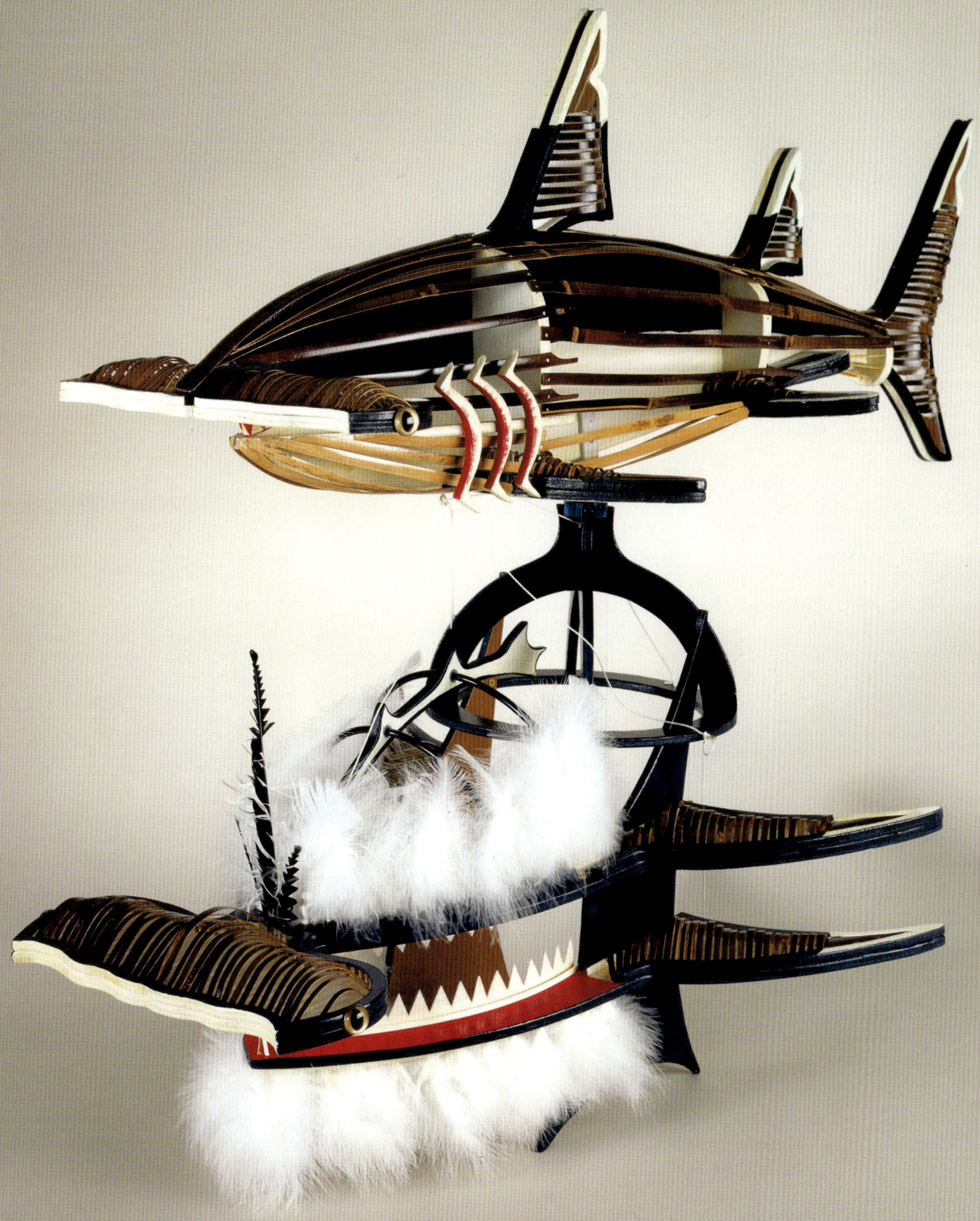

THANCOUPIE

BORN 1937
THANAQUITH
QUEENSLAND

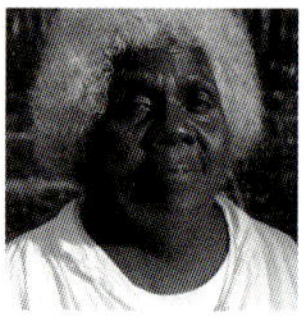

In 1971, after beginning her artistic career as a painter, Thancoupie travelled south from her coastal home in Napranum (Weipa), in far north Queensland, to study ceramics at East Sydney Technical College in Sydney. Thancoupie grew up at the Presbyterian Napranum Mission, where she experienced the use of clay in a ceremonial context. The opportunity to handle clay inspired her to complete her studies. Thancoupie is now Australia's foremost Aboriginal ceramicist, with a professional career spanning more than 30 years.

Thancoupie's strong Thanaquith background ensured a childhood rich in traditional customs, but many years of Christian influence and well-meaning but destructive assimilation policies had a significant impact on the continuation of Thanaquith culture. As a student, Thancoupie returned often to Napranum to learn of her ancestral histories from the old people of the community, with a view to preserving their stories through the design and decoration of her bold, sculptural forms.

During these years, Thancoupie designed a set of unique visual symbols and totemic characters that she continues to use to this day. The duality of the human and the natural world is integral to Aboriginal culture and ceremonial custom. Many of Thancoupie's characters are anthropomorphic, with creatures of the natural world showing human characteristics. She has translated her community's stories into a series of visual images, and decorates her stoneware with these narratives. Thancoupie refers to the end results as 'story pots'. These objects – both in their physical creation from earth, air, water and fire, and in their finished form as spherical story pots – embody the artist's relationship with her land, her culture and the natural world.

Thancoupie was one of the first generation of Aboriginal artists to explore art making in an academic environment, far from her people and home. She has created public art murals that can be seen in Brisbane, Sydney and Melbourne, as well as those executed when she was an artist-in-residence in Edmonton, Canada and Colorado, United States. Thancoupie features in many documentaries and has shown at scores of exhibitions nationally and internationally as a solo artist. Her life and work was the subject of a monograph published in 1982. In the early 1980s, she relocated from Sydney to Cairns, Queensland, where she produces ceramics from her base at Trinity Beach, continuing her work as an artist actively committed to the preservation of her distinct cultural heritage. NB

> **Cammbel and Paour exchange teeth** 1994
stoneware
27 x 24 cm

v left **Mosquito corroboree, two by two** 1994
stoneware
27 x 32 cm

v right **Mosquito corroboree** 1994
stoneware
32.4 x 34 cm

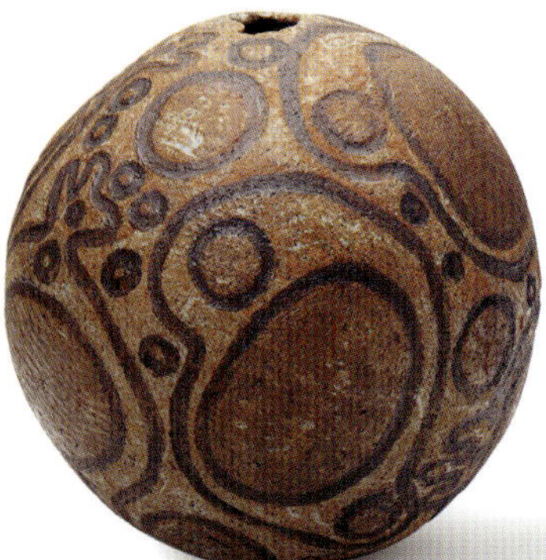

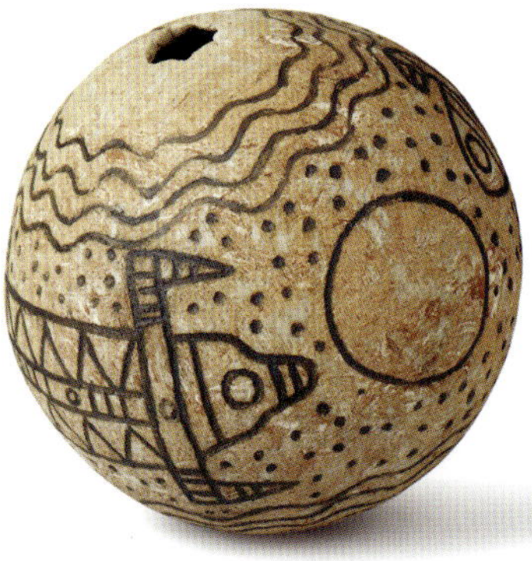

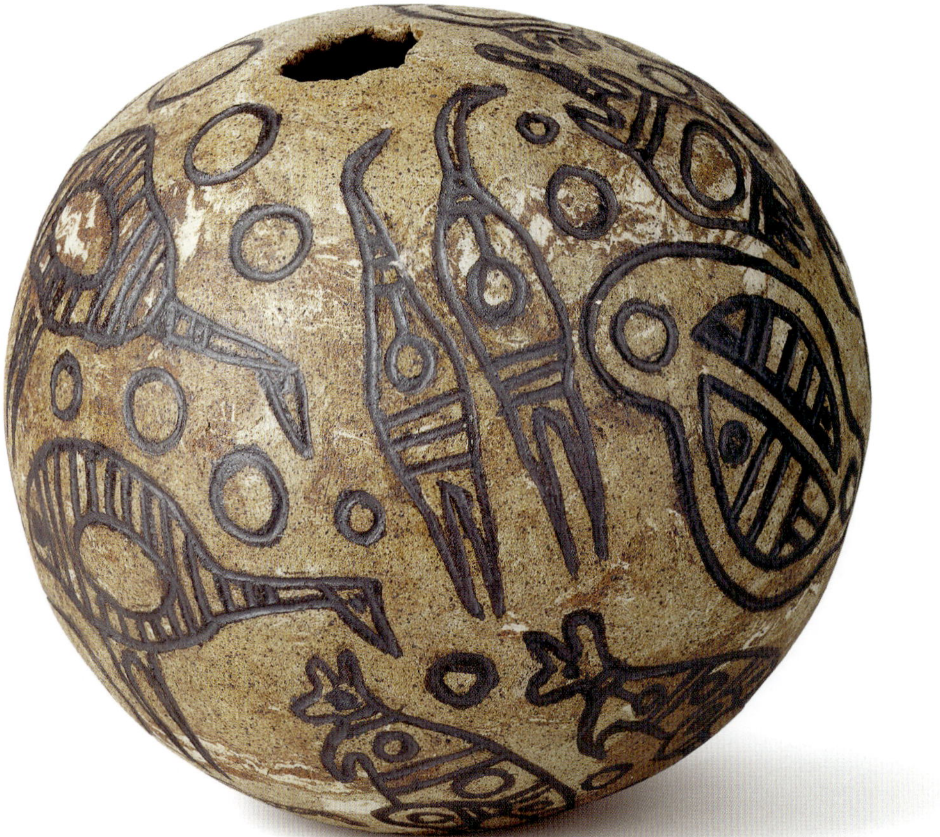

ROVER THOMAS

1926–1998
KUKATJA / WANGKAJUNGA
WESTERN AUSTRALIA

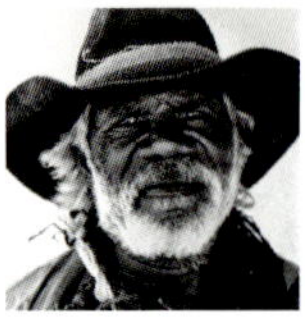

In late 1974, an elderly woman died on her way to hospital, following a car accident on the flooded road to Warmun (Turkey Creek), an Aboriginal community in the East Kimberley. After her death, the old woman travelled eastwards from the west coast of northern Australia. During her journey home, she met other spirit beings. She also witnessed the destruction of Darwin by Cyclone Tracey, understood to be the retributive act of the Rainbow Serpent, warning against the decline of Indigenous cultural practices. In a sequence of dream visitations, the old woman revealed her story to Thomas (who was her son, according to the regional Aboriginal kin system).

Thomas's revelation was the catalyst for the Gurirr Gurirr, a ceremony that recounted historic and contemporary events and associated sites throughout the East Kimberley. During public performances, dancers carried painted boards on their shoulders to illustrate the narrative. Today, the artists of Warmun still refer to their paintings on canvas as boards. Like Thomas and his pioneering fellow artists, the late Paddy Jaminji, George Mung Mung and Queenie McKenzie, contemporary Gija painters use locally mined ochres.

The afterlife journey of the old woman and its subsequent cultural interpretation may be understood as a metaphor for the conceptual logic that underpins much Aboriginal art. Nowhere has the merging of past and present, the spiritual and the physical, been more clearly realised than in Thomas's visionary paintings. His landscapes are corporeal, vacillating between figuration and abstraction to suggest the topography of the East Kimberley and the presence of unseen forces within it. In *Undubhill*, 1991, the route of the Great Northern highway passes by a Ngarrankarni shade tree. In Thomas's tour de force painting, *Two men dreaming*, c.1985, the form of an old ancestral man, turned to stone, is accentuated by the gleam of the rising moon. In 1994, the National Gallery of Australia, Canberra, staged a solo exhibition of Rover Thomas's work.

Although his paintings are now considered synonymous with East Kimberley art, his origins lie further to the south in the Great Sandy Desert, from where he travelled working as a stockman. His paintings have demonstrated the ability of art to not only transcend Indigenous cultural borders, but to also become a source of revelation for an international audience. This significance was not lost on Thomas, whose sighting of a Mark Rothko painting caused him to famously remark, 'That bugger paints like me!' HP

> **Two men dreaming** c.1985
natural pigments on canvas board
91 x 61 cm

v **Undubhill** 1991
natural pigments and bush gum on canvas
60 x 100 cm

> overleaf left **Country called Red Butte** 1984
natural pigments and bush gum on plywood
91 x 181 cm

> overleaf right **Untitled** 1984
natural pigments and bush gum on plywood
91 x 181 cm

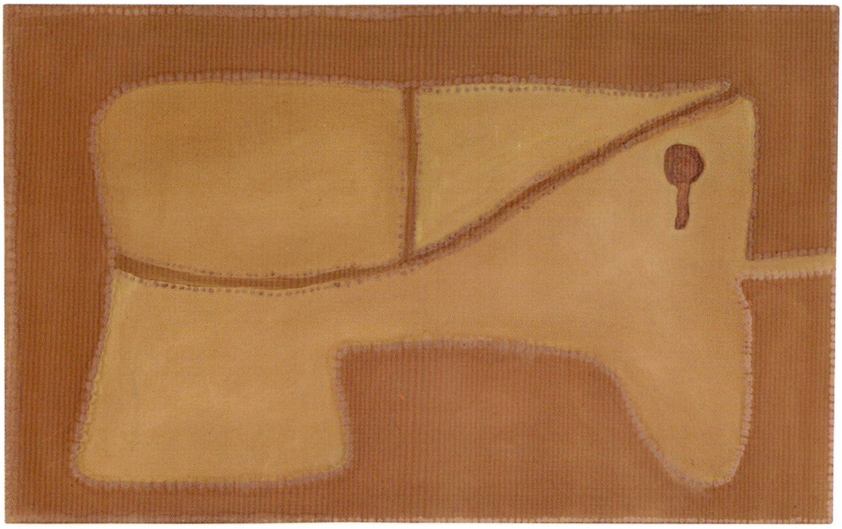

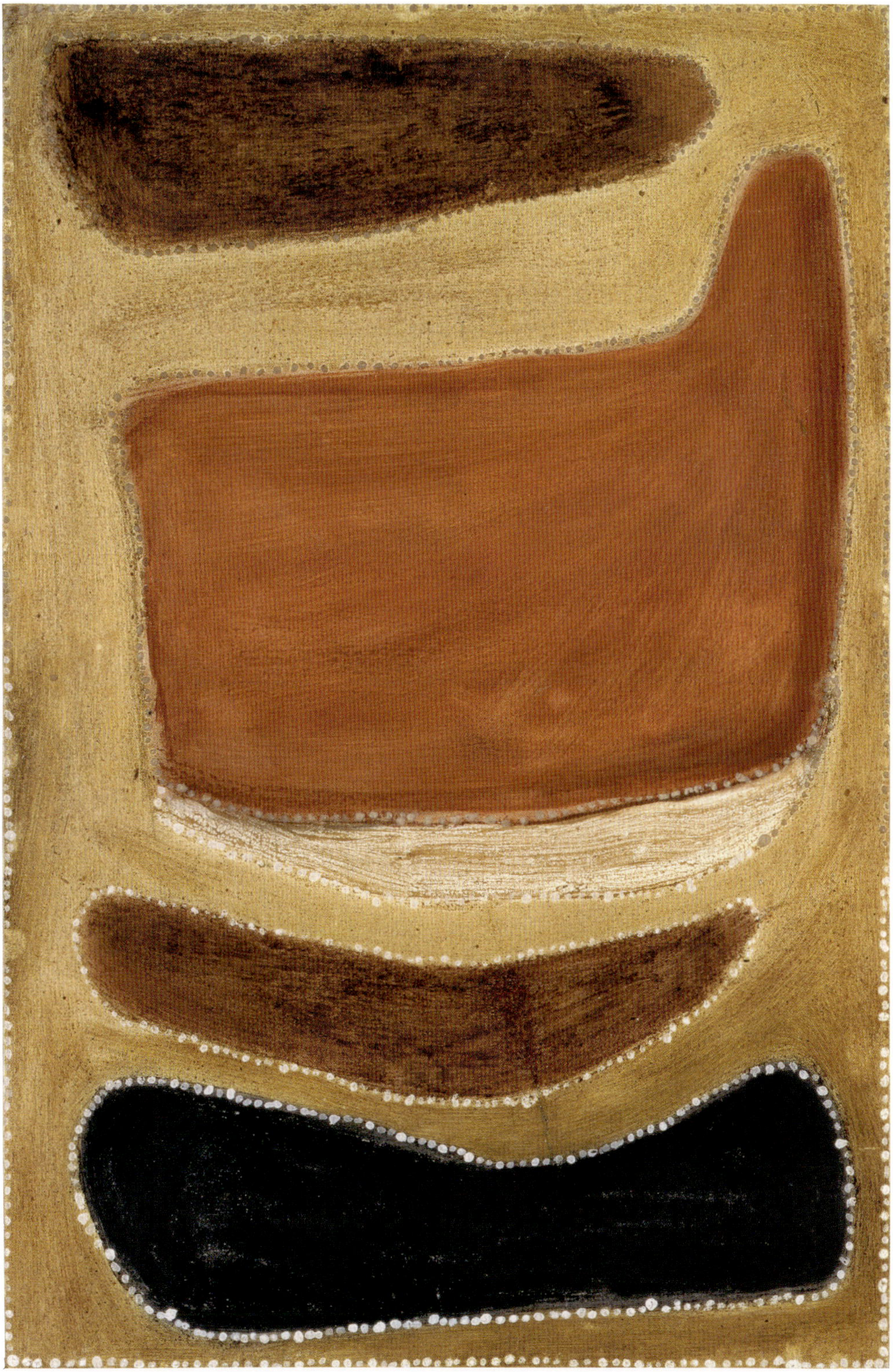

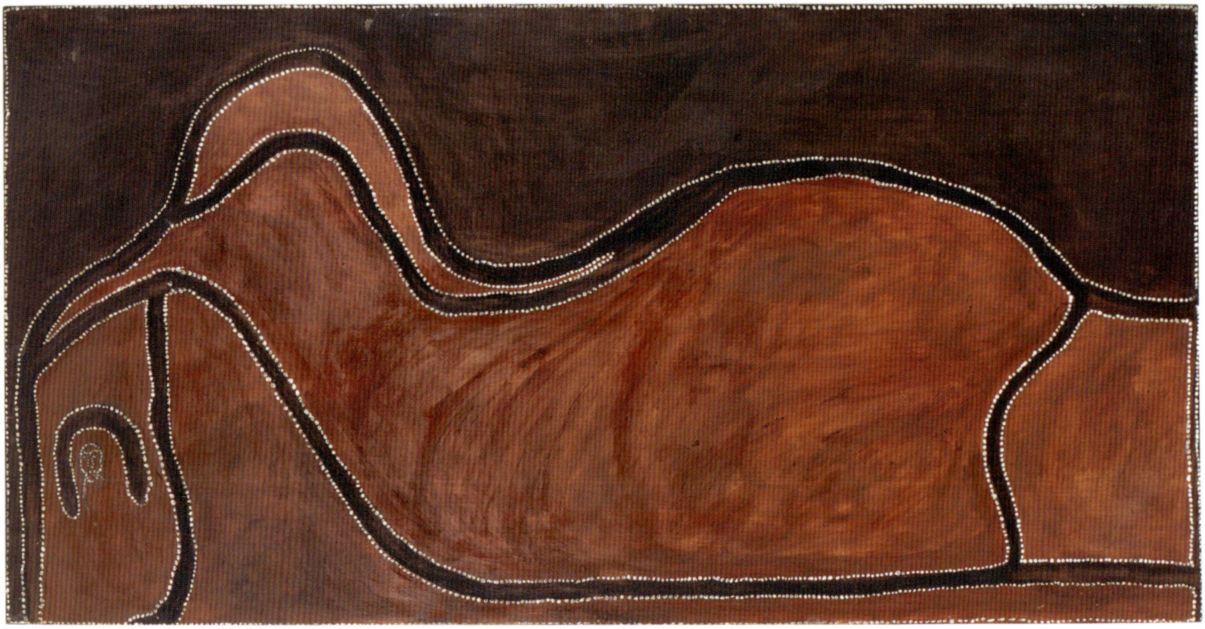

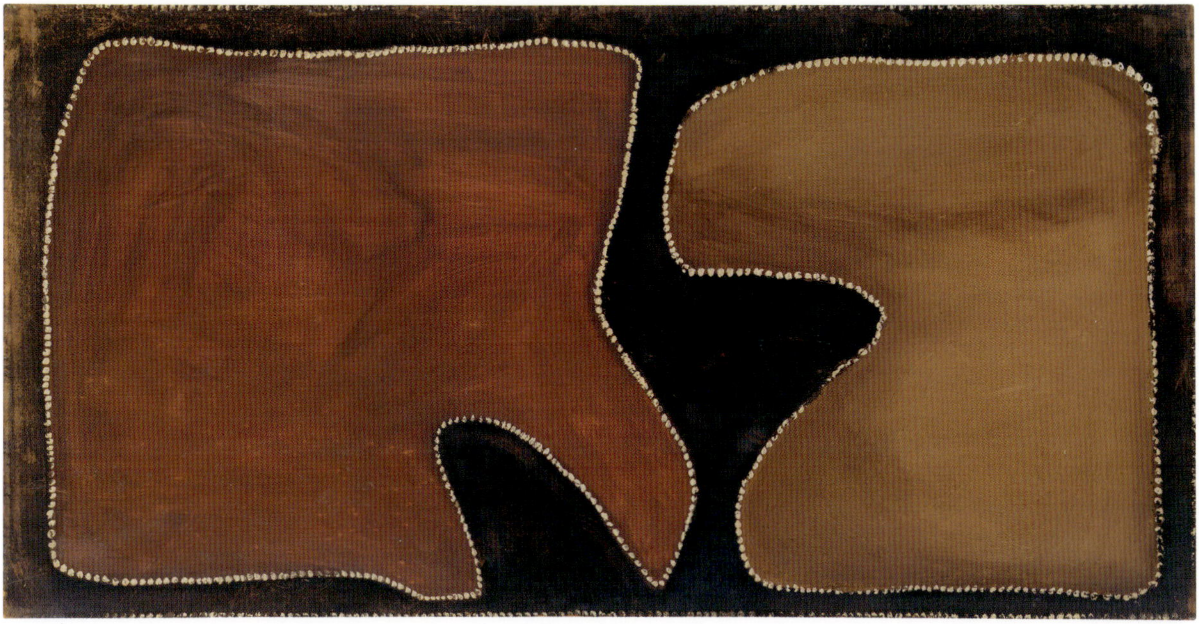

TIMMY TIMMS

c.1915–2000
GIJA
WESTERN AUSTRALIA

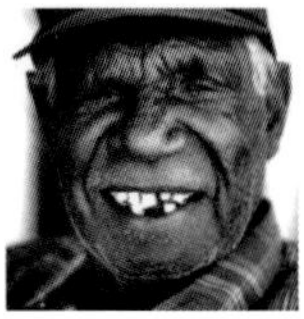

One of the most important keepers of Aboriginal law and culture among the Gija people, Timmy Timms came to painting very late in life, in the year 2000. He died having only created a handful of dramatic canvases that stand as a remarkable testament to his deep knowledge of and feeling for his culture and his country. In his art, as in his life, Timms's primary goal was to pass on to the younger generation his extensive knowledge of the Ngarrangkarni, ceremonies and history of his country. He was also an accomplished singer and dancer of several important forms of joonba (song and dance performances).

However, in one of his most dramatic works, *Bedford Downs massacre*, 2000, Timms does not portray the ancient stories of the Gija, but focuses on an incident from the violent early days of contact between the Aboriginal peoples of the East Kimberley and white settlers. With its spare, sinuous lines and large areas of ochre, the canvas reveals the site where a group of Gija people were massacred, sometime around 1924.

The men had been convicted by a local court of killing a bullock on Bedford Downs Station, and were sent back to the station with 'tickets' hung around their necks as a sign to the station owner that they were guilty. Some of the men discarded these tickets before they got back, but others chose to keep them. On their return, those who still had their tickets were taken to a remote location and told to chop wood. After a morning's work, the men were given a meal and told to eat quickly – the food was heavily poisoned with strychnine and all those who ate it died painful deaths. Their bodies were then burned with the wood they had chopped that morning. Two men, however, had refused to eat and made their escape. These two, along with two women who had followed the party and also witnessed the killings, returned to tell the story to their people.

Passed down through the generations both as oral narrative and in the form of a joonba, Timms relates the story of the Bedford Downs massacre, in visual form, to record this tragic event both for the Gija people and wider audiences. The joonba was recently staged as the performance *Fire Fire Burning Bright* at the Melbourne and Perth Festivals. EK

Bedford Downs massacre 2000
natural pigments on canvas
150 x 180 cm

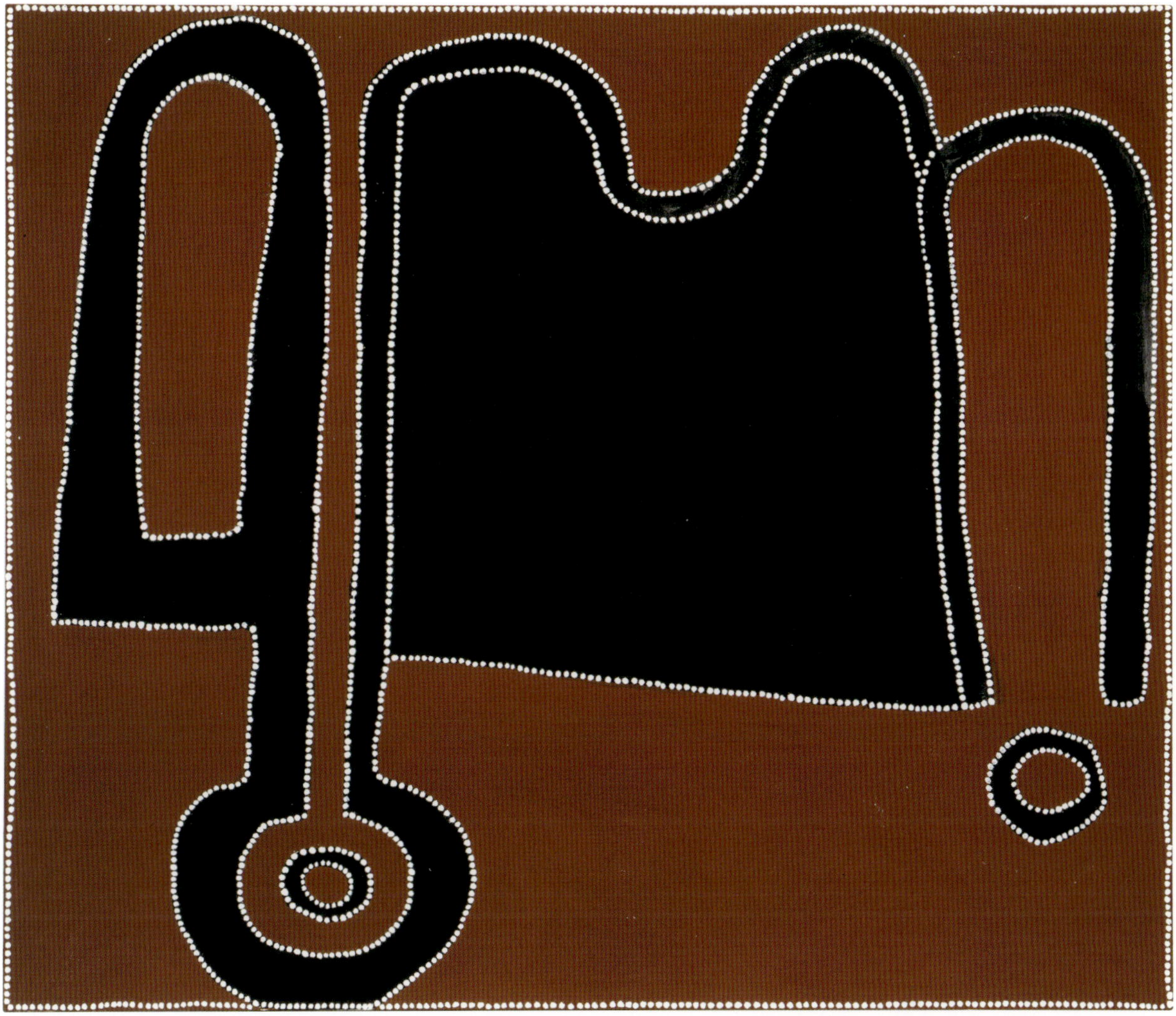

RONNIE TJAMPITJINPA

BORN c.1942
PINTUPI
NORTHERN TERRITORY / WESTERN AUSTRALIA

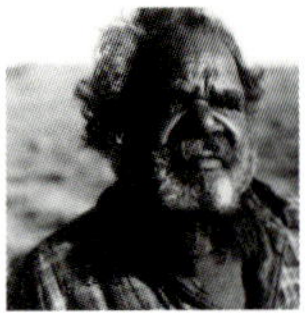

Ronnie Tjampitjinpa was born in Pintupi land at Muyinnga, about 100 kilometres west of the Kintore Range, just across the Western Australian border. He is the son of Uta Uta Tjangala's older brother, Minpuru Tjangala (c.1899–1976).

After his initiation into Pintupi law at the site of Yumari, Tjampitjinpa and his younger brother Smithy Zimran Tjampitjinpa walked into the Aboriginal community of Yuendumu. They later joined their parents and other siblings – who had come in to Ikuntji (Haasts Bluff) in 1956 from the Dover Hills/Yumari area – at the new settlement of Papunya. Tjampitjinpa worked as a labourer, assisting with the fencing of the aerodromes at Papunya and Ikuntji. He was one of the youngest of the group of men who began painting at the start of the Western Desert art movement in 1971, and was a founder of Paunya Tula Artists.

During the 1970s, Tjampitjinpa was preoccupied with returning to his traditional lands and became a strong advocate for the outstation movement, travelling between meetings in Papunya, Yuendumu, Wirrimanu (Balgo) and Mount Doreen Station. His goal was finally achieved with the establishment of the Walungurru (Kintore) settlement in 1981. Tjampitjinpa moved there with his young family in 1983, establishing an outstation at Ininti (Redbank) and serving as chairman of the Kintore Outstation Council. During this period, he emerged as one of Papunya Tula Artists' major painters, pioneering the bold, scaled-up, linear style that came to dominate many of the Walungurru painters' work during the 1990s. His distinctive aesthetic preoccupation is exemplified in the untitled works of 1994 and 2001. Now one of the last founding members of Papunya Tula Artists, Tjampitjinpa's career spans more than 30 years. He has had six solo exhibitions since 1989 in Australia, most recently at Utopia Art, Sydney.

Throughout the 1980s Tjampitjinpa worked devotedly on a land claim for Ininti, holding meetings in Darwin, Warmun (Turkey Creek), Utopia and many other places before finally abandoning political involvement as ' ... too much humbug for too long'.[1] Tjampitjinpa now wants ' ... to settle down and work for myself, just painting',[2] and resides on his outstation when not at Walungurru or in Mparntwe (Alice Springs). VJ

> **Untitled** 2001
synthetic polymer paint on canvas
183 x 244 cm

v **Untitled** 1994
synthetic polymer paint on canvas
183 x 152 cm

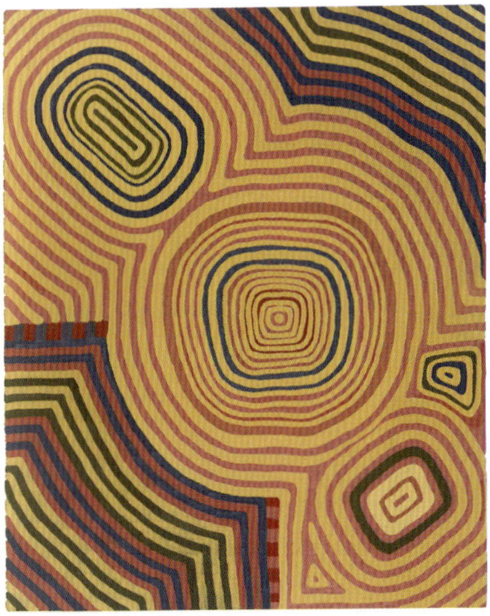

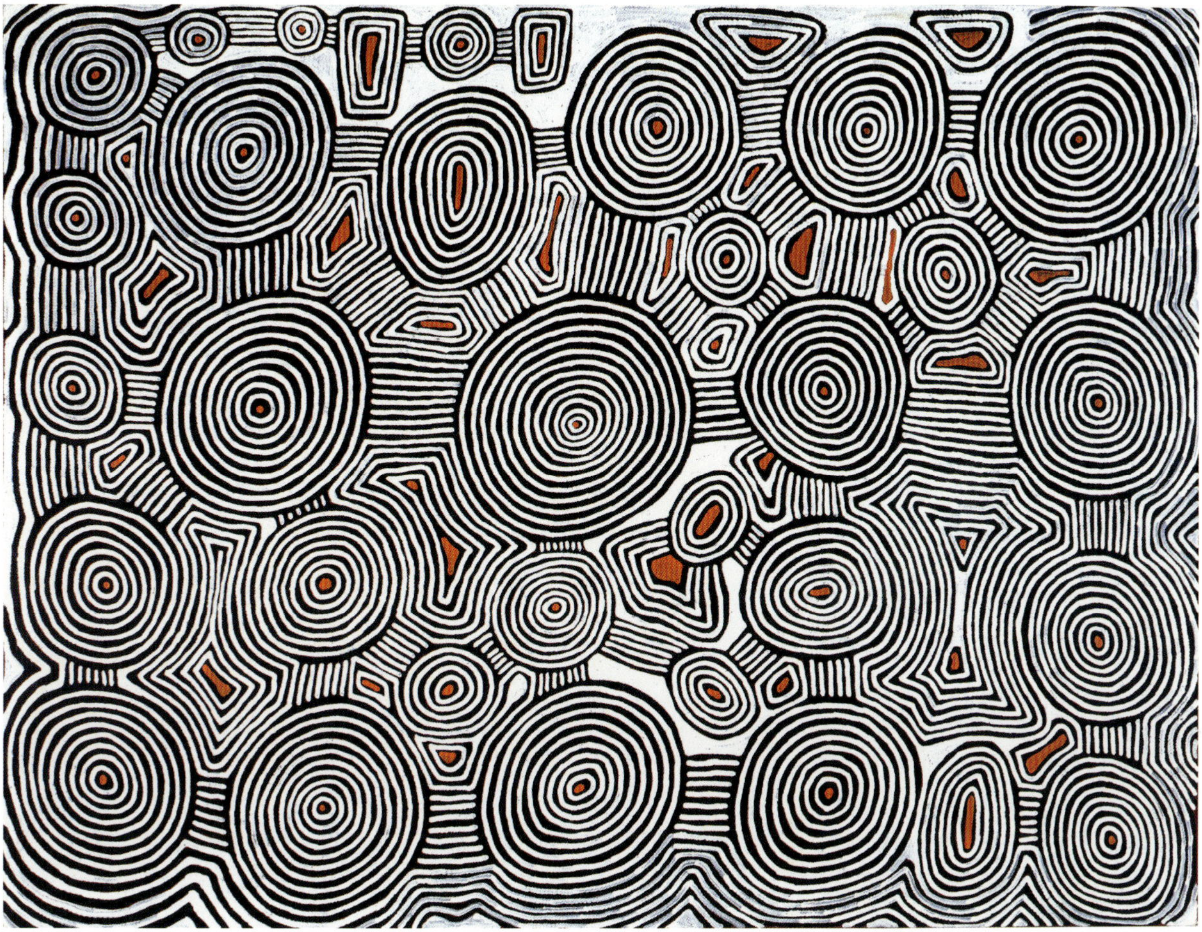

UTA UTA TJANGALA

c.1926–1990
PINTUPI
NORTHERN TERRITORY / WESTERN AUSTRALIA

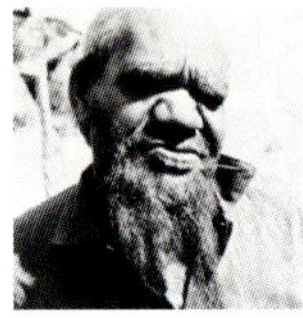

In the late 1950s, Uta Uta Tjangala led his family to Ikuntji (Haasts Bluff). It was his first contact with white people. He was later to move to the nearby government settlement of Papunya where, in 1971, he became one of the founding members of the Western Desert painting movement.

Uta Uta's work is characterised by its explosive energy, in which symbolic elements appear restlessly on the surface of the painting. His paintings pulse with heroic energy and rarely sit comfortably within the confines of a rectangular format. He was one of the most formidable and important of the Papunya Tula artists, with the capacity to tap the raw energy of the Tjukurrpa and give it visual form. Uta Uta was central to the establishment of the first phase painting at Papunya, when vivid representations of ceremonial details were laid down on hardboard. He was also an important innovator in the rapid stylisation of Pintupi painting in the second phase of its development (during 1972–75), and was one of the artists who established the conventions of Pintupi painting. He was, paradoxically, also the artist who pushed hardest at the boundaries of those conventions, disrupting a formal reading of his painting with incursions of idiosyncratic visual elements or vibrant, 'non-traditional' colours.

The inspiration for much of Uta Uta's work was the ancestral story of the illicit coupling of an old man and his mother-in-law at Yumari. The standing stones and trench-like rockholes at the site reappear in his paintings as bold Freudian iconography, and provide an exciting narrative quality to his work.

Uta Uta travelled widely in the late 1970s, visiting Aboriginal communities on the fringes of the Western Desert to advocate the mobilisation of desert people back to their homelands. In the mid-1980s he established an outstation at Muyin, in his traditional country.

Two of his monumental canvases, *Yumari*, 1981 and *Old Man at Yumari*, 1983, were exhibited together in 'Dreamings: Art of Aboriginal Australia' at the Asia Society Galleries, New York in 1988; this exhibition was seminal in gaining international recognition of Aboriginal art. Uta Uta's stature as a major artist was matched by his leadership in important social change amongst Aboriginal communities in the latter half of the twentieth century. Uta Uta Tjangala was a truly remarkable man whose best artwork provides a window to his passionate commitment to his culture, his country and his fierce engagement with life. JK

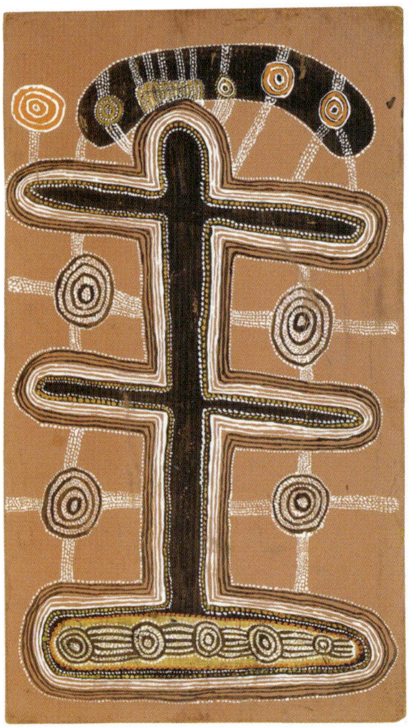

> **Untitled** 1972
synthetic polymer powder paint and natural pigments on hardboard
62.6 x 50.7 cm

v **Untitled** c.1971
synthetic polymer paint on hardboard
60.5 x 35 cm

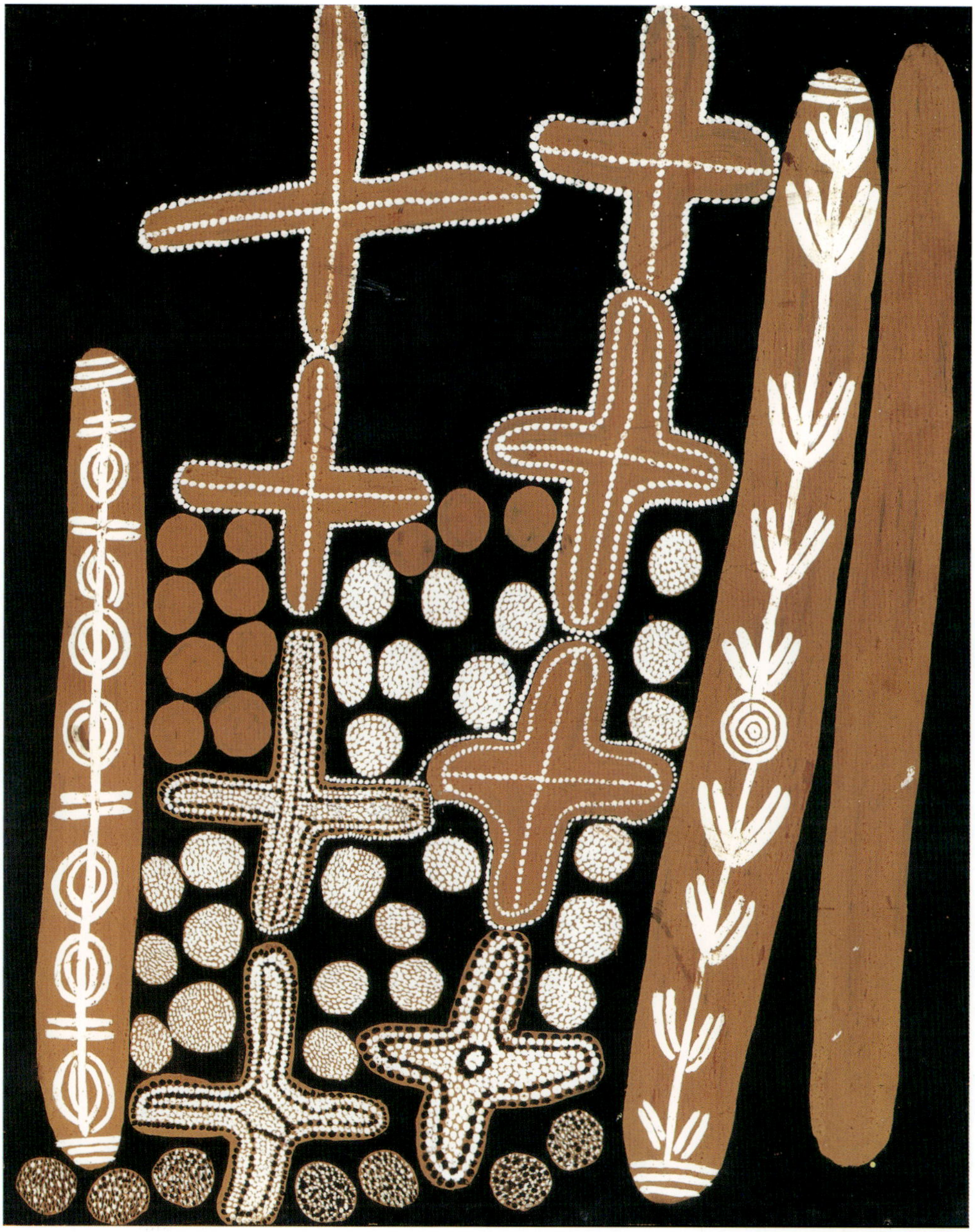

CLIFFORD POSSUM TJAPALTJARRI

c.1932–2002
ANMATYERR
NORTHERN TERRITORY

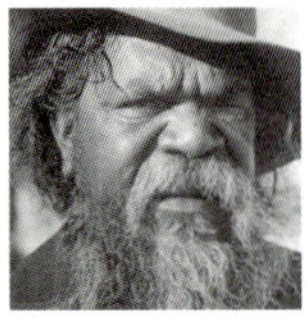

Clifford Possum Tjapaltjarri was born on Napperby Station about 200 kilometres north-west of Mparntwe (Alice Springs). Like many other Anmatyerr people, his family moved to the east region of their country following the Coniston Massacre of the mid-1920s. Tjapaltjarri's mother also raised Billy Stockman Tjapaltjarri, whose own mother was a victim of the massacre. Clifford Possum Tjapaltjarri started his working life at diverse stations across Central Australia, where he acquired his impressive linguistic repertoire of six Western Desert languages, including his native Anmatyerr, and a 'little bit English'.[1] He refined his skill as a woodcarver while continuing to work as a stockman.

Tjapaltjarri joined Papunya Tula Artists in February 1972 and was one of their founding directors. He rapidly distinguished himself as one of the company's most accomplished and inventive artists, an exponent of striking, multi-layered and meticulously rendered visual effects. He was chosen by Papunya Tula Artists to paint, with his brother Tim Leura Tjapaltjarri, the large canvas that became *Warlugulong*, 1976, for a BBC documentary, *Desert Dreamers*. The painting exceeded in size and narrative complexity anything hitherto produced by the Papunya painters. Its striking central fireburst depicts the Fire Dreaming site where Clifford Possum Tjapaltjarri's mother, Long Rose Nangala, was born. *Warlugulong* was one of the high points in the two brothers' artistic collaboration over the years, and also the first in Clifford Possum Tjapaltjarri's renowned series of monumental canvases of the late 1970s, which have been likened to vast encyclopedic 'maps' of his Tjukurrpa country.

Tjapaltjarri was chairperson of Papunya Tula Artists during the early 1980s. In 1988, the Institute of Contemporary Art in London organised a retrospective – it was Tjapaltjarri's first solo exhibition and the first time an Australian Aboriginal artist had been honoured in this way by the international art world. Over the next decade he would become the most widely travelled Aboriginal artist of his generation and an ambassador for Aboriginal art around the world.

In 2002 Clifford Possum Tjapaltjarri was appointed an Officer of the Order of Australia ' ... for service as a contributor to and pioneer of the development of the Western Desert art movement, and to the Indigenous community through interpretation of ancient traditions and cultural values.' VJ

> Clifford Possum Tjapaltjarri
& Tim Leura Tjapaltjarri
Warlugulong 1976
synthetic polymer paint on canvas
168.5 x 170.5 cm

v **Lungkata's two sons at Warlugulong** 1976
synthetic polymer paint on canvas board
70.5 x 55 cm

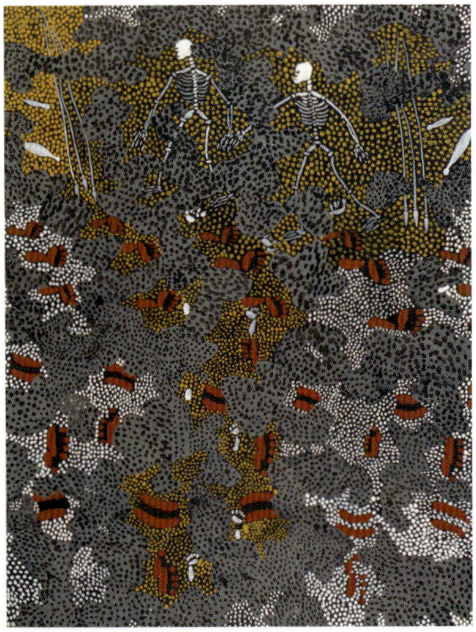

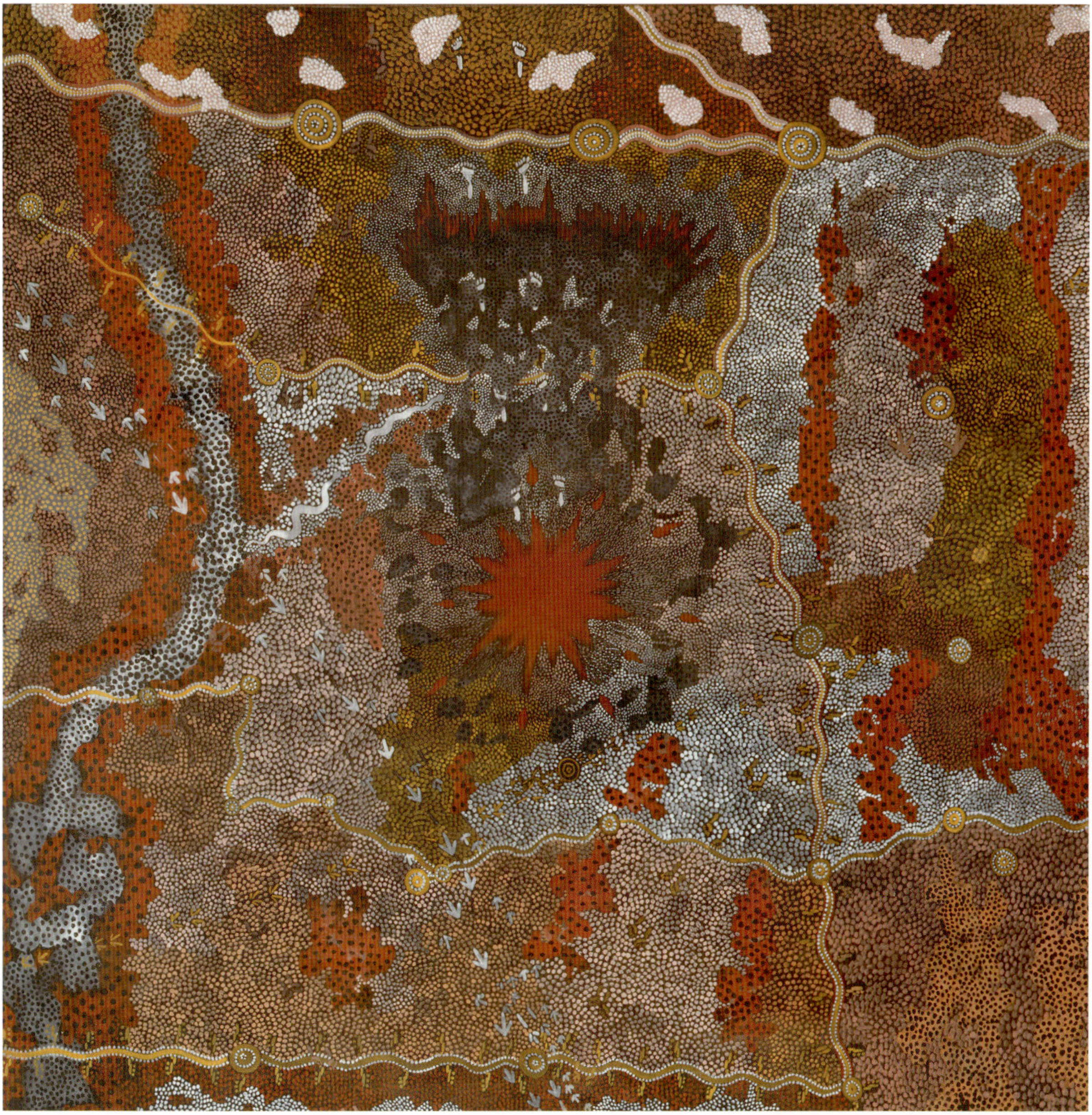

MICK NAMARARI TJAPALTJARRI

c.1926–1998
PINTUPI
NORTHERN TERRITORY

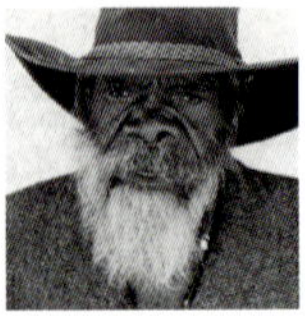

Mick Namarari Tjapaltjarri was one of the founding artists at Papunya in 1971. As a boy, following the death by spearing of his father and his mother's resulting suicide, he fled the desert, east to the safety of the Lutheran Hermannsburg Mission. Here he would have been aware of Albert Namatjira and his fellow Western Aranda landscape painters. While still a young man, Namarari worked on cattle stations and became familiar with non-Aboriginal people, such as 'Billy the Bunyip' MacNamara, from whom he took his (Aboriginalised) name, 'Namarari'. These life experiences, together with the observational skill associated with his extraordinary bushmanship, prepared him for his second career as an artist.

Namarari was a quiet and relatively inconspicuous character, often overshadowed by the more showy and dominant artists at Papunya. However, he painted assiduously for more than 25 years, building an oeuvre that is characterised by lightness of line and subtlety of tone. While many of his peers painted according to stylised conventions, Namarari's work is distinguished by an extraordinary range of visual inventions. In his first couple of years of painting, he explored figuration, giving the same weight to his depiction of ceremonial performers as to details of the ceremonial ground paintings and associated sacred objects. During the same period he created hypnotic depictions of his birthplace, Marnpi, using white pulsing lines to draw the eye into the vortex of an ancestral wind at the site. From the mid-1970s, he occasionally explored minimal representation, focusing on one tiny aspect of the activities of an ancestor; surprisingly, he would then change resolution in the next work, describing the topography of a much larger area. Despite his apparent reserve, the breadth and scope of his inventions over such a long period make him the most consistently brilliant of the Papunya Tula artists.

Namarari's paintings – *Untitled (Dingo dreaming at Nyunmanu)*, 1997, and *Untitled (Tjunginpa mouse dreaming)*, 1998 – were both created at the climax of his career, and depict in turn a detail of the ancestral activities of the Dingo and the Tjunginpa Tjukurrpa to create mesmerising visual rhythms. Both works exhibit Namarari's clarity of artistic conception and consistency of application, aspects of his work that have remained constant throughout his career and enabled him to continually improvise and expand his repertoire. JK

> **Untitled (Tjunginpa mouse dreaming)** 1998
synthetic polymer paint on canvas
152 x 122 cm

v **Untitled (Dingo dreaming at Nyunmanu)** 1997
synthetic polymer paint on canvas
153 x 120.9 cm

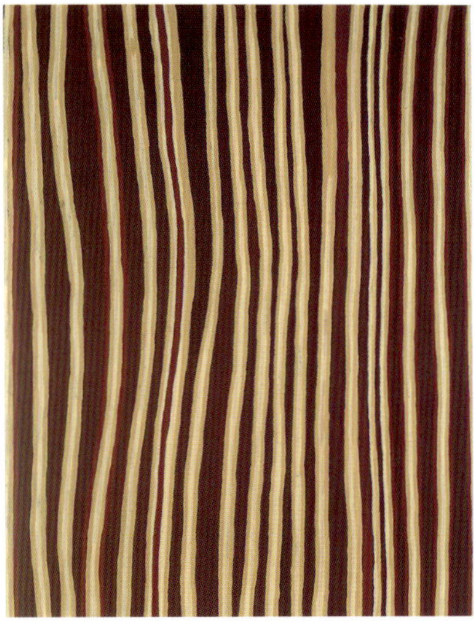

TIM LEURA TJAPALTJARRI

c.1929–1984
ANMATYERR
NORTHERN TERRITORY

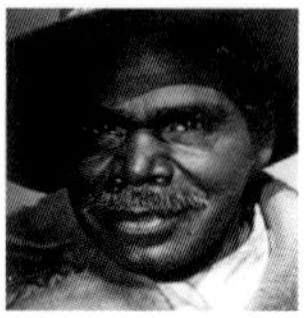

Tim Leura Tjapaltjarri was born in Napperby Creek and grew up around Napperby Station, around 200 kilometres north west of Mparntwe (Alice Springs), in his traditional Anmatyerr country. After working at Narwietooma Station as a stockman, he moved to Papunya in the late 1950s with his wife Daisy Leura Nakamarra and their young family, when the construction programme for the new settlement began.

Tjapaltjarri was already known in Central Australia as a brilliant craftsman in wood before the painting movement began in Papunya in 1971. He presented himself to schoolteacher Geoffrey Bardon and asked to do a painting. The two men became friends, and Tjapaltjarri went on to play a leading role in the emerging Papunya painting enterprise. Bardon recalls Tjapaltjarri encouraging his younger brother, Clifford Possum Tjapaltjarri (their mothers were sisters), to join the 'painting mob'. They went on to collaborate on some of the landmark paintings of the era, most notably the 1976 work, *Warlugulong*.

In the mid-1970s, Tim Leura Tjapaltjarri served on the Aboriginal Arts Board of the Australia Council as a Papunya Tula representative.

Bardon's book, *Papunya Tula: Art of the Western Desert*[1] contains a detailed map drawn by Tjapaltjarri. It shows his country and the sacred sites of the Rrpwamper (possum), Anek (yam), Rwang (fire), Lhwelk (blue-tongue lizard), Atwern (sun), Atay (moon) and Morning Star and other Tjukurrpa. Tjapaltjarri's paintings were often sombre in both colour and content, which some observers believe reflected the artist's profound sadness at the loss of the old ways of living. However, Dick Kimber, who knew Tjapaltjarri over a long period, contends that it was ' ... more a deep sense of family attachment, and strong recall of his father and grandfather and their association with the country'.[2]

The bold heraldic design of *Kooralia*, 1980, is in some ways atypical, but its subtle evocation of a moonbeam falling across the striped sands of the Napperby Creek bed exemplifies the artist's interest in atmospherics, particularly night effects.

Despite a painting career cut short by his untimely death, the paintings of Tjapaltjarri remain a telling influence on the work of many Western Desert artists. VJ

Kooralia 1980
synthetic polymer paint on canvas
188 x 155 cm

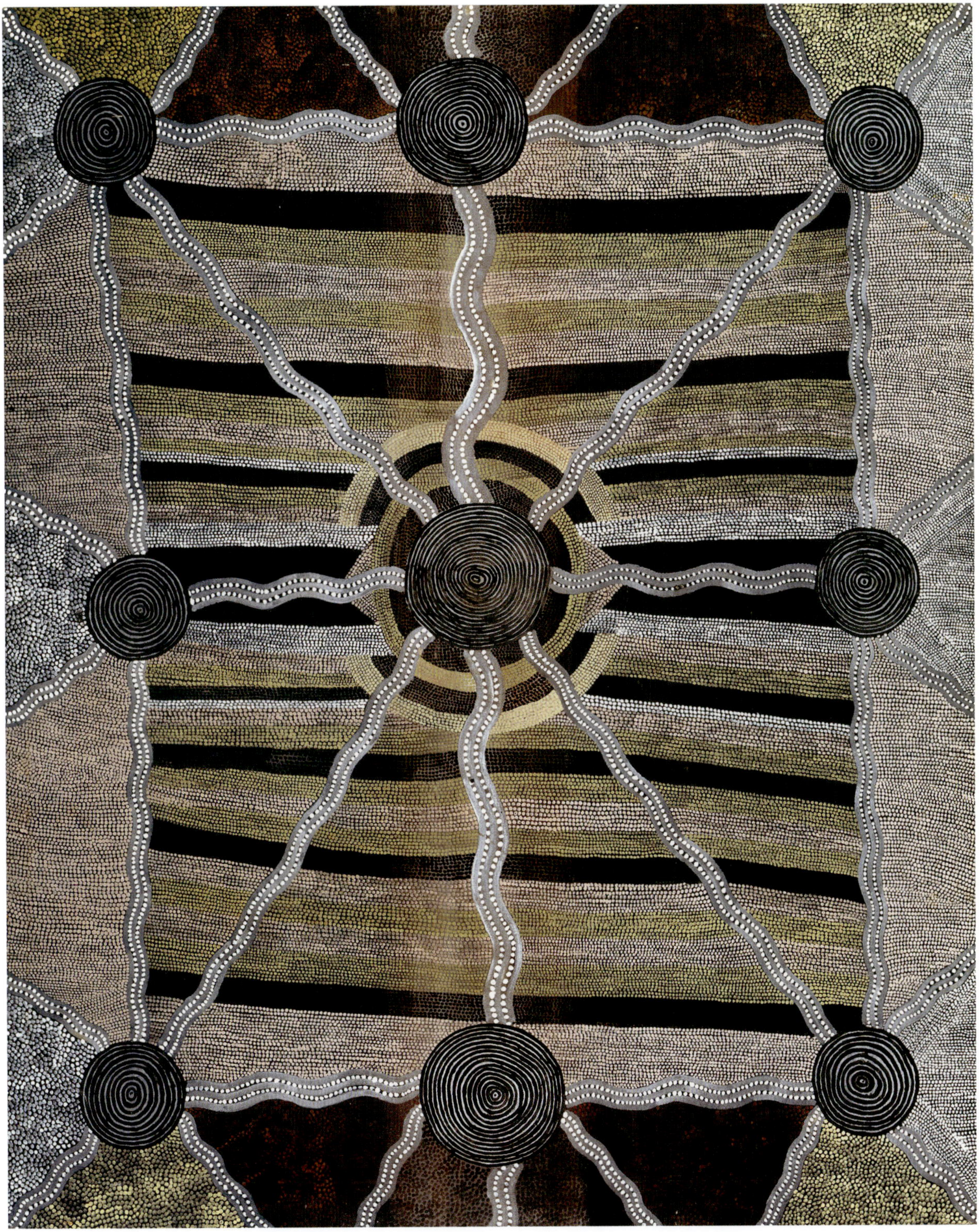

LONG TOM TJAPANANGKA

BORN c.1930
NGAATJATJARRA / PINTUPI
NORTHERN TERRITORY/
WESTERN AUSTRALIA

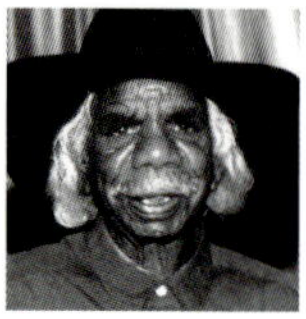

Long Tom Tjapanangka and his first wife Marlee Napurrula began painting for the Ikuntji Women's Centre in late 1993, following its opening in 1992. In recent years, Tjapanangka has also collaborated with his second wife, Mitjili Napurrula. Ikuntji (Haasts Bluff) is about 230 kilometres west of Mparntwe (Alice Springs) in the land of the Luritja people. The ancient ranges that dominate the landscape around the community offer a spectacle of rich natural beauty and immense ceremonial significance.

At the time of the proclamation of Haasts Bluff Aboriginal Reserve in 1940, Ikuntji was a ration depot. For Warlpiri, Pitjantjatjara, Pintupi and Arrernte people, it offered refuge from the harsh droughts of the early twentieth century, pastoral incursions into Aboriginal lands and the terror of the Coniston massacre. Today, the Ikuntji Arts Centre organises bush trips for the artists and their families back to their homelands. These journeys are a source of inspiration for painting and an opportunity to affirm traditional links with the land.

Tjapanangka's paintings celebrate the striking topography of the country he travelled through as a young man while working as a stockman and police tracker. The artist's stated intent is to paint for 'everyone', rather than making works of implicit sacred significance. Tjapanangka's method is akin to that of his contemporaries Emily Kame Kngwarreye, Kutuwulumi Purawarrampatu and Rover Thomas. Like the two distinguished women artists, Tjapanangka is diffident in the face of scrutiny from outsiders as to the 'meaning' of his work. And, like the late Rover Thomas, he lives and works as an artist far away from his birthplace on the Northern Territory and Western Australia border.

The inherent elusiveness of Tjapanangka's works is a direct contrast to their formal pictorial vigour. Although the abstract forms of tali (sandhills) and puli (rocks) that recur in Tjapanangka's paintings are features of the desert landscape, his artistic tendency towards the figurative is anomalous to classic Western Desert painting. His technique also diverges from that of the neighbouring Papunya Tula artists – his dense, clotted application of paint evokes a palpable sense of country. Tjapanangka's paintings present an idiosyncratic fusion of artistic influence that reflects the dynamism and cultural hybridity of the Ikuntji community. HP

> **Kanpaarka (centipede) Tjukurrpa** 1994
synthetic polymer paint on canvas
218.5 x 152.5 cm

v **Uluru and Putipulawa** 1994
synthetic polymer paint on paper
56 x 76cm

> overleaf
Big mob puli (rocks), other side of Mt Leibig 1998
synthetic polymer paint on canvas
150.5 x 300.5 cm

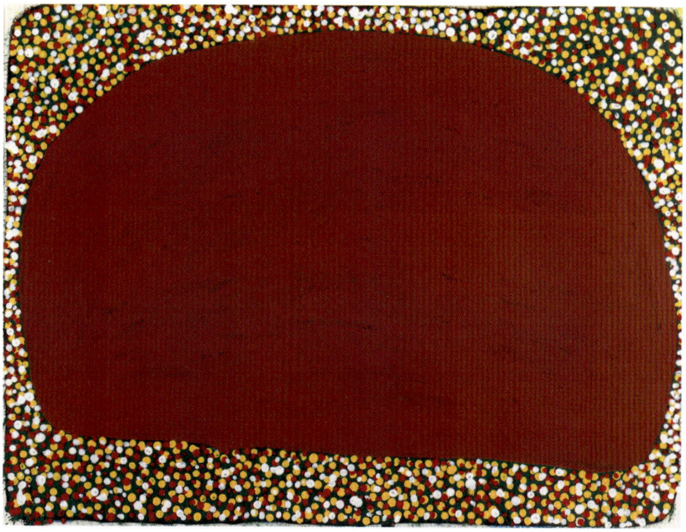

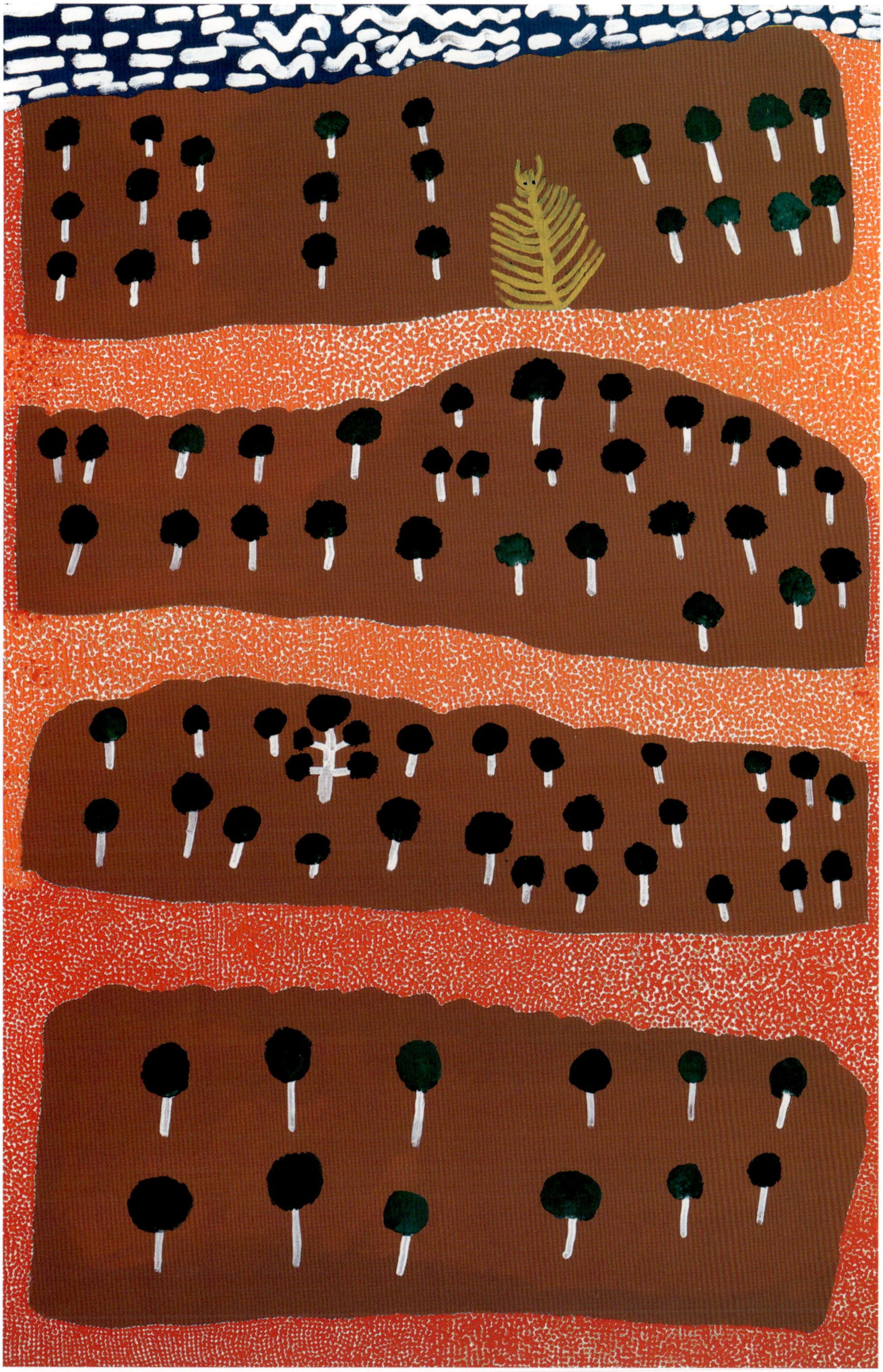

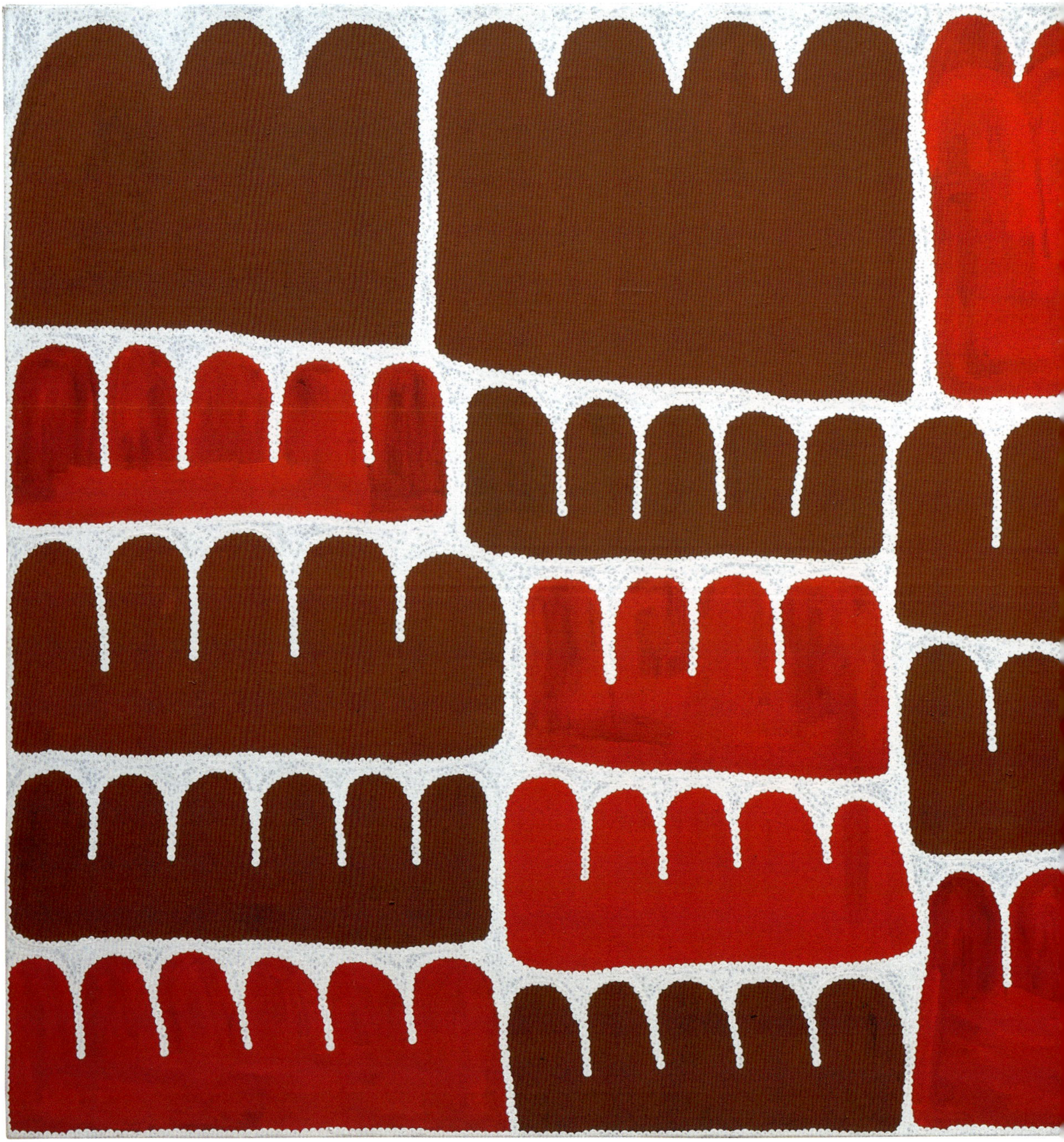

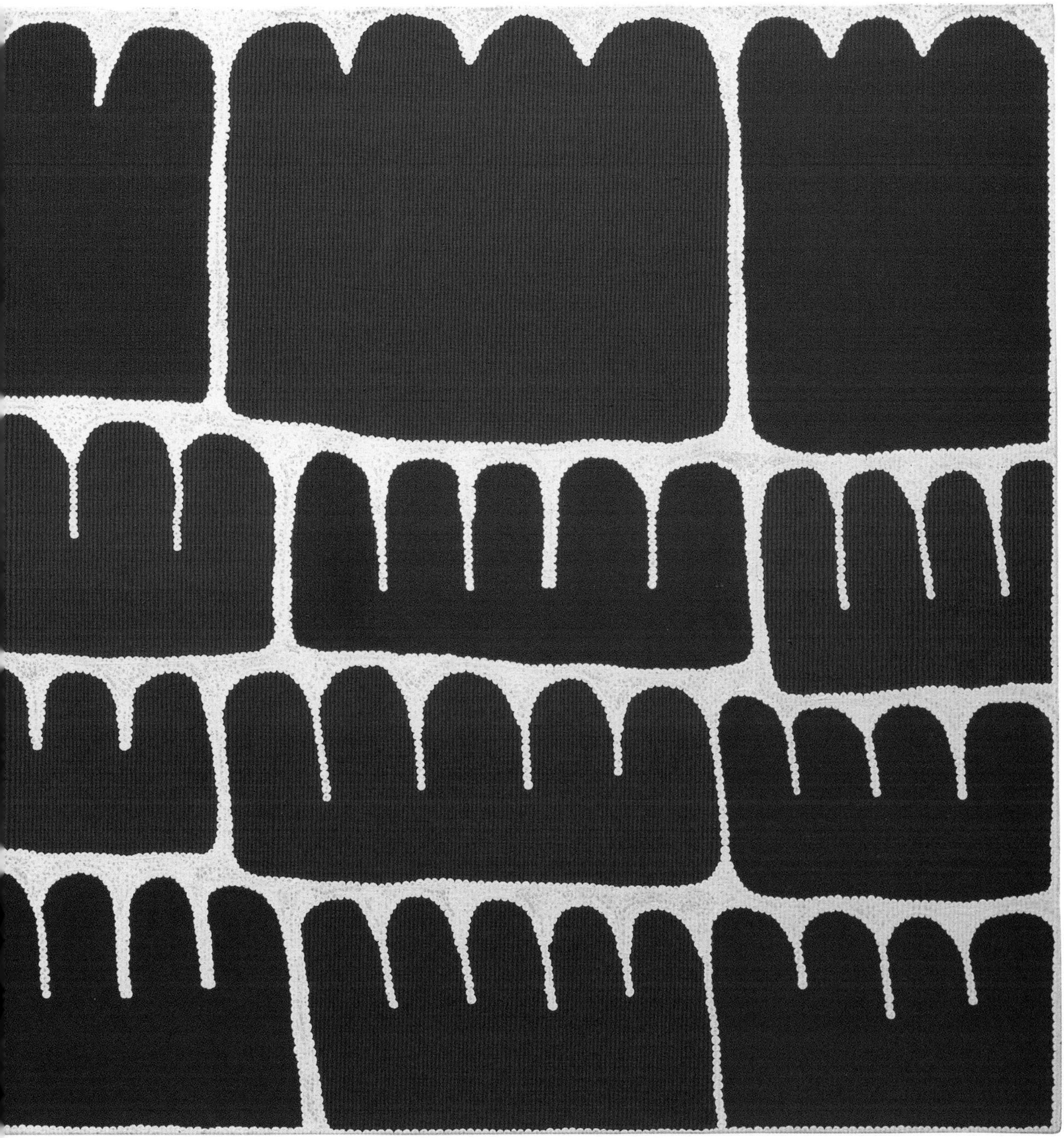

TJUMPO TJAPANANGKA

BORN c.1929
KUKATJA / PINTUPI
WESTERN AUSTRALIA

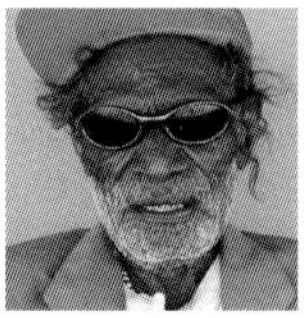

Kanapir, the place of Tjumpo Tjapanangka's birth, lies between the communities of Wirrimanu (Balgo) and Kiwirrkura in remote Western Australia. Tjapanangka's acrylic paintings, screenprints and occasional glass works reflect this geographic and artistic intersection. While his painting style is true to the Wirrimanu aesthetic, his work also signals the influence of the westernmost reach of the Papunya Tula Artists cooperative.

News of the genesis of Papunya Tula Artists – the art movement that formed when senior men began painting symbols of their cultural authority and knowledge onto found materials – reached Wirrimanu in 1971, via Pintupi community networks. However, reservations about the appropriateness of translating sacred information onto paintings for an outside audience initially held back the full-scale emergence of the Wirrimanu school. Following the exhibition, 'Aboriginal Art from the Great Sandy Desert', at the Art Gallery of Western Australia, Perth, in 1986–87, the Warlayirti art centre was established, and soon the explosive vigour and colour of Wirrimanu painting was capturing national attention.

Tjapanangka began painting in 1986. His early works adhered to the classic style of depicting the travels of the Tingari ancestors by painting interconnected circles, although with a Wirrimanu twist. He went on to develop a structure in his paintings that focuses on the spare arrangement of symbolic elements surrounded by a charged energy field of pulsating lines. His conservative use of colour highlights the key motifs and draws the eye through the composition in the manner of an animated narrative. *Wati Kutjarra*, 2002, relates the story of two ancestral brothers who travelled throughout the Western Desert teaching about the practical aspects of desert life: food gathering, hunting and fire management. The central roundel in the work represents the fire lit by the brothers where they lay down to rest. On either side of the ancestral camp fire – or rockhole, as it is known today – are the impressions left in the ground by the brothers, which remain as features of the landscape.

Tjapanangka is a formidable Western Desert personality whose charisma and maverick style are borne out in his paintings. An inveterate traveller, crisscrossing between the camps and outstations scattered throughout the deserts of Central Australia, he is immediately recognisable by his trademark wraparound sunglasses. Well-represented in the Warlayirti Artists gallery and the newly built cultural centre next door, Tjapanangka's art is an exemplar of the cultural verve and pride that wells from the heart of the Tanami and Great Sandy Deserts. HP

Wati Kutjarra 2002
synthetic polymer paint on canvas
180 x 120 cm

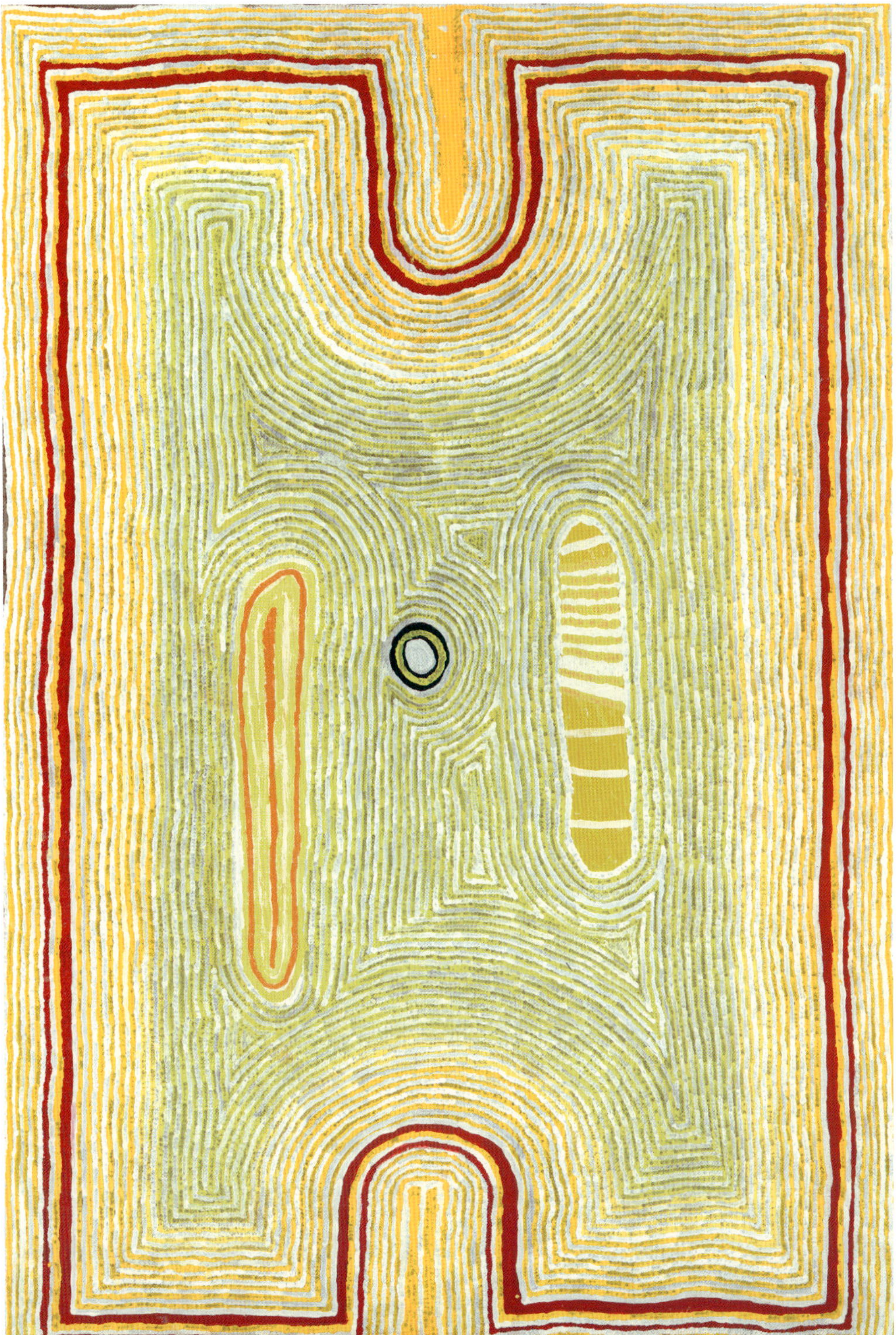

TIMMY PAYUNGKA TJAPANGATI

c.1940–2000
PINTUPI
NORTHERN TERRITORY / WESTERN AUSTRALIA

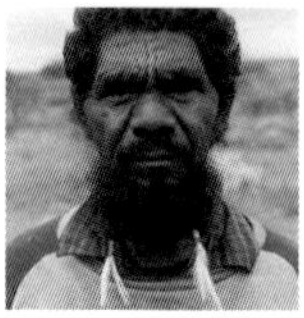

Timmy Payungka Tjapangati was among the first Pintupi men to begin painting on hardboard at Papunya in 1971. He had lived in his traditional country in the Gibson Desert to the west of the Wilkinkarra (Lake Mackay) saltpan before the drought of the late 1950s forced him and his family to walk to the distant ration station at Ikuntji (Haasts Bluff). After a short stay he returned to his country, where he contacted the government patrol officer Jeremy Long, with whom he returned east to the new government settlement at Papunya.

Tjapangati was working on the farm at Papunya when he and other Pintupi men took up the brush. In the late 1970s he spent much of his time with his relatives at Balgo Mission, to the north-west of Papunya, and did not paint for the market for extended periods. Tjapangati was a vital force behind the eventual return of the Pintupi to their traditional country of Kiwirrkura in the mid-1980s. At this time, he also became a key guardian for the 'new people', a group of nine Pintupi who had stayed isolated in the Gibson Desert for over 20 years, only making contact with their relatives again after seeing the smoke from their distant hunting fires.

Tjapangati was a highly individual painter among the Pintupi artists – figuration played a large part in his earlier works, with depictions of animals and people, their tracks and associated ceremonial detail. In the middle phase of his artistic development, while conforming to Pintupi conventions, his painting was characterised by compositional complexity and the use of unconventional chromatic and tonal arrangements.

The latter phase of his work is an assertion of his undoubted ceremonial authority. In *Tingari cycle at Wilkinkarra*, 1996, Tjapangati fills the picture space with the intricate 'key' patterns that are characteristically incised onto wooden objects associated with secret ceremonies, and the palette is reduced to a red ochre undercoat covered by a maze of black and white dotted lines. *Untitled*, 1998, is a similarly reductive work. It employs squared concentric elements, of a kind of geometry that had been eschewed by Pintupi artists in the 1970s and 1980s because it referred too closely to the secret patterns of the men's realm. In this work the squared elements are arranged in an informal grid. At the upper left of the work, just one square is left unfilled, begging us to question whether this was deliberate: its effect is of total visual power. JK

> **Untitled** 1998
synthetic polymer paint on canvas
152 x 122 cm

v **Tingari cycle at Wilkinkarra** 1996
synthetic polymer paint on canvas
153 x 122 cm

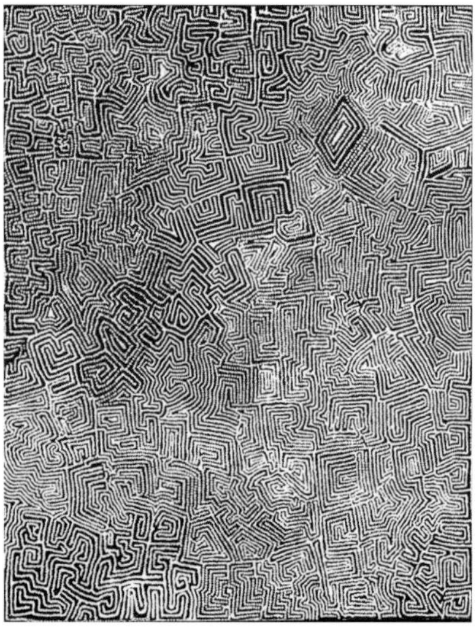

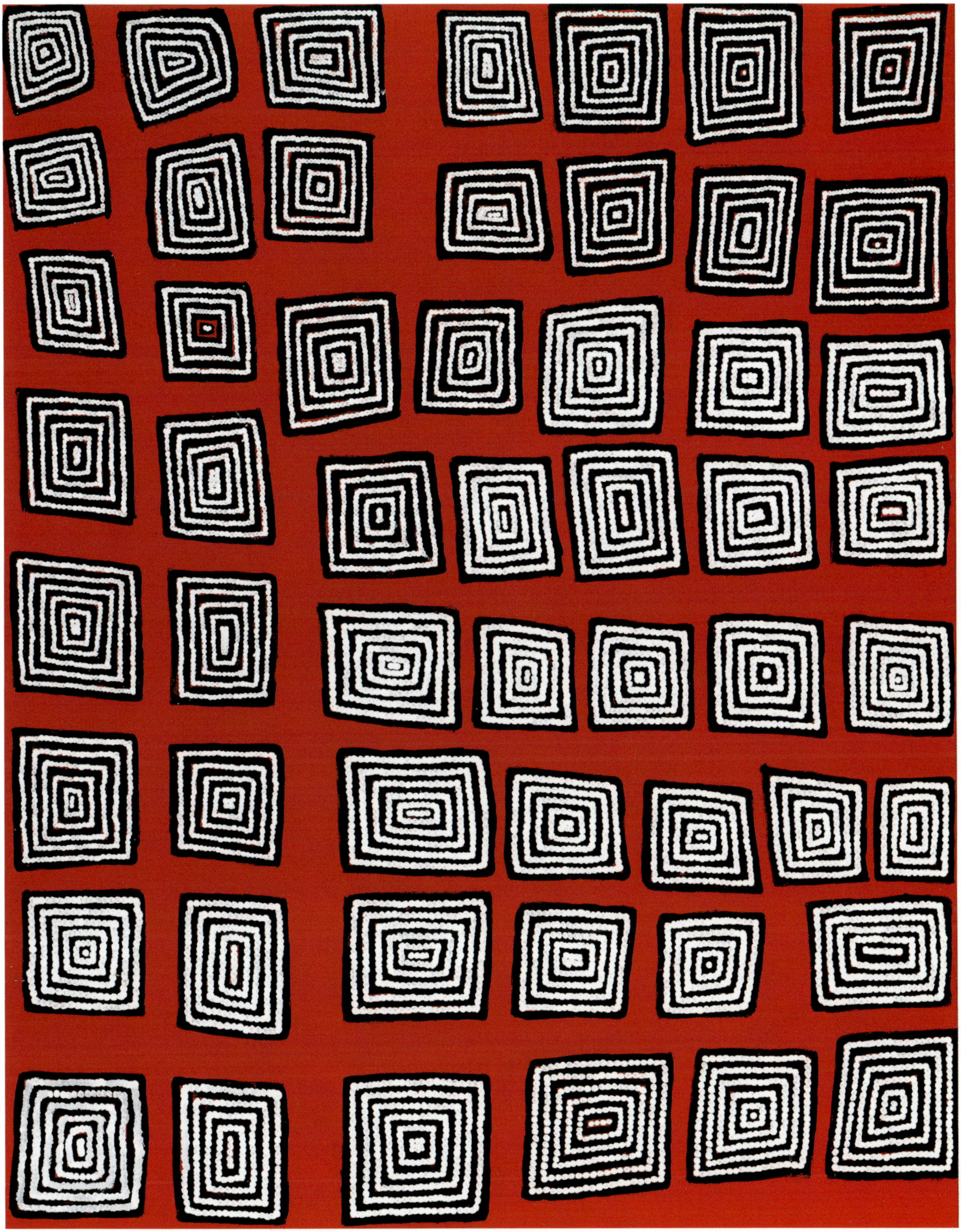

SHORTY LUNGKATA TJUNGURRAYI

c.1920–1987
PINTUPI
NORTHERN TERRITORY / WESTERN AUSTRALIA

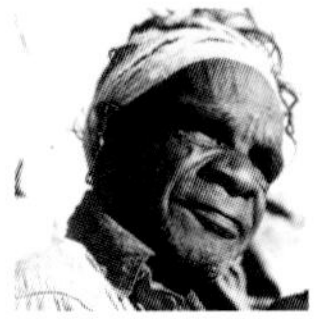

Shorty Lungkata Tjungurrayi was a man of quiet self-assurance and extraordinary presence. He grew up in the desert before travelling to Ikuntji (Haasts Bluff) around 1950. While he had a longer period of contact with non-Aboriginal people than some other Pintupi men of his age, he made little attempt to assimilate culturally or to learn English.

In 1960 he moved over the MacDonnell Ranges to Papunya, where the new settlement had been created. By the 1970s he was a powerful and sometimes feared ngangkari (traditional doctor). At Papunya, the Pintupi were marginalised, and there was almost continuous conflict between the people of various language groups clustered around the settlement. Lungkata was a forceful advocate for his people and more than once would proclaim his rights in a dance with spears in front of a large crowd in the community canteen. Because of the dire living conditions, he and his family chose to live on successive outstations to the west of the settlement, towards his traditional country.

Lungkata began painting in the Australian summer of 1971–72. His paintings are intensely concentrated; their energies are contained and inwardly focused. *Women's Dreaming* (*Two women*), 1972, is a magnificent example of his earliest work. It is spare and powerful, but with subtle details such as the interlocking of the dotted white lines that ensure the eye cannot rest completely on the imposing red ochre 'U' shapes representing the two women. Despite its pared back simplicity, this work resonates with the power of song – it is a moment of ephemeral ceremony enduring miraculously on hardboard.

From the mid-1970s, Lungkata's works became increasingly elaborate. His paintings often featured multiple sets of looping crescents building from a steady centre. In some instances he employed subtle modulations of tone and colour to support the pulsing rhythm of a work. During this phase, he was the only Papunya Tula artist to begin his roundels with ovals rather than circles, giving his painting an attenuated, slightly convex feel. By the end of the decade, he was creating monumental, authoritative works that were comprehensive representations of the several Tjukurrpa that cross his traditional country. His greatest works were created when the market demand for Western Desert art had not yet been realised and, consequently, Lungkata's significance as an artist should not be underestimated by the relative scarcity of his work. JK

Women's dreaming (Two women) 1972
synthetic polymer powder paint on hardboard
46 x 64 cm

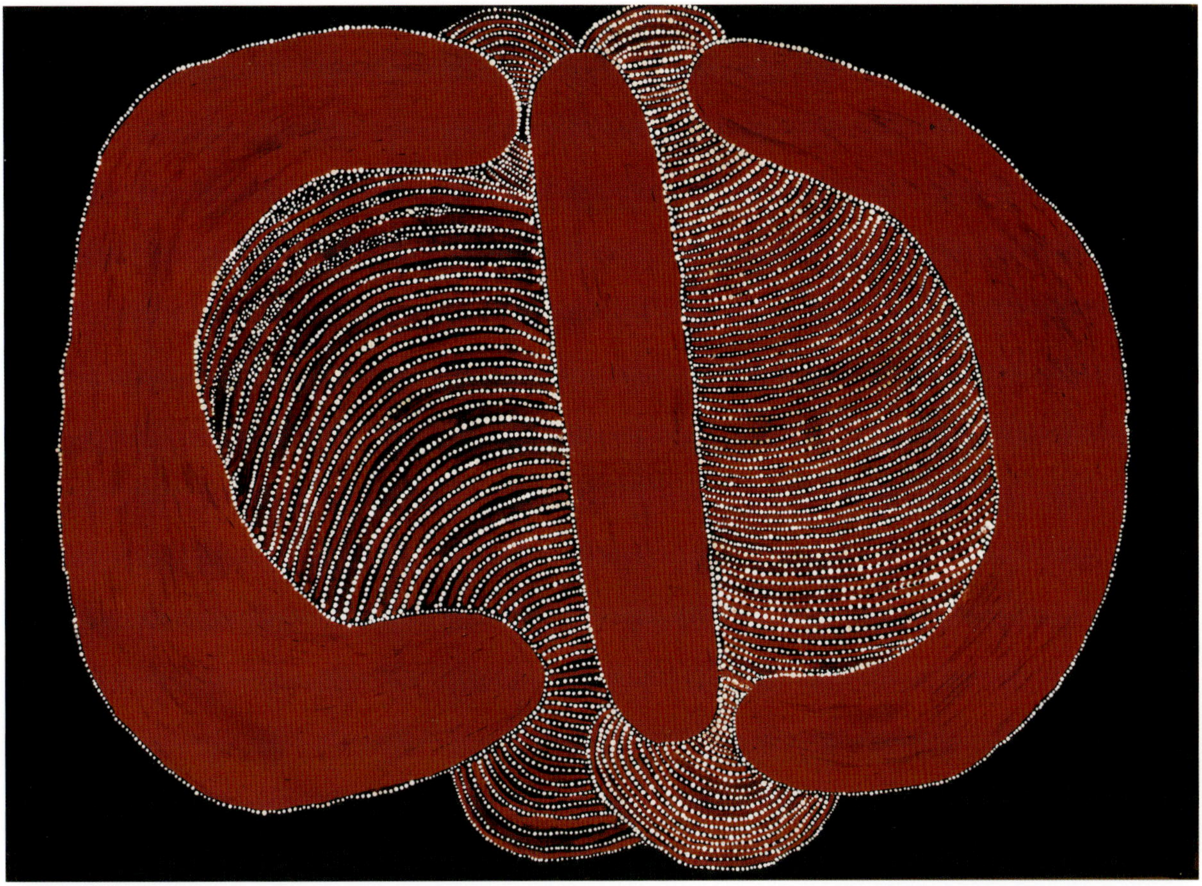

JOHNNY WARANGKULA TJUPURRULA

c.1920–2001
LURITJA
NORTHERN TERRITORY

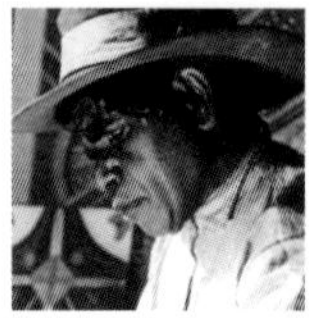

Born at Minjilpirri, south of the salt lake Wilkinkarra (Lake Mackay), Johnny Warangkula Tjupurrula's childhood was spent living a traditional lifestyle in the desert. Later, the family moved to Hermannsburg Mission, where Tjupurrula worked as a labourer constructing the airstrip. During this time, Tjupurrula passed through the initiation ceremonies for manhood. He then moved to Ikuntji (Haasts Bluff) for construction work, and later worked in Watiyawanu (Mount Liebig), Yuendumu and Mount Wedge. In 1954 he was chosen, along with Nosepeg Tjupurrula, to meet Queen Elizabeth II in Toowoomba, Queensland. In 1958 he travelled to the country around Wilkinkarra with Welfare Branch patrol officer Ted Evans, visiting Tjikari, a rockhole site north of Sandy Blight Junction. Tjupurrula had returned to Ikuntji when the bulk of the population was moved across to the new settlement of Papunya in 1960. For the rest of his life, Tjupurrula lived mostly in Papunya with his wife Gladys Napanangka and their extended family. His principal homeland site was Kalipinypa, a 'native' well north-west of Sandy Blight Junction.

Tjupurrula was serving on the Papunya Council when Geoffrey Bardon arrived at the settlement and began encouraging the older men to paint their traditional designs. Tjupurrula's work from the mid-1970s – such as *Emu Dreaming*, 1974 – is typical of the experimentation that marked the founding Papunya Tula artists' development of a simplified iconography. This more painterly approach signified their expanding encounter with the outside world. From the movement's earliest days, Tjupurrula developed a distinctive personal style of overdotting, often of several layers, creating effects that Bardon called 'tremulous illusion'.

'Johnny W' remained a major force in the movement until the mid-1980s, when his output was reduced by failing eyesight. In 1984, the inaugural Director of the National Gallery of Australia, Canberra, James Mollison chose to be photographed alongside Tjupurrula's large canvas *Yala Dreaming*, 1982, and declared the work of the Papunya artists to be the 'finest abstract art ever produced in this country'.[1] VJ

Emu Dreaming 1974
synthetic polymer paint on three-ply
50.7 x 45.4 cm

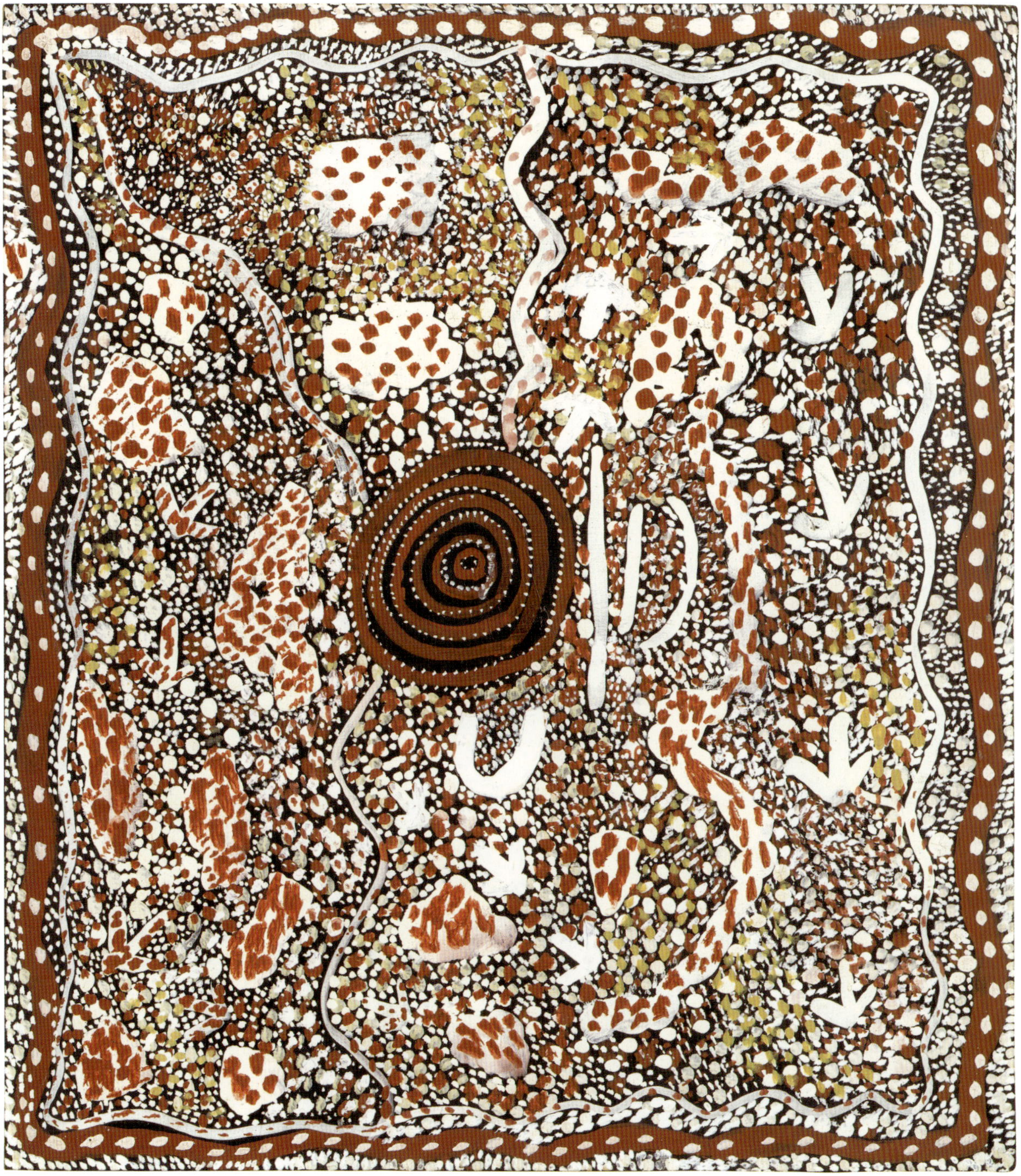

TURKEY TOLSON TJUPURRULA

c.1942–2001
PINTUPI
NORTHERN TERRITORY

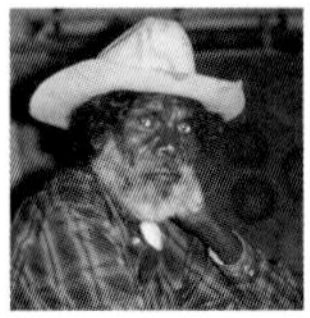

Turkey Tolson Tjupurrula was among the first of a slightly younger generation of artists to begin painting at Papunya in 1973. He had observed the work of older men, including Mick Namarari Tjapaltjarri, George Maxwell Tjangala and Ray Inkamala Tjampitjinpa, before picking up the brush himself. By the late 1970s he had developed into an accomplished artist in his own right and, because of his understanding of non-Aboriginal people and his command of English, was in a good position to be an effective cultural broker for his older relatives.

Tolson was born just outside Ikuntji (Haasts Bluff), soon after his family had migrated east out of the Gibson Desert. As a young man he honed his bush skills, trapping dingoes around the western MacDonnell Ranges with his father. In the 1970s and early 1980s, Tolson spent his time alternately in Papunya and at the outstation, Kungkayurnti. In 1985 he moved west to Walungurru (Kintore), which is just to the north of his ancestral country. He soon established an outstation at Yuwalki, along the route of the Kungka Kutjarra (Two Ancestral Women) that he depicts so often in his paintings.

Tolson's work developed through a succession of styles. His earlier, smaller works were modest, and conformed to the accepted conventions of the Pintupi artists. By the late 1970s, however, he had completed several large canvases in which the application of concentric circles and dotted bands was expressed to create an effect of mesmerising perfection. The 1980s was a period of visual exploration for the artist, his technical expertise allowing him to create subtle tonal effects combined with bold iconographic elements.

In 1990, Tolson painted *Straightening the spears at Ilyingaungau* – this work, now in the Art Gallery of South Australia, Adelaide, heralded in a new phase of minimalism in Papunya Tula art. Throughout the next decade he would occasionally represent the same site, using arbitrary variations of his dotted line to echo the irregularities of thin mulyati (acacia species) spears. *Straightening the spears*, 1999, is a fine example of these later works. Living at Yuwalki, Tolson regularly visited the small claypan, Ilyingaungau, or the cave site, Mitukatjirri, from where the ancestral warriors had travelled.

As chairperson of Papunya Tula Artists from 1985 to 1995, Tolson was a key contact between the public and the artists and their country, and his quiet confidence will be remembered by all who met him. JK

> **Straightening the spears** 1999
synthetic polymer paint on canvas
152 x 183 cm

v **Straightening the spears** 1998
woodcut
35 x 60 cm

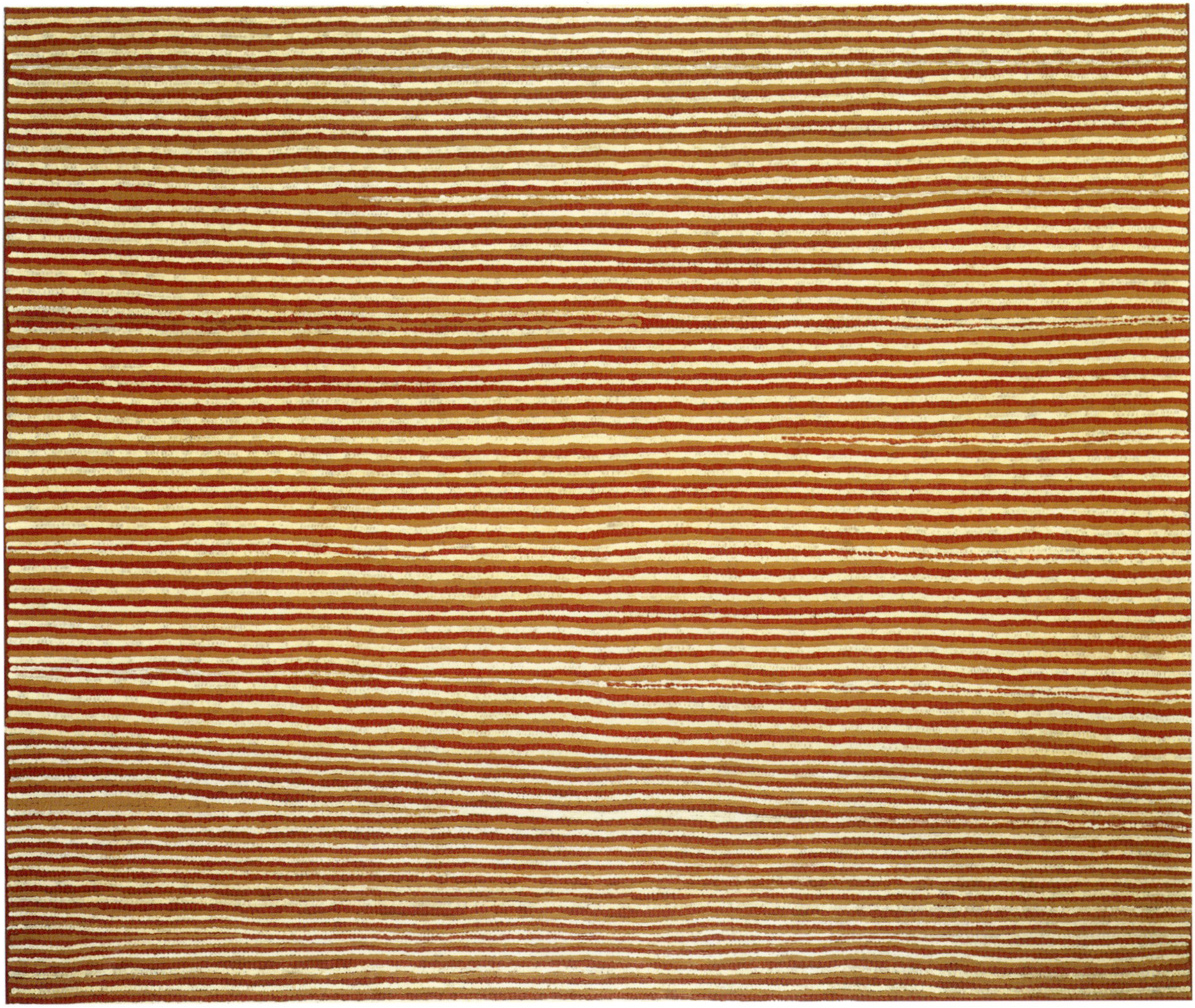

PRINCE OF WALES

1935–2002
LARRAKIA
NORTHERN TERRITORY

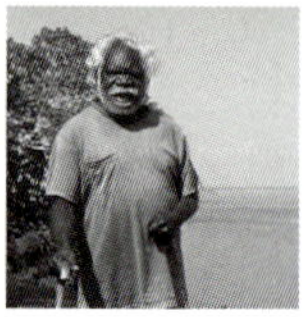

Larrakia painter, singer and dancer, Prince of Wales (Midpul) frequently camped with his family at Cullen Beach, Darwin. This once pristine harbour is now an upmarket, waterfront real estate and marina development. For Aboriginal people across the northernmost parts of Australia, however, its name remains notorious as a Westernisation of 'Kahlin', the compound where Aboriginal people rounded up from coastal camps and Aboriginal children who had been forcibly removed from their parents were detained. Prince of Wales's life was shaped by the destiny he shared with many people whose traditional lands were favoured for the establishment of non-Aboriginal settlements.

Prince's father, Imabul (Ichungarrabilluk) and also known as King George, resisted the encroaching colonisation of his people's land. By 1916, Darwin was prohibited to Aboriginal people, and Imabul lobbied strongly for the right of his people to live in their country. Sadly, his father passed away early in Prince's life, leaving his son to eventually inherit his traditional responsibilities to the Larrakia people. Prince grew up with his mother's people, the Wadjigiyn, at the Belyuen Aboriginal Reserve on the Cox Peninsula across the harbour from Darwin. Here he came to realise his father's legacy, proving his prowess as a singer and dancer. Prince was a celebrated performer, whether leading initiation ceremonies or performing for the Queen of England.

After suffering a stroke that restricted his movement, Prince moved to the Kulaluk beach community. A member of the Dangalaba clan of the Larrakia people, he was one of the original claimants in the 1977 Kenbi Land Claim. However, even though this land claim is now the longest-running in the history of the 1976 *Northern Territory Land Rights Act*, Prince did not live to see its resolution.

In taking up painting in 1995, Prince found a medium through which he could retain the essence of his active ceremonial life. His paintings have a musicality imparted by the lively staccato-effect of dots and intermittent bars, as if to be read like the sheet music for an improvised symphony. Prince's uninhibited use of colour belies the origins of these designs, which were passed on by his ancestors as marks on the bodies of ceremonial participants. His early works were painted on scraps of cardboard and other found materials, their compact size emulating the proportions of the body. In his last years, Prince 'upped the ante', scaling up his 'Body Marks' paintings to assert his cultural authority as a Larrakia elder, as embodied in his statement, '... I make the marks.'[1] HP

Body marks 2001
synthetic polymer paint on canvas
210 x 129 cm
> detail

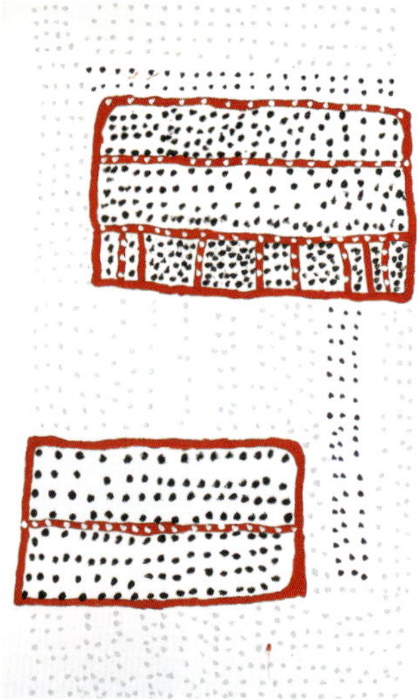

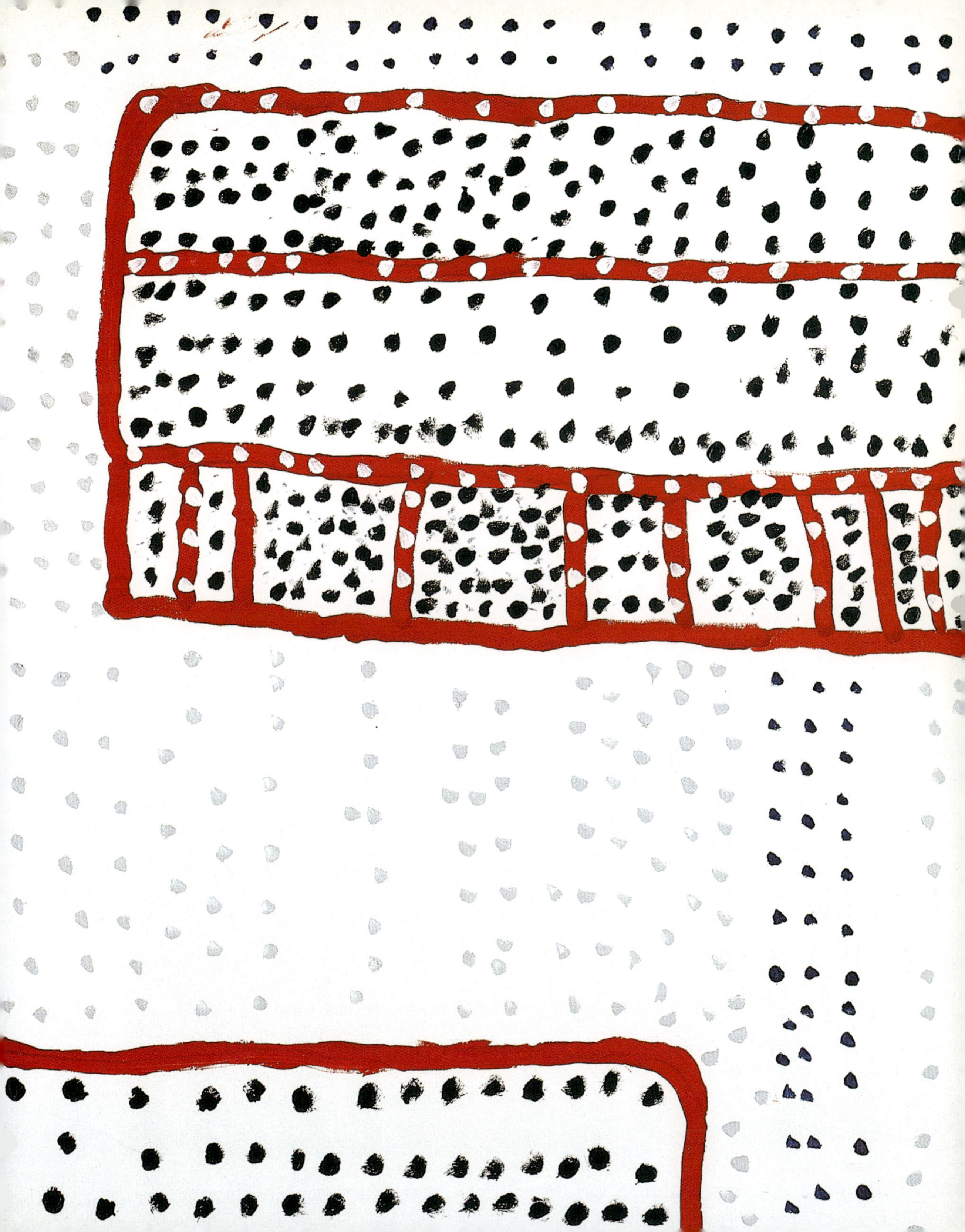

JUDY WATSON

BORN 1959
WAANYI
QUEENSLAND

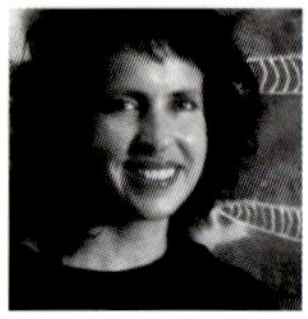

Judy Watson has described her experiences of travelling to her great-grandmother's country in north-west Queensland, as 'learning from the ground up'.[1] It is a philosophy she has transplanted on her several journeys and residencies abroad. In 1997 she represented Australia at the Venice Biennale, along with Emily Kame Kngwarreye and Yvonne Koolmatrie.

Watson's matrilineal link to the country of her ancestors has always been central to her printmaking and painting. The hidden histories of Indigenous experience on the colonial frontier – particularly those of women – continue to inspire her. Watson seeks the indelible impressions of past presence on the landscape – rubbings, engravings and incisions – and subtly inscribes them upon her work. Often using natural materials found in situ, she colours the canvas while it is laid wet on the ground, allowing the earth's contours to form a blueprint for the pigments pooling upon it. Forms of humans or natural features, as in *saltpan*, 1992, emerge from within. Watson does not frame her paintings, preferring to hang them so that they appear to float off the wall, or even spill onto the floor, their organic shapes suggesting a flayed hide.

Watson's series of prints from 1997, *our bones in your collections*, *our hair in your collections* and *our skin in your collections*, refers to the systematic dispossession and institutionalisation of Indigenous people and culture, catalogued in the ethnographic collections of museums around the world. When viewing the objects sourced from her country, Watson mused that those twined with human hair might include her own great-grandmother's hair and remembered being told that the old people used to be able to tell where a person was from by touching their hair.[2] In a process the artist describes as 'translation', Watson created the etchings from her drawings, yet was careful not to exactly replicate the objects and even concealed them behind a veil of chine collé. In so doing, she respectfully acknowledged their cultural significance, while enfolding these disenfranchised objects in a protective 'skin'.

Through her art, Watson repatriates the human artefacts and objects of collected cultures in museum storehouses, and reveals the 'skeletons' in colonial 'closets':

'I listen and hear those words a hundred
years away
That is my Grandmother's Mother's Country
it seeps down through blood and memory
and soaks
into the ground'[3] HP

> **saltpan** 1992
powder pigment and pastel on canvas
180 x 110 cm

v from left
our bones in your collections 1997
our hair in your collections 1997
our skin in your collections 1997
etching and chine collé
29.4 x 20.4 cm each

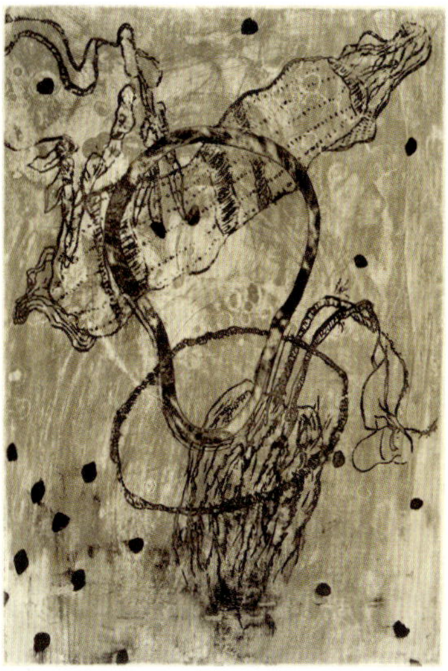
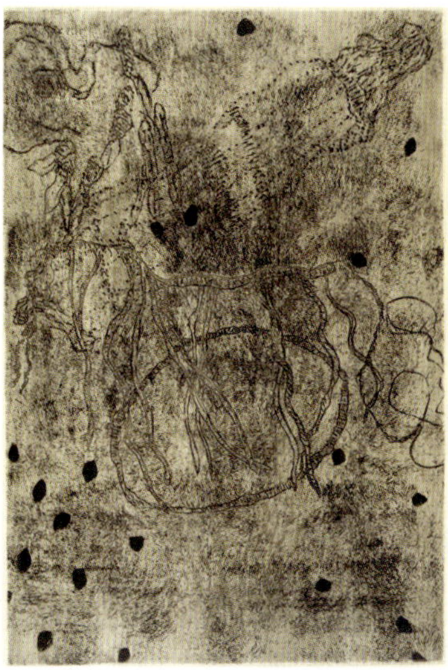
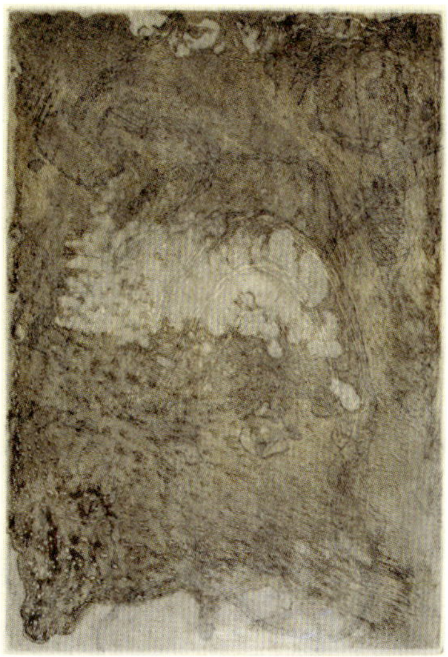

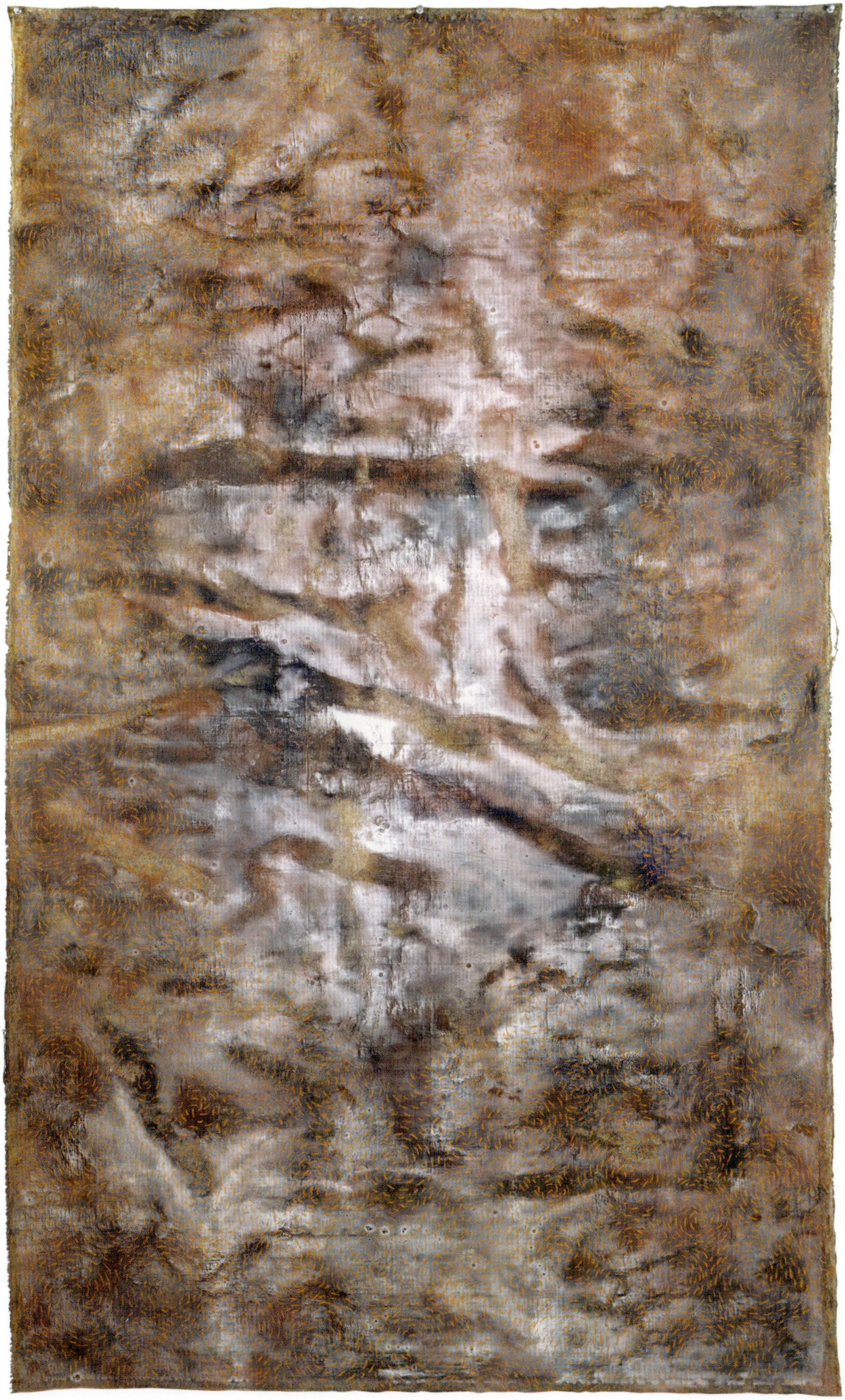

H. J. WEDGE

BORN 1957
WIRADJURI
NEW SOUTH WALES

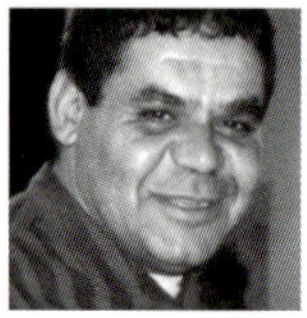

H. J. (Harry) Wedge was born on Erambie Mission near Cowra in central New South Wales, and draws on his experiences of mission life in his painting. Initially interested in photography, Wedge enrolled at the Eora Centre TAFE (Technical and Further Education) in Redfern, Sydney, in 1989. He soon transferred to painting in acrylic, the medium best suited to his artistic and communicative needs. With his surrealist style, Wedge's paintings seem to freeze a moment and draw out its raw emotive elements. After graduating, he joined the Boomalli Aboriginal Artists Cooperative, Sydney, and began exhibiting alongside such contemporaries as Ian Abdulla and Elaine Russell, launching his national and international career.

The Aboriginal tradition of oral history provides Wedge's framework, while his painting acts as a personal journal, compensating for the fact that he is illiterate. His work focuses on post-colonial narrative and examines current social and environmental issues. He has said that he tries ' ... to paint what I dream, what I hear on *A Current Affair*, things you can even hear people talking about on the train ... '.[1] His powerful paintings operate seductively, enchanting the viewer with signature lyrical figures that he combines with arresting political statements. His figures, refusing to be silenced, become social commentators and express the injustices of the past. In 1992 Wedge held a major solo exhibition, 'Wiradjuri Spirit Man', at Tandanya National Aboriginal Cultural Centre in Adelaide and at Boomalli in 1993. In 1996, the monograph *Wiradjuri Spirit Man* was published, containing a series of images accompanied by transcribed stories.

Wedge participated in the 25th Budapest Autumn Festival in 1993 with other Boomalli artists including Judy Watson and Fiona Foley. The same year, he was represented in Australian Perspecta 1993 and was artist-in-residence at the Art Gallery of New South Wales, Sydney, producing the narrative work *Stop and think*, 1993, which mixed cautionary tales with current social issues. Wedge was included in 'True Colours: Aboriginal and Torres Strait Islander Artists Raise the Flag', 1994, a major Boomalli exhibition that toured internationally and was curated by Hetti Perkins and Brenda L. Croft. In 2002, he participated in the Biennale of Sydney with his triptych, *Taken over the environment*, 2002, which tells the chronological story of the invasion of Australia. Wedge's interpretation of Australian history is a combination of fact and fiction occurring in dreamlike, sometimes nightmarish, sequences. JJ

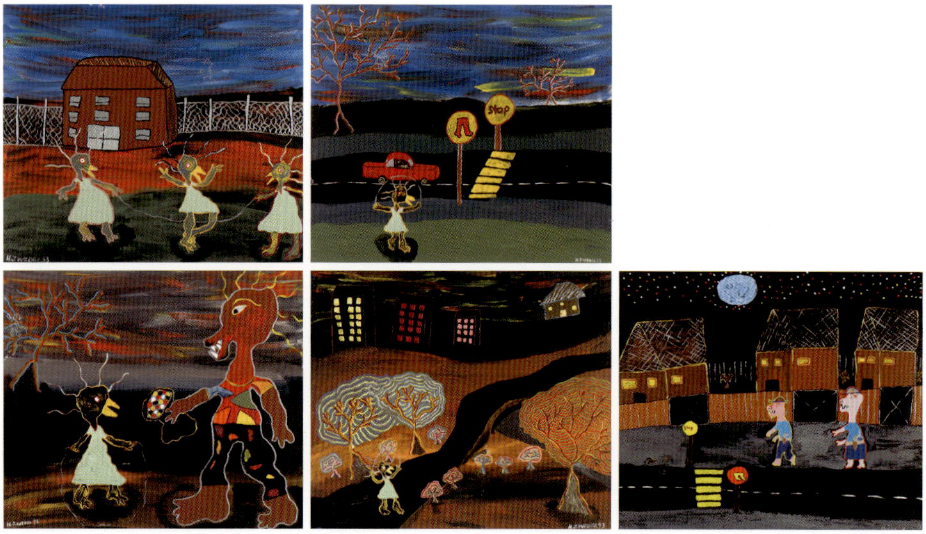

Stop and think 1993
five panels: synthetic polymer paint on canvas
76 x 456 cm overall
> detail

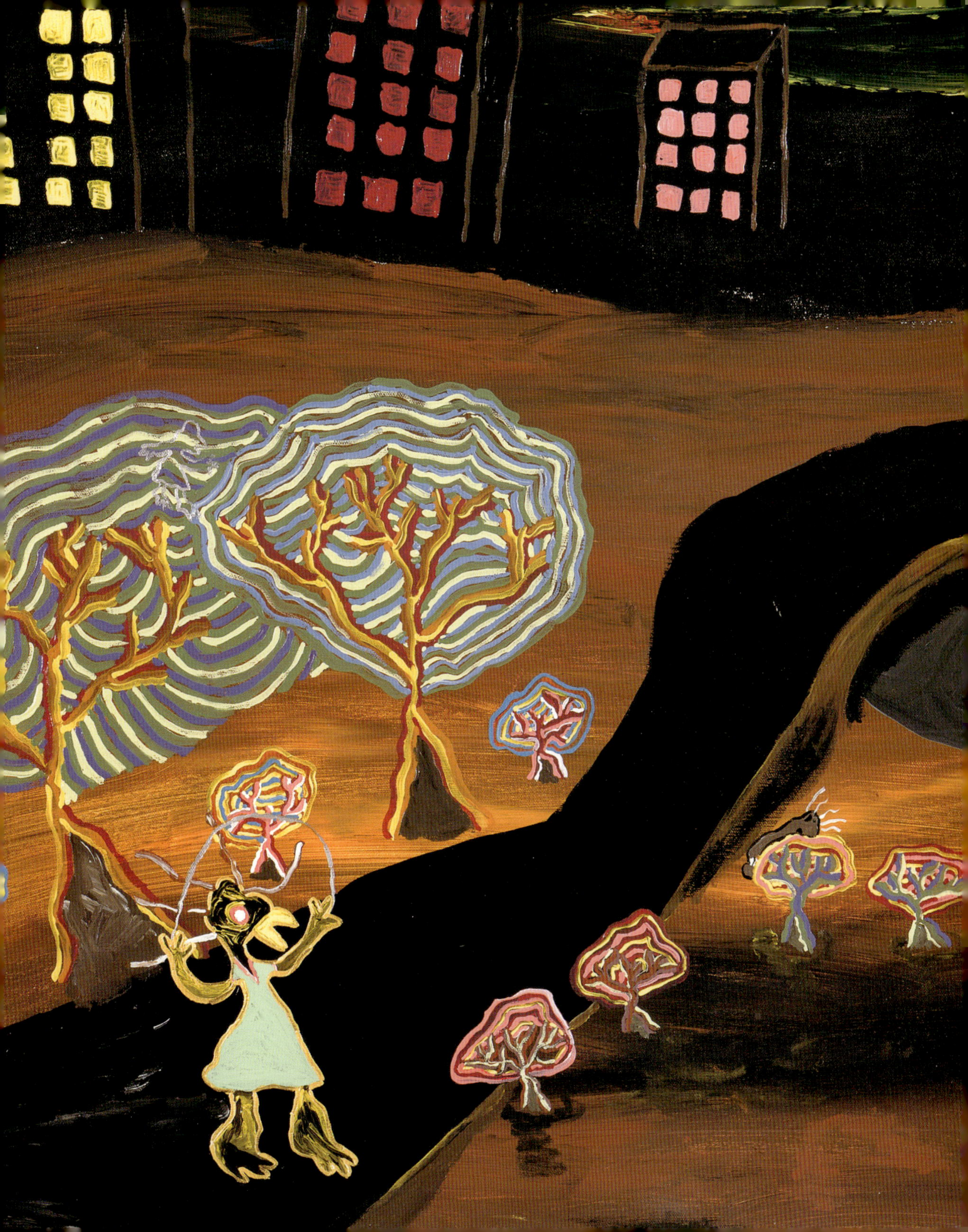

PEDRO WONAEAMIRRI

BORN 1974
TIWI
NORTHERN TERRITORY

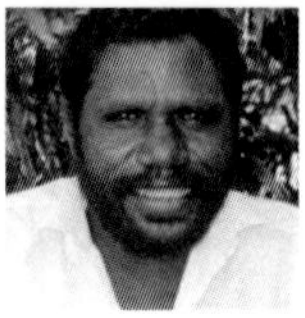

Pedro Wonaeamirri (Gurrumaiyuwa) was raised by his grandmother, Jacinta Wonaeamirri, at Pirlangimpi (Garden Point) on Melville Island; she taught him the traditional cultural practices of his grandfather. Wonaeamirri's artistic career began when he made his first ceremonial tutini or funerary pukumani pole for his father-in-law. Like many Tiwi artists, Wonaeamirri is an accomplished singer and dancer – key forms of expression in Tiwi culture. He maintained his art and dance practice during his secondary and tertiary education in Darwin, leading dance troupes and studying visual arts. In 1991 Wonaeamirri, aged 17, began working at Jilamara Arts and Crafts at Milikapiti on Melville Island both as an artist and in the leadership roles of president and vice-president. He worked alongside other noted Tiwi artists, such as Kutuwulumi Purawarrumpatu and Taracarijimo Freda Warlapinni.

Wonaeamirri is one of the few Tiwi people of his generation who speaks old or classic Tiwi. In his art practice, Wonaeamirri works within the strong Tiwi tradition of using pwoja (body designs), describing his works as an extension of the pukumani ceremonial body designs. His works are graphic expressions of dance and song that capture the essence of performance. Wonaeamirri has mastered the traditional techniques of painting in natural ochres collected from his country, rendered with kayimwagakimi (the traditional Tiwi ironwood comb), and refined the process into his own unique style. Strong fields of colour are illuminated with geometric 'dot' patterns painted on canvas, paper, barks and ironwood sculptures.

Wonaeamirri has travelled and exhibited nationally and internationally, and his work is represented in Australian state galleries and museums. In 1999 he was commissioned by the Art Gallery of New South Wales, Sydney, to create six ironwood pukumani poles from ochres, feathers and beeswax. These works were inspired by a visit to the Gallery in 1998, when Wonaeamirri studied the group of 17 tutini that were commissioned by Dr Stuart Scougall for the Art Gallery of New South Wales in 1959. This monumental group of sculptures was the first Aboriginal work to be accessioned as 'art' in a public gallery and, at the time they entered the Gallery's collection, their inclusion was regarded as controversial. Acting as a counterpoint to these, Wonaeamirri's tutini exemplify the connection of the contemporary artistic practices of Milikapiti with an illustrious past. JJ

from left:

Tutini 1999
natural pigments on ironwood
259.5 x 155 cm
252 x 22.5 cm
254 x 19 cm

Tutini with figure of Purukupali 1999
natural pigments on ironwood, feathers, beeswax
281 x 18 cm

Tutini 1999
natural pigments on ironwood
216 x 28 cm
241 x 21 cm

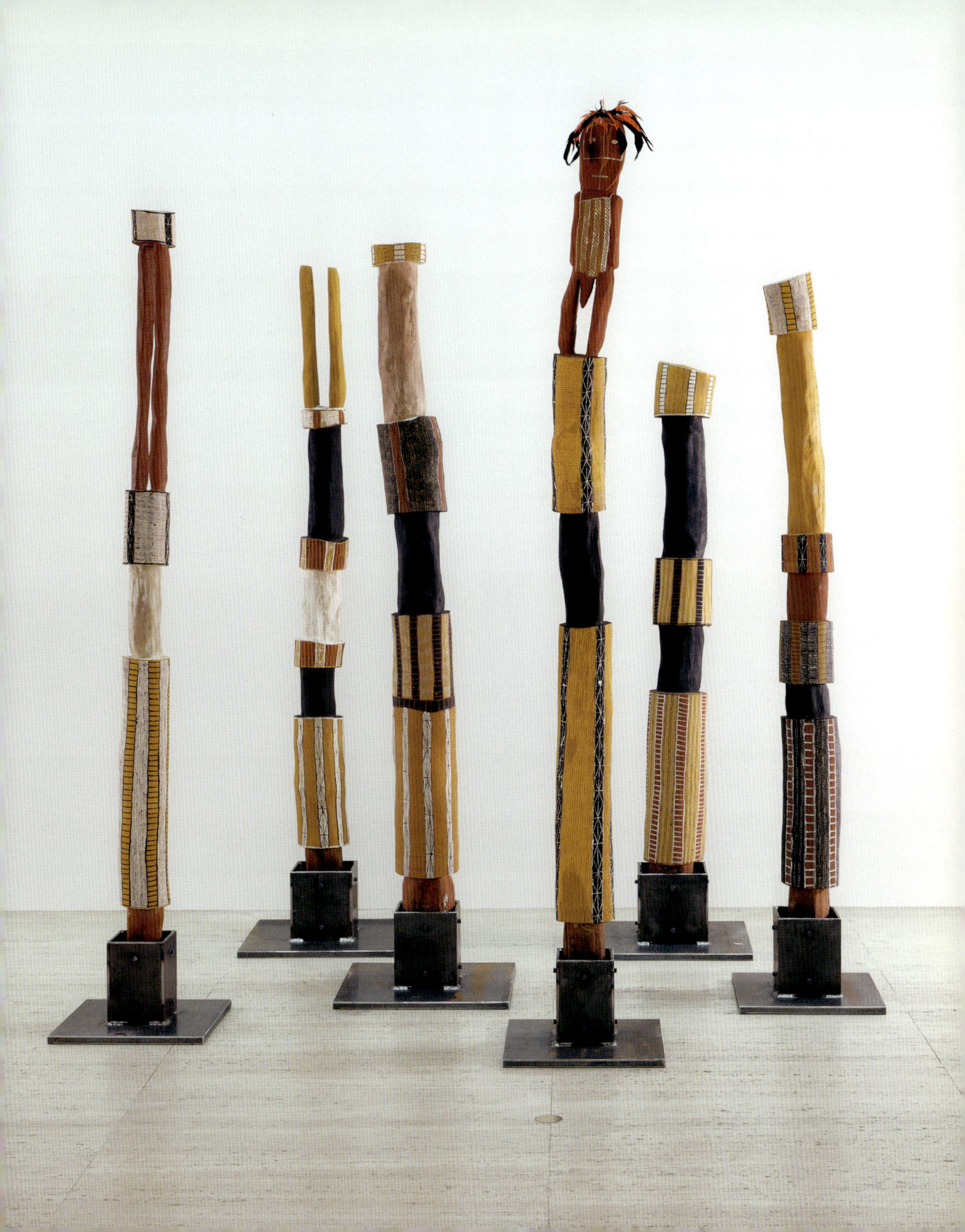

JABARRGWA WURRABADALUMBA

1896–c.1969
ANINDILYAKWA
NORTHERN TERRITORY

Jabarrgwa Wurrabadalumba was in his early fifties when he painted the bark, *Dugong hunt*, 1948. It is likely that the work was made at the request of anthropologist Charles Mountford, leader of the American–Australian Scientific Expedition to Arnhem Land in 1948. The published records of the expedition acknowledged a vigorous and distinctive art tradition at Groote Eylandt. Little effort was made to gather information on the artists, however, even though the expedition's intense campaign of collecting was inspired by a belief that it was assembling the work of a final generation of master artists. Like so many others, Wurrabadalumba is therefore known to us in only the barest biographical detail.

Wurrabadalumba, more widely known as Kneepad, belonged to the Bara, or north-west wind people, and was born on Groote Eylandt, near Bartaluma. This area is celebrated as a breeding ground for dugongs, a sea-mammal especially valued by Aboriginal people for its meat and for medicinal purposes. Essentially a sea people, the Groote Eylandters produced many bark and cave paintings that integrated their fishing experiences within a universal cosmology. In *Dugong hunt*, the artist captures the moment in a successful expedition when the spear-head finds its mark. It is a remarkably animated work, with harpoon rope swinging through the air, harpoonist with arms raised, securing the catch as his two companions keep the canoe on course, and a great, white-outlined dugong rises out of the water.

The painting illustrates many features of the rare 'middle period' Groote Eylandt barks. The background is a solid black, made from local manganese pigment, with the design laid on in white outline. Only four colours are used: white, yellow, red and black. In a reversal of east Arnhem Land practice, the complex details of the composition are found within the figures, while the surrounds are left bare and the images seem to float in space. The simple black background was characteristic of Groote Eylandt and to a particular period before the influx of manganese miners in the 1960s created a market for works with overall patterning and more complex compositions. This work, listed as one of the first acquisitions of Aboriginal art by the Art Gallery of New South Wales, Sydney, in 1956, is intensely engaging both in its strong linear conception and its spontaneity. SM

Dugong hunt 1948
natural pigments on bark
46 x 95 cm
> detail

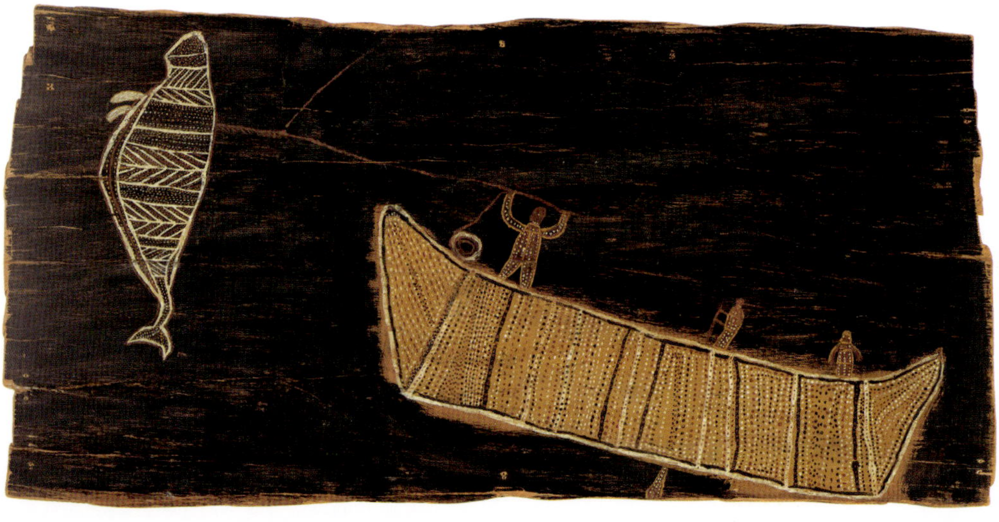

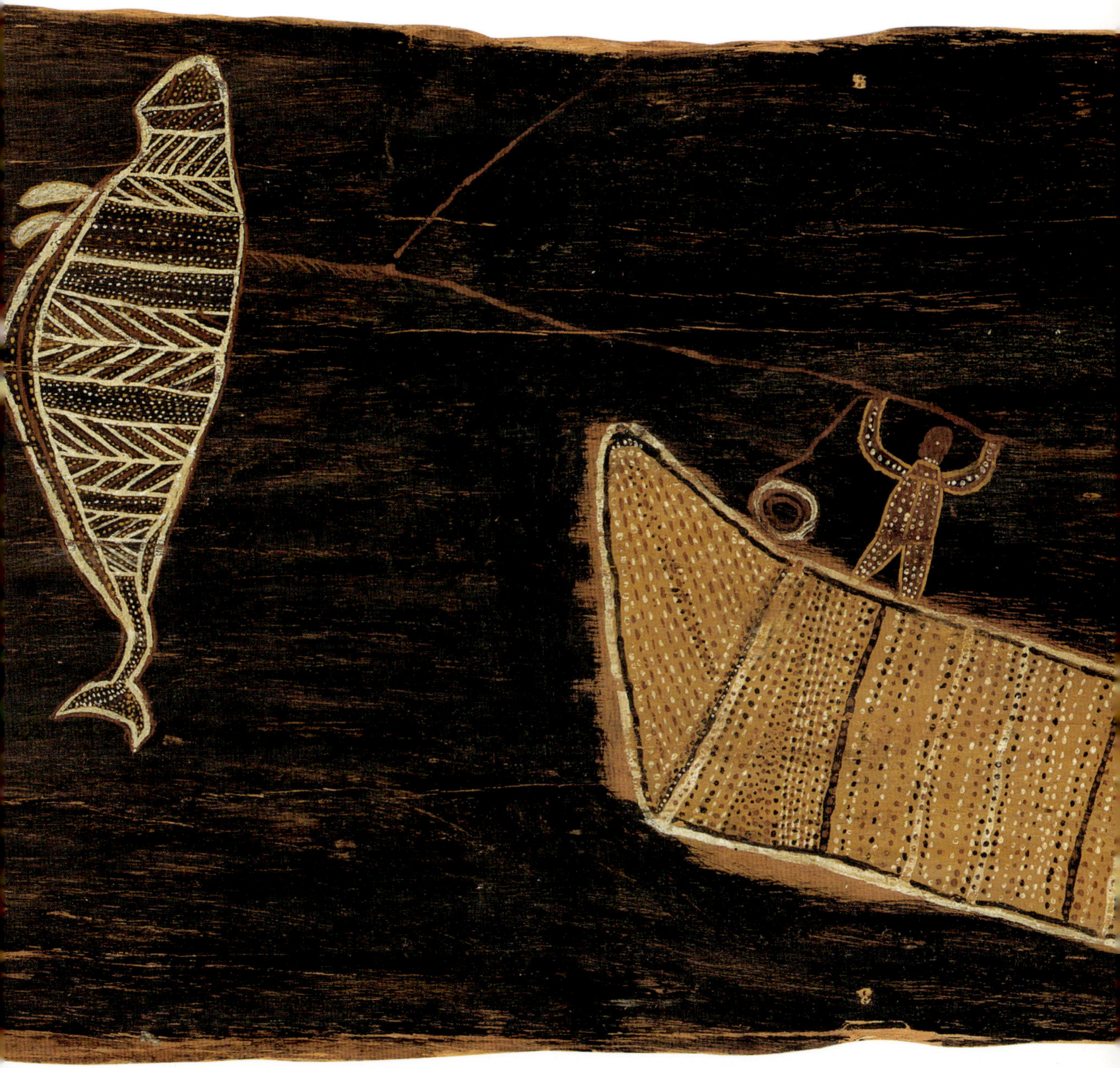

OWEN YALANDJA

BORN 1960
KUNINJKU
NORTHERN TERRITORY

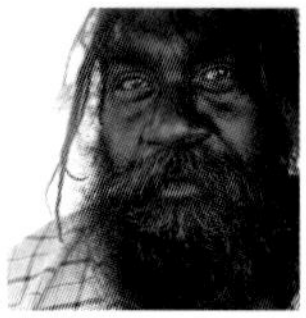

Owen Yalandja, like his brother Crusoe Kurddal, maintains his father Crusoe Kuningbal's patrimony of artistic inspiration in wood carving. Yalandja lives at Barrihdjowkkeng outstation, a camp established by his father and adjacent to a billabong that is a Yirridjdja moiety sacred site for the yawkyawk or young girl spirits. Yawkyawk live in this billabong and their shadows can occasionally be seen as they flee the smell of humans who approach the water. They are imagined to have been girls who transformed into mermaid-like figures with fish tails. While many bark painters in the region have depicted yawkyawk, Yalandja has developed the mimih form created by his father to create his own new form of carving, as in *Yawkyawk*, 1999. One innovative work from 1993 makes use of a natural fork in a tree to create the tail of a mermaid figure. More recently, Yalandja's sculptures have torsos that are much like that of the standard mimih, but with a tapering lower body and forked fish tail. Yalandja also asserts his unique approach by using a black background, as well as the more common red background to these figures. In the early 1990s, he experimented with the dot patterns his father taught him, and created new arrangements – first in arcs to suggest scales, and later, small 'v' shaped marks to suggest individual scales. He uses this graphic innovation to capture the scaly sheen of the watery being.

Yalandja now specialises in producing larger fine art pieces. He favours the wood of the kurrajong tree for carving because it has good strength across the grain, allowing him to incorporate three-dimensional carved elements without the concern that the trunk will split. Yalandja's recent innovations include the selection of more curvilinear tree trunks to give his figures a sinuous appearance. Very thin and waving trunks provide an even more attenuated form. These innovations in three-dimensional form are appropriate to the meaning of the figure, capturing as they do the sinuous movements of the yawkyawk's swimming form. LT

Yawkyawk 1999
Yawkyawk 1999
both natural pigments on Kurrajong wood
261.5 x 12.2 x 8.5 cm
227.5 x 9.8 x 8.4 cm

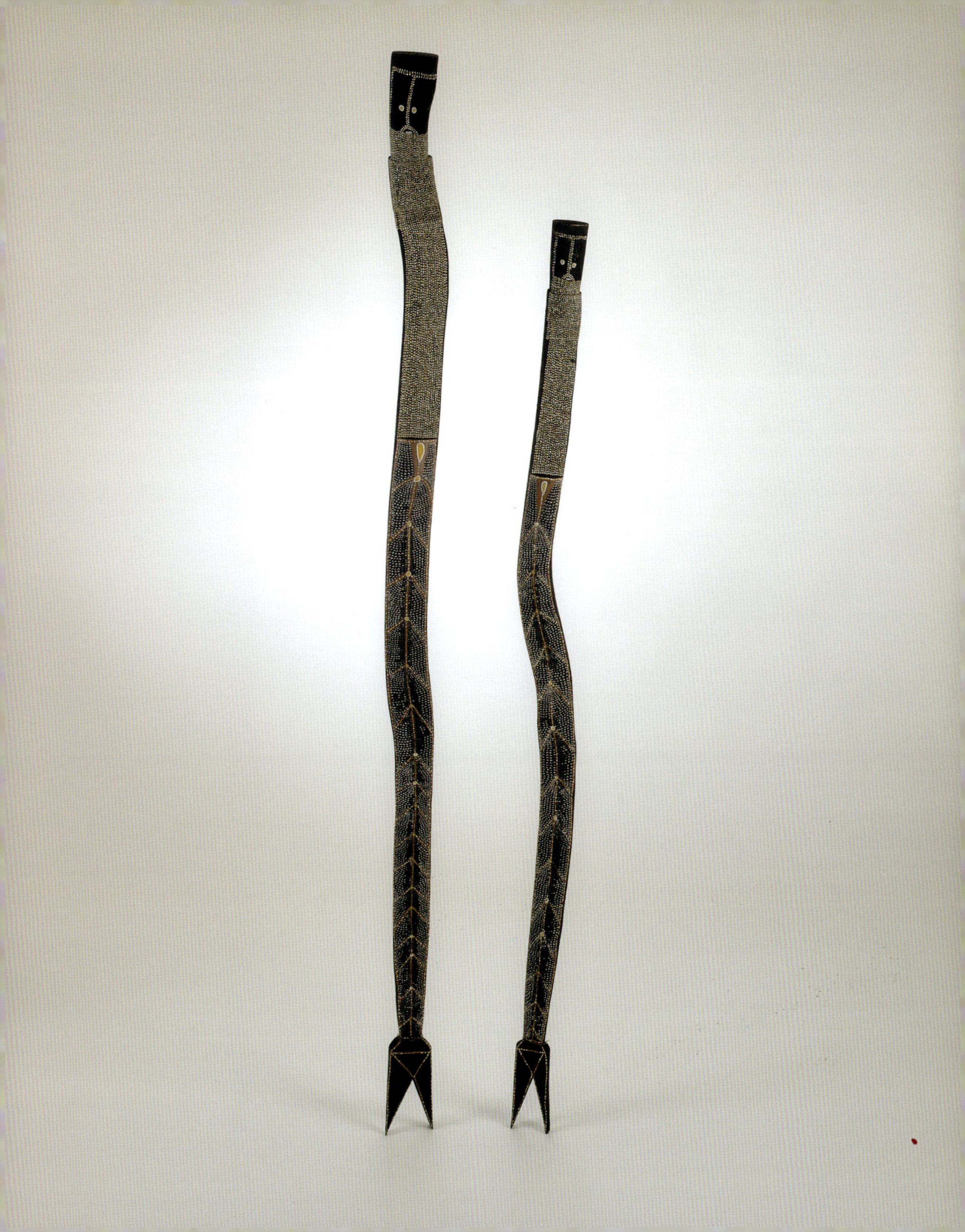

LENA YARINKURA

BORN 1961
REMBARRNGA / KUNE
NORTHERN TERRITORY

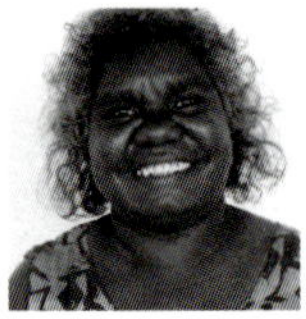

An innovative artist from central Arnhem Land, Lena Yarinkura learned how to weave from her mother, Lena Djamarrayku, with whom she collaborated on creating fibre animals. After mastering the traditional range of twined basketry, Yarinkura soon began experimenting with different shapes and stitch combinations. Before long, her woven sculptures had taken Northern Territory fibre craft and public ceremonial artefacts in a completely new direction.

Following her marriage in the mid-1980s to artist Bob Burruwal, Yarinkura ventured into bark painting and carving hollow log sculptures. This change in media and scale motivated a shift in her approach to fibre, and she started making the traditional long yam sculptures from paperbark bound by string (made from kurrajong tree bark), painting them with red and white ochres.

In the late 1980s, Yarinkura began producing near life-size representations of the major ancestral cycles told by the elders of western and central Arnhem Land. To illustrate the stories that belong to her husband and herself, Yarinkura makes paperbark and woven sculptures of a range of spirit figures, dogs, yawkyawk (mermaid-like spirits) and crocodiles. These installations, often decorated with ochre and feathers, have precedents in men's ceremonial objects that have rarely been seen after the 1960s – as well as the small spirit dolls held by women in Mularra ceremonies. Yarinkura's combining of the traditional with the non-traditional makes her work unique.

Each of Yarinkura's installations in the Art Gallery of New South Wales's collection tells a story.[1] The first is *Two brothers and Modjarrkki the Crocodile*, 1994. It recounts the tale of a crocodile hunt involving a man, his wife and the man's unmarried brother. When the younger brother caught a crocodile underwater, he used a rope to bind its snout, and the crocodile broke loose and killed the husband. The younger brother took responsibility for the widow and married his dead brother's wife. The second installation tells the story of *The tragedy of Bulanj and Balang*, 1994. Bulanj coveted another man's wife, whom he was forbidden to marry under customary law. He schemed to win her by offering to accompany her son Balang through his initiation ceremony. However, the boy died and, after many subterfuges, Bulanj was discovered with the white-ochred bones of the boy in a dilly bag. After a lengthy pursuit, the family eventually succeeded in the payback (revenge) killing of Bulanj for his crime. GA

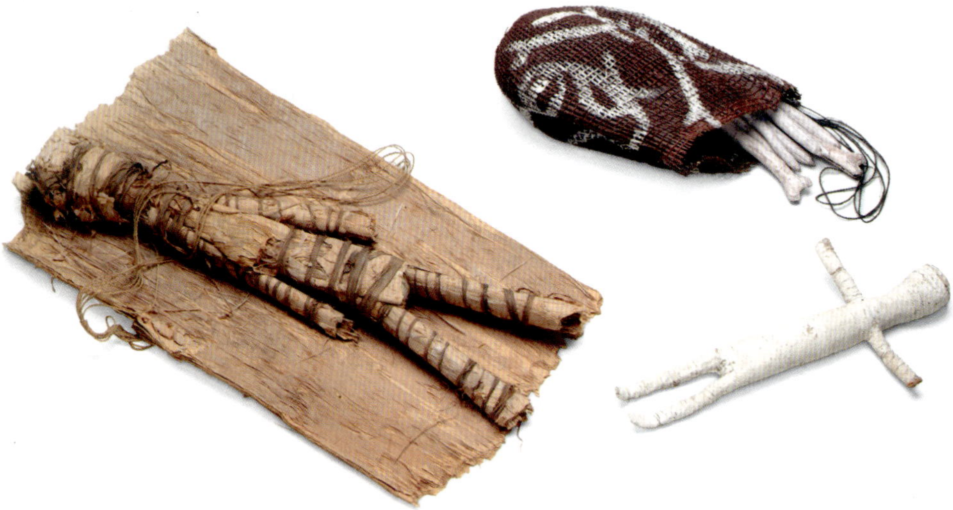

The tragedy of Bulanj and Balang 1994
six parts: paperbark, string, natural pigments
100 x 100 cm overall

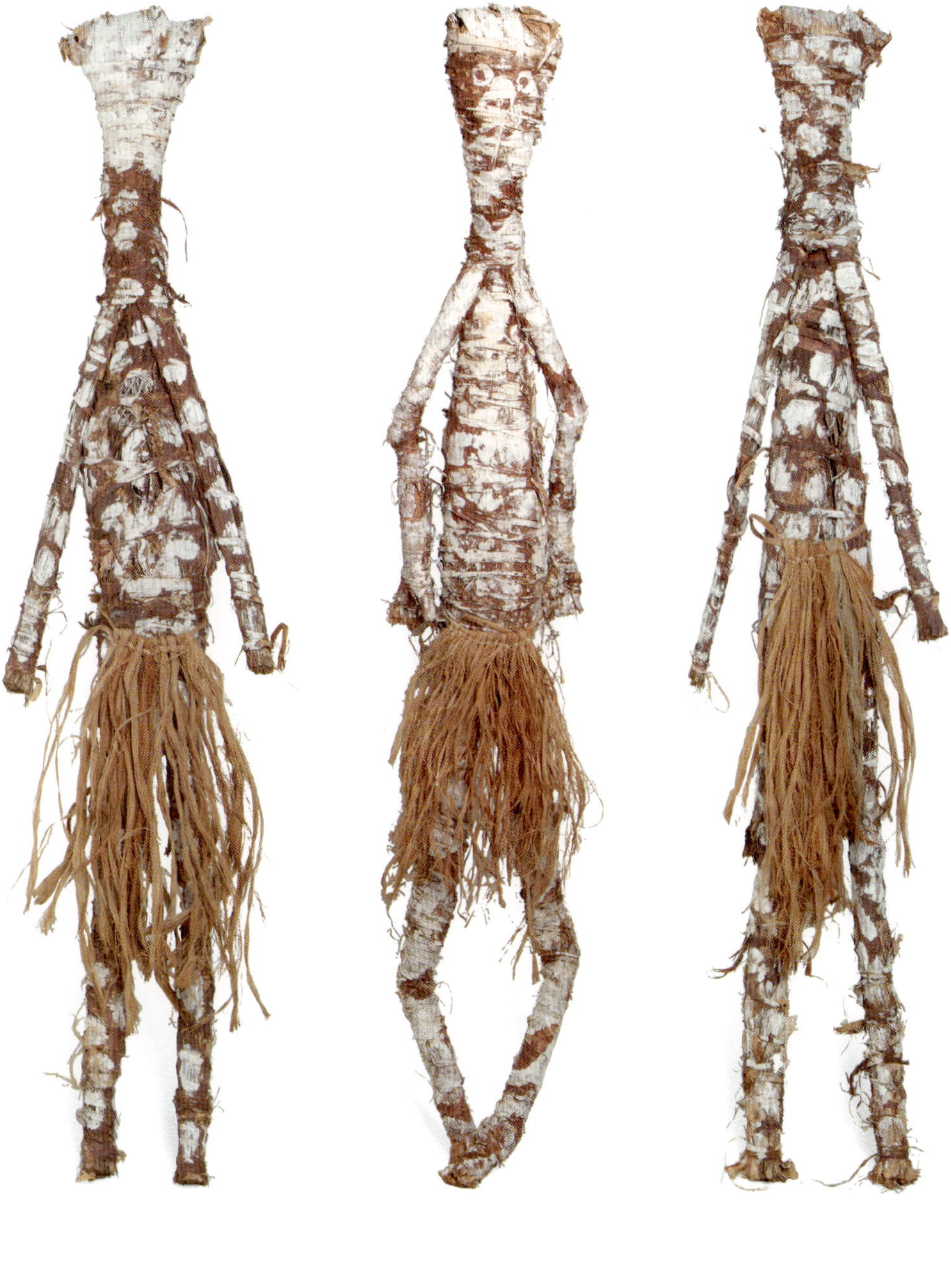

MUNGGURRAWUY YUNUPINGU

c.1907–1978
GUMATJ
NORTHERN TERRITORY

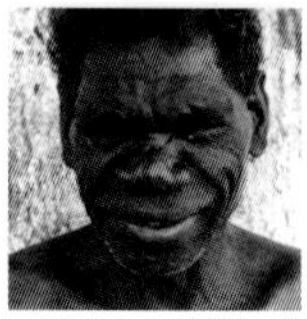

Biranybirany on Caledon Bay is the ancestral country for the three branches of the Gumatj clan, and is home to the major Gumatj totems: Baru (saltwater crocodile) and Gurtha (fire). It is also the homeland of the Yunupingu family. In 1959 – when Munggurawuy Yunupingu painted the Gumatj ancestral fire story on four large barks – he was ceremonial leader, custodian of knowledge and keeper of the law for the Gumatj clan of the Yirritja moiety in north-east Arnhem Land.

Lany'tjung story (*Crocodile and Bandicoot*), 1959, depicts the story of the ancestral fire that burnt across a huge swathe of eastern Arnhem Land, from Biranybirany to Melville Bay. During a ceremony near Caledon Bay, the fire on the ceremonial ground flared up, out of control, and raged northwards. Above this scene, Munggurawuy includes two images of Baru, making the association with the historical fire that caused the distinct markings on crocodiles' backs.

The patterns of diamond-shaped miny'tji (sacred clan designs) at the top left of the painting allude to Munggurrawuy's preoccupation with a missing canoe at the time he made this painting. By including this event with the ancestral story, he shows the relationship between the ancestral past and the present. Below this panel, Munggurawuy has painted a bandicoot running from one hollow log to another, showing that the bushfire has burnt itself out. The diamond shapes in this section represent flames and ashes, a swamp fire, leaves and grass aflame, sandbanks, a creek, footprints and sea-weed, which are all depicted in different configurations of miny'tji.

In *The Thunder Spirits* (*Birimbira*), 1961, Munggurawuy shows the Gumatj ancestors as two black serpents shooting bolts of lightning. The ancestor, Yumbulbul, is depicted revelling in the rain from a thundercloud below, with its black centre outlined in yellow and containing wavy lines representing rain. The top section of the painting reveals the different species of marine creatures that emerge after the rain. The miny'tji surrounding the stingray and the crocodile symbolises the sea.[1]

Munggurrawuy assisted Birrikitji Gumana and Narritjin Maymuru in painting the Yirritja church panels now housed in the Buku-Larrngay Mulka Museum at Yirrkala. He painted Yirritja designs on a bark petition presented to Federal Parliament in 1963, which outlined Yolngu grievances over the intrusion of mining interests in Arnhem Land. Munggurrawuy's children – particularly Gaymala, Galarrwuy and Mandawuy Yunupingu – have also distinguished themselves as Yolngu leaders in politics and the arts. KW

left **The Thunder Spirits (Birimbira)** 1961
natural pigments on bark
150.2 x 60.4 cm

right **Lany'tjung story (Crocodile and Bandicoot)** 1959
natural pigments on bark
193 x 72 cm

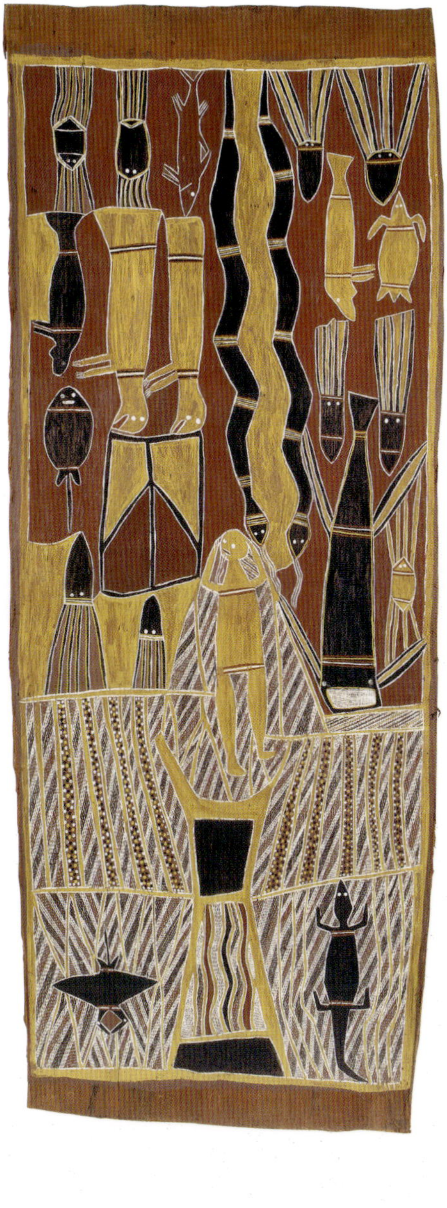

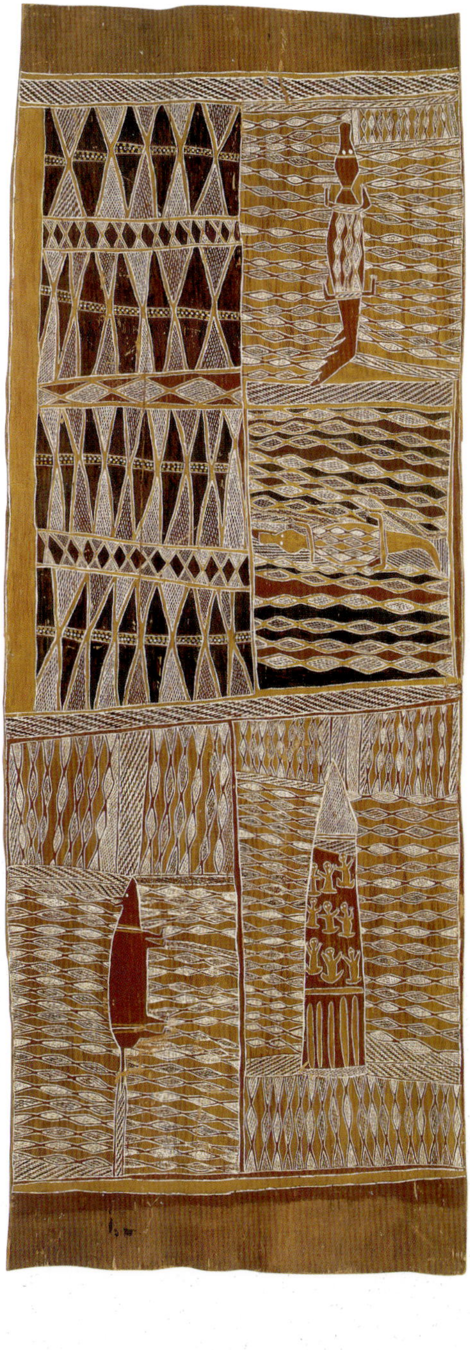

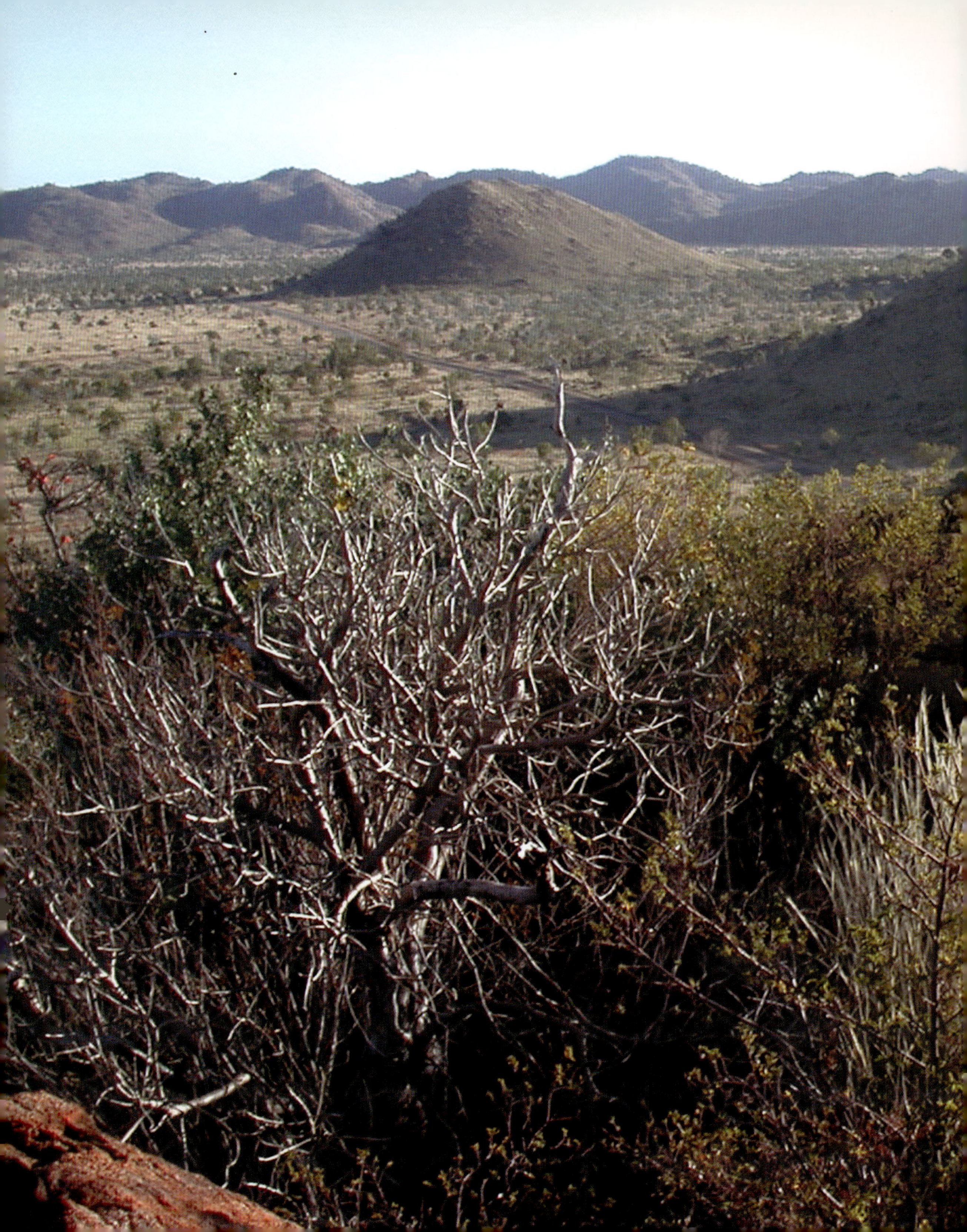

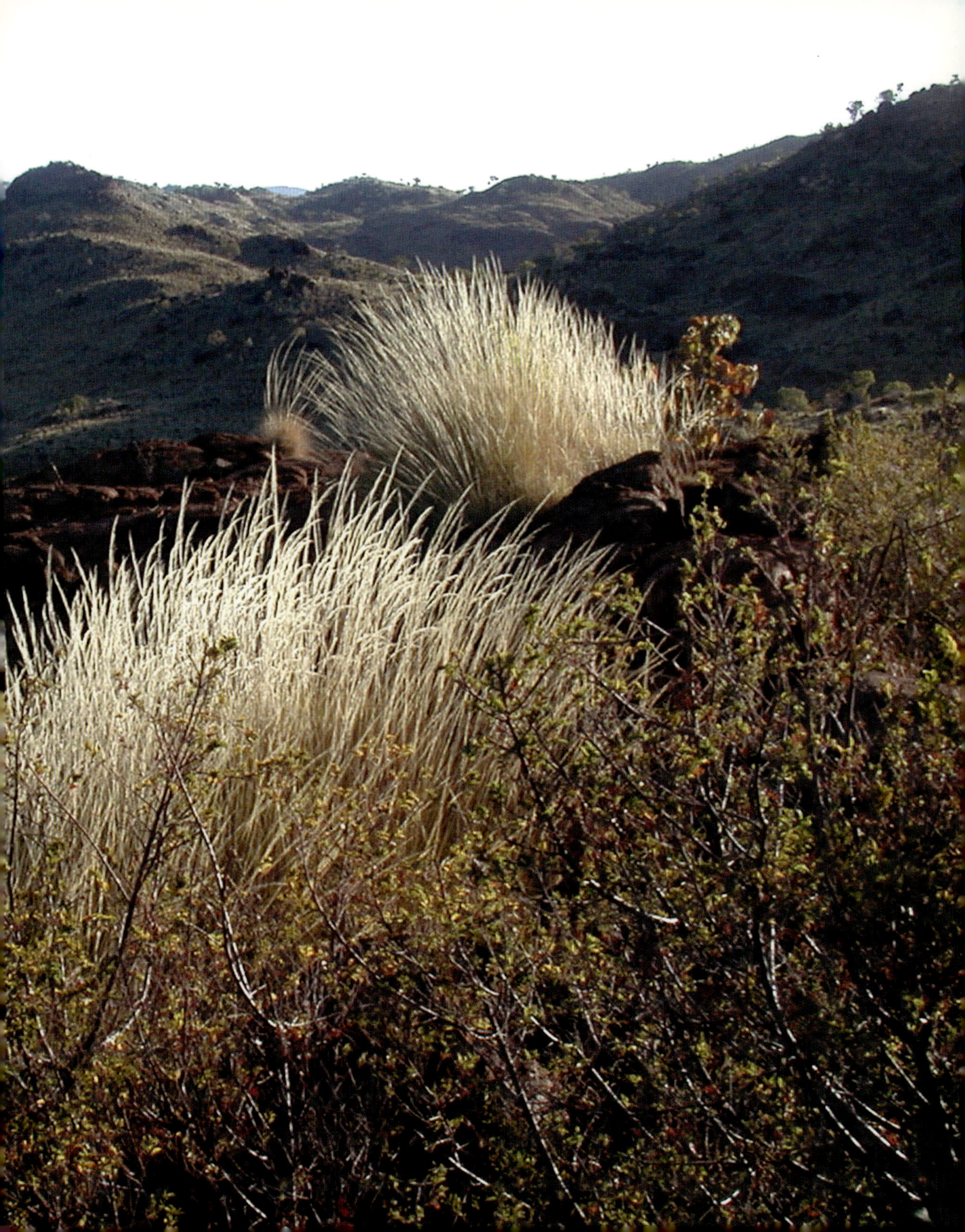

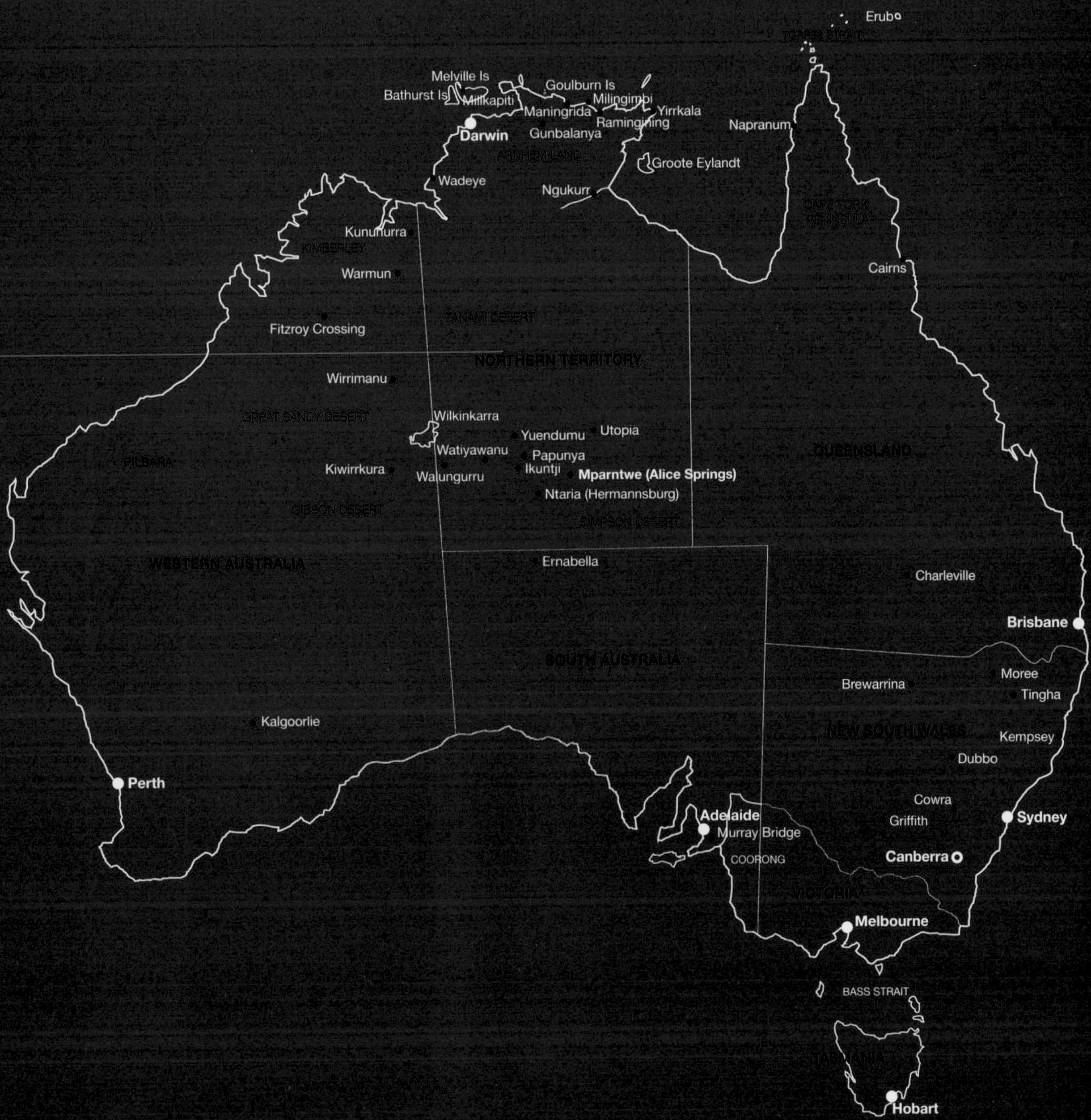
Erub
Melville Is
Bathurst Is
Milikapiti
Goulburn Is
Milingimbi
Maningrida
Yirrkala
Ramingining
Darwin
Gunbalanya
Napranum
ARNHEM LAND
Groote Eylandt
Wadeye
Ngukurr
Kununurra
KIMBERLEY
Warmun
Cairns
TANAMI DESERT
Fitzroy Crossing
NORTHERN TERRITORY
Wirrimanu
GREAT SANDY DESERT
Wilkinkarra
Yuendumu
Utopia
Watiyawanu
Papunya
QUEENSLAND
PILBARA
Kiwirrkura
Walungurru
Ikuntji
Mparntwe (Alice Springs)
Ntaria (Hermannsburg)
GIBSON DESERT
SIMPSON DESERT
WESTERN AUSTRALIA
Ernabella
Charleville
Brisbane
SOUTH AUSTRALIA
Moree
Brewarrina
Tingha
Kalgoorlie
NEW SOUTH WALES
Kempsey
Dubbo
Perth
Cowra
Adelaide
Griffith
Sydney
Murray Bridge
COORONG
Canberra
VICTORIA
Melbourne
BASS STRAIT
Hobart

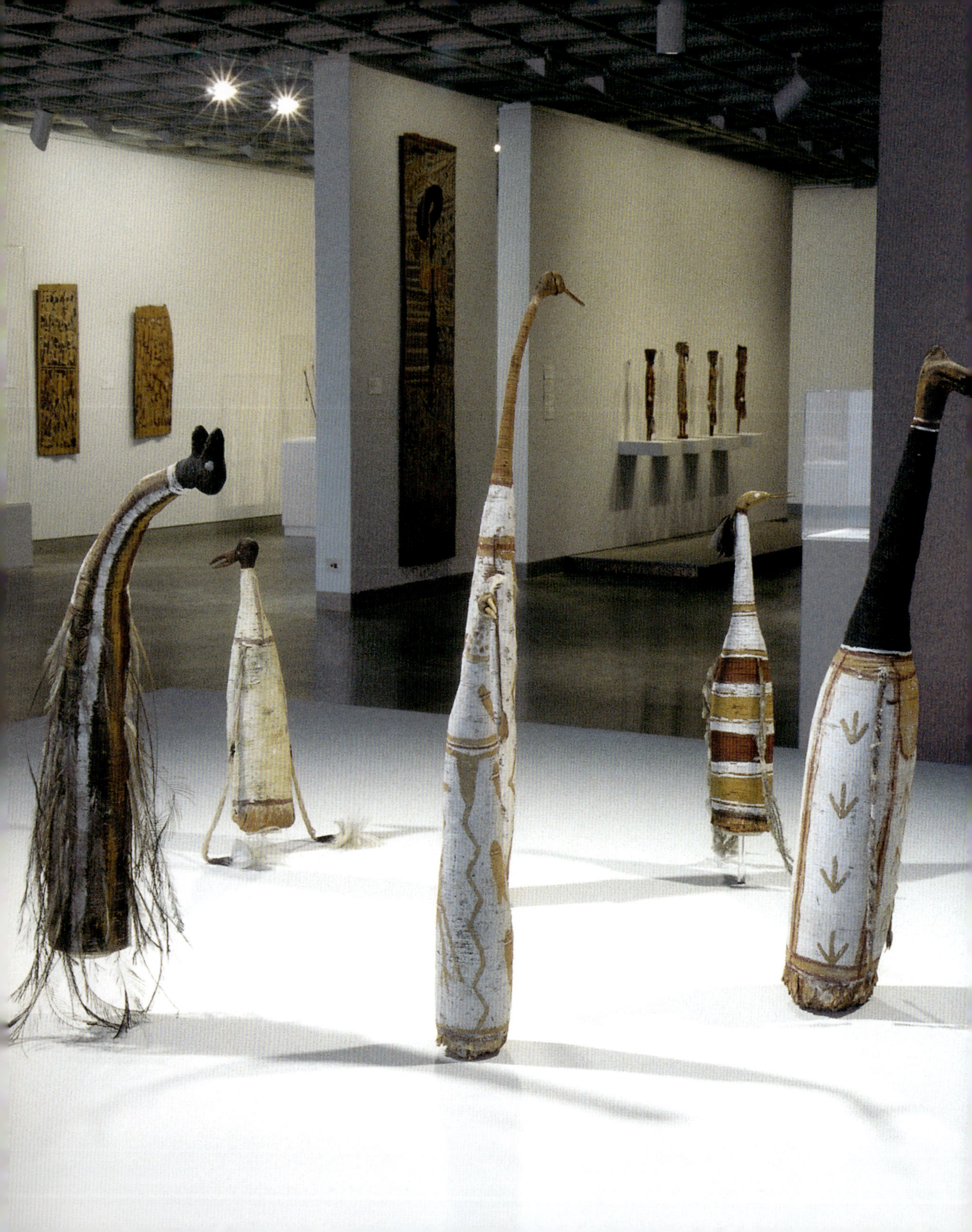

GLOSSARY

Aboriginal and Torres Strait Islander Arts Board of the Australia Council for the Arts assists Aboriginal and Torres Strait Islander people to claim, control and enhance their cultural inheritance through grants and the implementation of the Australia Council's National Aboriginal and Torres Strait Islander Arts Policy. Responsible for awarding the annual Red Ochre Award for outstanding contribution to the arts by an Indigenous person.

Aboriginal art centres community-based arts organisations primarily located in remote Aboriginal communities.

Aboriginal Artists Gallery the Sydney gallery of Aboriginal Arts Australia Limited (AAAL), established by the Aboriginal Development Commission to develop Aboriginal art markets within Australia and internationally. AAAL had its origins in Aboriginal Arts and Crafts Pty Limited, established in 1971, and ceased operations in 1991.

Aboriginal Tent Embassy first erected outside Parliament House in Canberra on Australia Day, 26 January 1972, as a protest against the Federal Government's failure to recognise Aboriginal land rights.

Aborigines Protection Board a New South Wales government agency established in 1883 that later became the Aboriginal Welfare Board (1940–69). Similar agencies operated in each state, each vested with the power to regulate the lives of Aboriginal people.

Altyerr/Akngganenty see Dreaming, terms used by Central Australian language groups including Anmatyerr.

Art advisers/art coordinators senior staff of an Aboriginal art centre.

Australia Council the Federal Government's arts funding and advisory body, established as a Commonwealth statutory authority under the *Australia Council Act*, 1975. The Australia Council uses a system of peer assessment through media-based boards to allocate public money for the arts, and awards fellowships each year to artists for outstanding achievement.

Australian Institute of Aboriginal and Torres Strait Islander Studies (AIATSIS) an independent Commonwealth Government statutory authority devoted to Aboriginal and Torres Strait Islander studies. It is Australia's premiere institution for information about the cultures and lifestyles of Aboriginal and Torres Strait Islander peoples.

Balanda originally a Malay word for Europeans of Dutch descent, as in 'Hollander'.

Geoffrey Bardon (1940–2003) a teacher who taught art and craft at Papunya from February 1971 to August 1972. Bardon was instrumental in the foundation of the Papunya School Painters Cooperative, which later became the Papunya Tula Artists company.

Coniston Massacre a police-led massacre, from August to October 1928, in the Lander River area of the Northern Territory in retaliation for the killing of trapper and prospector Frederick Brooks. Over the next year, police and locals indiscriminately killed hundreds of Warlpiri people in the surrounding regions. Clifford Possum Tjapaltjarri called this the 'killing times'. Those responsible for the massacre were exonerated.

Dreaming, Dreamings, Dreamtime a non-Indigenous term commonly used to describe the creative era when ancestral beings created the cultural, social and physical landscape of Aboriginal Australia. This period continues to influence the spiritual beliefs and cultural practices of Aboriginal people today. See also Altyerr/ Akngganenty, Ngarrangkarni, Tjukurrpa, Wangarr.

Eora Centre TAFE an educational and cultural institution for Indigenous students, established in Redfern in 1984, by the New South Wales Department of Technical and Further Education.

Film Australia a Federal Government-owned company that produces and distributes documentaries and educational programmes about issues of national interest to Australia.

Goori alternate spelling of Koori.

Koori a generic name for the Aboriginal people of New South Wales. Other regional terms include Murri, Nunga, Nyoongar, Yamitji, Yapa and Yolngu.

Land Rights a political movement led by Aboriginal activists advocating social justice and self-determination for Indigenous people through government recognition of the sovereignty of Indigenous people and their prior ownership of their land. Land claims may be based on traditional ownership or seek compensation for dispossession from traditional lands. The majority of successful claims have been made in the Northern Territory under the *Aboriginal Land Rights (NT) Act*, 1976.

Vincent Lingiari (1919–1988) a Gurindji elder who led a walk-off from Wave Hill Station on 23 August, 1966, to protest against discriminatory employment conditions on the largest cattle station in Australia. The strike lasted nine years and became a catalyst for the recognition of land rights.

Macassan people from Macassar in south Sulawesi, Indonesia, who traded with Aboriginal coastal communities of the Northern Territory for hundreds of years until banned by the Australian government in 1906.

Mission settlements established across Australia from the 1800s by religious and government agencies for Indigenous people who had been forcibly removed from their land. Missions generally took on the role of administering the government's assimilation policy. While some missions encouraged the commercialisation of Aboriginal culture, others repressed Indigenous ceremonies, languages and cultural beliefs. The term 'mission' is also applied to reserves and stations.

Moiety an anthropological term for the division of society and natural phenomena into two halves, as in the Yirritja and Dhuwa moieties of Arnhem Land, Northern Territory.

Native Title the entitlement of Indigenous people under common law to traditional land in accordance with the provisions of the Federal *Native Title Act*, 1993, which recognises the rights and interests in land and water that Indigenous people have under their traditional laws and customs. The High Court of Australia rejected the doctrine of terra nullius in the Mabo decision of 1992, and, in the subsequent Wik decision of 1996, found that Native Title can co-exist with other interests, such as pastoral leases.

Ngarrangkarni see Dreaming, a term used by East Kimberley language groups including Gija.

Nunga see Koori, a generic name for the Aboriginal people of South Australia.

Ochre natural earth pigments containing iron oxides used in traditional and contemporary art practice. Significant for both its spiritual qualities and use as a valuable trade item.

Outstation small Aboriginal settlements of family members living on their traditional land.

Pukumani the funerary ceremony of the Tiwi people of Bathurst and Melville Islands, which commemorates the death of the ancestor, Purukuparli. Also used generally to refer cultural practice and associated objects of a restricted nature.

Redfern an inner-city suburb of Sydney centred around Eveleigh Street, with a significant Aboriginal population. The site of important Aboriginal initiatives in health, welfare and legal services.

Reserve see Mission

Stolen Generations a term used to describe the thousands of Aboriginal children forcibly removed from their parents in accordance with government assimilation policy up until the 1970s. Many children were indentured into domestic servitude and were never reunited with their families. This deplorable part of Australia's history is yet to be formally recognised by the Australian government.

Donald Thomson (1901–1970) an anthropologist who studied and worked with the Yolngu people in Arnhem Land in the 1930s and the Pintupi people in the Central Desert in the 1950s and 1960s. Served on the Aborigines Welfare Board of Victoria and was a foundation member of the Australia Institute of Aboriginal Studies in 1964 (now AIATSIS).

Tingari a Tjukurrpa, regionally specific to the Western Desert, referring to travelling ancestors involved in post-initiatory activity of a secret sacred nature. Generally depicted as interconnected concentric circles in ceremonial and contemporary painting.

Tjukurrpa see Dreaming, a term used by Western Desert language groups including the Pintupi, Warlpiri, Luritja and Anmatyerr.

Tranby Aboriginal College, Indigenous adult training institution in Sydney.

Trepang sea cucumber

Wangarr see Dreaming, a term used by Arnhem Land language groups.

Wik decision, see Native Title

Yolngu see Koori, a generic name for Aboriginal people of central and eastern Arnhem Land.

CONTRIBUTORS

George Alexander (GA)
George Alexander writes fiction as well as art criticism and is Coordinator of Contemporary Art Education at the Art Gallery of New South Wales.

Natasha Brook (NB)
Natasha Brook trained in Sydney as a graphic designer, studied Fine Arts (painting) and has worked as a freelance writer and designer. She spent 2001 in Alice Springs painting and studying the Arrernte language and culture.

Deborah Edwards (DE)
Deborah Edwards worked at Sydney University and the Queensland Art Gallery before joining the Art Gallery of New South Wales. She was appointed Curator of Australian Art in 1992, and has curated various exhibitions and written publications on Godfrey Miller, Rayner Hoff and his school, Rosalie Gascoigne, and the monograph and retrospective exhibition on Robert Klippel in 2002.

Hannah Fink (HF)
Hannah Fink is a former editor of *Art AsiaPacific* and *Art and Australia* magazines, and co-editor with Hetti Perkins of *Papunya Tula: Genesis and Genius*.

Vivien Johnson (VJ)
Dr Vivien Johnson is a Sydney writer and sociologist. She curated the Clifford Possum retrospective for the Art Gallery of South Australia. She is a senior ARC Research Fellow, based at the Centre for Cross-Cultural Research at the Australian National University, writing the history of the Papunya Tula artists.

Jonathan Jones (JJ)
Jonathan Jones is a member of the Kamilaroi and Wiradjuri communities and was curator at Boomalli Aboriginal Artists Cooperative from 2000 to 2002, working on projects such as an international exchange with First Nations in Canada. He is an installation artist exhibiting nationally and internationally and currently works at the Art Gallery of New South Wales as Coordinator Aboriginal and Torres Strait Islander Art Programmes.

John Kean (JK)
John Kean was an art adviser for Papunya Tula Artists from mid-1977 to the end of 1979. In 1990, as the inaugural Exhibition Coordinator at Tandanya National Aboriginal Cultural Institute, he curated 'East to West: Land in Papunya Tula Painting'. He is currently Producer at Museum Victoria.

Eric Kjellgren (EK)
Eric Kjellgren is the Evelyn A. J. Hall and John A. Friede Assistant Curator for Oceanic Art at the Metropolitan Museum of Art in New York where he has curated exhibitions on the art of Easter Island and Borneo. Dr Kjellgren has worked extensively with contemporary Aboriginal painters in the East Kimberley. A former Fulbright scholar, he has served as Secretary of the Pacific Arts Association since 1999 and was recently made a Fellow of the Royal Geographical Society.

Steven Miller (SM)
Steven Miller is Archivist, Art Gallery of New South Wales.

Howard Morphy (HM)
Howard Morphy is Professor and Director of the Centre for Cross-Cultural Research at the Australian National University. He has published widely in the anthropology of art, aesthetics, performance, museum anthropology, visual anthropology and religion. His books include *Ancestral Connections: Art and an Aboriginal System of Knowledge*, University of Chicago Press and *Aboriginal Art*, Phaidon.

Hetti Perkins (HP)
Hetti Perkins is a member of the Arrernte and Kalkadoon communities of Central Australia and Queensland, now living in Sydney. She was co-curator with Brenda L. Croft of 'fluent', Australia's representative exhibition at the 1997 Venice Biennale, and was a member of the selection committee of the 2000 Biennale of Sydney. She is Curator, Aboriginal and Torres Strait Islander Art at the Art Gallery of New South Wales.

Luke Taylor (LT)
Luke Taylor is currently Director of Research at the Australian Institute of Aboriginal and Torres Strait Islander Studies and Adjunct Professor with the Centre for Cross-Cultural Research at the Australian National University. Previously he was Curator and then Senior Curator in the Gallery of Aboriginal Australia at the National Museum of Australia from 1990 to 2000. He is an anthropologist who specialises in research with Aboriginal and Torres Strait Islander artists and has written a number of books on Aboriginal art.

Wayne Tunnicliffe (WT)
Wayne Tunnicliffe is Curator of Contemporary Australian Art at the Art Gallery of New South Wales. He has written extensively on contemporary Australian practice and curated many exhibitions. Recent projects have included solo exhibitions by Tracey Emin and Simryn Gill and the group show 'BitterSweet'. In 1999 he co-curated 'Talkback' with Hetti Perkins as part of Australian Perspecta.

Ken Watson (KW)
Ken Watson is Assistant Curator of Aboriginal and Torres Strait Islander Art at the Art Gallery of New South Wales.

LIST OF WORKS

Ian Abdulla

Swimming before school 1995
synthetic polymer paint on canvas
160 x 240 cm
Mollie Gowing Acquisition Fund for Contemporary Aboriginal Art 1996
219.1996
© Ian W. Abdulla, courtesy Greenaway Art Gallery

Paddy Bedford

Untitled (Emu) 1999
natural pigments on canvas
122.2 x 135.3 cm
Mollie Gowing Acquisition Fund for Contemporary Aboriginal Art 1999
60.1999

Untitled (Old Bedford) 1999
natural pigments on canvas
122.5 x 135.1 cm
Mollie Gowing Acquisition Fund for Contemporary Aboriginal Art 1999
61.1999
© Paddy Bedford, courtesy Jirrawun Aboriginal Art Corporation

Richard Bell

Pigeonholes 1992
13 photographic panels on composition board
76 x 292 cm overall
Purchased 1993
389.1993

Devine inspiration 1993
synthetic polymer paint and collage on canvas
239.6 x 149.6 cm
Purchased with funds provided by the Contemporary Collection Benefactors 1993
549.1993
© Richard Bell, courtesy Fireworks Gallery

Billy Benn

In the bush Barrow Creek way c.1996
synthetic polymer paint on flexi panel
30 x 244 cm
Purchased 2002
304.2002
© Billy Benn, courtesy Bindi Centa Arts

Binyinyuwuy

Trees and flying fox camp c.1950s
natural pigments on bark
48 x 29.5 cm
Purchased 1962
10.1962

Rain in the trees c.1959
natural pigments on bark
74 x 39.4 cm
Purchased 1962
7.1962

Yirritja honey bee design (Niwuda) c.1960
natural pigments on bark
74.5 x 35 cm
Gift of Dr Stuart Scougall 1960
48.1960
© The Binyinyuwuy Estate

Mervyn Bishop

Life and death dash 1971
gelatin silver photograph
40.4 x 30.1 cm
Hallmark Cards Australian Photography Collection Fund 1991
168.1991
© Mervyn Bishop and *The Sydney Morning Herald*

Prime Minister Gough Whitlam pours soil into the hands of traditional landowner Vincent Lingiari, Northern Territory 1975
printed 1999
type R3 photograph
30.5 x 30.5 cm
Hallmark Cards Australian Photography Collection Fund 1991
58.2000
© Mervyn Bishop and Department of Aboriginal Affairs, Viscopy Ltd

Girl pours tea, Burnt Bridge 1988
gelatin silver photograph
30.1 x 40.4 cm
Hallmark Cards Australian Photography Collection Fund 1991
174.1991
© Mervyn Bishop, Viscopy Ltd

John Bulunbulun

Journey of the Guwaynang 2000
natural pigments on eucalyptus bark
217 x 97 cm
Mollie Gowing Acquisition Fund for Contemporary Aboriginal Art 2001
360.2001
© John Bulunbulun, courtesy Maningrida Arts and Culture and Viscopy Ltd

Nym Bunduck & Kevin Bunduck

Emus feeding 1961
natural pigments on bark
78.8 x 179 cm
Gift of Dr Stuart Scougall 1961
22.1961
© Estate of Kevin and Nym Bunduck, courtesy Kardu Numida Council

Robert Campbell Jnr

Sunset over the Macleay overlooking Euroka 1990
synthetic polymer paint on canvas
118 x 197.5 cm
Mollie Gowing Acquisition Fund for Contemporary Aboriginal Art 1997
285.1997

Map of the massacres of blacks on the Macleay Valley 1990
synthetic polymer paint on canvas
78.8 x 114.3 cm
Purchased 1994
559.1994
© Estate of Robert Campbell Jnr

Robert Ambrose Cole

Untitled 1993
Untitled 1993
both synthetic polymer paint on paper on canvas
76.5 x 58 cm
77.5 x 57 cm
Mollie Gowing Acquisition Fund for Contemporary Aboriginal Art 1993
312–313.1993
© Estate of Robert Ambrose Cole, courtesy Utopia Art Sydney

Brenda L. Croft

Shane Phillips and Noel Collett, Eveleigh Street, Redfern 1992
duratran, light box
180 x 270 x 20 cm
Gift of Brenda L. Croft 2000
166.2000.2

Mary Mumbulla and Murri Craigie 1993
R3 colour photograph
99.5 x 120.5 cm
Purchased 1993
391.1993
© Brenda L. Croft, Viscopy Ltd

Destiny Deacon

Dreaming in urban areas 1993
colour polaroid laser copies
62.5 x 56.5 cm overall
Purchased 1993
393.1993

Waiting for Goddess 1994
colour bubble-jet print from polaroid photograph
69.8 x 56.7 cm
Purchased 1996
371.1996
© Destiny Deacon, courtesy Roslyn Oxley9 Gallery

Dawidi Djulwarak

Snakes and fish anticipating rain c.1950s
natural pigments on bark
44 x 17 cm
Purchased 1962
5.1962
© Estate of Dawidi Djulwarak

Kevin Gilbert

Christmas Eve in the land of the dispossessed 1968
printed 1990
linocut
45 x 63 cm
Purchased 1993
310.1993
© Estate of Kevin Gilbert

Willie Gudabi

Gabal ritual 1990
synthetic polymer paint on canvas
126.1 x 92.1 cm
Gift of Margaret Tuckson 1992
22.1992

Willie Gudabi & Moima Willie
Dead man ceremony 1993
synthetic polymer paint on canvas
237 x 136 cm
Mollie Gowing Acquisition Fund for Contemporary Aboriginal Art 1993
546.1993
© Estate of Willie Gudabi, courtesy Alcaston Gallery

Philip Gudthaykudthay

Badurru and Dindin (Hollow log and dilly bag) 1985
natural pigments on wood
169 x 14 cm/29.8 x 15.2 cm
Purchased 1985
223.1985–224.1985

Badurru (Hollow log) 1986
natural pigments on wood
148.5 x 13.7 x 13.7 cm
Purchased 1986
246.1986

Badurru (Hollow log) 1986
natural pigments on wood
153 x 14 x 14 cm
Purchased 1986
247.1986
© Philip Gudthaykudthay, Viscopy Ltd

Mithinarri Gurruwiwi

Djaykung (File snakes) c.1960
natural pigments on bark
280 x 70 cm
Gift of Professor Harry Messel 1987
392.1987

Wuyal the Honey Man c.1960
natural pigments on bark
116 x 40 cm
Gift of Harry Messel 1989
67.1989
© Estate of Mithinarri Gurruwiwi, courtesy Buku-Larrngay Mulka Arts

Roy Kennedy

Mossgiel Weigh Station 2001
etching
12.3 x 20.2 cm
Mollie Gowing Acquisition Fund for Contemporary Aboriginal Art 2001
449.2001

Pepper Tree Avenue 2001
etching
23 x 28.7 cm
Mollie Gowing Acquisition Fund for Contemporary Aboriginal Art 2001
450.2001
© Roy Kennedy

Emily Kame Kngwarreye

Untitled (Alhalker) 1992
synthetic polymer paint on canvas
165 x 480 cm
Mollie Gowing Acquisition Fund for Contemporary Aboriginal Art 1992
229.1992

Untitled (Awely) 1994
triptych: synthetic polymer paint on paper laminated to canvas
100.7 x 213 cm overall
Purchased 1994
567.1994
© Estate of Emily Kame Kngwarreye, Viscopy Ltd

Yvonne Koolmatrie

Eel trap 1997
sedge rushes (Lepidosperma canesens)
168 x 59 x 59 cm
Mollie Gowing Acquisition Fund for Contemporary Aboriginal Art 1999
97.1999
© Yvonne Koolmatrie

Anchor Kulunba

Mandjabu (Conical fish trap) 1985
wood, milil vine
290 x 48 x 70 cm
Purchased 1985
222.1985
© Estate of Anchor Kulunba, courtesy Maningrida Arts and Culture

Crusoe Kurddal

Mimih spirits c.1985
natural pigments on wood
272 x 15 x 15 cm
270 x 14 x 14 cm
314 x 19.5 x 14 cm
Purchased 1985
80–81.1985, 180.1985
© Crusoe Kurddal, courtesy Maningrida Arts and Culture and Viscopy Ltd

Queenie McKenzie

Untitled c.1994
natural pigments on canvas
80 x 100 cm
Gift of Christopher Hodges and Helen Eager 2002
192.2002
© Estate of Queenie McKenzie, courtesy Red Rock Art

Dr Pantjiti Mary McLean

Hunting grounds 1993
synthetic polymer paint, charcoal and ochre on paper
138.5 x 261 cm
Mollie Gowing Acquisition Fund for Contemporary Aboriginal Art 1993
547.1993
© Dr Pantjiti Mary McLean

Dr David Malangi

Food pattern of trees c.1960
natural pigments on bark
57.5 x 31.1 cm
Purchased 1962
4.1962

Gunmirringu funeral scene 1983
natural pigments on bark
156 x 73.7 cm
Purchased 1984
126.1984
© Estate of Dr David Malangi, Viscopy Ltd

Samuel Manggudja

Figure with long fingers 1960
natural pigments on bark
34.5 x 103.5 cm
Gift of Dr Stuart Scougall 1961
9.1961

Man with leprosy 1961
natural pigments on bark
75 x 39.7 cm
Gift of Dr Stuart Scougall 1961
10.1961
© Estate of Samuel Manggudja, courtesy Injalak Arts

Banduk Marika

Miyapunuwuy Yarru Yan – Turtle hunting at Dhambaliya (Bremer Island) 1987
linocut
28.7 x 48.2 cm
Purchased 1988
12.1988

Wawalak Wulay, Djan'kawu Creation 1987
linocut
23.3 x 41.4 cm
Purchased 1988
13.1988
© Banduk Marika, Viscopy Ltd

Mawalan Marika

Djan'kawu creation story 1959
natural pigments on bark
188 x 64.8 cm
Gift of Dr Stuart Scougall 1959
68.1959

Djan'kawu, ancestral being of the Dhuwa moiety 1960
Djan'kawu, ancestral being of the Dhuwa moiety 1960
both wood, human hair, bark fibre, parakeet feathers, white feathers, natural pigments
74.3 cm
81 cm
Gifts of Dr Stuart Scougall 1960
7–8.1960
© Estate of Mawalan Marika

Wandjuk Marika

Djan'kawu Story (The sun rising) 1959
natural pigments on bark
44.8 x 32.4 cm
Gift of Dr Stuart Scougall 1959
50.1959

Sea life (Dreaming of the artist's mother) 1959
natural pigments on bark
102.9 x 62.9 cm
Gift of Dr Stuart Scougall 1959
56.1959
© Estate of Wandjuk Marika

John Mawurndjul

Yawkyawk (Young girl's spirit) 1985
Yawkyawk (Young girl's spirit) 1985
both natural pigments on bark
50.5 x 27 cm
47.5 x 25.9 cm
Purchased 1985
216.1985.1–2

Mardayin ceremony 2000
natural pigments on bark
170 x 78 cm
Don Mitchell Bequest Fund 2000
538.2000
© John Mawurndjul, courtesy Maningrida Arts and Culture and Viscopy Ltd

Galuma Maymuru

Nyapilingu ga Guwak 1999
natural earth pigments on wood
130.5 cm
Purchased with funds provided by the Mollie Gowing Acquisition Fund for Contemporary Aboriginal Art and the New Perspectives Fund 1999
99.1999

Sacred digging stick 1999
natural earth pigments on wood
113 cm
Purchased with funds provided by the Mollie Gowing Acquisition Fund for Contemporary Aboriginal Art and the New Perspectives Fund 1999
98.1999
© Galuma Maymuru, courtesy Buku-Larrngay Mulka Arts

Narritjin Maymuru

Djert (The sea eagle) c.1958
natural pigments on bark
90 x 47 cm
Purchased 1999
137.1999
© Estate of Narritjin Maymuru, courtesy Buku-Larrngay Mulka Arts

Ricky Maynard

Wik Elder, Arthur 2000
gelatin silver photograph
96.1 x 121.4 cm
Purchased under the terms of the Annette Dupree Bequest 2002
206.2002.3

Wik Elder, Gladys 2000
gelatin silver photograph
95.3 x 121.7 cm
Purchased with funds provided by Stephen Grant and Bridget Pirrie 2002
150.2002.1
© Ricky Maynard, courtesy Stills Gallery

Tracey Moffatt

Something More 1
from the series 'Something More' 1989
cibachrome photograph
103 x 133 cm
Hallmark Cards Australian Photography Collection Fund 1989
334.1989

Birth certificate, 1962
Doll birth, 1972
Useless, 1974
from the series 'Scarred for life' 1994
photolithographs
80 x 60 cm each
Purchased 1996
128.1996.9, 128.1996.5, 128.1996.3
© Tracey Moffatt, courtesy Roslyn Oxley9 Gallery

Sally Morgan

Citizenship 1987
screenprint
58.7 x 36.3 cm
Purchased 1988
217.1988
© Sally Morgan

Ginger Riley Munduwalawala

Nyamiyukanji, the river country 1997
synthetic polymer paint on canvas
185 x 201.5 cm
Purchased 2002
301.2002

Ngak Ngak and the Ruined City 1998
synthetic polymer paint on canvas
193 x 249.3 cm
Purchased under the terms of the Florence Turner Blake Bequest 1999
58.1999
© Estate of Ginger Riley Munduwalawala, courtesy Alcaston Gallery

Mäw' Mununggurr

Banumbirr (Morning Star ceremony) 1948
natural pigments on bark
120.6 x 64.2 cm
Gift of Dr Stuart Scougall 1960
36.1960

The Morning Star ceremony c.1960
natural pigments on bark
120.6 x 64.2 cm
Gift of Dr Stuart Scougall 1960
37.1960
© Estate of Mäw' Mununggurr, courtesy Buku-Larrngay Mulka Arts

Wonggu Mununggurr (attrib.)

Untitled c.1930s
natural pigments on bark
69.5 x 72 cm bark
Purchased with funds provided by the Art Gallery Society of New South Wales 1997
357.1997
© Estate of Wonggu Mununggurr, courtesy Buku-Larrngay Mulka Arts

Albert Namatjira

Palm Valley c.1940s
watercolour
37 x 54.2 cm
Purchased 1986
93.1986

Catherine Creek, Northern Territory c.1950
watercolour
37 x 37 cm
Purchased 2001
358.2001
© Legend Press

Eubena Nampitjin

Pinyu 1991
synthetic polymer paint on canvas
100 x 50 cm
Purchased 2003
2.2003
© Eubena Nampitjin, courtesy Warlayirti Artists

Inyuwa Nampitjinpa

Untitled (Pukunya) 1999
synthetic polymer paint on canvas
153 x 122 cm
Purchased with funds provided by the Leo Christie Emerging Artists Fund 1999
139.1999
© Estate of Inyuwa Nampitjinpa, Aboriginal Artists Agency Ltd

Makinti Napanangka

Untitled 2000
synthetic polymer paint on canvas
153 x 122 cm
Mollie Gowing Acquisition Fund for Contemporary Aboriginal Art 2000
516.2000
© Makinti Napanangka, Aboriginal Artists Agency Ltd

Mitjili Napurrula

Nullanulla and alcatjari (bush sultanas), Ualki 1994
synthetic polymer paint on canvas
91 x 137 cm
Purchased 1994
569.1994

Untitled 1999
synthetic polymer paint on canvas
183 x 198 cm
Mollie Gowing Acquisition Fund for Contemporary Aboriginal Art 2000
213.2000
© Mitjili Napurrula, courtesy Ikuntji Arts Centre

Ningura Napurrula

Untitled (Wirrulnga) 2000
synthetic polymer paint on canvas
183 x 244 cm
Patricia Lucille Bernard Bequest Fund 2001
151.2001
© Ningura Napurrula, Aboriginal Artists Agency Ltd

Dula Ngurruwutthun

Untitled 2001
natural pigments on bark
181 x 105 cm
Purchased 2001
445.2001
© Estate of Dula Ngurruwutthun, courtesy Buku-Larrngay Mulka Arts

Jimmy Njiminjuma

Yawkyawk 2000
natural pigments on bark
157 x 63 cm
Mollie Gowing Acquisition Fund for Contemporary Aboriginal Art 2001
446.2001
© Jimmy Njiminjuma, courtesy Maningrida Arts and Culture and Viscopy Ltd

Lin Onus

Fruit bats 1991
polychromed fibreglass sculptures, polychromed wooden disks, Hills Hoist clothes line
250 x 250 x 250 cm overall
Purchased 1993
395.1993
© Estate of Lin Onus, Viscopy Ltd

Otto Pareroultja

Untitled landscape c.1950s
watercolour
33.5 x 28 cm
Purchased 2001
359.2001

The hills behind Hermannsburg c.1954
watercolour
31 x 52 cm
Purchased 1996
573.1996
© Estate of Otto Pareroultja

Rusty Peters

Waterbrain 2002
8 panels: natural pigments on canvas
180 x 1200 cm overall
Purchased 2002
97.2002
© Rusty Peters, courtesy Jirrawun Aboriginal Arts Corporation

Gloria Tamerre Petyarre

Awely for the mountain devil lizard (Twenty-one women) 1996
21 panels: synthetic polymer paint on canvas
294 x 490 cm overall
Gift of Yuana and Stephen Hesketh 1997
376.1997
© Gloria Tamerre Petyarre, courtesy Utopia Art Sydney

Kutuwulumi Purawarrumpatu

Untitled 1997
natural pigments on canvas
92 x 94 cm
Purchased with funds provided by the Friends of Yiribana 1998
47.1998

Untitled 1997
natural pigments on paper
57 x 75.5 cm
Purchased with funds provided by the Friends of Yiribana 1998
49.1998

Untitled 1997
etching
19.5 x 88.4 cm
Mollie Gowing Acquisition Fund for Contemporary Aboriginal Art 1999
9.1999
© The Estate of Kutuwulumi Purawarrumpatu, courtesy Jilamara Arts and Crafts

Rea
Blue moon I saw you standing alone…
Green, I wish I could be seen
Mum, she said can I have an orange
Red there's a gun at my head
She was in the midst of a purple patch or else she could have been standing in her mother's kitchen
Yellow reminds me of the roses which I put on my Uncle's grave
from the series 'Highly coloured – my life is coloured by my colour I–VI'
1994
computer-generated photographs on perspex
185 x 58.5 cm each
Purchased with funds provided by the Young Friends of the Art Gallery Society of New South Wales 1994
573.1994.1–6
© Rea

Michael Riley
Maria 1985
gelatin silver photograph
45.5 x 47.9 cm
Mollie Gowing Acquisition Fund for Contemporary Aboriginal Art 1999
12.1999

Untitled (crucified hands)
Untitled (row of eight fish)
Untitled (water)
from the series 'Sacrifice' 1992
gelatin silver photographs
22.5 x 15.5 cm
15.5 x 22 cm
15.5 x 22 cm
Purchased 1993
396–398.1993
© Michael Riley

Elaine Russell
Inspection day 1994
synthetic polymer paint on cardboard
73.5 x 99.9 cm
Purchased with funds provided by the Australian Collection Benefactors 1995
19.1995

Lachlan River, our childhood dreams 1994
synthetic polymer paint on cardboard
73.2 x 99.9 cm
Purchased with funds provided by the Australian Collection Benefactors 1995
20.1995
© Elaine Russell

Nyirlpirr Spider Snell
Kurtal 1996
synthetic polymer paint on paper
74.5 x 105 cm
Purchased 1997
284.1997
© Nyirlpirr Spider Snell, courtesy Mangkaja Arts Resource Agency

Ken Thaiday
Beizam (shark) dance mask 1996
plywood, black bamboo, string, plastic, paint, glass, feathers
86.7 x 106 x 71 cm
Mollie Gowing Acquisition Fund for Contemporary Aboriginal Art 1997
4.1997
© Ken Thaiday

Thancoupie
Cammbel and Paour exchange teeth 1994
stoneware
27 x 24 cm
Mollie Gowing Acquisition Fund for Contemporary Aboriginal Art 1995
95.1995

Mosquito corroboree 1994
stoneware
32.4 x 34 cm
Mollie Gowing Acquisition Fund for Contemporary Aboriginal Art 1995
94.1995

Mosquito corroboree, two by two
1994
stoneware
27 x 32 cm
Gift of Dr and Mrs Ronald K. Faithfull 2001
461.2001
© Thancoupie

Rover Thomas
Country called Red Butte 1984
natural pigments and bush gum on plywood
91 x 181 cm
Purchased under the terms of the Florence Turner Blake Bequest 1995
98.1995

Untitled 1984
natural pigments and bush gum on plywood
91 x 181 cm
Purchased under the terms of the Florence Turner Blake Bequest 1995
99.1995

Two men dreaming c.1985
natural pigments on canvas board
91 x 61 cm
Purchased 2000
37.2000

Undubhill 1991
natural pigments and bush gum on canvas
60 x 100 cm
Purchased under the terms of the Florence Turner Blake Bequest 1995
96.1995
© Estate of Rover Thomas, courtesy Warmun Art Centre

Timmy Timms
Bedford Downs massacre 2000
natural pigments on canvas
150 x 180 cm
D. G. Wilson Bequest Fund 2000
545.2000
© Estate of Timmy Timms, courtesy Jirrawun Aboriginal Arts Corporation

Ronnie Tjampitjinpa
Untitled 1994
synthetic polymer paint on canvas
183 x 152 cm
Purchased 1994
215.1994

Untitled 2001
synthetic polymer paint on canvas
183 x 244 cm
Purchased 2002
140.2002
© Ronnie Tjampitjinpa, Aboriginal Artists Agency Ltd

Uta Uta Tjangala
Untitled c.1971
synthetic polymer paint on hardboard
60.5 x 35 cm
Katherine Mabel Reid Bequest 1998
50.1998

Untitled 1972
synthetic polymer powder paint and natural pigments on hardboard
62.6 x 50.7 cm
Purchased 1999
138.1999
© Estate of Uta Uta Tjangala, Aboriginal Artists Agency Ltd

Clifford Possum Tjapaltjarri
Lungkata's two sons at Warlugulong 1976
synthetic polymer paint on canvas board
70.5 x 55 cm
Mollie Gowing Acquisition Fund for Contemporary Aboriginal Art 1996
308.1996
© Estate of Clifford Possum Tjapaltjarri, Aboriginal Artists Agency Ltd

Clifford Possum Tjapaltjarri
& Tim Leura Tjapaltjarri
Warlugulong 1976
synthetic polymer paint on canvas
168.5 x 170.5 cm
Purchased 1981
321.1981
© Aboriginal Artists Agency Ltd

Mick Namarari Tjapaltjarri
Untitled (Dingo dreaming at Nyunmanu) 1997
synthetic polymer paint on canvas
153 x 120.9 cm
Purchased 1999
1.1999

Untitled (Tjunginpa mouse dreaming) 1998
synthetic polymer paint on canvas
152 x 122 cm
Purchased with funds provided by the Art Gallery Society of New South Wales 1999
82.1999
© Estate of Mick Namarari Tjapaltjarri, Aboriginal Artists Agency Ltd

Tim Leura Tjapaltjarri
Kooralia 1980
synthetic polymer paint on canvas
188 x 155 cm
Gift of the Art Gallery Society of New South Wales 1995
482.1995
© Estate of Tim Leura Tjapaltjarri, Aboriginal Artists Agency Ltd

Long Tom Tjapanangka
Kanpaarka (centipede) Tjukurrpa
1994
synthetic polymer paint on canvas
218.5 x 152.5 cm
Patricia Lucille Bernard Bequest Fund 2001
150.2001

Uluru and Putipulawa 1994
synthetic polymer paint on paper
56 x 76cm
Purchased 1994
578.1994

Big mob puli (rocks), other side of Mt Leibig 1998
synthetic polymer paint on canvas
150.5 x 300.5 cm
D. G. Wilson Bequest Fund 1998
245.1998
© Long Tom Tjapanangka, courtesy Ikuntji Arts Centre

Tjumpo Tjapanangka

Wati Kutjarra 2002
synthetic polymer paint on canvas
180 x 120 cm
Mollie Gowing Acquisition Fund for Contemporary Aboriginal Art 2003
66.2003
© Tjumpo Tjapananagka, courtesy Warlayirti Artists

Timmy Payungka Tjapangati

Tingari cycle at Wilkinkarra 1996
synthetic polymer paint on canvas
153 x 122 cm
Mollie Gowing Acquisition Fund for Contemporary Aboriginal Art 2000
318.2000

Untitled 1998
synthetic polymer paint on canvas
152 x 122 cm
Mollie Gowing Acquisition Fund for Contemporary Aboriginal Art 2000
215.2000
© Estate of Timmy Payungka Tjapangati, Aboriginal Artists Agency Ltd

Shorty Lungkata Tjungurrayi

Women's dreaming (Two women) 1972
synthetic polymer powder paint on hardboard
46 x 64 cm
Purchased with funds provided by the Art Gallery Society of New South Wales 2002
302.2002
© Estate of Shorty Lungkata Tjungurrayi, Aboriginal Artists Agency Ltd

Johnny Warangkula Tjupurrula

Emu Dreaming 1974
synthetic polymer paint on three-ply
50.7 x 45.4 cm
Purchased 1997
268.1997
© Estate of Johnny Warangkula Tjupurrula, Aboriginal Artists Agency Ltd

Turkey Tolson Tjupurrula

Straightening the spears 1998
woodcut
35 x 60 cm
Mollie Gowing Acquisition Fund for Contemporary Aboriginal Art 1999
62.1999.1

Straightening the spears 1999
synthetic polymer paint on canvas
152 x 183 cm
Mollie Gowing Acquisition Fund for Contemporary Aboriginal Art 2000
218.2000
© Estate of Turkey Tolson Tjupurrula, Aboriginal Artists Agency Ltd

Prince of Wales

Body marks 2001
synthetic polymer paint on canvas
210 x 129 cm
Purchased 2002
275.2002
© Estate of Prince of Wales, courtesy Karen Brown Gallery

Judy Watson

saltpan 1992
powder pigment and pastel on canvas
180 x 110 cm
Mollie Gowing Acquisition Fund for Contemporary Aboriginal Art 1993
232.1993

our bones in your collections
our hair in your collections
our skin in your collections
1997
etching and chine collé
29.4 x 20.4 cm each
Mollie Gowing Acquisition Fund for Contemporary Aboriginal Art 1998
242–244.1998
© Judy Watson, Viscopy Ltd

H. J. Wedge

Stop and think 1993
5 panels: synthetic polymer paint on canvas
76 x 456 cm overall
Purchased 1994
217.1994
© H.J. Wedge

Pedro Wonaeamirri

Tutini with figure of Purukupali 1999
natural pigments on ironwood, feathers, beeswax
281 x 18 cm

Tutini 1999
natural pigments on ironwood
259.5 x 155 cm
216 x 28 cm
254 x 19 cm
252 x 22.5 cm
241 x 21 cm
Mollie Gowing Acquisition Fund for Contemporary Aboriginal Art 1999
176–181.1999
© Pedro Wonaeamirri, courtesy Jilamara Arts and Crafts

Jabarrgwa Wurrabadalumba

Dugong hunt 1948
natural pigments on bark
46 x 95 cm
Gift of the Commonwealth Government 1956
9266
© Estate of Jabarrgwa Wurrabadalumba, courtesy Anindilyakwa Land Council

Owen Yalandja

Yawkyawk 1999
Yawkyawk 1999
natural pigments on Kurrajong wood
261.5 x 12.2 x 8.5 cm
227.5 x 9.8 x 8.4 cm
Mollie Gowing Acquisition Fund for Contemporary Aboriginal Art 2000
78–79.2000
© Owen Yalandja, courtesy Maningrida Arts and Culture and Viscopy Ltd

Lena Yarinkura

The tragedy of Bulanj and Balang 1994
6 parts: paperbark, string, natural pigments
100 x 100 cm overall
Purchased 1995
28.1995
© Lena Yarinkura, courtesy Maningrida Arts and Culture and Viscopy Ltd

Munggurrawuy Yunupingu

Lany'tjung story (Crocodile and Bandicoot) 1959
natural pigments on bark
193 x 72 cm
Gift of Dr Stuart Scougall 1959
61.1959

The Thunder Spirits (Birimbira) 1961
natural pigments on bark
150.2 x 60.4 cm
Gift of Dr Stuart Scougall 1961
19.1961
© Estate of Munggurrawuy Yunupingu, courtesy Buku-Larrngay Mulka Arts

NOTES

Introduction

1. Hetti Perkins and Clare Williamson, *Blakness: Blak City Culture!*, exhibition catalogue, Australian Centre for Contemporary Art, Melbourne, and Boomalli Aboriginal Artists Cooperative, Sydney, 1994.
2. Galarrwuy Yunupingu, 'Indigenous Art in the Olympic Age', in Hannah Fink and Hetti Perkins (eds), *Art & Australia: Olympic Arts Festival Special Issue*, vol. 35, no. 1, 1997, p. 66.
3. ibid., p. 65.

Ian Abdulla

1. Ian Abdulla, *As I Grew Older*, Omnibus Books, South Australia, 1993; Ian Abdulla, *Tucker*, Omnibus Books, South Australia, 1994; Ian Abdulla, *Elvis Has Left the Building*, Wakefield Press, South Australia, 2003.

Richard Bell

1. Richard Bell, artist's statement, 'Bell's Theorem', November 2002, Art Gallery of New South Wales Archive, Sydney.
2. ibid.
3. *Richard Bell: Aboriginal art, it's a white thing*, exhibition catalogue, Fire-Works Gallery, Brisbane, 2002, u.p.
4. Victoria Lynn (ed.), *Australian Perspecta 1993*, exhibition catalogue, Art Gallery of New South Wales, Sydney, 1993, p. 8.

Billy Benn

1. Information provided by Bindi Centa Arts, Alice Springs.

Binyinyuwuy

1. Ann E. Wells, *Milingimbi, Ten Years in the Crocodile Islands of Arnhem Land*, Angus and Robertson, Sydney, 1963, p. 230.

John Bulunbulun

1. *Bulun Bulun*, exhibition catalogue, Christine Abrahams Gallery, Melbourne, September 1984, u.p.

Robert Ambrose Cole

1. Robert Ambrose Cole, quoted in Christopher Hodges, 'Robert Ambrose Cole', in Victoria Lynn (ed.), *Australian Perspecta 1993*, exhibition catalogue, Art Gallery of New South Wales, Sydney, 1993, p. 22.

Brenda L. Croft

1. Brenda L. Croft, artist's statement, in Anthony Bond (ed.), *9th Biennale of Sydney: The boundary rider*, exhibition catalogue, The Biennale of Sydney, Sydney, 1992, p. 192.

Destiny Deacon

1. Destiny Deacon, in Linda Michael, 'Destiny Deacon', *Das lied von der erde*, exhibition catalogue, Museum Fridericianum, Kassel, Germany, 2000, pp. 76–77.

Dawidi Djulwarak

1. Dawidi Djulwarak was known as Djulwarak, following the death of the elder Dawidi Djulwarak, and was also later known as Dawidi (2) Djulwarak.

Kevin Gilbert

1. Jane Barney and Trevor Smith, *Breath of Life*, exhibition catalogue, Canberra Contemporary Art Space, Canberra, 1996, p.13f.
2. ibid., p. 40.

Philip Gudthaykudthay

1. Philip Gudthaykudthay, quoted in Djon Mundine, 'Philip Gudthaykudthay: Aspects of his world', in *Painting and Sculpture from Ramingining by Jimmy Wululu and Philip Gudthaykudthay*, exhibition catalogue, Drill Hall Gallery, Canberra, 1992, u.p.

Roy Kennedy

1. Roy Kennedy, artist's statement, *Eora Student Exhibition 2001*, exhibition catalogue, Eora Centre TAFE, Sydney, 2001.
2. ibid.
3. ibid.

Yvonne Koolmatrie

1. As Koolmatrie's father was adopted into a white family, he was exempt from official recognition as an Aboriginal person. In effect this meant that her family were also considered by the law as white and therefore not able to associate with Aboriginal communities after 6pm. As they were not eligible for government welfare programmes, such as rations or housing on the missions, they led a fringe dwellers' existence, with seasonal work being their only means of survival.
2. Yvonne Koolmatrie, quoted in Doreen Mellor, 'Yvonne Koolmatrie', in Brenda L. Croft (ed.), *Beyond the Pale: Contemporary Indigenous art, Adelaide Biennial of Australian Art 2000*, exhibition catalogue, Art Gallery of South Australia, Adelaide, 2000, p. 43.
3. Yvonne Koolmatrie, in John Kean, *Murrundi: Three River Murray stories*, exhibition catalogue, Contemporary Art Centre of South Australia, Adelaide, 1993, u.p.

Anchor Kulunba

1. See J. C. Altman, 'Eastern Gunwinggu Fish Trapping at Gunbatgarri', *Beagle* 1 (7), 1983, pp. 59–71; and J. C. Altman, *Hunter-gatherers Today: An Aboriginal economy in north Australia*, Australian Institute of Aboriginal and Torres Strait Islander Studies, Canberra, 1987.

Samuel Manggudja

1. R. M. Berndt, C. H. Berndt and J. E. Stanton, *Aboriginal Australian Art: A visual perspective*, Methuen Australia, Sydney, 1982, p. 52.
2. Aboriginal Arts Board of the Australia Council, *Oenpelli Bark Painting*, Ure Smith, Sydney, 1979.

Wandjuk Marika

1. J. Isaacs, *Wandjuk Marika, Life Story*, University of Queensland Press, St Lucia, Queensland, 1995, p. 110.

Galuma Maymuru

1. Galuma Maymuru, artist's statement, *Galuma Maymuru: In memory of Narritjin*, exhibition catalogue, William Mora Galleries, Melbourne, 1999.
2. ibid.

Ricky Maynard

1. Ricky Maynard, artist's statement, *Returning to Places that Name Us*, exhibition catalogue, Stills Gallery, Sydney, 2001.
2. ibid.
3. ibid.

Tracey Moffatt

1. Tracey Moffatt, interviewed by Michael Cathcart, *Arts National*, radio programme, ABC Radio, Melbourne, 9 January 2001.

Sally Morgan

1. Sally Morgan, *My Place*, Fremantle Arts Centre Press, Western Australia, 1987.
2. Jill Milroy, *The Art of Sally Morgan*, Viking, Ringwood, Victoria, 1996, p. 8.

Ginger Riley Munduwalawala

1. Judith Ryan, *Ginger Riley*, exhibition catalogue, National Gallery of Victoria, Melbourne, 1997, p. 11.
2. 'Gulf country' is a colloquial reference to the Gulf of Carpentaria region.

Albert Namatjira

1. Judith Ryan, 'A Transplanted Landscape Idiom – Albert Namatjira and the Hermannsberg School', in Judith Ryan, *Mythscapes: Aboriginal art of the desert from the National Gallery of Victoria*, exhibition catalogue, National Gallery of Victoria, Melbourne, 1989, pp. 18–23; Ian Burn and Ann Stephens, 'The Transfiguration of Albert Namatjira', *Age Monthly Review*, November 1986, and 'Namatjira's White Mask', in Jane Hardy, J. V. S. Megaw and M. Ruth Megaw (eds), *The Heritage of Namatjira: The watercolourists of Central*

Australia, William Heinemann Australia, Melbourne, 1992, pp. 249–282.

Eubena Nampitjin
1. Christine Watson, 'Eubena Nampitjin: Animating landforms, enlivening the palette', in Rebecca Coates et al., *In Place (Out of Time): Contemporary art in Australia*, Museum of Modern Art, Oxford, 1997, p. 21.

Mitjili Napurrula
1. Mitjili Napurrula, artist's statement, 1994, Art Gallery of New South Wales Archive, Sydney.

Dula Ngurruwutthun
1. Dula Ngurruwuthun, quoted in Buku-Larrngay Mulka Centre, *Saltwater, Yirrkala Bark Paintings of Sea Country, Recognising Indigenous Sea Rights*, exhibition catalogue, Buku-Larrngay Mulka Centre in association with Jennifer Isaacs Publishing, Yirrkala, Northern Territory, 1999, p. 12.
2. Information provided by Buku-Larrngay Mulka Arts.

Otto Pareroultja
1. T. G. H. Strehlow, *Rex Battarbee, Artist and Founder of the Aboriginal Art Movement in Central Australia*, Legend Press, Sydney, 1957, pp. 30–31.
2. Rex Battarbee, *Modern Australian Aboriginal Art*, Angus & Robertson, Sydney, 1951, pp. 6–7.

Rusty Peters
1. See Cath Bowdler, *Two Laws … One Big Spirit*, exhibition catalogue, 24HR Art, Northern Territory Centre for Contemporary Art, Darwin, 2000.

Kutuwulumi Purawarrumpatu
1. Kutuwulumi Purawarrumpatu, artist's statement, Jilamara Arts and Crafts, Milikapiti, Northern Territory, 1998.

Rea
1. Art Gallery of New South Wales, *Yiribana*, Art Gallery of New South Wales, Sydney, 1994, p. 130.

Michael Riley
1. 'Dreamings: Art of Aboriginal Australia', Asia Society Galleries, New York, 1988.

Elaine Russell
1. Biographical statement, Boomalli Aboriginal Artists Cooperative, Sydney, 1993.

Ronnie Tjampitjinpa
1. Personal communication to the author, September – October, 2000.
2. ibid.

Clifford Possum Tjapaltjarri
1. Vivien Johnson, *The Art of Clifford Possum Tjapaltjarri*, Craftsman House, Sydney, 1994, p. 147.

Tim Leura Tjapaltjarri
1. Geoffrey Bardon, *Papunya Tula: Art of the Western Desert*, McPhee Gribble Australia, Melbourne, 1991.
2. Personal communication to the author, c. June 2002.

Johnny Warangkula Tjupurrula
1. *Sydney Morning Herald*, 26 January, 1984.

Prince of Wales
1. Prince of Wales, artist's statement, Karen Brown Gallery, Darwin, 1997.

Judy Watson
1. *Identities, Art from Australia; contemporary Australian art to Taiwan*, exhibition catalogue, Taipei Fine Arts Museum, Taipei, Taiwan, 1993, p. 153.
2. Personal communication to the author, May 1997.
3. Judy Watson, artist statement, in *Wiyana/ Perisferia (Periphery)*, exhibition catalogue, Boomalli Aboriginal Artists Cooperative at The Performance Space, Sydney, 1992.

H. J. Wedge
1. Biographical statement, recorded and transcribed by Antonia Carver, in Hannah Fink (ed.), *H. J. Wedge, Wiradjuri Spirit Man*, Craftsman House in association with Boomalli Aboriginal Artists Cooperative, Roseville East, New South Wales, 1996, p. 41.

Lena Yarinkura
1. Artist's statement, audiotape, recorded 21 October 1994 and 15 November 1994, Maningrida Arts and Culture, Northern Territory.

Munggurrawuy Yunupingu
1. Art Gallery of New South Wales Archive, Sydney.

BIBLIOGRAPHY

BOOKS AND EXHIBITION CATALOGUES

Aboriginal Arts Board of the Australia Council, *Oenpelli Bark Painting*, Ure Smith, Sydney, 1979

Altman, J. C., *Hunter-gatherers Today: An Aboriginal economy in north Australia*, Australian Institute of Aboriginal and Torres Strait Islander Studies, Canberra, 1987

Altman, J. C., McGuigan, Chris and Yu, Peter, *The Aboriginal Arts and Crafts Industry: Report of the review committee*, Department of Aboriginal Affairs, AGPS, Canberra, 1989

Amadio, Nadine, *Albert Namatjira: The life and work of an Australian painter*, Macmillan, South Melbourne, Victoria, 1986

A material thing: Objects from the collection, exhibition catalogue, Art Gallery of New South Wales, Sydney, 1998

Art Gallery of New South Wales, *One Sun, One Moon: Indigenous art in Australia*, Art Gallery of New South Wales, Sydney [forthcoming]

Art Gallery of New South Wales, *Yiribana: An introduction to the Aboriginal and Torres Strait Islander Collection*, Art Gallery of New South Wales, Sydney, 1994

Australian Collection Focus: Warlugulong 1976, exhibition catalogue, Art Gallery of New South Wales, Sydney, 1999

Bardon, Geoffrey, *Papunya Tula: Art of the Western Desert*, McPhee Gribble Australia, Melbourne, 1991

Battarbee, Rex, *Modern Australian Aboriginal Art*, Angus & Robertson, Sydney, 1951

Berndt, R. M., Berndt, C. H. and Stanton, J. E., *Aboriginal Australian Art: A visual perspective*, Methuen Australia, Sydney, 1982

Berndt, R. M., *An Exhibition of Australian Aboriginal Art: Arnhem Land paintings on bark and carved human figures*, exhibition catalogue, Art Gallery of Western Australia, Festival of Perth Committee, Perth, 1957

Berndt, R. M., *Djanggawul: An Aboriginal religious cult of north-eastern Arnhem Land*, Routledge & Kegan Paul Ltd, London, 1952

Bond, Anthony (ed.), *9th Biennale of Sydney: The boundary rider*, exhibition catalogue, The Biennale of Sydney, Sydney, 1992

Brandl, Eric Joseph, *Australian Aboriginal Paintings in Western and Central Arnhem Land: Temporal sequences and elements of style in Cadell River and Deaf Adder Creek Art*, Australian Institute of Aboriginal Studies, Canberra, 1973

Brody, Anne Marie (ed.), *Stories: Eleven Aboriginal artists, works from the Holmes à Court collection*, Craftsman House, Sydney, 1997

Buku-Larrngay Mulka Centre, *Saltwater, Yirrkala Bark Paintings of Sea Country, Recognising Indigenous Sea Rights*, exhibition catalogue, Buku-Larrngay Mulka Centre in association with Jennifer Isaacs Publishing, Yirrkala, Northern Territory, 1999

Caruana, Wally, *Aboriginal Art*, Thames and Hudson, London and New York, 2003

Caruana, Wally, *Painted Objects from Arnhem Land*, exhibition catalogue, Australian National Gallery, Canberra, 1986

Caruana, W. et al., *The Eye of the Storm: Eight contemporary Indigenous Australian artists*, National Gallery of Australia, Canberra / National Gallery of Modern Art, New Delhi, 1996

Caruana, Wally (ed.), *Windows on the Dreaming: Aboriginal paintings in the Australian National Gallery*, Australian National Gallery and Ellsyd Press, Sydney, 1989

Cawte, John, *The Universe of the Warramirri: Art, medicine, and religion in Arnhem Land*, New South Wales University Press, Kensington, New South Wales, c.1993

Coates, Rebecca et al., *In Place (Out of Time): Contemporary art in Australia*, Museum of Modern Art, Oxford, 1997

Cochrane, G., *The Crafts Movement in Australia: A history*, New South Wales University Press, Kensington, New South Wales, 1992

Contemporary Aboriginal Art: The Robert Holmes à Court Collection, exhibition catalogue, Heytesbury Holdings Ltd, Perth, 1990

Cowan, James, *Wirrimanu: Aboriginal art from the Balgo Hills*, Craftsman House, Sydney, 1994

Cowan, James, *Balgo: New directions*, Craftsman House, Sydney, 1999

Croft, Brenda L. (ed.), *Beyond the Pale: Contemporary Indigenous art, Adelaide Biennial of Australian Art 2000*, exhibition catalogue, Art Gallery of South Australia, Adelaide, 2000

Demozay, Marion (ed.), *Gatherings: Contemporary Aboriginal and Torres Strait Islander Art from Queensland Australia*, Keeaira Press, Southport, Queensland, 2001

Elkin, A. P., Berndt, R. M. and Berndt, C. H., *Art in Arnhem Land*, Cheshire, Melbourne, 1959

Engberg, Juliana and McDonald, Ewen (eds), *All This and Heaven Too: 1998 Adelaide Biennial of Australian art*, exhibition catalogue, Art Gallery of South Australia, Adelaide, 1998

Fink, Hannah (ed.), *H. J. Wedge, Wiradjuri Spirit Man*, Craftsman House in association with Boomalli Aboriginal Artists Cooperative, Roseville East, New South Wales, 1996

Fluent, 47th Venice Biennale, 1997, exhibition catalogue, Art Gallery of New South Wales, Sydney, 1997

Garside, Sioux, *Aboriginal Bark Paintings from Arnhem Land*, exhibition catalogue, Newcastle Region Art Gallery, Newcastle, New South Wales, 1984

Hardy, Jane, Megaw, J.V.S. and Megaw, M. Ruth (eds), *The Heritage of Namatjira: The watercolourists of Central Australia*, William Heinemann, Port Melbourne, 1992

Horton, David (ed.), *The Encyclopaedia of Aboriginal Australia*, Aboriginal Studies Press for the Australian Institute of Aboriginal and Torres Strait Islander Studies, Canberra, 1994

Hutcherson, Gillian, *Djalkiri Wänga – The Land Is My Foundation: Fifty years of Aboriginal art from Yirrkala, northeast Arnhem Land*, University of Western Australia, Berndt Museum of Anthropology, Occasional Paper no. 4, Vanguard Press, Perth, 1995

Identities: Art from Australia; Contemporary Australian Art to Taiwan, exhibition catalogue, Taipei Fine Arts Museum, Taipei, Taiwan, 1993

Indigenous Art: Art Gallery of Western Australia, Art Gallery of Western Australia, Perth, 2001

Isaacs, J., *Aboriginality: Contemporary Aboriginal paintings and prints*, University of Queensland Press, Brisbane, 1989

Isaacs, J., *Thancoupie the Potter*, Aboriginal Artists Agency, Sydney, 1982

Isaacs, J., *Wandjuk Marika, Life Story*, University of Queensland Press, St Lucia, Queensland, 1995

Izett, Erica and Mahood, Kim, *Eubena Nampitjin*, exhibition catalogue, Alcaston Gallery, Melbourne, 2002

Johnson, Vivien, *Aboriginal Artists of the Western Desert: A biographical dictionary*, Craftsman House, East Roseville, New South Wales, 1994

Johnson, Vivien, *Clifford Possum Tjapaltjari*, exhibition catalogue, Art Gallery of South Australia, 2003

Johnson, Vivien, *Dreamings of the Desert: Aboriginal dot painting of the Western Desert*, Art Gallery of South Australia, Adelaide, 1996

Johnson, Vivien, *Lives of the Papunya Tula Artists* [forthcoming]

Johnson, Vivien, *The Art of Clifford Possum Tjapaltjarri*, Craftsman House, Sydney, 1994

Kean, John (ed.), *East to West: Land in Papunya Tula painting*, Tandanya Aboriginal Cultural Institute, Adelaide, 1990

Kean, John, *Mary McLean – Hunting Grounds*, exhibition catalogue, Fremantle Arts Centre, Perth, 1995

Kerr, Joan and Holder, Jo (eds), *Past Present: The national women's art anthology*, Craftsman House, Sydney, 1999

Kleinart, Sylvia and Neale, Margo (eds), *Oxford Companion to Aboriginal Art and Culture*, Oxford University Press, South Melbourne, 2000

Luthi, Bernhard (ed.), *Aratjara – Art of the First Australians: Traditional and contemporary works by Aboriginal and Torres Strait Islander artists*, exhibition catalogue, Kunstsammlung Nordrhein – Westfalen, Dusseldorf, 1993

Lynn, Victoria (ed.), *Australian Perspecta 1991*, exhibition catalogue, Art Gallery of New South Wales, Sydney, 1991

Lynn, Victoria (ed.), *Australian Perspecta 1993*, exhibition catalogue, Art Gallery of New South Wales, Sydney, 1993

McDonald, Helen, *Erotic Ambiguities, The Female Nude in Art*, Routledge, London, 2001

Michaels, Eric, *Bad Aboriginal Art: Tradition, media and technological horizons*, Allen and Unwin, Sydney, 1994

Milroy, Jill, *The Art of Sally Morgan*, Viking, Ringwood, Victoria, 1996

Morphy, Howard, *Aboriginal Art*, Phaidon Press, London, 1998

Morphy, Howard, *Ancestral Connections: Art and an Aboriginal system of knowledge*, Chicago: University of Chicago Press, Chicago, 1991

Morphy, Howard and Smith Boles, Margot (eds), *Art from the Land: Dialogues with the Kluge-Ruhe Collection of Australian Aboriginal art*, University of Virginia, Charlottesville, Virginia, c.1999

Mountford, Charles P., *Aboriginal Art*, Longmans, London, 1961

Mountford, Charles P., *Aboriginal Conception Beliefs*, Hyland House, Melbourne, 1981

Mountford, Charles P., *Records of the American–Australian Scientific Expedition to Arnhem Land 1: Art, myth and symbolism*, Melbourne University Press, Melbourne, 1956

Mountford, Charles P., *Records of the American–Australian Scientific Expedition to Arnhem Land 2: Anthropology and nutrition*, Melbourne University Press, Melbourne, 1960

Mountford, Charles P., *The Tiwi: Their art, myth and ceremony*, Phoenix House, London, 1958

Mundine, Djon, *The Native Born – Objects and Representations from Ramingining, Arnhem Land*, exhibition catalogue, Museum of Contemporary Art in association with Bula'bula Arts, Ramingining, Northern Territory, 2000

Myers, Fred R., *Painting Culture: The making of an Aboriginal high art*, Duke University Press, Durham and London, 2002

Neale, M. et al., *Emily Kame Kngwarreye: Alhalkere – paintings from Utopia*, exhibition catalogue, Queensland Art Gallery, Brisbane, 1998

Newton, Gael and Moffatt, Tracey, *Tracey Moffatt: Fever Pitch*, Piper Press, Sydney, 1995

O'Ferrall, Michael A., *Art from the Great Sandy Desert*, Art Gallery of Western Australia, Perth, 1987

Oliver, Tony (ed.), *Blood on the Spinifex*, exhibition catalogue, The Ian Potter Museum of Art, University of Melbourne, Melbourne, 2002

Painted Dreams: Western Desert Paintings from the Johnson Collection, exhibiton catalogue, Art Gallery of New South Wales, Sydney, 1995

Perkins, Hetti (ed.), *Aboriginal Women's Exhibition*, exhibition catalogue, Art Gallery of New South Wales, Sydney, 1991

Perkins, Hetti and Fink, Hannah (eds), *Papunya Tula: Genesis and Genius*, exhibition catalogue, Art Gallery of New South Wales, Sydney, 2000

Phillips, Sandra (ed.), *Racism, Representation and Photography*, Inner City Education Centre Cooperative, Sydney, 1994

Pinchin, Rebecca (ed.), *Yarns from the Talbragar Reserve*, exhibition catalogue, Dubbo Regional Gallery, Dubbo, New South Wales, 1999

Quaill, Avril, *A Koori Perspective Tour: An Artspace touring exhibition*, exhibition catalogue, Artspace, Sydney, 1990

Ryan, Judith, *Ginger Riley*, exhibition catalogue, National Gallery of Victoria, Melbourne, 1997

Ryan, Judith, *Images of Power: Aboriginal Art from the Kimberley*, exhibition catalogue, National Gallery of Victoria, Melbourne, 1993

Ryan, Judith, *Mythscapes: Aboriginal art of the desert from the National Gallery of Victoria*, exhibition catalogue, National Gallery of Victoria, Melbourne, 1989

Ryan, Judith, *Spirit in Land: Bark paintings from Arnhem Land in the National Gallery of Victoria*, exhibition catalogue, National Gallery of Victoria, Melbourne, 1990

Ryan, Judith and Healy, Robyn (eds), *Raiki Wara: Long Cloth from Aboriginal Australia and the Torres Strait*, exhibition catalogue, National Gallery of Victoria, Melbourne, 1998

Seear, Lynne (ed.), *Asia-Pacific Triennial of Contemporary Art 2002*, exhibition catalogue, Queensland Art Gallery, Brisbane, 2002

Strehlow, T. G. H., *Rex Battarbee, Artist and Founder of the Aboriginal Art Movement in Central Australia*, Legend Press, Sydney, 1957

Sullivan, Graeme, *Seeing Australia – Views of Artists*

and Artwriters, Piper Press, Sydney, 1994

Sutton, Peter (ed.), *Dreamings: The art of Aboriginal Australia*, Viking, in association with The Asia Society Galleries, New York, 1988

Taylor, Penny (ed.), *After 200 Years: Photographic essays of Aboriginal and Islander Australia Today*, Australian Institute of Aboriginal Studies, Aboriginal Studies Press, Canberra, 1988

Teffer, Nicola and Tunnicliffe, Wayne (eds), *Living Here Now – Art and Politics, Australian Perspecta 1999*, exhibition catalogue, Art Gallery of New South Wales, Sydney, 1999

Thomas, Rover et al., *Roads Cross: The Paintings of Rover Thomas*, exhibition catalogue, National Gallery of Australia, Canberra, 1994

Tjalaminu Mia, *Daughters of the Dreaming – Sisters Together Strong*, exhibition catalogue, Art Gallery of Western Australia, Perth, 1997

True Stories: Art of the East Kimberley, exhibition cataolgue, Art Gallery of New South Wales, Sydney, 2003

Turner, Caroline and Devenport, Rhana, *The Second Asia-Pacific Triennial of Contemporary Art*, exhibition catalogue, Queensland Art Gallery, Brisbane, 1996

Wells, Ann E., *Milingimbi, Ten Years in the Crocodile Islands of Arnhem Land*, Angus and Robertson, Sydney, 1963

West, Margie K. C. (ed.), *The Inspired Dream: Life as art in Aboriginal Australia*, exhibition catalogue, Queensland Art Gallery, Brisbane, 1988

Wiyana/Perisferia (Periphery), exhibition catalogue, Boomalli Aboriginal Artists Cooperative at The Performance Space, Sydney, 1992

Wright, Felicity and Morphy, Frances, *The Art & Craft Centre Story*, Aboriginal and Torres Strait Islander Commission, Woden, ACT, 2000

JOURNALS, ARTICLES AND OTHER MEDIA

Ashburn, Liz, 'REA is for Resistance', *World Art*, no. 3, 1996, pp. 12–14

Barber, Kim, 'All the World: The 1958 and 1959 Paintings of Nym Bandak', *artonview*, Spring 2000, pp. 26–31

Carver, Antonia, 'A Moving Out of Place, About Time', *Art and Australia*, vol. 35, no. 3, 1998, pp. 438–439

Contemporary Australian Aboriginal Art, *Artlink*, special issue, vol. 10, nos.1 and 2, 1992

Fraser, Virginia, 'Destiny's Dollys', *Photofile*, no. 40, November 1993, p. 7

Gennochio, Ben, 'Dreaming in Urban Areas: Activism and audience in urban Aboriginal art', *Eyeline*, no. 35, Summer, 1997/98, pp. 34–36

Kerr, Joan, 'Colonial Quotations', *Art and Australia*, vol. 33, no. 3, Autumn, 1996, p. 376

Kimber, R. G., 'Kumantjayi T. P. Tjapaltjarri' (obituary), *The Australian*, 5 June 2000, p. 10

Kimber, R. G., 'M. N. Tjapaltjarri' (obituary), *Art and Australia*, vol. 36, no. 3, 1999, p. 397

Kjellgren, Eric, 'Mingmarriya: Art as autobiography in the paintings of Queenie McKenzie', *Pacific Arts*, 23 and 24, 2001, pp. 11–20

Langton, Marcia, 'The Valley of the Dolls: Black humour in the art of Destiny Deacon', *Art and Australia*, vol. 35, no. 1, 1997, p. 100

Langton, Marcia, '"Well I Heard It on the Radio and I Saw It on the Television …": an essay for the Australian Film Commission on the politics and aesthetics of filmmaking by and about Aboriginal people and things', Australian Film Commission, Sydney, 1993

Mundine, Djon, 'La Quinta Bienial de la Habana', *Art and Asia Pacific*, vol. 2, no. 1, January, 1995, p. 38

Narritjin at Djarrakpi, Parts 1 and 3, film recording, directed by Ian Dunlop, Film Australia, Sydney, 1981

Narritjin in Canberra, film recording, directed by Ian Dunlop, Film Australia, Sydney, 1981

Newton, Gael, 'See the woman with the red dress on ... and on … and on … ', *Art and Asia Pacific*, vol. 1, no. 2, 1994, p. 96

Reconciliation: Indigenous art from the 21st century, *Artlink*, vol. 20, no.1, 2000

Stewart, Garry, 'Shall We Dance', *Artforce*, Australia Council for the Arts, Sydney, Summer, 1998/99, iss. 101, pp. 10–11

The Festival of the Dreaming: Aboriginal and Torres Strait Islander Art issue, *Art and Australia*, vol. 35, no. 1, 1997

WEBSITES

www.aiatsis.gov.au – Australian Institute of Aboriginal and Torres Strait Islander Studies

www.fatsil.org – Aboriginal and Torres Strait Islander Corporation of Languages

www.ga.gov.au – Geoscience Australia, the National agency for geoscience research and geospatial information

INDEX

PORTRAIT PHOTOGRAPHY

Ian Abdulla Mick Bradley, courtesy Greenaway Art Gallery
Paddy Bedford Katie Wilson
Richard Bell courtesy Fire-Works Gallery
Billy Benn Neridah Stockley, courtesy Mwerre Anthurre – Bindi Centa Arts
Mervyn Bishop courtesy Mervyn Bishop and ATSIC
John Bulunbulun Kellie Austin, courtesy Maningrida Arts and Culture
Kevin Bunduck courtesy Kanamkek-Yile Ngala Museum
Nym Bunduck courtesy Kanamkek-Yile Ngala Museum
Robert Campbell Jnr courtesy Roslyn Oxley9 Gallery
Robert Ambrose Cole courtesy Utopia Art Sydney
Brenda L. Croft courtesy Brenda L. Croft
Destiny Deacon courtesy Roslyn Oxley9 Gallery
Kevin Gilbert courtesy Eleanor Gilbert
Willie Gudabi courtesy Alcaston Gallery
Mithinari Gurruwiwi courtesy Howard Morphy
Roy Kennedy courtesy Brenda L. Croft
Emily Kame Kngwarreye Rick Stevens, courtesy the Fairfax Photo Library
Yvonne Koolmatrie Brenda L. Croft
Anchor Kulunba Altman Collection, courtesy AV archives, AIATSIS
Crusoe Kurddal Kellie Austin, courtesy Maningrida Arts and Culture
Queenie McKenzie Art Gallery of New South Wales archive
Dr Pantitji Mary McLean Nalda Searles
Dr David Malangi courtesy Margie West, Museum and Art Gallery of the Northern Territory
Samuel Manggudja Dr Peter Carroll, courtesy Injalak Arts and Crafts, Gunbalanya and the Aboriginal Arts Board of the Australia Council
Banduk Marika courtesy Buku-Larrngay Mulka Arts
Mawalan Marika Margaret Tuckson, Art Gallery of New South Wales archive
Wandjuk Marika Margaret Tuckson, Art Gallery of New South Wales archive
John Mawurndjul Kellie Austin, courtesy Maningrida Arts and Culture
Galuma Maymuru courtesy Buk-Larrngay Mulka Arts
Narritjin Maymuru courtesy Howard Morphy
Ricky Maynard courtesy Stills Gallery
Tracey Moffatt courtesy Roslyn Oxley9 Gallery
Sally Morgan courtesy Sally Morgan
Ginger Riley Munduwalawala courtesy Alcaston Gallery
Mäw' Mununggurr courtesy Howard Morphy
Albert Namatjira courtesy News Limited
Eubena Nampitjin courtesy Warlayirti Artists
Inyuwa Nampitjinpa Paul Sweeney, courtesy Papunya Tula Artists
Makinti Napanangka Paul Sweeney, courtesy Papunya Tula Artists
Mitjili Napurrula courtesy Ikuntji Arts Centre
Ningura Napurrula Paul Sweeney, courtesy Papunya Tula Artists
Dula Ngurruwutthun courtesy Colin and Liz Laverty
Jimmy Njiminjuma Art Gallery of New South Wales archive
Lin Onus Andrew Chapman
Otto Pareroultja Rex Battarbee, first published in Rex Battarbee, *Modern Australian Aboriginal Art*, Angus and Robertson, Sydney, 1951
Rusty Peters Katie Wilson
Gloria Tamerre Petyarre courtesy Utopia Art Sydney
Kutuwulumi Purawarrumpatu Diana Stewart, Jilamara Arts and Crafts
Rea courtesy Rea
Michael Riley courtesy Boomalli Aboriginal Artists Cooperative
Elaine Russell courtesy Elaine Russell
Nyirlpirr Spider Snell Karen Dayman, courtesy Mangkaja Arts Resource Agency
Ken Thaiday courtesy Ken Thaiday
Thancoupie Kerry Trapnell
Rover Thomas Martin van der Wal, courtesy AV archives, AIATSIS
Timmy Timms Leon Morris, courtesy Jirrawun Aboriginal Arts Corporation
Ronnie Tjampitjinpa Paul Sweeney, courtesy Papunya Tula Artists
Uta Uta Tjangala Jeremy Long, courtesy AV archives, AIATSIS
Clifford Possum Tjapaltjarri John Corker
Mick Namarari Tjapaltjarri Paul Sweeney, courtesy Papunya Tula Artists
Tim Leura Tjapaltjarri Alan Scott, courtesy the Geoffrey Bardon Estate
Long Tom Tjapanangka courtesy Margie West, Museum and Art Gallery of the Northern Territory
Tjumpo Tjapanangka courtesy Warlayirti Artists
Timmy Payungka Tjapangati R.G. Kimber
Shorty Lungkata Tjungurrayi Alan Scott, courtesy the Geoffrey Bardon Estate
Johnny Warangkula Tjupurrula Alan Scott, courtesy the Geoffrey Bardon Estate
Turkey Tolson Tjupurrula Paul Sweeney, courtesy Papunya Tula Artists
Prince of Wales courtesy Karen Brown Gallery
Judy Watson Jenni Carter, Art Gallery of New South Wales
H. J. Wedge courtesy Boomalli Aboriginal Artists Cooperative
Pedro Wonaeamirri Diana Stewart, courtesy Jilamara Arts and Crafts
Owen Yalandja Kellie Austin, courtesy Maningrida Arts and Culture
Lena Yarinkura Kellie Austin, courtesy Maningrida Arts and Culture
Munggurrawuy Yunupingu Margaret Tuckson, Art Gallery of New South Wales archive

ACKNOWLEDGMENTS

The Art Gallery of New South Wales would firstly like to acknowledge the artists, their families and communities.

The realisation of this project has been made possible with the support of the following staff of the Art Gallery of New South Wales: Judy Annear, Tony Bond, Mark Boxshall, Cherith Devenish, Anne Flanagan, Richard Harling, Jo Hein, Deborah Jones, Denise Mimmocchi and Barry Pearce.

We would also like to thank and acknowledge the assistance of the following individuals: Brian Aarons, Deborah Barber, Kim Barber, Ace Bourke, Karen Brown, Kathleen Brown, Felix Bunduck, Peter Carroll, Mark Crocombe, Brenda L. Croft, Trisha Dann, Karen Dayman, Philippa Deveson, Robert Edwards, Hannah Fink, Eleanor Gilbert, Jenny Green, Paul Greenaway, Amanda Hall, Tamelyn Hall, Carolynne Hamdorf, Alana Harris, Christopher Hodges, Jennifer Isaacs, Karen Jackson, Susan Jenkins, Kevin Kelly, Beverly Knight, Frances Kofod, Apolline Kohen, Colin and Liz Laverty, Djon Mundine, Anthony Murphy, Tony Oliver, Jo Onus, Tiriki Onus, Roslyn Oxley, Rudy Panozzo, Kerry Reid Gilbert, Sandra Reynolds, Brian Robinson, Amanda Rowell, Gabriella Roy, Judy Ryan, Carolyn Sanders, Merryn Schriever, Marielle Schwerin, Belinda Scott, Nalda Searles, Naomi Sharp, John Stanton, Diana Stewart, Neridah Stockley, Will Stubbs, Paul Sweeney, Samantha Tongi, Margaret Tuckson, Cynthia Tupicoff, Lesley Turner, Margie West and Stephen Williamson.

Tradition Today: Indigenous art in Australia
Art Gallery of New South Wales
Published by the Art Gallery of New South Wales, Sydney, Australia
© 2004, Art Gallery of New South Wales, Sydney, Australia

Any copy of this book issued by the publishers is sold subject to the condition that it shall not by way of trade or otherwise be lent, resold, hired out or otherwise circulated without the publisher's prior consent in any form of binding or cover other than that in which it is published and without a similar condition, including these words being imposed on a subsequent publisher. All rights reserved. No part of this publication may be reproduced or transmitted in any form or by any means, electronic or mechanical, including photocopying, recording, or any other information storage and retrieval system, without prior permission in writing from the publisher.

© 2004 Individual essays, George Alexander, Natasha Brook, Deborah Edwards, Hannah Fink, Vivien Johnson, Jonathan Jones, John Kean, Eric Kjellgren, Steven Miller, Howard Morphy, Hetti Perkins, Luke Taylor, Wayne Tunnicliffe and Ken Watson
© All artworks remain the copyright of the artists and are reproduced with permission
© All photographs are subject to copyright and have been reproduced with permission

All information in this book was correct at time of printing and permission has been sought to reproduce all material contained herein.

Art Gallery of New South Wales.
Tradition today : indigenous art in Australia / Art Gallery of New South Wales.
Includes bibliography (p. 198–200) and index.
ISBN: 0-7347-6344-1

1. Art Gallery of New South Wales--Catalogs.
2. Art–New South Wales--Sydney--Catalogs.
3. Art, Australian aboriginal--Catalogs.
4. Artists, Australian aboriginal. I. Title.

708.99441

Curatorial management **Hetti Perkins, Ken Watson, Jonathan Jones**
Project coordinator **Cara Pinchbeck**
Editor **Theresa Willsteed**
Consulting editor **Dinah Dysart**
Research assistants **Julia Pucci, Anna Kaneider**
Design **Analiese Cairis**
Production **Catherine Ferrari**
Prepress **Spitting Image, Sydney**
Printing **Imago**

Cover detail:
Long Tom Tjapanangka
Big mob puli (rocks), other side of Mt Leibig 1998
D. G. Wilson Bequest Fund 1998
© Long Tom Tjapanangka, courtesy Ikuntji Arts Centre

The Art Gallery of New South Wales gratefully acknowledges the assistance of ATSIC, the Aboriginal and Torres Strait Islander Commission, towards this publication and Qantas Airways for its ongoing support of the Yiribana Gallery of Aboriginal and Torres Strait Islander Art.

ATSIC

QANTAS

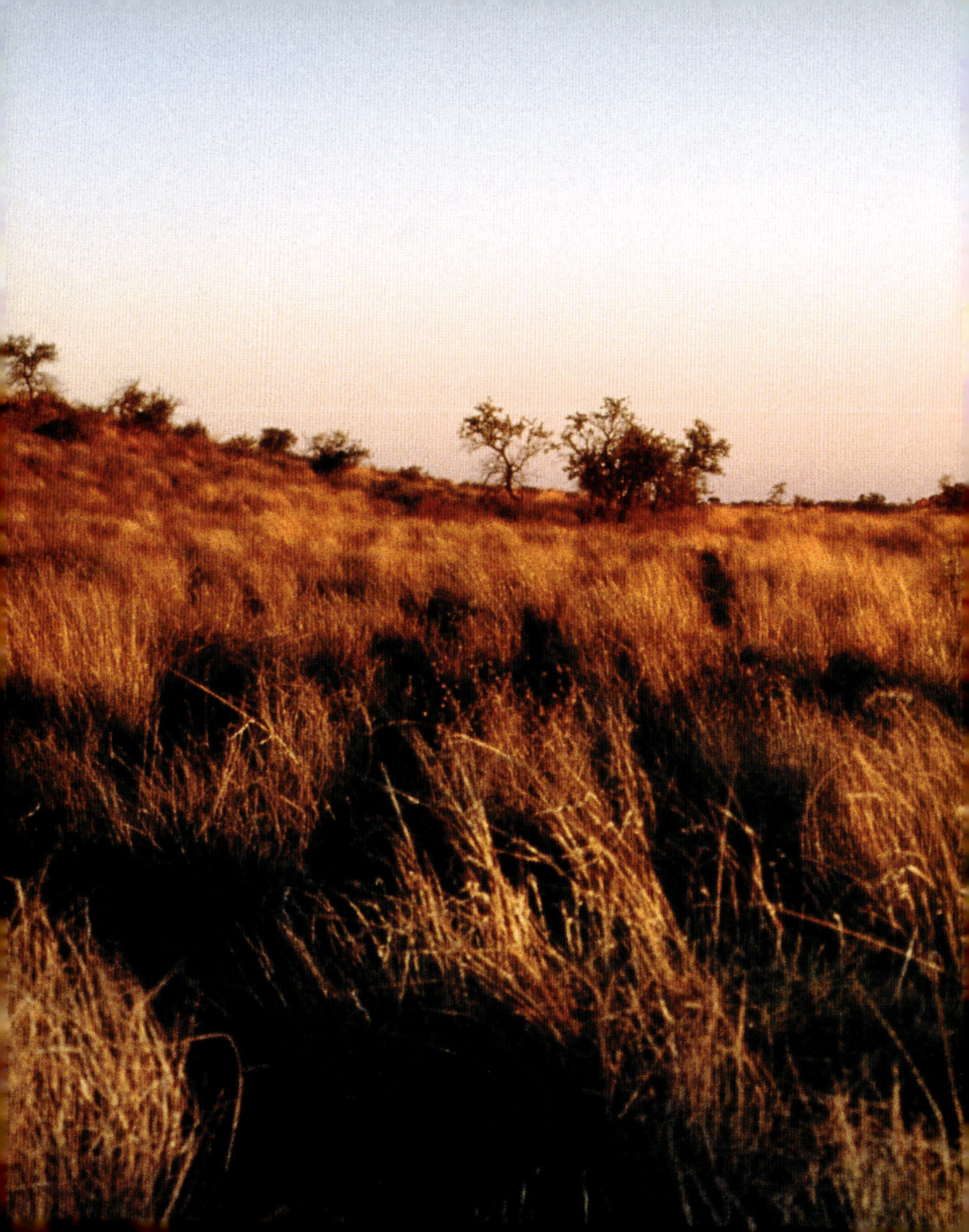

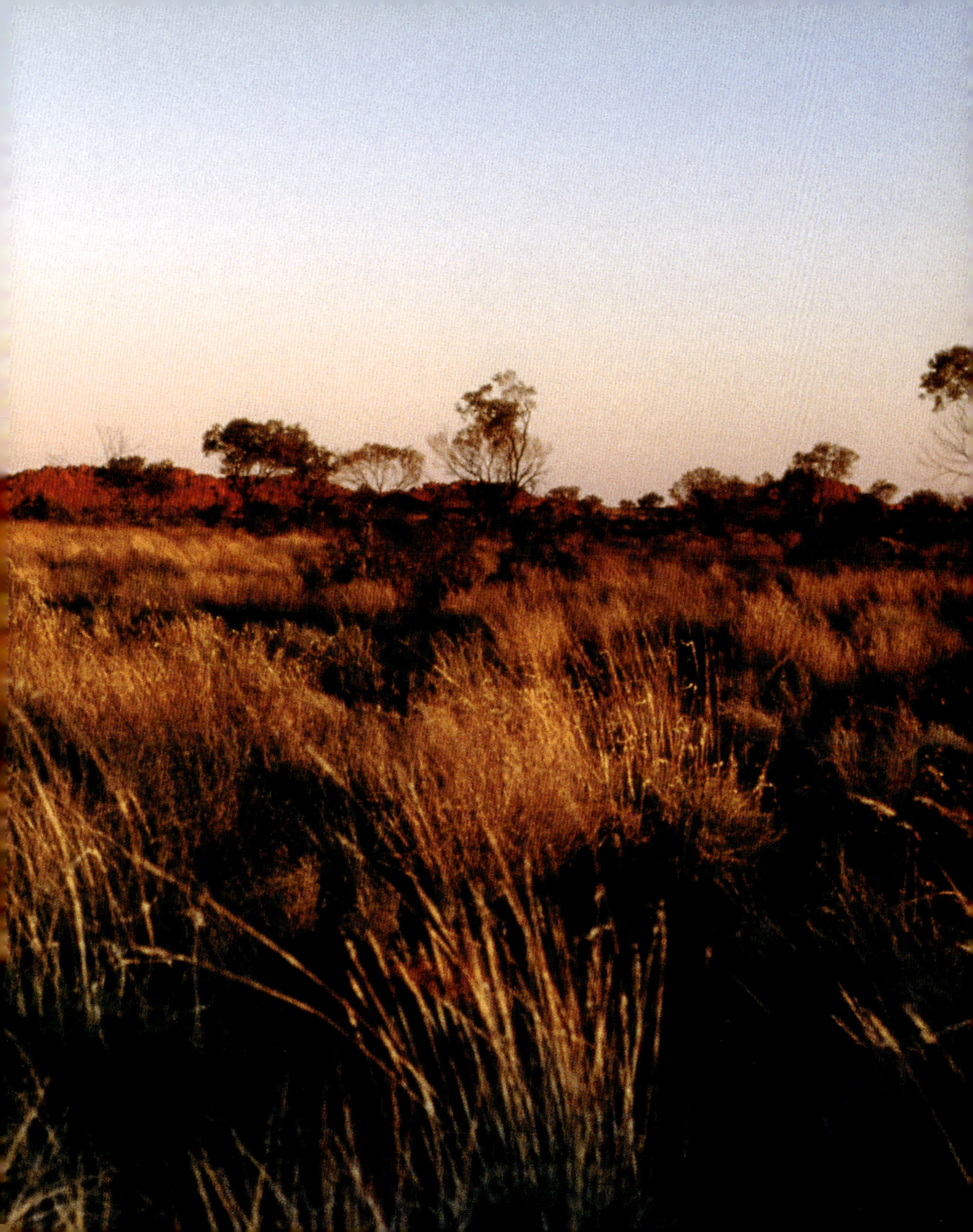

PAINTING MEANS TO US COUNTRY, THAT'S WHY PEOPLE PAINT.

WE ARE BORN WITH IT WE GOT IT ON OUR BODY. ON OUR BONES —
WE ARE BORN WITH IT — IT IS ON OUR SKIN.